LANGUAGES OF TRIBAL AND INDIGENOUS PEOPLES OF INDIA

THE ETHNIC SPACE

MLBD SERIES IN LINGUISTICS

General Editor
DHANESH JAIN

Volume X

LANGUAGES OF TRIBAL AND INDIGENOUS PEOPLES OF INDIA

THE ETHNIC SPACE

Edited By

ANVITA ABBI

MOTILAL BANARSIDASS PUBLISHERS
PRIVATE LIMITED • DELHI

First Edition: Delhi, 1997

ISBN: 81-208-1374-x

Also Available at:

MOTILAL BANARSIDASS

41 U.A. Bungalow Road, Jawahar Nagar, Delhi 110 007
8 Mahalaxmi Chamber, Warden Road, Mumbai 400 026
120 Royapettah High Road, Mylapore, Chennai 600 004
Sanas Plaza, Subhash Nagar, Pune 411 002
16 St. Mark's Road, Bangalore 560 001
8 Camac Street, Calcutta 700 017
Ashok Rajpath, Patna 800 004
Chowk, Varanasi 221 001

PRINTED IN INDIA

BY JAINENDRA PRAKASH JAIN AT SHRI JAINENDRA PRESS,
A-45 NARAIN, PHASE-I, NEW DELHI 110 028
AND PUBLISHED BY NARENDRA PRAKASH JAIN FOR
MOTILAL BANARASIDASS PUBLISHERS PRIVATE LIMITED,
BUNGALOW ROAD, DELHI 110 007

DEDICATION

To my Guru
JAMES W. GAIR
Who taught me to untie the knots
of Linguistic Structures

PREFACE

It was the summer of 1990 in Simla where I had been invited to be a Fellow for conducting research work on the shared linguistic features of Indian languages. The assignment drew me close to languages that are lesser known among the linguists at large. The ambiance of Summer hills, colleagues and friends at the Indian Institute of Advanced Study, Rashtrapati Niwas gave me the appropriate atmosphere to think about minority languages and languages of the small speech communities. My personal involvement in conducting and teaching a course in Field Methods in Jawaharlal Nehru University every year had already exposed me to the magnificent structures these languages possessed. On discussing these sructures with friends like M.L. Khubchandani and U.N. Singh (then residents of the IIAS, Simla) it became clear that there are lot of similarities between these languages which need to be further explored. Also visiting several libraries and book stores, I realized that there is not a single book on the shelf which discusses about all the five language families from the tribal language perspective. Thus grew the need for a volume totally devoted to the issues of the tribal and indigenous languages of India. It was felt that the linguists and intellectuals dealing with language issues should be requested to contribute a paper each on the language/s they had been working in.

In true sense, hence, this volume grew out of love for tribal languages, languages that have been long ignored by Indian bureaucracy and polity but not by ethnologists and linguists. It took quite a while to prepare this volume as some of the contributors were too busy to send in their papers by the deadline. Nonetheless it was thought wise to wait than follow the strict deadline schedule lest we would have missed some important contributions.

The volume never got any financial support from any government or private body, though in anticipation of receiving one, we wasted more than two years. It is ironical that like languages of these small speech communities, the work on these languages are also ignored, despite the declaration of 'the year of the indigenous people' and 'promotion of the scheduled tribes' and various other government banners that we see year-after-year. In such a dismal atmosphere, it is really courageous for Motilal Banarsidass Publishers Pvt. Ltd. to undertake the publication of this volume. I am thankful to Shri Narendra Prakash Jain and his advisors who agreed to publish such a difficult book. Thanks are due to my students Avatans who painstakingly prepared the language index and to Nina who assisted me in editing parts of this volume. Special thanks are due to Peter Hook who solidly supported the idea of bringing out a book of this type. But for his encouragement I would have hesitated to tread this ground. Finally our gratitude to all those Ādivāsīs who made this book possible by being helpful, cooperative, friendly and above all, by allowing us to have a glance at their world-view.

Anvita Abbi
Jawaharlal Nehru University
New Delhi

March 2, 1996

CONTENTS

LIST OF ILLUSTRATIONS

FIGURES AND ILLUSTRATIONS

LIST OF TABLES

MAPS

I

IN SEARCH OF IDENTITY

Dreaming of you in bed
I woke and took to the road.
Stumbling the stone
On the village road I remembered
I remembered my caste, my gotra
And stood transfixed.

(Munda Song)

'The Awakened Wind'—Sitakant Mahapatra

CHAPTER 1

INTRODUCTION

Anvita Abbi

The peace-loving, self-contented *Ādivāsis* or the tribals have lived on this soil for thousands of years. These traditional lovers of natural environment who have a creative outlet in dance, painting and clay-modelling, are thus part of the national heritage. The advent of industrialization and modernization threatened to displace them by gross neglect and apathy towards their essential 'tribal' nature. To ward off this imminent danger, they instinctively took recourse to the adherence in two basic factors of their existence. Firstly, they fell back on Nature, the forest for shelter and sustenance. Secondly, they reafirmed their allegiance to their 'tongue', correctly recognizing their language as the basic mark of their identity as a people.

For a long time we had been contemplating to bring forth the reality, the simplicity and the abstractness manifested in the languages of this part of our society. Though these tribal languages have not been used to express 'modern' aspects of our life, they do contain an inbuilt mechanism to modernize themselves to meet the modern educational requirement. Not all of us are aware of this potential of these languages. One word of caution. The term 'tribal languages' should not be equated with primitive or underdeveloped languages. The word *tribal* is used in this volume to refer to the languages of those communities that are listed as 'tribals' in the Constitution of India vide Article 342. In other words, 'tribe' in India is an administrative concept. This reminds us of what Pt. Jawaharlal Nehru said once:

> But I am sure that to think of the tribals and non-tribals as people qualitatively different is wrong. Take the description in our Constitution of the Scheduled Castes. As you know, it is rather arbitrary. Government after consideration, decide whether a particular caste is a Scheduled Caste or not. It is not possible to draw a hard and fast line. That is why we aim ultimately at removal of all these appellations, descriptions and names which ideologically and physically separate the people as the Depressed Classes, the Harijans, the Scheduled Castes, the Scheduled Tribes and so on.
>
> (Inaugural Address at the Tribal Affairs Conference held on Dec. 4, 1959 in New Delhi)

The tribal communities living in different areas of the country can be conveniently divided into five territorial groupings:1) the Himalayan region consisting of Assam, Meghalaya, Arunachal Pradesh, Nagaland, Manipur, Mizoram, Tripura, hills of Uttar Pradesh and Himachal Pradesh; 2) Middle India having 55% tribal population which consists of Bihar, West Bengal, Orissa and Madhya Pradesh (The major tribal area of this region is asking for an autonomous state of Jharkhand currently; 3) Western India consisting of Rajasthan, Maharashtra, Gujarat, Goa, Dadra and Nagar Haveli; 4) South India which has 6.4% tribal population consisting of Karnataka, Andhra Pradesh, Tamil Nadu and Kerala; and 5) Islands such as Andaman, Nicobar and Lakshadweep.

According to 1981 Census, the population of the Scheduled Tribes was 51.63 million comprising almost 8% of the total population of the country. The distribution of the Scheduled Tribe population varies a great deal from region to region. There are States such as Nagaland where tribal population is 85% of the total State population, and there are others such as Madhya Pradesh that alone houses one-fourth of the total scheduled tribe population of India. Just as we divide five distinct regions of tribal population in India similarly tribal languages of the country also fall into five distinct language family groupings.

They are Andamanese, Austro-Asiatic, Dravidian, Indo-Aryan and Tibeto-Burman. We have tried to cover all these language families in this volume covering thus our investigative span from Himalayan ranges in the North to down South in the Andaman Islands in the Bay of Bengal. Our sole aim has been to bring forth the research in these tribal languages to help to bridge intellectual gulf between cultures.

The linguistic research in modern Indian languages has been more or less on the pattern of American and European insights into the linguistic theory. This has not helped us get to know the languages of the indigenous people. The requirement to undertake linguistic research into the logics of tribal languages and realization that they have equal scientific validity with our own thinking habits cannot be undermined.

Our readers would find that distinct and seemingly strange grammars of various tribal languages are little windows through which we can see a distinct and different mode of perceiving and conceiving the world as seen by these speech communities. The age-old multilingual mosaic of India has generated a unique kind of language contact situation. The 'tolerance of other' philosophy has been applicable to the linguistic situation of the country as well. Minority languages, tribal languages and lesser known languages have been in contact with the so-called 'major' languages leading to often generated ethnic and linguistic conflicts. Such linguistic conflicts, however, do not last long and soon a compromise is achieved. As a result, these languages adopt some of the structures of the dominant languages. Such an adoption, interestingly is not detrimental to their growth. This kind of language contact situation helps in strengthening India as a Linguistic Area. Contact-induced changes might lead to language contraction but we see that in case of India, these contracted languages have important social utility.

The research papers in the current volume are organized into seven broad sections. Part I is 'In Search of Identity'. Are there any tribal specific characteristics that help one identify languages as tribal or non-tribal? Several related enquiries are made by Annamalai (Chap. 2). When we talk of tribal languages, do we refer to the languages of an isolated population living in jungles, or those of in minority or those who do not belong to the *jāti* system of Hindu society. Similar questions are raised by Emeneau (Chap. 3) in his paper. He advocates for a firmer methodology, better and more data, large body of tests and above all, the requirements that a linguist discovering this area should also be an ethnologist.

A feast of information regarding tribes and subtribes, the various languages (449 in total) spoken by them and the exact area of speech are given by K.S. Singh (Chap. 4). His article might serve as encyclopedic in nature as the listing, in addition to being complete, is based on the first-hand data acquired in the mammoth project 'Peoples of India' conducted by him recently.

Indian Census has been of a great value to indicate not only the population figure of tribals in the country but also to represent the quantitative aspect of mother tongue speakers and bilinguals. Unfortunately, the information for bilingualism ceased to be sought after the 1961 Census. Khubchandani (Chap. 5) in his paper critically evaluates the Census figures of last three decades of mother tongues spoken among tribals and reaches a very significant judgement about 'language shift' and 'language persistance'. He is concerned about the various tribal movements currently at work in the country and strongly opines that ethnic identity should be channelised in a positive manner to enrich nation's heritage. Related to Khubchandani's concern is Imtiaz Hasnain's (Chap. 6) enquiry into the existing language planning with regard to tribal and minority languages. He believes in multidisciplinary field of language planning where there is a dialectical relationship between subjective and objective factors.

The beauty of Indian linguistic scene is characterized by the presence of several languages and several language families in a particular region. One such region is South Orissa and Jharkhand. The former houses languages of Central Dravidian family, Austro-Asiatic (Munda) family and Indo-Aryan family while the latter is signified by Indo-Aryan, North Dravidian and Austro-Asiatic (Munda) families. Part II is devoted solely to the contact and convergence issues emerging in such areas. Mohanty (Chap. 7) discusses the phonological aspect of linguistic convergence while Israel (Chap. 8), details the morphological changes that have been brought into languages in contact (particularly in Kui). Language contact generally works like a pendulum. On the one hand of this pendulum is the state of language contraction while on the other extreme lies language conflation. This paradoxical situation exists in most of the cases of tribal languages in contact in South Asia. Abbi (Chap. 9) examines two tribal languages of distinct families (Austro-Asiatic and North Dravidian) spoken in Jharkhand in contact with dominant languages of Indo-Aryan family, and tries to establish that language contact (inclusive of language shift and loss at times) in such areas has given a new lease of life to the dominated languages as these languages have shown strong evidence of movement towards areal typological homogeneity.

The next five parts of the volume are devoted to unravel the mysteries of linguistic structures of specific language families, i.e. Indo-Aryan, Dravidian, Austro-Asiatic (Munda and Mon-Khmer), Tibeto-Burman and Andamanese.

Readers would find only one paper under part III but it is a well researched and interesting paper by Claus Peter Zoller on Baṅgāṇi, a language of the Western Pahāṛi subgroup of Indo-Aryan. His subject of enquiry is the grammar of poetics of Baṅgāṇi version of the Mahābhārata called *Pɔ̃ḍuaṇ*. A very neat synthesis of diachronic and synchronic analysis is presented which, despite the discussion of linguistic intricacies, does not mar the vision of the readers from seeing the complete harmony, unity and beauty of the narrative poems. Readers particularly interested in more material on Indo-Aryan languages can refer to relevant articles in part II and part I.

Andronov (Chap.11) analyses first person pronominals in Brāhuī (North Dravidian language spoken in Baluchistan) and tense from in Goṇḍī (a Central Dravidian language). Brāhuī, as any linguist working in the area of Indian linguistics is aware of, is very significant from the point of view of Historical and Areal Linguistics. If we add to this the fact that the language area is almost unapproachable for us and thus whatever data is available is too precious to be ignored, then this particular article, readers would agree with me, would serve as a catalyst.

The next article (Chap.12) by Christianne Pilot-Raichoor is an extensive study of the abstract nature of the Baḍaga verb stem, a language of Nilgiri Hills. Contrary to the theory of dominant-language-power Baḍaga shows influence of neighbouring tribal languages but not that of Kannada. The results of the research might initiate the readers to explore the bilingual patterns of Baḍaga community. 'Numeral classifiers in Malto' contributed by B.P. Mahapatra (Chap.13) raises some fundamental questions in the theories of cognition and iconicity.

All the language of Austro-Asiatic family fall under 'Scheduled Tribe Languages', and paradoxically this is the only group that has no representation at all in the Eigth Schedule of the Constitution of India. Interestingly, the languages of this group represent the communities which were the original inhabitants of India. The two major branches Munda and Mon-Khmer of the Austro-Asiatic language family are separated from each other politically, socially and geographically. Contributors to Part V of the volume wrestle with the concepts of language universals with regard to the languages of this family. The age old dichotomy of noun and verb in the so-called sophisticated languages such as English and Hindi is challenged by Bhat (Chap.14) as he opines that compartmentalization of words into various grammatical categories is absent in the Munda languages.

He proposes an idealized language type which does not make any such distinction between nouns and verbs; instead it has a nuclear predicate with all the information incorporated regarding participant roles, modification, temporal and spatial relations. Now this calls for an altogether different perspective and world-view of looking at languages and their grammars. This was long overdue, as the *mot-phrase* characteristic of Munda, as well as that of Tibeto-Burman languages perhaps will help us delimit one basic characteristic feature of these two language families from the rest. Moreover, Bhat's article substantiated by others in this part and the next might set a path for a new linguistic theory in future. To establish the correctness of this prediction one has to wait and watch. The next article by Arlene Zide (Chap.15) on Gorum falls in the same line where she analyses the pronominal and nominal incorporation into the predicate structure. The next essay 'Sora Noun Inflection' (Chap.16), by S. Starosta is a contribution both to linguistic theory and Austro-Asiatic linguistics. This paper is a lexicase description of the inflectional categories of Sora nouns. Starosta's framework might prove applicable to all languages of this family or to all those languages that are typologically similar to Sora.

Norman Zide's paper on Gutob-Remo-Gtʌ? (languages of Koraput Munda, Chap. 17) is the result of extensive analysis of the painstaking data collected by several people in Koraput District of Orissa and in the adjacent areas of Andhra Pradesh. Incorporation is also the feature of these languages as Norman Zide unfolds the structures marked by subject prefixes and enclitic subject markers. M. Istitiaq's is an important article (Chap. 18) on the sociology of language that discusses the raison de être of language shift and language maintenance among Santals and Mundas. He suggests a typology of language shift and maintenance towards the end of his paper which helps identify the position of Santali and Munda.

The next two papers deal with a language belonging to Mon-Khmer branch of this family: Khasi spoken in Meghalaya. Nagraja's enquiry (Chap. 19) into the varying word-order in distinct dialects of Khasi raises a very fundamental issue in Typological Linguistics. How should one define a type if the language concerned and its dialects show conflicting patterns? The paper would also motivate readers to raise further enquiry into the language/dialect question. Interestingly barring Kashmiri, Khasi is the only SVO type language of India. However, the dialects of Khasi show traits of SOV as well as of VSO. The next article (Chap. 20) would give an insight into a different 'experience' or a distinct "world view" of Khasis as examined by Mayjee Philip in her work on 'Compounds'. The possibility of various Khasi collocational elements in compound-formations are unparallelled in other Indian languages.

There are five papers in the next part (VI) which is devoted to the languages of the Tibeto-Burman family. The Himalayan languages are generally grouped into "pronominalised" and "nonprominalised" languages, the former being characterised by language contact-induced changes. Sharma (Chap. 21) discusses a very wide range of tribal languages (all rather inapproachable due to hilly terrains and snow covered mountains of Western Himalayan group). Pronominal incorporation of Munda type is evident in these Tibeto-Himalayan languages.

The next three articles by Yashwanta Singh on 'Negation' (Chap. 22) in Kuki-Chin and Naga languages, Subbarao and Lalitha's work on 'Passive in Mizo' (Chap. 23) as well as A. Abbi and Ahum Victor's study (Chap. 24) of 'Expressive Morphology' cover a wide span of the number and nature of languages. The former two deal with the syntactic aspect and the latter discusses the phonological and morpho-semantic aspects of widely used expressive words. Kailash Aggarwal in 'Script and Ethnolinguistic Identity' (Chap. 25) examines and describes the fascinating case of Manipuri script, the associated conflicts, revival of traditional orthography and interplay of bureaucrats and language loyalists. Manipuri is no longer scheduled as a tribal language. It has been incorporated into the VIII Schedule recently. We have included this paper in the volume for two reasons. First, this is the most common indigenous language that the tribals of the North East learn it as an L2, and hence is used by a large number of tribals. Second, the plight of Meitei (Manipuri) script is shared by many of the lesser known languages of India.

Finally, we have an enquiry into a very important and not-so-much-worked-upon language of India's fifth language family, i.e. Andamanese. The geographical barriers of the sea, along with socio-cultural barriers have shoved this language family into isolation. Among the very few linguists working on this language, Manoharan's contribution (Chap. 26) has really enriched the volume. His discussion of 'Pronominal prefixes and formative affixes' in Andamanese again raises the question as in what many ways a single word can be conflated to manifest the meaning of a whole sentence. I believe the languages of indigenous people of India will force us to rethink about the universal applicability and validity of a typical noun/verb distinction generally found in Indo-European languages and dialects. The greatest power of the tribal languages that one is immediately struck with is the simplicity and brevity of their grammatical structures. They are the ideal languages for 'modernization' and perhaps can help us in devising a computer language.

This volume is just a glimpse of the structures of the tribal languages of India. Many more languages are still waiting for linguists to do serious and proper analysis. In an intense and stable language contact situation most of the Indian tribal languages have no longer remained isolated. The infiltration of neighbouring dominant languages as well as other minority languages and their structures have brought tremendous changes in the tribal languages and experiences of their speakers. The present papers are nevertheless the first collection of essays that we know of devoted to the descriptions of the tribal and indigenous languages, language change, language demography, sociology of language, languages in contact and the social status of the indigenous peoples of India. To peep into the experiences and the world-views, there is no other way but to study the languages of these indigenous speech communities.

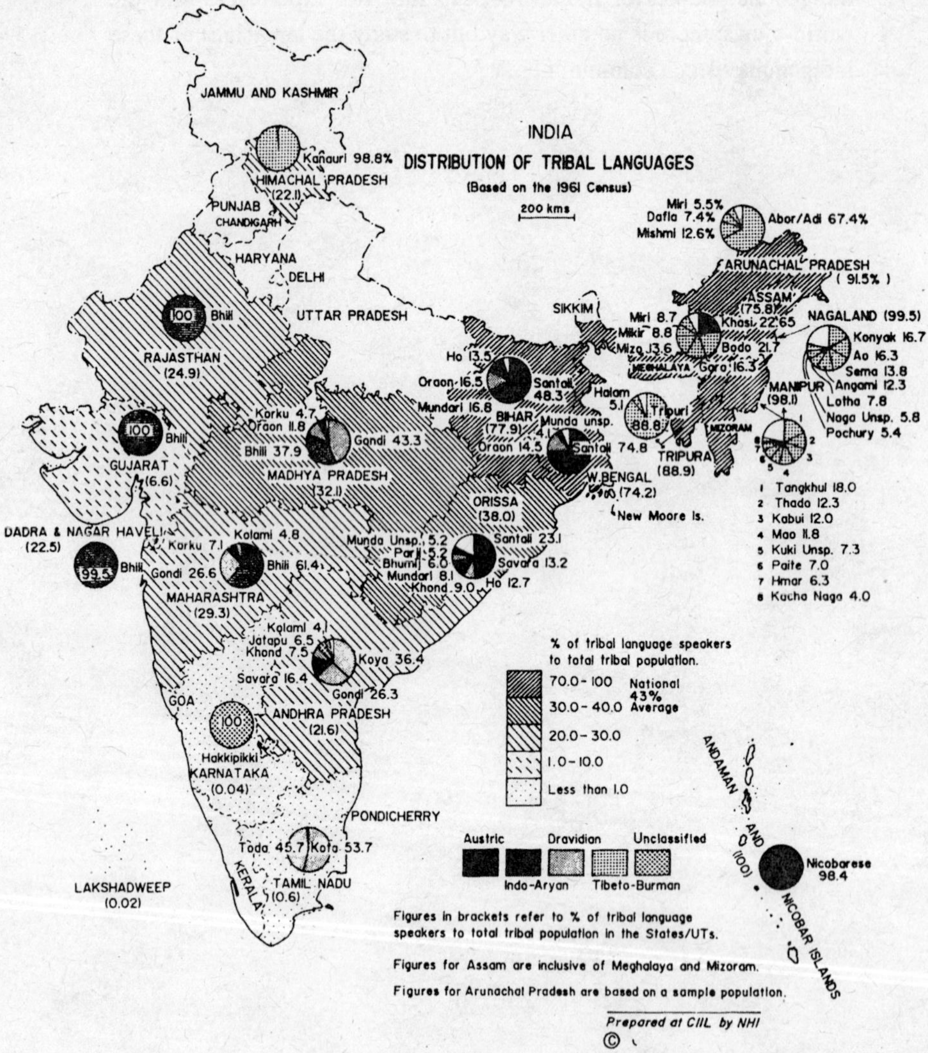

SPACE FOR MAP

CHAPTER 2

QUESTIONS ON THE LINGUISTIC CHARACTERISTICS OF THE TRIBAL LANGUAGES OF INDIA

E. Annamalai

Introduction

It is an interesting question whether the term 'tribal' in tribal languages of India can be linguistically characterised. Another related question is what percentage of the tribal linguistic characteristics has become Indian, in the sense that they are shared areawise by non-tribal Indian languages. Though these two questions are independent of each other, a situation can arise when the linguistic features common to the tribal languages of India are those areal features shared by all Indian languages. In such a case the first question is vacuous and can be raised only diachronically, with reference to a stage before convergence. It is also, however, possible that synchronically there are features of tribal languages not shared by non-tribal languages, but are found in all or most of the tribal languages of India. This paper is concerned about them.

Legally and administratively, the term 'tribal' in tribal languages does not have any linguistic connotation. The Indian Constitution does not define or make any special provision for the tribal languages. The tribal languages are those spoken natively by the tribal communities,[1] which are scheduled as per Article 342 of the Constitution by the President and Parliament. The Constitutional provisions to safeguard the interests of scheduled tribes including their cultural interests will also help their native languages. A tribal community is defined for the purpose of scheduling on the basis of various historical, socio-economic and cultural parameters (and language may be one of the cultural parameters). There is no linguistic definition of a tribal language.

Nevertheless, in the popular and bureaucratic world view, a tribal language is linguistically perceived as "a speech without grammar". Tribal language in this perception is a misnomer and there are only tribal dialects. By that it does not mean that tribal languages do not have a script or a grammar book—i.e., not codified in a visual medium and a metalanguage—but it means that they are not a system. The absurdity of this view is obvious to any linguist who has attempted to describe a tribal language and confronted the complexity of its system. It should also be obvious that without being a system, shared between speakers, communication through a language is not possible at all.

Linguistic Diversity and Language Families

If the grammars of the tribal languages are not deficient as a system, are they different from the grammars of non-tribal languages? The grammar of every language is different; otherwise they will not be autonomous systems and called different languages, linguistically.[2] It is a difficult question and the difficulty increases when we try to identify common differentiating linguistic features for all the tribal languages of India. The tribal languages of India belong to four genetic families, viz. Indo-European, Dravidian, Austro-Asiatic and Sino-Tibetan. The number of tribal mothertongues and languages according to 1961 Census distribution familywise is given below:[3]

TABLE 1
Distribution of Tribal Mothertongues and languages, 1961

	No. of mother-tongues	No. of languages	% to total no. of tribal languages	% to total no. of languages in the family	% to all languages of India
Indo European	36	1	1.08	1.85	0.50
Dravidian	35	9	9.78	45.00	4.48
Austro-Asiatic	64	19	20.65	95.00	9.45
Sino-Tibetan	159	63	68.48	64.29	31.34
Total	294	92			45.77

It should be noted that it is the tribal languages which widen the scope of genetic families in India. For example, the presence of Kempti in Arunachal Pradesh being a Thai language makes Tibeto-Burman an inadequate description and enlarges this family into Sino-Tibetan. Similarly Khasi in Meghalaya and Car-Nicobarese in Andaman and Nicobar Islands make Munda into Austro-Asiatic Tribal languages like Onge in Andaman and Nicobar Islands suggest a possibility of a fifth linguistic family, viz., Negrito. Thus the tribal languages add to India's linguistic diversity genetically. They also have a large share in the demographic composition of languages being close to half of the languages of India.[4]

Of these four families, the Austro-Asiatic and Sino-Tibetan languages are almost entirely tribal.[5] Therefore, it is not possible to distinguish between tribal and non-tribal linguistic features in these languages. Among the Sino-Tibetan languages, there is only one language (Manipuri) which is a scheduled language. About 40 per cent of them are neither scheduled nor tribal languages as per legal and administrative definition, but it is likely that they share linguistically more with tribal languages.

The Question of Identification

There is an empirical problem to the task of identifying tribal linguistic features, which is that some tribal languages are linguistically, dialects of a non-tribal language. For example, Jenu Kuruba. The speech of Jenu Kurubas in Karnataka identified as a primitive tribe, is a dialect of Kannada. The problem of dialect-language continuum is an unsolved-one with reference to some tribal languages like the Irula and Badaga in the Nilgiris. This makes it difficult to have a sharp boundary between tribal and non-tribal languages.

A methodological problem is that there will be always some exceptions to any generalisation. This, however, does not make any generalisation untenable empirically. When we speak of common linguistic features of all tribal languages of India, we have in mind the "family resemblance" in the Wittgensteinian sense. As the meaning of a word does not inclusively define all the characteristics of all the objects it refers to, the common features of tribal languages are not inclusive of all of them with reference to each feature.

Language reflects the social, cultural and ecological patterns and preferences of the community which speaks it. The question about differentiating linguistic features of tribal languages can then be reframed as to what are the common social, cultural and ecological features of tribal communities which differentiate them from non-tribal communities. That such differentiating non-linguistic features exist in the tribal communities is assumed to be true. We shall then explore how they are reflected in the tribal languages. In general, any such reflection can be seen in grammatical categories than in grammatical processes.

It is unclear how grammar reflects them. There is however enough evidence that they are reflected in the deictic categories, social and spatial. But, what is common in the grammatical categories among the tribal languages of India is unexplored. We shall not follow this route at the moment.

We shall take up the second question raised in the beginning of the paper and ask whether any of the areal features of Indian languages can be considered tribal. That is, whether any of the shared features of Indian languages are distinctively tribal which have converged. Historically it would mean that such features will belong to Sino-Tibetan and Austro-Asiatic languages, which are almost entirely tribal. Features like classifier system are largely restricted to contiguous non-tribal languages in contact with tribal languages and are not areal covering the country. But the converse of non-tribal linguistic features shared by tribal languages, i.e., Sino-Tibetan and Austro-Asiatic languages, like compound or explicator verb system (Abbi and Gopalakrishnan 1991) has areal spread covering the whole country.

These cannot be considered tribal linguistic features. Moreover, there is a methodological problem. The temporal dimension of convergence between tribal and non-tribal languages may refer to such a remote past that it will not be meaningful to extrapolate the present day tribal/non-tribal distinction of languages to the linguistic state of the languages of that time. That is, all the communities speaking the languages in contact might have been tribal at that historical period when convergence took place. We will not therefore follow this course.

The reflection of social, cultural and ecological patterns and preferences of a community on its language is more prominent in the lexicon than in the grammar. The question then is whether there are lexical features specific to the tribal languages of India. From the published dictionaries of tribal languages, it seems that they are less polysemous than the non-tribal languages. But this may be the result of the lexicographer's limitation, who is a non-native speaker, is limited to oral sources and to elicitation techniques rather than the fact of the language. The natural and cultural domains for specialized vocabulary in tribal languages are different from those of non-tribal languages and they belong to their speakers' immediate life experience, like having separate words for different kinds of rice, fish, basket, wind, terrain, etc. A comparison of lexical domains and lexical distinctions in them between tribal and non-tribal languages will throw light on this. There is another difference about the lexical domains with reference to their shared knowledge. The specialized vocabularies are normally shared by the whole community in tribal languages[6] whereas they are used only by particular professional groups in non-tribal languages. Thus there are no different registers in tribal languages used only by different specialized professions such as with legal terms and medical terms and or like traditional occupational terms of weavers, masons and farmers. Specialised vocabulary in the sense of technical vocabulary is part of the general vocabulary in tribal languages.

This takes us to the 'use of language' from grammar and lexicon. The use of language affects its structure not in terms of its grammar but in terms of its discourse. It is said that language of informal discourse is structurally more paratactic than syntactic and is operationally more pragmatic than semantic (Tannen, 1984). Since the tribal languages are used largely in informal situations, it will be interesting to see if they exhibit these properties in their use. Unfortunately, there are no studies on discourse in the tribal languages of India.

We could not go far in identifying differentiating linguistic features of tribal languages with reference to grammar, but can suggest a greater possibility in the lexicon and discourse.

We shall now see whether there are any differentiating features in the linguistic behaviour of the speakers of tribal languages. There are more bilinguals among the tribal language speakers than among the non-tribal language speakers; tribal bilingualism is 50 per cent more than national average bilingualism. Higher incidence of bilingualism is however, true of all linguistic minorities. Tribal bilingualism is perhaps less than minority bilingualism in India indicating a language shift towards majority languages and isolation of tribals. The gender difference in bilingualism is absent among the tribals. As many males are bilinguals than females among the tribal language speakers, whereas among the non-tribal language speakers, the female bilinguals are only half of the male bilinguals (Annamalai, 1990). Another feature of tribal bilingualism is that it is relatively unstable as mentioned earlier unlike the Indian bilingualism in general. Less than half of the tribals have reported a tribal language as their mothertongue indicating a language shift[7] (Itagi et al, 1986) or at least shift in linguistic identity.

The Ladder of Development

We shall now look at the developmental scale of language to see whether the tribal languages belong to a particular niche in the scale. Ferguson (1971) has a four point developmental scale for writing as below:

W0—not used for normal written purposes

W1—used for normal written purposes

W2—original research in physical sciences regularly published

W3—Languages in which translations and resumes of scientific work in other languages are regularly published.

Normal written purposes include use of written language for ordinary interpersonal epistolary purposes, in popular periodicals and newspapers and in books originally written and not translated from other languages.

The tribal languages of India belong to W0 and W1. But most non-tribal Indian languages also are at W1. The scale can be extended to other aspects of development like the number of domains of use and kinds of discourse forms. However, the tribal languages of India include languages like Mizo and Khasi, which are languages of administration at the State level, of education at the college level and of literary creation in the recent past. Therefore, the place in the developmental scale does not help us to characterise generally the tribal languages of India. Moreover, the kind of state of development attributed to tribal languages is common to minor languages also, which are not tribal such as Tulu and Kodagu. The state of development of a language is related to the technological, economic and political development of the community which speaks it. Therefore, any linguistic characterisation of tribal languages on this parameter will ultimately amount to characterising them on the basis of the nature of the community, as we started with.

The Geographic Context

Finally, we shall ask the question whether the tribal languages of India exhibit any geolinguistic characteristics, i.e. have a geographic distribution specific to them. Roy Burman (1972) hypothesises that the tribal communities perform "either bridge or buffer roles between more powerful politico-cultural entities". It means that they are in the periphery of dominant communities. This is reflected in the distribution of tribal languages as well (see the Map). The tribal languages are spoken largely in the hilly regions and between dominant Indo-Aryan and Dravidian languages in Central India and between dominant Indian Chinese, and Burmese languages in the North East. It will be interesting to study the linguistic consequences of the bridge and buffer functions of the tribal communities, particularly with reference to convergence and languages shift.[8]

This discussion shows that it is almost as if there are no linguistic features which characterise exclusively only the tribal languages of India and inclusively all of them. The tribal languages of India are not a special kind of languages which could be linguistically characterized as a homogneous group except as languages of a special kind of people who are historically, geographically, politically, socially and culturally differentiated from other people.

NOTES

1. It is not the case that all mother tongues of tribals are tribal languages, as they have non-tribal languages as mother-tongues. As per 1981 Census, only 37 per cent of the tribals speak a tribal mother tongue. Also, there are not as many tribal languages as there are tribal communities. The number of tribal mother tongues is half of the number of tribal communities and the number of tribal languages is only 1/6th of them. (Annamalai, 1990).
2. Languages, however, may be defined socio-culturally and politically and not grammatically and thus two speech forms with same grammar may be called separate languages like Hindi and Urdu.
3. Mother tongues are what the speakers report to the census enumerator, which may be perceived as an identity marker and they are classified into languages on linguistic grounds by census officers. The figures are not final because of the problem of distinction between dialect and language, of differences in grouping mother tongues into languages and of mother tongues unclassified yet as to their genetic affliation. According to the same census, unclassified mother tongues are 521. According to one analysis, after identifying some unclassified mother tongues, the number of tribal mother tongues is 304 and tribal languages is 101. Linguists differ in the count of languages. For example, Zvelebil (1990) lists only 18 Dravidian tribal languages out of 24 languages of this family.
4. Though the tribal languages constitute 46 per cent of the languages of India, tribal language speakers (as mothertongue) constitute about 3 per cent of the population (3.34 in 1961 and 2.87 in 1981).
5. The figures in column 4 of the preceding table are not 100 per cent for those two families because of the number of languages which are non-scheduled and non-tribal. It is for this reason the number of languages in Indo-Aryan and Dravidian families is also low. The number of such languages are Indo-Aryan 42, Dravidian 7, Austro-Asiatic 1 and Sino-Tibetan 35. This is because of the way a tribe is defined as mentioned in the beginning of the paper.
6. It is not quite true because there are special linguistic events like oracles whose vocabulary is not shared by the common man, ritual events like an initiation ceremony where special vocabulary is used for and by the initiated and social groups like women who use a special vocabulary among themselves.
7. It was 43 per cent in 1961 and came down to 37 per cent in 1981 indicating continuing increase of language shift. In 1961, of 57 per cent tribals who had a non-tribal language as their mother tongue, 49 per cent had a scheduled language and 8 per cent a non-scheduled and non-tribal.

8. The map was conceived, designed and drawn by N.H. Itagi. I am grateful to him. The copyright of the map is with the CIIL. It should not be reproduced in any manner without written permission from the CIIL.

REFERENCES

Abbi, Anvita and Devi Gopalakrishnan, 1991. Semantics of explicator compound verbs in South Asian Languages. *Language Sciences* 13:2. 161-80.

Annamalai, E., 1990. Linguistic dominance and cultural dominance. A study of tribal bilingualism in India. In D.P. Pattanayak (ed.) *Multilingualism in India.* Clevedon: Multilingual Matters Ltd.

Ferguson, Charles 1971. The language factor in national development, in Dil, Anwar S. (ed.), *Language Structure and Language Use: Essays by Charles A. Ferguson.* Stanford: Stanford University Press.

Itagi, N.H., B.D. Jayaram and V. Vani, 1986. *Communication Potential in the Tribal Population of Assam and Madhya Pradesh.* Mysore: CIIL.

Roy Burman, B.K., 1972. Distribution of the scheduled tribes of India: An exploratory geo-cultural appraisal. In Chandrashekar (ed). *Economic and Socio-Cultural Dimensions of Regionalisation: An Indo-USSR Collaborative Study.* New Delhi: Office of the Registrar General.

Tannen, Deborah (ed.), 1984. *Coherence in Spoken and Written Discourse.* Norwood, N.J. Ablex.

Zvelelbil, Kamil V., 1990. *Dravidian Linguistics: An Introduction.* Pondicherry: Pondicherry Institute of Linguistics and Culture.

CHAPTER 3

LINGUISTICS AND INDIAN TRIBAL LANGUAGES

M.B. Emeneau

Introduction

My Indian linguistic experience, apart from its beginnings in Sanskrit and the historical relations of Indo-Aryan to the Indo-European language family, has been 'tribal'. If I may be pardoned for being in some ways over-personal and anecdotal in this paper, I shall attempt to generate from my experience some statements which may be elementary but which must certainly be kept in mind by any investigator of 'tribal languages'.

The Problem of Definition

Our first question must be: What is the meaning of 'tribal' in a linguistic context? For India, this is difficult to answer. Many ethnographers (in the beginning chiefly from the non-Indian world) have struggled with the problem of defining 'tribalism' in the Indian context. I must rely on them, and especially on Mandelbaum 1970, who in *Society in India,* pp. 573-619, struggled valiantly with the problem of 'recurrent change through...tribal movements'. He identified several salient features of 'tribalism': much more stress, as compared with the social units of Hinduism, on kinship as the overriding factor in the unit's organization; reliance in some cases on swidden ('slash-and-burn') agricultural economy; lack of the asceticism so prominent in Hinduism, with a consequent fondness for the 'pleasures of the senses...in food, alcoholic drink, sex, song, or dance [i.e. at funerals, ritual occasions, etc.'], (p. 583). These factors certainly are weighty. However, I would like to concentrate on a feature of Hinduism that is lacking among the tribes and has often enough been stressed by students of Hinduism. It is that the communities that are contained within 'Hinduism', whether they are high or low in the Hindu hierarchy, are definable by the values, moral or otherwise, including the values of the caste system, that are laid down by the written codes of the system. These codes are, of course, contained within the corpus of written literature in the *Sanskrit* language, as controlled (i.e. composed and interpreted) by a special community, who are regarded as the apex of the hierarchy, viz. the brahmins. When modern ethnographers, Indian or non-Indian, refer to 'Sanskritization' as a process by which a community low in the hierarchy can attain a higher rank, the meaning is usually only that some (item or) items having higher token value are adopted from the total corpus and thereby some amelioration in ranking is achieved. Does all this mean merely that 'tribals' are non-literate and thus cut off from the Sanskritic, written codes of Hinduism? Certainly not in theory only the brahmins (and exceptionally a few from other top communities) are literate in this sense within Hinduism. But it seems, and has been so expressed, that all communities within Hinduism, even those farthest from exercising any control or attempting any interpretation of the written code, are under the control of the system. This may well provide us with the most important section of our desired definition. Hindu communities are within the system; they are the jātis. The 'tribals' are outside the system; they are not jātis.

However, as soon as we attempt to be more definite, it begins to be evident that we have not solved the definition problem. When we begin to fill in characteristics of the jāti system, the difficulties appear. A jāti is, with the most minor of exceptions, an endogamous community (a caste is usually a cluster of jātis)—but, with the same proviso about exceptions, so is a tribe in India. A jāti, or a caste, frequently is characterized by its practice and/or monopoly of a special occupation—the brahmins as a cluster of many ritually-specialized endogamous jātis, the blacksmiths as a cluster of many iron-working endogamous jātis, etc. As linguistic scholars, we must recognize that difference of dialect or language is often a differentiating mark of jātis endogamous as against an Oriya-speaking fisherman jāti. We are familiar with the Saurashtran silk-weaving endogamous jāti in Tamil-Nadu, or the Indo-Aryan-speaking endogamous blacksmith-musicians: in Burushaski-speaking Hunza.

As soon as we turn ethnographer, we find that we have established, not an opposition between jātis and tribes neatly separated by two sets of characteristics, but a cultural continuum. There are many rather pure jāti communities at one end, characterized by many strong features of Hinduism, but at the other end hardly any pure tribal communities, without any jāti characteristics, and in some areas tribals are under pressure, or in some sense pressure themselves, to undergo Sanskritization and take on jāti characteristics.

Areal considerations enter into the matter, e.g., the communities of the Nilgiris of South India, very isolated geographically on their 7000 foot, non-tropical plateau, are in some respects tribal, non-jāti in their characteristics, so much so that for a century at least of scholarly enquiry the Todas were taken to be typically tribal. But, it has been pointed out that the three (or four) central communities of the area showed in aboriginal times many jāti characteristics, both individually and in their relations to one another; see in general Mandelbaum 1970, especially pp. 599-603; for the Todas, Walker 1986, passim; for the Badagas, who were a jāti people when they came to the Nilgiris in the 15th century and there adopted some tribal characteristics, Madelbaum, *op. cit.*, p. 588, and Paul Hockings quoted there, and Hockings 1980. Similarly, the Central Indian tribes, who are in many ways more tribal in their characteristics than the Nilgiri tribes (e.g., more generally practising in the past slash-and-burn agriculture), are yet not untouched by jāti characteristics. It has been pointed out (Elwin, 1951, pp. 25 ff.) that, aboriginally and even more in modern times, many of these tribes depended on Hindu artisan/weaver jātis for the manufacture of their garments; e.g., 'a number of tribes, especially in Orissa, use cloth woven for them by Hindu weavers from yarn spun by themselves....When the Saora yarn is ready it is taken to a Pano neibhbour for weaving....The Saora, who deeply mistrusts his Pano friend, sits over him as he works, instructing him at every turn....' .

The Task of a Linguist

However 'tribal' is defined, we as linguistic scholars must make it our first duty to collect the languages of the tribes of the Indian subcontinent. We must collect data and present the learned world with descriptions of the languages, whether in an old-fashioned mode or in the newer transformational-generative style. Whatever the mode adopted, we must strive to present all features of the language, phonological, morphological, syntactic, lexical. And, though this may sound elementary, texts are urgently needed (and not merely sentences); the good old grammar of Kui by the missionary Winfield has not yet been supplemented by texts in sufficient bulk to allow a really good analysis of the verb forms used when there is an object, direct or indirect, in the 1st or 2nd person. We are going to be most interested in the languages of such areas as the Nilgiris and the non-jāti hills and jungles, often very inaccessible, of Central India; on the peripheries are the Assamese area and the sub-Himalayan tracts of the north; isolated internally are certain areas in the Western Ghats from the Konkan area south all the way to southern Kerala. I too, as a Dravidianist, am not going to allow myself to be debarred from the Muslim tribal area of Baluchistan where live the Dravidian speaking Brahui. The languages involved belong to all the major families of the area—Indo-Aryan, Dravidian, Munda and its Austro-Asiatic congeners in Assam, Tibeto-Burman, and Iranian. Adequate comparative-historical work on these families will only be achieved when descriptive work on many tribal languages has been added to what we already have in the record, whether literary or non-literary. It would be invidious to specify remaining gaps—but not so to point out what is obvious, that work on Indo-Aryan is the farthest advanced so far (Masica, 1991).

Language Contact and Structural Convergences

Comparative-historical research will have to take much account of 'areal linguistic' contacts and resulting convergences. This may be expected between any of the languages that are geographically contiguous. Though something has already been achieved, e.g. identification in the demonstrative pronouns of the results of contact between Dravidian, Munda, and Indo-Aryan in Central India, it is a sobering thought to realize how little research of this nature has been undertaken in that area so far. Since bilingualism or multilingualism is the operative social factor in such matters, it is discouraging to realize how little we know so far that bears on this (Census data are very unsatisfactory).

It will have to be taken into account also that the tribal communities have for many centuries (perhaps millennia?) been in contact, more or less close, with jāti communities, even if these latter were not always of a high rank. Linguistically, this implies contact of the tribal languages with the major Indian languages, in some dialect or other. For the Central Indian tribes this means Telugu, Marathi, Hindi, Halbi, or Oriya. Even the Nilgiri languages Kota and Toda have not been unaffected by contact with Tamil, Malayalam, or Kannaḍa, quite apart from the close contact over recent centuries with the immigrant Badaga offshoot of Kannaḍa. It will at times be difficult to differentiate the effects of tribal contacts from those between tribal and nontribal communities. It hardly needs to be pointed out that, if there is postulation of centuries-old contact with a major language, the cooperation of linguistic historians (philologists) of the major languages will be necessary to identify and explicate the results of such contacts. This has hardly been envisaged so far, except for Telugu and the tribal languages which have been in contact with it over the centuries (an interest of our colleague, Bh. Krishnamurti). One lexical item which was early identified (by my late colleague in the work on the Dravidian etymological dictionary, T. Burrow) is the Parji item *ḍukki* 'cultivated upland field' (DEDR 688 **uṛ-*'to plow'), which with its non-Parji but clearly Telugu metaphony must be an early borrowing from Telugu, which in the record has only the later form *dukki* 'plowing, tillage' (with the development within Telugu **ḍ- > d-*). One of the most recent discoveries (by Bh. Krishnamurti; DEDR, p. viii) is that (DEDR 2582 'parrot') Gondi *siṛī,* Konḍa *siṛa,* Pengo *hiṛa* are borrowed from (DEDR 1584) pre-Telugu **ciḷi,* which is a representative of Proto-Dravidian **kiḷi* with Telugu palatalization of **k.*

In my previous studies I have come to the conclusion that in defining a linguistic area lexical borrowings are secondary to structural convergences, phonological, syntactic, morphological. Lexical borrowings can be observed between any two languages, whether contiguous or (in the modern mode of extended communications) non-contiguous; Chinese words for 'tea' are used worldwide without thereby having any relevance for areal study. However, once a linguistic area has been identified for the proper reasons, lexical studies may again become relevant.

It can be difficult, restricting ourselves to tribal languages, to identify structural convergences. This difficulty results really from our lack of many details so far. It has been shown that the Dravidian Brahui language in Baluchistan, through the speakers' close political and cultural relations with the Iranian Balochi speakers, has become in many respects thoroughly Iranianized. Its vowel system is no longer Dravidian, but Balochi; it has lost the Dravidian gender system; it makes no distinction between inclusive and exclusive in the 1st plural pronouns; it has a system of pronominal suffixes, quite separate from the verbal pronominal inflections, which is general Iranian and NW Indo-Aryan in type, but in detail is closest to that of the contiguous Rāxšānī Balochi (the system is Iranian, but the morphemes are Dravidian in origin); it has in the verb an aspect system (not yet completely clarified) which is Iranian, and which in one of the aspects involves a prefix *a-*, which is borrowed from Balochi (prefixing is not a Dravidian trait); a conjunction (subordinator) *ki* is Iranian in origin (Masica, 1991, p. 414), and has usages exactly corresponding to those of Balochi. All these traits were identified by myself (Emeneau 1962) and later confirmed by the Iranianist J. Elfenbein (1982) from his much more exact knowledge of Balochi, along with an additional trait, the use in Brahui of a Balochi case suffix -ā 'motion to or from'. This is in fact the most conspicuous and best known instance so far of contact and structural convergence in the case of tribal languages. The efficient cause, bilingualism, is well-known as holding between these two communities, but even so, demographic fieldwork is still much needed in this case.

In the Nilgiris little has been identified of this kind. The retention in Kota, Toda, and several of the more marginal tribal languages, of the three-way contrast between dental, alveolar, and retroflex stops and other consonants is well-known; even though it is retention rather than innovation, it can be regarded as a type of convergence. But the whole subject is overshadowed by the general historical hypothesis about Kota and Toda, that they split off from South Dravidian, or more specifically pre-Tamil, about two millennia ago (they do not show the palatalization of the initial velar stop before front vowels, which happened in Tamil prior to all the records of that language). This assumes that they are coequal members of a subgroup, having split after arrival in the isolation of the Nilgiris. But they have developmental features in common, perhaps most conspicuously the phonological feature of loss of short vowels and change of **i* to *y* in non-initial syllables of the word. The question arises as to whether this change took place before the split of the subgroup, or whether it took place in one language and diffused into the other (convergence), or whether indeed (what seems implausible) it took place independently in the two languages after they split. No evidence has been identified so far that would lead towards an answer to this question. In fact, the situation has been stated too simply; these two Nilgiri languages are not the only Dravidian languages in which this kind of loss of vowels has occurred, and even colloquial Tamil shows a great deal of it. Similarly, Toda and Kota alone show use of the general South Dravidian verbal past stem in other paradigms than the past.

But a few Nilgiri studies have been profitable. Notable is the demonstration that Badaga shows convergence with Toda and Kota in having a class of verbs with intransitive/transitive contrast carried by contrasting past tense suffixes **-nt-* and **-tt-*, a trait of South Dravidian (including the Nilgiri group) which Kannaḍa, of which Badaga is an offshoot, is quite without (Emeneau 1967, pp. 365-413, especially 392-4).

In the Central Indian tribal area Dravidian and Munda languages show some tempting convergence in the demonstrative pronominal forms. Analysis was attempted, but without any sure conclusions about direction of diffusion in Emeneau 1980. Much new data and reanalysis on the Munda side (unpublished paper by Norman H. Zide) have shown the need for reworking of the Dravidian material; Zide's paper finds diffusion from Dravidian sources into some of the Munda languages. This subject however is not yet exhausted. So far as I know, much more work needs to be done in this area.

Lexical Convergences

On shifting our attention from structural convergences to lexical items, we find again that little has been done so far. Investigation is difficult when the languages belong to the same language family, most difficult if they belong to the same subgroup or to closely related subgroups. This last is the case of the Nilgiri languages; even so, a first step has been taken by Zvelebil (1980) in a paper entitled 'A plea for Nilgiri areal studies', and several instances have been found in which the original source of diffusion has been identified. A recent (still unpublished) study by myself of names of botanical species found only in the non-tropical Nilgiri plateau has identified several items which may have originated in Toda-Kota and been borrowed into Badaga. Much easier is the identification of the source of borrowing when languages belong to different families. The simplest situation is that when two languages are involved. Such is the Brahui-Balochi pair, and here there has been sufficient study on both the Dravidian and the Iranian sides to identify many lexical borrowings in both directions. Those from Balochi to Brahui forming the great majority but still there being a respectable minority of borrowings from Brahui into Balochi.

In the Central Indian tribal area, with its two, or even three language families, even though structural convergences have so far tended to elude identification, two studies of lexical items have been made by myself. I would refer to 'The right hand is the "eating hand"' (Emeneau 1987.263-73) and 'Joking relationships in India: a linguistic note' (Emeneau 1992.73-83). Both are concerned with matters that require some ethnographic knowledge (or should one say 'sophistication'?).

The first is known to every inhabitant of the Indian sub-continent by indoctrination from childhood. The linguistic identification of the right hand as the 'eating hand' (literally 'hand with which one eats' or the like) turned up after much search in the lexicon, word-lists, etc., assisted by the entries in CDIAL, DED/DEDR, and Pinnow 1959. The languages which have such lexical items are a great bloc, not entirely continuous, but concentrated in what can be roughly identified as Central India, and made up of such Dravidian languages as Parji, the group Gondi to Kui-Kuwi, Kuṛux and Malto, to which Telugu is to be added, and many Munda languages both Southern and Northern. The contiguous Oriya ('less-than-standard' colloquial), dialectal Hindi, and Lamani-Banjara as recorded in Pune, and even normal Gujarati are to be added. This is to be interpreted as a linguistic areal-feature. But no morphology or forms can be reconstructed, even within any one of the families. In Dravidian the verbs involved are three in numbers: **tin-* 'to eat', **uṇ-* 'to eat, drink', and in Telugu *kuḍi-* 'to drink, eat' (which ceased to be used as a verb in this meaning in the 14th-15th centuries), and various types of morphology seen in the verbal attribute forms are very divergent. The data can only be interpreted as the results of a calquing process spreading from language to language, and even if Telugu provides an early date (its item must have been formed before the verb meaning became extinct), no definite chronology or language of origin can be found (so far). The calquing process must still be going on, since for Dravidian Parji and Munda Santali and Mundari doublets have been recorded, one the 'eating' form and the other an older form, not further analyzable, than as meaning 'right hand'.

The other study, on joking relationships, turned out much less satisfactory. For ethnologists this relationship is the relaxed social one that holds in North India in some castes between a woman and her husband's younger brothers and between a man and his wife's younger sisters. The ethnologists have not in fact settled on a statement of the incidence of this relationship in the various castes, and we know all too little of where or how it is found tribally. It is possible that in South India and in various tribes of Central India it holds between cross-cousins. I found (I hope correctly—but my necessary use of interpreters as intermediaries may have misled me) that the Kolams, in a Marathi-speaking area of Central India, used for 'cross-cousin' terms that meant literally 'person with whom one laughs/who laughs with one'. Those who collected information on others of the languages of the subgroup Kolami-Naiki of Chanda-Parji-Gadaba found similar terms (but the classes of persons so denominated vary somewhat in the recordings, and the ethnographic data are clearly faulty). This Dravidian subgroup splits into two sub-subgroups (about 200 miles apart) and each uses a different verb meaning 'to laugh'. One neighboring Gondi dialect (Muria) uses an equivalent term, with a historically third verb, and the very distant Kuṛux uses still another verb in an equivalent term. In the Munda family in two distinct areas (but related spatially to the Dravidian areas) equivalent terms are reported based on two different verbs. Again calquing would seem to be the explanation, but no definite sources or historical relations are evident.

Conclusions: The Need for Ethno-Semantic Material

From these two studies it would seem that we need not only a firmer methodology, but also a certainly better or more adequate data, including texts. It should however be clear that in studying tribal languages we must be ethnologists, in order at least, to know what our tribals are talking about and what they mean. I end with what I think is a very instructive incident in my study of the Toda language in the Nilgiris. The language is aberrantly difficult enough to begin with. The ethnology of the Todas, aberrant too, was thought to have been very adequately described by Rivers (1906). However, in my recording of song texts, a unit *poḷy o·ḷ ṇo·ṡ̌ky* appeared (Emeneau 1971; concordance, p. 929); *no·ṡ̌ky* means 'shame' (DEDR 3639, cf. Kannaḍa *nācike,* Kota *na·ckm*). This song-unit, as it turned out when my records of songs had become sufficiently large, is used as the formula whenever shame is mentioned as being felt, e.g. especially in song 138.2 (1971, p. 435 f.) when a woman feels this after her husband talks of divorcing her because of her lack of sons. But what was *poḷy o·ḷ* 'the people of the *poḷy*'? The word *poḷy* was already well-known as the term for the dairy-building and also as the specific word for a Badaga house (as opposed to *a·s* 'a Toda house'); it is in DEDR 4018, derived from **paḻḻi,* which means basically 'hamlet, small settlement' or 'house'. The known Toda meanings seemed to yield no sense in this song-unit, nor did River's *püliol* (a very defective recording) which he defined as 'relatives whose intermarriage is prohibited'.

A certain amount of probing (my interpreters were Christian Todas) produced the meaning 'the people of a matrilineage'—most unexpected since River's account of social organization made it very clear that the Todas were organized in partilineages which are all-important in the economic and ritual aspects of the culture and are exogamous. It turned out that they are also organized in matrilineages, whicn are exogamous, making the marriage rules and use of kinship terms even more complicated than Rivers had found. There are manifestations of 'shame' or 'embarrasment' towards this matrilineal organization—hence the use of this phrase 'shame before/about one's matrilineal relatives' as the song formula for any 'shame'. From this shame resulted the concealment of the matrilineages from Rivers, and the attempt of one of my informants to avoid the subject and the substitution of other phrases by my Christian informant/interpreter in song 230.28 (Emeneau 1971, pp. 694, 821). My published material on the matrilineages was an important ethnological addition to what had been known about Toda culture, and a lexical addition gained by ethnological investigation. If it was doubted by Yalman (1967), Prince Peter's fieldwork had backed up and validated mine (Peter 1951), and Walker's fieldwork (1986) further authenticated it. Also the theoretical work on Dravidian kinship by Trautmann (1981) finds it valid.

The moral is, as I stated earlier: careful ethnography is an essential ingredient of lexical work with tribals.

REFERENCES

CDIAL = R.L. Turner, 1966. *A Comparative Dictionary of the Indo-Aryan Languages.* London: Oxford University Press.

DEDR = T. Burrow and M.B. Emeneau 1984. *A Dravidian Etymological Dictionary,* 2nd ed. Oxford: Clarendon Press.

Elfenbein, J., 1982. 'Notes on the Balochi-Brahui Linguistic Commensality'. *Transactions of the Philological Society* 1982.77-98.

Elwin, Verrier, 1951. *The tribal art of Middle India.* Bombay: Oxford University Press.

Emeneau, M.B., 1962, *Brahui and Dravidian Comparative Grammar.* (University of California Publications in Linguistics, 27.) Berkeley and Los Angeles: University of California Press:

—, 1967. 'The South Dravidian languages', *JAOS* 87.365-413.

—, 1971. *Toda Songs.* Oxford: Clarendon Press.

—, 1980. 'Indian pronominal demonstrative pronouns—a revision', *Proceedings of the Sixth Annual Meeting of the Berkeley Linguistics Society*, 20-27.

—, 1987. 'The right hand is the "eating hand"', *Dimensions of Social Life: Essays in Honor of David G. Mandelbaum* (ed. Paul Hockings; Berlin: Mouton de Gruyter), 263-73.

—, 1992. 'Joking relationships in India: a linguistic note', *Dimensions of Sociolinguistics in South Asia: papers in Memory of Gerald Kelley* (eds. Edward C. Dimock, Jr. Braj B. Kachru, Bh. Krishnamurti; New Delhi: Oxford & IBH Publishing Co.), 73-83.

Hockings, Paul, 1980. *Ancient Hindu refugees: Badaga Social History*, 1550-1975. Delhi: Vikas Publishing House.

Mandelbaum, David G., 1970. *Society in India*. Berkeley and Los Angeles: University of California Press.

Masica, Colin P., 1991. *The Indo-Aryan Languages*. Cambridge: Cambridge University Press.

Peter, H.R.H. Prince of Greece and Denmark, 1951. 'The mother sibs of the Todas of the Nilgiris', *Eastern Anthropologist* 5.65-73.

Pinnow, Heinz-Jürgen, 1959. *Versuch Einer Historischen Lautlehre der Kharia-Sprache*. Wiesbaden: Otto Harrassowitz.

Rivers, W.H.R., 1906. *The Todas*. London: Macmillan and Co.

Trautmann, Thomas R., 1981. *Dravidian kinship*. Cambridge: Cambridge University Press.

Walker, Anthony R., 1986. *The Toda of South India: A New Look*. Delhi: Hindustan Publishing Co.

Winfield, W.W., 1928. *A Grammar of the Kui Language*. Calcutta: Asiatic Society of Bengal.

—, 1929. *A Vocabulary of the Kui Language (Kui-English)*. Calcutta: Asiatic Society of Bengal.

Yalman, Nur, 1967. *Under The Bo Tree: Studies in Caste, Kinship, and Marriage in the Interior of Ceylon*. Berkeley and Los Angeles: University of California Press.

Zvelebil, Kamil V., 1980. 'A plea for Nilgiri areal studies', *IJDL, International Journal of Dravidian Linguistics* 9.1-22.

CHAPTER 4

THE SCHEDULED TRIBES AND THEIR LANGUAGES

K.S. Singh

Introduction

The question whether the Scheduled Tribes of India can be described as indigenous populations has been widely debated. The indigenous populations have been defined[1] as those consisting of the existing descendants of the people who inhabited the present territory of the country wholly or partially, and those who were reduced subsequently to non-dominant colonial conditions by the people of a different culture. These indigenous people have lived more in conformity with their particular social, economic and cultural customs and traditions than with the institutions of the country of which they now form part, under a state structure which incorporates national, social and cultural categories of the other sections of the populations which are predominant. This concept of the indigenous people is more applicable to Australia and the Americas than the ancient and pluralistic societies of Indias. The concept of tribes in India is an administrative, jural and political concept which is applied to such sections of the populations as are relatively isolated. Secondly, according to the dominant view, the major racial types in India such as the Cacausoid, Proto-

Austroloid or Austroloid, Mongoloid and Negrito came from outside and made India their home. India became a melting pot. Many of the so called backward and isolated communities moved up the social ladder and acquired political power and founded the states like the Gonds, Bhils, Nagvansis, Kacharis, Ahoms etc. As ethnographers discovered, many castes rose from tribal matrices. However, there were also many relatively isolated communities who sank into the social morass, and were exploited. Such communities are subsumed by the constitutional categories of Scheduled Tribes, Scheduled Castes and other educationally and specially backward classes. In recent years the pressure on resources like land, forest and water of the Scheduled Tribes has mounted and they have been displaced. Their land has been taken away. A great deal of their culture and traditional institutions have been eroded. Yet, some of the tribes have made use of the democratic processes to acquire political power. They control the states in the Northeast and occupy high position in middle India where tribes are present in sizeable numbers. In many such areas they are demanding the application of the Sixth Schedule of the Constitution to acquire a measure of political authority, a share in regional structure of power. Recent studies also suggest that a great deal of autonomy in terms of culture has survived. However, the key issue today is the protection of the tribal people against exploitation, guaranteeing their rights in their resources so that they are able to develop according to their genius and aspirations.

There is a provision for the protection of the distinctive language, script and culture of the minorities. Although the word 'minority' is not defined in the Constitution, it may be presumed that the tribes, for such purposes, are included among the ethnic, religious or linguistic minorities.

The People of India

In a recent survey under 'The People of India' project conducted by the Anthropological Survey of India, 461 tribal communities have been identified all over the country, of which 174 are subgroups. Many of the latter are as good as discrete categories. The total population of Scheduled Tribes in the country stands at 51,628,638 (1981 census). They constitute 7.76 per cent of the total population (1981 census). They are speread in all states except Punjab and Haryana and in all Union Territories except Chandigarh, Delhi and Pondicherry. Out of their total population in the country, 93.80 per cent are returned from rural areas, whereas only 6.20 per cent are urbanised. Their largest concentration is in Madhya Pradesh (23.22 per cent), followed by Orissa (11.46 per cent), Bihar (11.26 per cent), Maharashtra (11.18 per cent), Gujarat (9.39 per cent), Rajasthan (8.10 per cent), Andhra Pradesh (6.15 per cent) and West Bengal (5.95 per cent). The small population is returned from Goa, Daman and Diu (0.02 per cent), Andaman and Nicobar Islands (0.04 per cent), Lakshadweep (0.07 per cent), Sikkim (0.14 per cent), Dadra and Nagar Haveli (0.16 per cent), etc.

Tribals subsist on forest, fishing, agriculture and horticulture. Some of them are involved in shifting cultivation. In the post-colonial period there has been a trend towards occupational diversity. Ecological degradation has severly curtailed the traditional occupation of the tribal communities. For instance, the number of the tribes practising hunting and gathering has declined by 44 per cent. On the other hand, there is a rise in the incidence of terrace cultivation (52 per cent) and settled cultivation (42 per cent). The evidence suggests that the tribals are settling down as peasants. As many as 32.67 per cent of the tribals professions are returned as agricultural labourers.

The size of the tribal communities is also an important factor. There are communities with a very large population of 3 to 7 million. The largest tribes are the Gond (7,449,193), Bhil (7,367,973), Santal (4,260,842), Mina (2,087,075) and Oraon (1,871,995). A few tribes such as Haisa Tangsa, Hotang Tangsa, Katin Tangsa, etc., have returned only a single soul (1981 Census). The Bomdo, Jambo Karka, Kongbo etc., have between two to ten persons. The Andamanese including all subgroups have only 42 persons; other small groups are the Jarwas (31), Chaimal (18), Onges (97), Aranadan (236), Kochuvelan (53) etc. The 1981 Census has thus recorded five tribes with a single soul, 17 tribes with a population of 2-10 persons, 16 tribes with that of 11-50 persons, nine tribes with 51-100, and 17 tribes with 101-500 persons.

A notable feature of the People of India project has been the generation of information on languages and dialects spoken by different communities of India including the tribals. We collected information on the languages/dialects spoken within a family or kin group and those spoken outside. The picture that emerges from the analysis of our data is an interesting one. We have identified the langustes/dialects spoken by 449 tribes/subtribes and their segments (See Appendix I).

Major Findings

We may now discuss the major findings. First, though Indo-Aryan languages are spoken by a vast majority of the tribal communities, those speaking Dravidian and Tibeto-Burman languages are not fewer in terms of number of communities. According to our study the tribal communities speaking Indo-Aryan languages are 163, Dravidian 107, Tibeto-Burman 143 (including Siamese-Chinese 1), Austro-Asiatic 30 and those speaking Andamanese are only 4 (Appendix II).

The total number of languages claimed by the tribal communities as their mother tongue is about 200 only. Almost half of these belong to the Tibeto-Burman family of languages. Fifty four languages belong to the Indo-Aryan family of languages; twentynine belong to the Dravidian family of languages; twenty to the Austro-Asiatic family of languages and the Andamanese languages family is represented by four languages that are spoken in the Andaman groups of Islands as mentioned earlier.

Many tribal communities speak their tribal languages (269). Almost as many of them (223) speak the Scheduled languages and their variants. One hundred and forty seven tribal communities speak the 10 Scheduled languages such as Assamese (6), Bengali (6), Gujarati (18), Hindi (13), Kannada (16), Malayalam (17), Marathi (15), Oriya (23), Tamil (12) and Telugu (21). Variants of the respective Scheduled language spoken by the tribal communities are as follows: Bengali (2), Hindi (64), Malayalam (1), Oriya (3), Sindhi (1) and Tamil (5).

Out of the 623 tribal communities (state and union territorywise) taken up for study by us, only 123 communities (19.47 per cent) have been reported as monolingual. The highest number of monolingual communities are found in Madhya Pradesh (23), followed by Andhra Pradesh (13), Gujarat (12), and Orissa (11).

The tribal communities of India speak in total 55 languages including Nagamese and Nafamese for intergroup communication. Most of the tribal communities are linguistically heterogeneous. Only a few are linguistically homogenous, the ethnic boundary being coterminous with their linguistic boundary (Annamalai, 1990).

While Indian bilingualism is reported to be stable, thanks to our mother-tongue loyalties and reluctance to identify our bilingual affiliation, tribal bilingualism is described as relatively unstable (Annamalai, 1990: 3) owing to their exposure to other communities and the rapid pace of change. Tribal mother tongue speakers are only 12.8 million against their population of 29.9 million in 1961. The incidence of bilingualism, even trilingualism, among the tribal communities studied by us in situations of language contact, is much higher than generally believed. For instance, most of the tribes are bilingual in regional or state or scheduled language. They are trilingual in English or in the *lingua franca* in some regions that has emerged such as Nafamese, Nagamese, Deshi and Sadri. This shows the extent of acculturation and opening up of tribal people in their region to the influences and processes from outside their society. Both tribal males and tribal females are highly bilingual to the extent of 56 per cent and 44 per cent respectively, the gender difference being only 12 per cent which shows the mobility of tribal men and women. The male speakers of non-tribal mother tongues are 12 per cent and the female speakers only 6 per cent. Another interesting point made by the linguists is that tribal bilingualism is entirely rural; non-tribal bilingualism is higher in urban areas. The tribals are not so much bilingual in other tribal languages as in the scheduled languages such as Assamese, Bengali, Hindi, English etc., as mentioned earlier.

Many tribal languages are losing ground. There has been substantial shifting of languages. It is reported about Bhili (M. Ishtiaq) that there is only one district, that is Dungarpur in Rajasthan where Bhili is spoken by cent per cent Bhils. In the heartland of the Bhil region in districts of Banswara, Ratlam, Jhabua and Dhulia there is language maintenance, but elsewhere Bhili has suffered substantial erosion. There are 32 districts out of 53 districts in which cent per cent Bhils have declared non-tribal language or the local language as their mothertongue. Among the Gonds also, many subgroups have given up

Gondi language and switched over to the regional languages. The only tribes who have relatively held out, appear to be Mundari and Oraon speaking tribal groups in middle India.

NOTES

1. Based on the material contributed to the World Guide of Ethnic Minorities and Indigenous Peoples for El Collegio De Mexico, February 1991.

REFERENCES

Singh, K.S., 1994. *The Scheduled Tribes, People of India,* Vol. III, Oxford University Press, New Delhi.

Singh, K.S. and S. Manoharan, 1993. *The Languages and Scripts. People of India.* Vol IX, Oxford Univeristy Press.

Annamalai, E. *Linguistic Dominance and Cultural Dominance : A Study of Tribal Bilingualisms in India.* Presidential Address, XVIII, All India Conference of Dravidian Linguistics, April 19-21, 1990, CIIL, Mysore

Ishtiaq, M. Language change and maintenance among the Bhils in India. *International Journal of Dravidian Linguistics,* Vol. XXI, No. I.

APPENDIX I

The Scheduled Tribes, Their Languages and Distribution

	Sub-Tribe	Language Spoken	State/Union Territory
	1	2	3
	Adi	Adi	Arunachal Pradesh
1	Adi, Ashing	Ashing	Arunachal Pradesh
2	Adi, Bokar	Bokar	Arunachal Pradesh
3	Adi, Bori	Bori	Arunachal Pradesh
4	Adi, Gallong	Gallong	Arunachal Pradesh
5	Adi, Karko	Karko	Arunachal Pradesh
6	Adi, Komkar	Komkar	Arunachal Pradesh

	1	2	3
7	Adi, Milang	Milang	Arunachal Pradesh
8	Adi, Minyong	Minyong	Arunachal Pradesh
9	Adi, Padam	Padam	Arunachal Pradesh
10	Adi, Pailibo	Pailibo	Arunachal Pradesh
11	Adi, Pangi	Pangi	Arunachal Pradesh
12	Adi, Pasi	Pasi	Arunachal Pradesh
13	Adi, Ramo	Ramo	Arunachal Pradesh
14	Adi, Shimong	Shimong	Arunachal Pradesh
15	Adi, Tangam	Tangam	Arunachal Pradesh
16	Adiyan	Kannada	Kerala
17	Agariya	Chhattisgarhi	Madhya Pradesh
18	Aimol	Aimol	Manipur
19	Aka	Hrusso	Arunachal Pradesh
20	Anal	Anal	Manipur
21	Andh	Marathi	Andhra Pradesh
		Marathi	Maharashtra
22	Apatani	Apatani	Arunachal Pradesh
23	Aranadan	Malayalam	Kerala
24	Asur	Asuri	Bihar
		Asuri	Madhya Pradesh
		Asuri	West Bengal
25	Bagatha	Telgu	Andhra Pradesh
		Oriya	Orissa
26	Baiga	Hindi	Madhya Pradesh
27	Bakarwal	Gujjari	Jammu and Kashmir

1		2	3
28	Balti	Balti	Jammu and Kashmir
29	Bangni	Bangni	Arunachal Pradesh
30	Banjara	Banjari	Orissa
31	Barda	Marathi	Maharashtra
		Gujarati	Gujarat
32	Barodia	Marathi	Gujarat
33	Bathudi	Hindi	Bihar
		Oriya	Orissa
34	Bavcha	Gujarati	Gujarat
35	Beda	Ladakhi	Jammu and Kashmir
36	Bedia	Panchpargania	Bihar
		Kudmali	West Bengal
37	Bentho Oriya	Oriya	Andhra Pradesh
38	Bhaina	Chhattisgarhi	Madhya Pradesh
39	Bharia	Hindi	Madhya Pradesh
40	Bharwad	Gujarati	Gujarat
41	Bhatra	Bhatri	Madhya Pradesh
42	Bhil	Bhili	Gujarat
		Bhili	Madhya Pradesh
		Bhili	Maharashtra
		Bhili	Tripura
		Bhili	Maharashtra
43	Bhil, Barela	Rathi	Madhya Pradesh
44	Bhil, Dungri Garasia	Bhili	Gujarat
45	Bhil, Mavchi	Mavchi	Maharashtra
46	Bhil, Tadvi	Bhili	Maharashtra

	1	2	3
47	Bhil, Vasave	Bhili	Gujarat
48	Bhil, Gametia	Mewari	Rajasthan
49	Bhil, Kataria	Wagri	Rajasthan
50	Bhil, Mama	Wagri	Rajasthan
51	Bhil, Mina	Braj Basha	Madhya Pradesh
		Wagri	Rajasthan
52	Bhil, Bhilala	Bhili	Madhya Pradesh
		Bhili	Maharashtra
53	Bhoksa	Hindi	Uttar Pradesh
54	Bhotia	Bhotia	Sikkim
		Bhotia	Uttar Pradesh
		Bhotia	West Bengal
55	Bhottada	Basturia	Orissa
56	Bhuinya	Oriya	Orissa
57	Bhuinya Pauri	Oriya	Orissa
58	Bhumia	Jabalpuri	Madhya Pradesh
		Oriya	Orissa
59	Bhumij	Bhumij	Bihar
		Bhumij	Orissa
		Bengali	West Bengal
60	Bhunjia	Bhunjia	Madhya Pradesh
		Bhunjia	Orissa
61	Biar	Chhattisgarhi	Madhya Pradesh
62	Binjhal	Sambalpuri	Orissa

1	2	3
63 Binjhia	Sadri	Bihar
	Oriya	Orissa
64 Binjhwar	Chhattisgarhi	Madhya Pradesh
	Hindi	Maharashtra
65 Birhor	Birhor	Bihar
	Chhattisgarhi	Madhya Pradesh
	Birhor	Orissa
	Birhor	West Bengal
66 Birjia	Birjia	Bihar
	Birjia	West Bengal
67 Bodh	Bhotia	Himachal Pradesh
	Ladakhi	Jammu and Kashmir
68 Bondo	Bondo	Orissa
69 Broq-Pa	Shina	Jammu and Kashmir
70 Chakma	Chakma	Assam
	Chakma	Mizoram
	Chakma	Tripura
71 Changpa	Changpa	Jammu and Kashmir
72 Charan	Gujarati	Gujarat
73 Chaudhuri/Chaudhri	Gujarati	Gujarat
74 Chenchu	Telugu	Andhra Pradesh
75 Chero	Sadri	Bihar
	Sadri	West Bengal
76 Chik Baraik	Nagpuri	Bihar
	Panchpargania	West Bengal

1	2	3
77 Chiru	Chiru	Manipur
78 Chote	Chote	Manipur
79 Dal	Kui	Orissa
80 Damor	Wagri	Rajasthan
81 Deori	Deori	Arunachal Pradesh
	Deori	Assam
82 Dhanka	Dhanki	Gujarat
	Gujarati	Maharashtra
	Hindi	Rajasthan
83 Dhanwar	Chhattisgarhi	Madhya Pradesh
	Marathi	Maharashtra
84 Dharua	Kudmali	Orissa
85 Dhodia	Dhodia	Dadra and Nagar Hevali
	Dhodia	Daman and Diu
	Dhodia	Gujarat
	Gujarati	Maharashtra
86 Didayi	Didayi	Andhra Pradesh
	Didayi	Orissa
87 Dokhpa/Drokpa	Droskhat(Dokpa)	Jammu and Kashmir
88 Drukpa/Dukpa	Bhotia	Sikkim
	Bhotia	West Bengal
89 Dubla	Gujarati	Dadra and Nagar Haveli
	Gujarati	Daman and Diu
	Gujarati	Gujarat
	Gujarati	Maharashtra

	1	2	3
90	Eravallan	Tamil	Kerala
		Tamil	Tamil Nadu
91	Gadaba	Gadaba	Andhra Pradesh
		Bhatri	Madhya Pradesh
		Gutob	Orissa
	Gaddi	Gadiali	Himachal Pradesh
92	Gaddi (Brahman)	Gadiali	Himachal Pradesh
93	Gaddi (Rajput)	Gadiali	Himachal Pradesh
94	Gamit	Gamit	Gujarat
		Konkani	Maharashtra
95	Gangte	Gangte	Manipur
96	Gara	Ladakhi	Jammu and Kashmir
97	Garasia/Girasia	Garasia	Rajasthan
98	Garo	Garo	Assam
		Garo	Meghalaya
		Garo	Nagaland
		Garo	Tripura
		Garo	West Bengal
99	Gond	Gondi	Andhra Pradesh
		Sadri	Bihar
		Gondi	Orissa
100	Gond, Abuj Maria	Maria	Madhya Pradesh
101	Gond, Amat Gond	Chhattisgarhi	Madhya Pradesh
102	Gond, Arakh	Naiki	Maharashtra
103	Gond, Bada Maria	Maria	Maharashtra
104	Gond, Bis.Horn Maria	Maria	Madhya Pradesh

	1	2	3
105	Gond,Chota Maria	Maria	Maharashtra
106	Gond, Dheria Gond	Chhattisgarhi	Madhya Pradesh
107	Gond, Dhulia	Bundhelkhandi	Madhya Pradesh
108	Gond, Dhur Gond	Chhattisgarhi	Madhya Pradesh
109	Gond, Dhurwa	Parji	Madhya Pradesh
110	Gond, Dorla	Gondi	Madhya Pradesh
111	Gond, Govari	Marathi	Maharashtra
112	Gond, Jhare Gond	Gondi	Maharashtra
113	Gond, Kandra Gond	Chhattisgarhi	Madhya Pradesh
114	Gond, Khatola Gond	Hindi	Madhya Pradesh
115	Gond, Kol Bhuta	Hindi	Madhya Pradesh
116	Gond, Mana	Marathi	Maharashtra
117	Gond, Mannewar	Telugu	Maharashtra
118	Gond, Maria Gond	Maria	Maharashtra
119	Gond, Muria	Gondi	Madhya Pradesh
120	Gond, Nagwanshi	Chhattisgarhi	Madhya Pradesh
121	Gond, Naikpod	Telugu	Maharashtra
122	Gond, Ojha	Gondi	Madhya Pradesh
123	Gond, Paharia Gond	Chhattisgarhi	Madhya Pradesh
124	Gond, Raj Gond	Chhattisgarhi	Madhya Pradesh
		Gondi	Maharashtra
125	Gond, Raja Muria	Gondi	Madhya Pradesh
126	Gond, Sabaria Gond	Telugu	Madhya Pradesh
127	Gond, Sargujhia Gond	Chhattisgarhi	Madhya Pradesh
128	Gond, Sargujhia Gond	Chhattisgarhi	Madhya Pradesh

	1	2	3
129	Gond, Sonjhari	Laria	Maharashtra
130	Gond, Thatia	Gondi	Madhya Pradesh
131	Gond/Gondaru	Kannada	Karnataka
132	Gorait	Sadri	Bihar
133	Goudu	Oriya	Andhra Prasesh
134	Gowdalu	Tulu/Kannada	Karnataka
135	Great Andamanese	Andamanese	Andaman and Nicobar Islands
136	Gujjar	Gujjari	Himachal Pradesh
		Parimu	Jammu and Kashmir
137	Hajong	Assamese	Assam
		Hajong	Meghalaya
138	Hakkipikki	Wagri	Karnataka
139	Halam	Halam	Assam
140	Halam, Kaipeng	Halam	Tripura
141	Halam, Kaipeng	Halam	Tripura
142	Halam, Molsgom	Halam	Tripura
143	Halam, Rupini	Kakbarak	Tripura
144	Halba	Halbi	Madhya Pradesh
		Marathi	Maharashtra
		Halbi	Orissa
145	Halba Nagbansi	Halbi	Madhya Pradesh
146	Hansala/Hasalaru	Tulu	Karnataka
147	Hill Miri	Miri	Arunachal Pradesh
	Hill Pulaya	Tamil	Kerala

	1	2	3
148	Hill Pulaya (Karavazhi)	Tamil	Kerala
149	Hill Pulaya (Kurumba)	Tamil	Kerala
150	Hmar	Hmar	Assam
		Hmar	Manipur
		Duhlian-Twang	Mizoram
151	Ho	Ho	Bihar
		Ho	Orissa
		Ho	West Bengal
152	Irular	Tamil	Kerala
		Irula	Tamil Nadu
		Tamil	Karnataka
153	Jaintia	Khasi	Meghalaya
		Khasi	Assam
154	Jamatia	Kakbarak	Tripura
155	Jarawa	Jarawa	Andaman and Nicobar Islands
156	Jatapu	Kuvi (Jatapu)	Andhra Pradesh
		Kuvi (Jatapu)	Orissa
157	Jaunsari	Jaunsari	Uttar Pradesh
158	Juang	Juang	Orissa
159	Kachari	Kachari	Nagaland
160	Kachari, Bodo	Bodo	Assam
		Bodo	Meghalaya
161	Kachari, Burman	Dimasa	Assam

	1	2	3
162	Kachari, Dimasa	Dimasa	Assam
163	Kachari, Hojai	Dimasa	Assam
164	Kachari, Madahi	Bodo	Assam
165	Kachari, Mech	Assamese	Assam
		Bodo	West Bengal
166	Kachari, Sonowal	Assamese	Assam
167	Kadar	Kadar	Kerala
		Tamil	Tamil Nadu
168	Kagati	Kagati	Sikkim
169	Kamar	Chhattisgarhi	Madhya Pradesh
170	Kammara (Ozulu)	Telugu	Andhra Pradesh
171	Kandha Gauda	Kui	Orissa
172	Kanikkar	Malayalam	Kerala
173	Kaniyar	Kannada	Karnataka
		Malayalam	Tamil Nadu
174	Karbi/Mikir	Karbi	Arunachal Pradesh
		Karbi	Assam
		Karbi	Meghalaya
		Karbi	Nagaland
175	Karmali	Khotta	Bihar
176	Katkari/Kathodi	Kokni	Dadra and Nagar Haveli
		Marathi	Gujarat
		Marathi	Maharashtra
		Marathi	Rajasthan

	1	2	3
177	Kattunayakkan	Kannada	Kerala
		Kannada	Tamil Nadu
178	Kawar (Cherwa)	Chhattisgarhi	Madhya Pradesh
179	Kawar (Rathia)	Chhattisgarhi	Madhya Pradesh
180	Kawar (Tanwar)	Chhattisgarhi	Madhya Pradesh
181	Kawar/Kanwar	Chhattisgarhi	Madhya Pradesh
		Chhattisgarhi	Maharashtra
182	Khairwar	Chhattisgarhi	Madhya Pradesh
183	Khamba	Khamba	Arunachal Pradesh
184	Khamiyang	Assamese	Arunachal Pradesh
185	Khampa	Khampa	Himachal Pradesh
186	Khampti	Khampti-Shan	Arunachal Pradesh
187	Kharia	Kharia	Bihar
		Kharia	Madhya Pradesh
		Marathi	Maharashtra
		Kharia	Orissa
		Oriya	West Bengal
188	Kharwar	Sadri	Bihar
		Sadri	Orissa
		Khotta	West Bengal
189	Khasi	Khasi	Meghalaya
		Khasi	Tripura
190	Khasi (Bhoi)	Khasi	Assam
		Khasi	Meghalaya
191	Khasi (Khyntrian)	Khasi	Meghalaya

	1	2	3
192	Khasi (Lyngam)	Khasi	Assam
		Khasi	Meghalaya
193	Khasi (War)	Khasi	Meghalaya
194	Khasi Muslim	Khasi	Meghalaya
195	Khow/Bugun	Bugun	Arunachal Pradesh
196	Kinnaura	Kinnauri	Himachal Pradesh
197	Kir	Gujarati	Madhya Pradesh
198	Kisan	Sadri	Bihar
		Kisan	Orissa
		Sadri	West Bengal
199	Koch	Koch	Meghalaya
200	Kochu Velan	Malayalam	Kerala
201	Kodaku	Korwa	Madhya Pradesh
202	Koirao	Maram	Manipur
203	Koireng	Koireng	Manipur
204	Kokna	Kokni	Dadra and Nagar Haveli
		Kokni	Gujarat
		Kokni	Maharashtra
205	Kol	Hindi	Madhya Pradesh
		Hindi	Maharashtra
206	Kol Lohar	Oriya	Orissa
207	Kolam	Kolami	Andhra Pradesh
		Kolami	Maharashtra
208	Koli (Chunvalia)	Gujarati	Gujarat
209	Koli (Mahadev)	Marathi	Maharashtra

	1	2	3
210	Koli (Malhar)	Marathi	Maharashtra
211	Koli (Talapada)	Gujarati	Gujarat
212	Koli Dhor/ Kolga/ Kolcha	Konkani	Dadra and Nagar Haveli
		Marathi	Gujarat
		Marathi	Karnataka
		Marathi	Maharashtra
213	Kom	Kom	Manipur
214	Konda Dora	Konda	Andhra Pradesh
		Telugu	Orissa
215	Konda Kammara	Telugu	Andhra Pradesh
216	Konda Kapu	Telugu	Andhra Pradesh
217	Konda Reddi	Telugu	Andhra Pradesh
		Telugu	Tamil Nadu
218	Kondh	Kuvi	Andhra Pradesh
		Kuvi	Orissa
219	Kondh (Dongaria)	Kuvi	Orissa
220	Kondh (Sitha)	Kui	Orissa
221	Kora	Khotta	Bihar
		Oriya	Orissa
		Khotta	West Bengal
222	Koraga	Koraga	Karnataka
		Koraga	Kerala
223	Korku	Korku	Madhya Pradesh
		Korku	Maharashtra

	1	2	3
224	Korku (Bawaria)	Korku	Madhya Pradesh
225	Korwa	Sadri	Bihar
		Chhattisgarhi	Madhya Pradesh
		Sadri	Orissa
226	Kota	Kota	Tamil Nadu
227	Kotia/Kotiya/Kutiya	Oriya	Orissa
		Oriya	Andhra Pradesh
228	Kotwalia/Kotwal	Kotwalia	Gujarat
		Kotwalia	Maharashtra
229	Koya	Malayalam	Lakshadweep
230	Koya/Konda Rajulu	Koi (Koya)	Andhra Pradesh
		Telugu	Maharashtra
		Koi	Orissa
231	Koya Dora	Telugu	Andhra Pradesh
232	Koya/Konda Rajulu	Koi (Koya)	Andhra Pradesh
		Koi (Koya)	Madhya Pradesh
		Koi (Koya)	Orissa
233	Kudiya	Tulu	Karnataka
		Tulu	Kerala
234	Kuki	Kuki	Assam
		Kuki	Nagaland
		Kuki	Tripura
235	Kuli	Oriya	Orissa
236	Kuliya/Muliga	Oriya	Andhra Pradesh
237	Kunbi	Gujarati	Gujarat

	1	2	3
238	Kurichchan/Kurichian	Kannada	Tamil Nadu
		Malayalam	Kerala
239	Kuruman	Kannada	Tamil Nadu
240	Kurumba, Mullu Kuruman	Kannada	Kerala
241	Kurumba, Urali Kuruman	Kannada	Kerala
242	Kurumba	Kannada	Kerala
		Kannada	Tamil Nadu
243	Kurumba, Alu Kurumba	Kannada	Tamil Nadu
244	Kurumba, Jenu Kuruba	Kannada	Karnataka
245	Kurumba, Kadu Kuruba	Kannada	Karnataka
246	Kurumba, Mullu Kurumba	Kannada	Karnataka
247	Kuvi Kandh	Kuvi	Orissa
248	Lahaula	Lahauli	Himachal Pradesh
249	Lalung	Lalung	Assam
		Lalung	Mehgalaya
250	Lambadi	Lambani	Andhra Pradesh
251	Lamgang	Lamgang	Manipur
252	Lepcha	Lepcha (Rong)	Sikkim
		Lepcha	West Bengal
253	Lisu	Lisu	Arunachal Pradesh

	1	2	3
254	Lodha	Lodha	Orissa
		Lodha	West Bengal
255	Lohara	Sadri	Bihar
		Bengali	West Bengal
256	Mag	Mag	Tripura
257	Maha Malasar	Tamil	Kerala
		Tamil	Tamil Nadu
258	Mahli	Sadri	Bihar
		Thar	Orissa
		Bengali	West Bengal
259	Majhi	Bundhelkhandi	Madhya Pradesh
260	Majhwar	Chhattisgarhi	Madhya Pradesh
261	Mal Paharia	Bengali	Bihar
		Malto	West Bengal
262	Mala Kuravan	Malayalam	Tamil Nadu
263	Mala Pandaran	Tamil	Kerala
264	Malai Arayan	Malayalam	Kerala
265	Malai Vedan	Malayalam	Tamil Nadu
266	Malaikudi/Maleru	Tulu	Karnataka
		Tulu	Kerala
267	Malasar	Tamil	Kerala
		Tamil	Tamil Nadu
268	Malayali	Tamil	Kerala
269	Malayan (Kongu)	Malayalam	Kerala
270	Malayan (Nattu)	Malayalam	Kerala

	1	2	3
271	Malis	Oriya	Andhra Pradesh
272	Malmi	Malayalam	Lakshadweep
273	Man	Assamese	Assam
		Assamese	Meghalaya
274	Manikfan	Mahal	Lakshadweep
275	Mannan	Tamil	Kerala
		Tamil	Tamil Nadu
276	Manne Dora	Telugu	Andhra Pradesh
277	Marathi	Marathi	Karnataka
		Marathi	Kerala
278	Matya	Telugu	Orissa
279	Mawasi	Hindi	Madhya Pradesh
280	Meda	Kodagu	Karnataka
281	Melacheri	Malayalam	Lakshadweep
282	Memba	Memba	Arunachal Pradesh
283	Miji	Sajalong	Arunachal Pradesh
	Mina		
284	Mina, Chaukidar	Dhundhari	Rajasthan
285	Mina, Zamindari	Dhundhari	Rajasthan
286	Mirdha	Kurukh	Orissa
287	Mishing	Mishing	Arunachal Pradesh
		Mishing	Assam
288	Mishmi Digaru	Mishmi	Arunachal Pradesh
289	Mishmi, Idu	Mishmi	Arunachal Pradesh

	1	2	3
290	Mishmi, Miju	Mishmi	Arunachal Pradesh
	Mizo		
291	Mizo, Bawm	Bawm	Mizoram
292	Mizo, Biate	Biate	Meghalaya
		Biate	Mizoram
293	Mizo, Hualngo	Hualngo	Mizoram
294	Mizo, Lushai	Duhlian-Twang	Mizoram
		Lushai	Tripura
295	Mizo, Mara/Lakher	Lakher (Mara)	Mizoram
296	Mizo, Paite	Paite	Manipur
		Paite	Mizoram
297	Mizo, Pang	Pang	Mizoram
298	Mizo, Pawai	Lai Hawlh	Mizoram
299	Mizo, Ralte	Ralte	Mizoram
300	Mizo, Tlau	Duhlian-Twang	Mizoram
301	Mon	Ladakhi	Jammu and Kashmir
302	Monpa (But)	Monpa	Arunachal Pradesh
303	Monpa (Chugpa)	Monpa	Arunachal Pradesh
304	Monpa (Dirang)	Monpa	Arunachal Pradesh
305	Monpa (Kalaktang)	Monpa	Arunachal Pradesh
306	Monpa (Lishpa)	Monpa	Arunachal Pradesh
307	Monpa (Tawang)	Monpa	Arunachal Pradesh
308	Monsang	Monsang	Manipur
309	Moyon	Moyon	Manipur
310	Mudugar	Muduga	Kerala

	1	2	3
311	Muduvan/Mutuvan	Tamil	Kerala
		Tamil	Tamil Nadu
312	Mukha Dora	Telugu	Andhra Pradesh
313	Munda	Mundari	Bihar
		Bhatri	Madhya Pradesh
		Mundari	Orissa
		Mundari	Tripura
		Mundari	West Bengal
314	Na	Na	Arunachal Pradesh
315	Naga, Angami	Angami	Nagaland
316	Naga, Ao	Ao	Nagaland
317	Naga, Chakhesang	Chakhesang	Nagaland
318	Naga, Chang	Chang	Nagaland
319	Naga, Jeme/Zeme	Zemi	Assam
320	Naga, Kabui/Rongmei	Kabui	Assam
		Kabui	Nagaland
		Kabui	Manipur
321	Naga, Kacha	Kacha Naga	Manipur
322	Naga, Khiamngan	Khiamngan	Nagaland
323	Naga, Konyak	Konyak	Assam
		Konyak	Nagaland
324	Naga, Lotha	Lotha	Nagaland
325	Naga, Mao	Mao	Manipur
326	Naga, Maram	Maram	Manipur
327	Naga, Maring	Maring	Manipur

	1	2	3
328	Naga, Phom	Phom	Nagaland
329	Naga, Pochury	Pochury	Nagaland
330	Naga, Rengma	Rengma	Assam
		Rengma	Nagaland
331	Naga, Sangtam	Sangtam	Nagaland
332	Naga, Sema	Sema	Assam
		Sema	Nagaland
333	Naga, Tangkhul	Tangkhul	Manipur
334	Naga, Yimchunger	Yimchungre	Nagaland
335	Naga, Zeliang	Zeliang	Nagaland
336	Nagesia	Sadri	Madhya Pradesh
		Sadri	West Bengal
337	Nahal	Nimari	Madhya Pradesh
		Korku	Maharashtra
338	Naika/Naikda	Marathi	Maharashtra
		Naikadi	Gujarat
339	Nayak	Telugu	Andhra Pradesh
340	Nayaka	Kannada	Karnataka
341	Nicobarese	Nicobarese	Andaman and Nicobar Islands
342	Nishi/Dafla	Nishi	Arunachal Pradesh
343	Noatia	Kakbarak	Tripura
344	Nocte	Nocte	Arunachal Pradesh
		Nocte	Assam
345	Omanatya	Oriya	Orissa

	1	2	3
346	Onge	Onge	Andaman and Nicobar Islands
347	Oraon	Kurukh	Bihar
		Kurukh	Madhya Pradesh
		Sadri	Maharashtra
		Kurukh	Orissa
		Kurukh	Tripura
		Kurukh	West Bengal
348	Padhar	Gujarati	Gujarat
349	Paliyan	Tamil	Kerala
		Tamil	Tamil Nadu
350	Pando	Chhattisgarhi	Madhya Pradesh
351	Pangwal Brahman	Pangwali	Himachal Pradesh
352	Pangwal Rajput	Pangwali	Himachal Pradesh
353	Panika	Hindi	Madhya Pradesh
354	Paniyan	Malayalam	Kerala
		Malayalam	Tamil Nadu
355	Pao	Bundhelkhandi	Madhya Pradesh
356	Paradhi	Kachchi	Gujarat
357	Pardhi	Gujarati	Maharashtra
358	Paradhi (Phanse)	Marathi	Maharashtra
359	Paradhi (Takankar)	Marwari	Maharashtra
360	Paradhi/Nahar Paradhi	Kachchi	Gujarat
		Gondi	Madhya Pradesh
361	Pardhan	Gondi	Andhra Pradesh
		Gondi	Madhya Pradesh

	1	2	3
362	Parenga	Oriya	Orissa
363	Parhaiya	Baigani	Bihar
364	Paroja	Parji	Andhra Pradesh
		Parji	Orissa
365	Paroja (Pengo)	Pengo	Orissa
366	Patelia	Gujarati	Gujarat
		Gujarati	Madhya Pradesh
		Gujarati	Rajasthan
367	Pathiri Kurichian	Malayalam	Kerala
368	Pentia	Oriya	Orissa
369	Pnar/Syteng	Khasi	Mizoram
370	Pomla	Gujarati	Gujarat
	Purig-Pa (A Territorial Identity)		
371	Rabari	Gujarati	Gujarat
372	Rabha	Assamese	Assam
		Bodo	Meghalaya
		Bengali	West Bengal
373	Raji	Jangali	Uttar Pradesh
374	Rajuar	Oriya	Orissa
375	Rathawa	Gujarati	Gujarat
376	Rathi	Gadiali	Himachal Pradesh
377	Raveri	Mahal	Lakshadweep
378	Reddy Dora	Telugu	Andhra Pradesh

	1	2	3
379	Riang	Riang	Assam
		Riang	Mizoram
		Riang	Tripura
380	Rona	Oriya	Andhra Pradesh
381	Saharia	Hindi	Madhya Pradesh
		Harauti	Rajasthan
382	Santal	Santali	Bihar
		Santali	Orissa
		Santali	Tripura
		Santali	West Bengal
383	Saora	Saora	Andhra Pradesh
		Saora	Madhya Pradesh
		Saora	Orissa
		Bengali	West Bengal
384	Saora (Jora)/Malhar	Saora	Orissa
385	Saora (Lanjia)	Saora	Orissa
386	Saunta	Chhattisgarhi	Madhya Pradesh
387	Saur	Hindi	Madhya Pradesh
388	Sauria Paharia	Malto	Bihar
389	Savar	Savara	Orissa
390	Savara/Savara Kapu	Telugu	Andhra Pradesh
391	Sentinelese	Sentinelese	Andaman and Nicobar Islands
392	Sherdukpen	Sherdukpen	Arunachal Pradesh
393	Sherpa	Sherpa	West Bengal
394	Sholagar (Urali)	Soliga	Tamil Nadu

	1	2	3
395	Shompen	Shompen	Andaman and Nicobar Islands
396	Siddi	Gujarati	Daman and Diu
		Gujarati	Gujarat
397	Singpho	Singpho	Arunachal Pradesh
		Singpho	Assam
398	Soliga/Soligar	Soliga/Kannada	Karnataka
		Soliga	Tamil Nadu
399	Sonr	Bundhelkhandi	Madhya Pradesh
400	Sounti	Oriya	Orissa
401	Sugali	Banjari	Andhra Pradesh
402	Sulung	Sulung	Arunachal Pradesh
403	Swangla	Manchat	Himachal Pradesh
404	Tagin	Tagin	Arunachal Pradesh
	Tangsa	Tangsa	Arunachal Pradesh
405	Tangsa, Havi	Tangsa	Arunachal Pradesh
406	Tangsa, Jugli	Tangsa	Arunachal Pradesh
407	Tangsa, Kimsing	Tangsa	Arunachal Pradesh
408	Tangsa, Lungchang	Tangsa	Arunachal Pradesh
409	Tangsa, Lungphi	Tangsa	Arunachal Pradesh
410	Tangsa, Lungri	Tangsa	Arunachal Pradesh
411	Tangsa, Morang	Tangsa	Arunachal Pradesh
412	Tangsa, Mosang	Tangsa	Arunachal Pradesh
413	Tangsa, Muklom	Tangsa	Arunachal Pradesh
414	Tangsa, Ronrang	Tangsa	Arunachal Pradesh
415	Tangsa, Sangwal	Tangsa	Arunachal Pradesh

	1	2	3
416	Tangsa, Sankey	Tangsa	Arunachal Pradesh
417	Tangsa, Tikhak	Tangsa	Arunachal Pradesh
418	Tangsa, Tonglim	Tangsa	Arunachal Pradesh
419	Tangsa, Yongkuk	Tangsa	Arunachal Pradesh
420	Thado	Thado	Assam
		Thado	Manipur
		Thado	Mizoram
421	Thakru	Mahal	Lakshadweep
422	Thakrufan	Mahal	Lakshadweep
423	Thakur	Marathi	Maharashtra
424	Tharu	Tharu	Uttar Pradesh
425	Tharua	Oriya	Orissa
426	Thoti	Gondi	Maharashtra
427	Tibetan	Tibetan	Sikkim
428	Toda	Toda	Tamil Nadu
429	Toda Christian	Toda	Tamil Nadu
430	Toto	Toto	West Bengal
431	Tripuri	Kakbarak	Tripura
432	Uchai	Kakbarak	Tripura
433	Ulladan	Malayalam	Kerala
434	Urali	Malayalam	Kerala
435	Vaghri	Sarhodi	Gujarat
436	Vaiphei	Vaiphei	Manipur
437	Valmiki	Telugu	Andhra Pradesh
		Kannada	Karnataka

	1	2	3
438	Varli	Varli	Dadra and Nagar Haveli
		Varli	Gujarat
		Varli	Maharashtra
439	Wancho	Wancho	Arunachal Pradesh
440	Yanadi	Telugu	Andhra Pradesh
441	Yanadi (Challa)	Telugu	Andhra Pradesh
442	Yerava	Yerava	Karnataka
443	Yerukula	Yerukula	Andhra Pradesh
444	Yerukula, Kappara-latippa	Yerukula	Andhra Pradesh
445	Yerukula, Katherollu	Yerukula	Andhra Pradesh
446	Yerukula, Korcha	Yerukula	Andhra Pradesh
447	Yerukula, Kuncheti	Yerukula	Andhra Pradesh
448	Zakhring/Meyer	Zakharing (Meyer)	Arunachal Pradesh
449	Zou	Zou	Manipur

APPENDIX II

Languages Spoken by Tribes

Indo-Aryan Family: 1. Assamese 2. Baigani 3. Banjari 4. Bengali 5. Bhatri 6. Bhili 7. Bhunjia 8. Chakma 9. Chhattisgarhi 10. Dhanki 11. Dhodia 12. Dhundhari 13. Gadiali 14. Gamit/Gavti 15. Garasia/Girasia 16. Gojri/Gujjari 17. Gujarati 18. Hajong 19. Halbi 20. Harauti 21. Hindi 22. Jaunsari 23. Kachchi 24. Khotta 25. Kinnui 26. Kokni 27. Konkani 28. Kotwalia 29. Kudamali/Kudmali 30. Thar 31. Lambani 32. Laria 33. Magahi 34. Mahl 35. Marathi 36. Mavchi

37. Mewari 38. Nagpuri 39. Naikadi 40. Nimari 41. Oriya 42. Rathi 43. Sarhodi 44. Shina 45. Tharu 46. Wagri 47. Warli.

Tibeto-Burman Family: 1. Adi Ashing 2. Adi Bokar 3. Adi Bori 4. Adi Gallong 5. Adi Komkar 6. Adi Milang 7. Adi Minyong 8. Adi Padam 9. Adi Karko 10. Pailibo 11. Adi Pangi 12. Adi Pasi 13. Adi Ramo 14. Adi Shimong 15. Adi Tangam 16. Aimol 17. Anal 18. Angami 19. Ao 20. Apatani 21. Balti 22. Bangni/Dafla 23. Bawm 24. Bhotia 25. Biate 26. Bodo 27. Bugun 28. Chakhesang 29. Champa 30. Chang 31. Chiru 32. Chote 33. Chung 34. Dalu 35. Deori 36. Dokpa/Droskat 37. Duhlian-Twang 38. Gangte 39. Garo 40. Halam 41. Hmar 42. Hrusso/Aka 43. Hualngo 44. Kabui 45. Kachari 46. Kagati 47. Kak barak 48. Khamba 49. Khampa 50. Khiamngan 51. Koch 52. Koireng 53. Konyak 54. Kuki 55. Ladakhi 56. Lahauli 57. Lai Hawlh 58. Lakher/Mara 59. Lalung 60. Lamgang 61. Lepcha 62. Lisu 63. Lotha 64. Lushai/Mizo 65. Mag/Mogh 66. Mao 67. Maram 68. Maring 69. Memba 70. Mikir 71. Miri 72. Mishing 73. Mishmi 74. Monpa 75. Monsang 76. Moyon 77. Na 78. Naga 79. Sherdukpen 80. Nishi 81. Nocte 82. Paite 83. Pang 84. Phom 85. Pochury 86. Ralte 87. Rengma 88. Riang 89. Sajalong/Miju 90. Sangtam 91. Sema 92. Sherpa 93. Singpho 94. Sulung 95. Tagin 96. Tangsa 97. Thado 98. Tangkhul 99. Tibetan 100. Toto 101. Vaiphei 102. Wancho 103. Yimchungre 104. Zakhring/Meyer 105. Zemi 106. Zou.

Dravidian Family: 1. Dhurwa 2. Gadaba 3. Gondi 4. Kadar 5. Kannada 6. Kodagu 7. Kolami 8. Koraga 9. Kota 10. Koya/Koi 11. Kui 12. Kurukh 13. Kuvi 14. Malayalam 15. Malto 16. Maria 17. Naiki 18. Parji 19. Pengo 20. Tamil 21. Telugu 22. Toda 23. Tulu 24. Yerava 25. Yerukula.

Austro-Asiatic Family: 1. Asuri 2. Bhumij 3. Birhor 4. Birjia 5. Bondo 6. Diday 7. Gutob 8. Ho 9. Juang 10. Kharia 11. Khasi 12. Kherwari 13. Korku 14. Korwa 15. Kurmi 16. Lodha 17. Mundari 18. Nicobarese 19. Santali 20. Saora/Savara 21. Shompen 22. Thar.

Andamanese Family: 1. Andamanese 2. Jarawa 3. Onge 4. Santinelese.

Siamese-Chinese Family: 1. Khampti

Unclassified: 1. Manchat.

CHAPTER 5

DEMOGRAPHIC INDICATORS OF LANGUAGE PERSISTENCE AND SHIFT AMONG TRIBALS:

A SOCIOLINGUISTIC PERSPECTIVE

Lachman M. Khubchandani

Introduction

In the contemporary climate of development, various traditional and modernising factors affect the issues of identity, the sense of belonging, among tribal societies, and the changing patterns of intra-tribal and intertribal communications among them. This study draws attention to one of the sociocultural indicators (namely, mothertongue claims in the census) signifying the direction of continuity and change among tribal societies in the country. How is this dynamics affecting the sociocultural profile of tribal communities? How is the awareness of belonging to a distinct culture reflected through various processes of acculturation, particularly, claims in decadal census about one's mothertongue, identity through the 'ancestral' language or switching over to the language dominant in the region?

The paper[1] critically reviews the trends of tribal assimilation into the mainstream or of their assertion to a distinct identity. It is based on a more comprehensive study aimed at acquiring a 'grassroots' understanding of tribal societies through their claims of identity and communication in the changed circumstances.

According to the 1981 census, nearly 300 tribal groups in the country comprise 7.9 per cent of the total population; 53.8 million population is notified as belonging to the Scheduled Tribes out of the country's total population of 685 million. In 1950, at the time of formulating the Schedule, the tribal groups comprised over 6 per cent of the total population (cf. 1951 Census). The tribal awareness, in this respect, has significantly grown over the four decades in independent India.

Tribal Language Claims

Most of the tribals, with the exception of the North-East, Andaman & Nicobar Islands and Lakshadweep, live in the midst of sweeping non-tribal populations. During the course of history, though nearly half of the tribal societies still maintain a distinct language as a mark of their identity (49 per cent in 1971, reduced to 42 per cent in 1981), a large section of them tend to switch over to the surrounding non-tribal languages as their mothertongue or retain both languages (ancestral and non-tribal) in home environments, a characteristic feature of plurilingual India (cf. Khubchandani 1983, 1991a).

The 1971 and 1981 census list 81 tribal languages whose population is over 10,000 each: 54 languages of Tibeto-Burman family (4.3 million speakers in 1981), 14 belonging to Austrio family (7.9 million), 11 to Dravidian (4.6 million), and two to Indo-Aryan (5.0 million) families. The total number of those identified with tribal languages is enumerated 22.3 million in 1981 Census (18.4 million in 1971, and 14.7 million in 1961).

A large section of tribals representing Austric, Dravidian and Indo-Aryan languages are spread throughout the central belt of the country, interspersed with vast non-tribal populations. Hence tribal languages in this area are charged with minimum functional load (restricted largely to the home environment) and serving primarily as a mark of group identity. In everyday life activities, these languages are, thus, open to the pressures of assimilation from major regional languages.

On the other hand, tribals representing Tibeto-Burman languages, though constituting a smaller section of the total tribal population (roughly eight percent), exclusively dominate in most parts of the North-East region (along with Khasi, an Austric language). In Assam and Tripura, where the speakers of tribal languages form a 'powerful' minority, they are now becoming quite conscious of their 'ancestral' dominance in the region in recent past specially during the period of Ahom rulers.[2] In recent decades, with a relatively autonomous political set up, many tribal languages in the region are exposed to various functions in diverse sociocultural, educational and mass media settings. Consequently, the pressures of language shift in the region have been somewhat arrested.

There are four tribal languages claimed by over one million speakers each in the country in the 1981 Census:

Bhili, Indo-Aryan, 4.45 million
Santali, Austric, 4.21 million
Gondi, Dravidian, 1.96 million
Kurukh, Dravidian, 1.26 million

In addition, as many as 21 classified tribal languages are spoken by populations between one hundred thousand and one million each: 7 Austric, 9 Tibeto-Burman, 4 Dravidian, and 1 Indo-Aryan. See Table 1:

TABLE 1

Classified Tribal Languages of India 1981

Austric	**Thousands**		**Thousands**
Ho	802	Munda	349
Mundari	753	Savara	235
Khasi	632	Kharia	198
Korku	363		
Tibeto-Burman			
Bodo	858*	Miri	239*
Tripuri	491	Dafla (Nissi)	140
Garo	408	Abor (Adi)	120
Lushai	385	Ao	106
Mikir	157*		

Austric	Thousands		Thousands
Dravidian			
Kui	508	Khond	204
Koya	242	Kisan	155
Indo-Aryan			
Halabi[3]	525		

*Figures of Bodo, Mikir and Miri languages speakers are based on the projected estimates as per the growth rate registered during the decade 1961-71.

Remaining 56 languages (out of the total of 81, enumerated in 1971 and 1981 censuses) are spoken by the population of 10-100 thousand each: 6 Austric, 45 Tibeto-Burman and 5 Dravidian. A bulk of 'other languages' population, 546 thousand in 1981 Census, comprises of such languages which are claimed by less than 10,000 each. It is assumed that most of these belong to the tribal category.

Regional Language Claims

In recent decades various modernisation processes have accelerated the pace of assimilation. The ratio of non-tribal mother tongue claims has increased from 51 per cent (in 1971) to 58 per cent (in 1981). About 12 per cent tribals retain certain hybrid varieties, with the Indo-Aryan base (Lamani or Lambadi, Banjari, Sadri, Khortha, Dangi, Bhatri) or the Dravidian base (Vadari, Yerukula), as their mother-tongues.

The 1961 Census records over 30 such distinct 'tribal' vernaculars. The 1971 Census enumerates 20 of them spoken by more than ten thousand speakers each; total claims amounting to nearly 4.7 million, i.e. 12 per cent of the total tribal population. A bulk of them belong to Indo-Aryan languages (95 per cent), and rest (5 per cent) to Dravidian languages. Prominent tribal vernaculars and their dominant regions, along with the major language with which they are clubbed together, are listed in Table 2.

TABLE 2

'Tribal' Vernaculars of Major Non-Tribal Languages: 1961 and 1971

'Tribal' Vernaculars	Mothertongue speakers 1971 (thousands)	Region
BIHARI (HINDI)		
Sadan/Sadri	807	Bihar, W. Bengal, Madhya Pradesh
Khortha/Khotta	504	Bihar
Nagapuria	335	Bihar
Gawari Panchparganis	21	Bihar
(Tamaria)	18	Bihar
Tharu	11	Bihar
RAJASTHANI (HINDI)		
Lamani	1,203	Andhra Pradesh, Maharashtra
Banjari	472	Karnataka, Maharashtra, Madhya Pradesh
PAHARI (HINDI)		
Bharmauri/Gaddi	70	Himachal Pradesh
CHHATTISGARHI (HINDI)		
Laria	46*	Madhya Pradesh, Orissa
Binjhwari	13	Madhya Pradesh
Baigani	11	Madhya Pradesh
MARATHI[4]		
Kamari	10	Madhya Pradesh
Katkari	5*	Gujarat, Maharashtra
Thakri	4*	Maharashtra
Kathodi	1.6*	Gujarat, Maharashtra
Koli	Neg.	Dadra, Nagar Haveli

'Tribal' Vernaculars	Mothertongue speakers 1971 (thousands)	Region
KHANDESHI		
Ahirani	364	Maharashtra
Dangi	81	Gujarat
BENGALI		
Malpaharia	99	W Bengal, Assam
Chakma	69	Tripura, Mizoram
Haijong	24	Meghalaya
ORIYA		
Bhatri	104	Madhya Pradesh
Saunti	2*	Orissa
KANNADA		
Badaga	105	Tamil Nadu
Kuruba/Kurumba	8	Karnataka, Tamil Nadu
Soliga	2*	Andhra Pradesh, Tamil Nadu
Naiki	1.2*	Karnataka
TELUGU		
Vadari	36	Maharashtra, Karnataka
Chenchu	Neg.	Andhra Pradesh
Yenadi	Neg.	Andhra Pradesh
TAMIL		
Yerukula	68	Andhra Pradesh
Irula/Irulinga	5	Tamil Nadu
MALAYALAM		
Yerava	11	Karnataka
Pania	5*	Kerala, Tamil Nadu

*As per the returns of 1961 Census.

The 1961 Census provides a breakdown of the tribal population (about 40 per cent) identified with dominant regional languages in the country, in addition to those claiming tribal vernaculars, as shown in Table 3:

TABLE 3
Regional Language Claims of Tribals: 1961

Languages	State(s)	Tribal claims: 1961 (thousands)	Percentage to total speakers of the language
Hindi		6.810	
Hindi	HUP Region	4,718	3.8
Rajasthani	Rajasthan	1,314	8.8
Chattisgarhi	MP	546	18.4
Awadhi (Baghelkhandi)	UP, MP	94	16.9
Bhojpuri	Bihar	72	0.9
Magahi	Bihar	12	0.4
Chameali	HP	42	95.5
Pahari	HP	12	1.2
Gujarati	Gujarat	2,529	12.6
Oriya	Orissa	2,213	14.2
Marathi	Maharashtra	1,684	5.1
Telugu	Andhra Pradesh	913	2.4
Assamese	Assam	459	6.8
Bengali	W. Bengal, Tripura	454	1.4
Tamil	Tamil Nadu	268	0.9
Malayalam	Kerala	196	1.2
Kannada	Karnataka	118	0.7
Tulu	Karnataka	29	3.1
Nepali	W. Bengal, Sikkim	18	1.8
Konkani	Goa, Daman & Diu	4	0.3
Kodagu (Coorgi)	Karnataka	0.7	0.9

Vitality of Ancestral Languages

In this context, vitality indices of different languages are worked out on the scale indicating the intensity of retention of an ancestral language in relation to the strength of the tribe by the same/similar name, as per the claims of 1971 Census. At one end of the scale, there are over 30 such languages whose mothertongue speakers exceed the strength of the tribe bearing the same name. These languages are marked by a greater intensity of functions, qualifying for the role of somewhat restricated 'contact' languages in respective regions. Many languages of the North-East Khasi, Garo, Miri, Tripuri, Lushai, Mikir, Tangkhpul, Lepcha, Dafla (Nissi), Monpa, Kabui, Mao, Paite, Nocte, Hmar, Halam, Mech and a few prominent languages of the Centre-East (Santali, Ho) and of the Centre-West (Korku, Halabi, Kolami) come under this category.

Mothertongue claims of a few 'tribal' vernaculars of non-tribal languages also exceed the strength of the corresponding tribes; Lamani claims are ninefold higher than the Sugali and Andh tribes in Andhra Pradesh, followed by Chakma, Haijong (varieties of Bengali), and Bhatri (a variety of Oriya).

At the second rung of the scale, a few more languages of the North-East are retained by over 80 per cent of the respective tribe namely Bodo, Thado, Wancho, Zou, Kuki, Lakher, Vaiphei, Mogh.

Next on the scale come Bhili in the Centre-West and Kurukh, Kharia, Koya, Juang, and Bhutia in the Centre-East, showing parallel trends of retaining ancestral languages (between 50-80 per cent) as well as of assimilating with the non-tribal languages of the region.

Moving towards the assimilatory drift, Gondi, a prominent language of the Centre-West and many languages of the Centre-East (Kisan, Parji, Jatapu, Munda, Saora, Khond, Gadaba), along with a Tibeto-Burman language Rabha in Assam, indicate feeble signs of maintenance. The strength of those claiming different varieties of Bhili (such as Varli, Garasia, Gamit, Kokna, Dhodia) is also considerably reduced.

At the other end of the scale where the forces of assimilation are prominent, a few tribal languages such as, Dimass, Lalung in Assam; Bhumij, Konda in the Centre-East and tribal vernaculars mostly in the South (Soliga, Irular, Paina), register the retention rate less than 20 per cent.

A few tribes claim the retention rate of their ancestral variety less than one per cent: such as, Panki (Chhattisgarhi), Lohara, Pardhan, Dhanka (Bhili), Agaria and Kharwar (both Munda), Yenadi and Chenchu (both Telugu).

A cursory glance comparing tribal languages on the vitality scale during 1961-71 reveals the attitudes favouring a gradual language shift. Many tribal languages do not keep the pace *vis-à-vis* the growth of the tribal community bearing the same name. As in the case of Kharia tribe, despite the increase in absolute numbers claiming Kharia as mothertongue (191 thousand in 1971 against 177 thousand in 1961), the language retention rate (vitality index) is reduced from 86 to 71. Similarly, the vitality index of Miri is also reduced from 84 in 1961 to 68 in 1971 Census.

The Bhumij, Parji and Savara indices show a sharp decline. Bhumij speakers are reduced from 142 thousand in 1961 to 52 thousand in 1971; whereas, Bhumij tribe records the growth from 308 thousand to 441 thousand during the same period, drastically reducing the Bhumij language index from 46 to 12. The Parji vitality index (the language of the Paroja tribe) is also reduced from 68 to 45, and the Savara index from 61 to 45.

A sharp increase in the vitality index of Bodo in Assam during the 1961-71 decade signifies the growing consciousness of the Bodo distinct identity, increasing from 56 in 1961 to 91 in 1971. The upward swing in the case of Ho language from 130 in 1961 to 140 in 1970 reveals its increasing prominence in the Chotanagpur region, attracting smaller tribes to claim it as mothertongue.

Language Maintenance and Language Shift

The intensity of language assimilation with major regional languages among tribal communities varies in different states, characterising differential pressures of maintenance and shift in ancestral languages, as is shown in Table 4. One can identify following significant trends in this regard:

1. **Strong tendency to maintain tribal language identity:** In Manipur, Meghalaya, and Andaman and Nicobar Islands almost all tribal communities retain their ancestral mother tongues. In remaining states of the North-East (Nagaland, Mizoram, Tripura, Arunachal, Assam) and Dadra and Nagar Haveli the number of tribals claimings their distinct mothertongues is quite high (83-89 per cent). These languages are also favourably disposed as contact languages in respective regions.

2. **Coexistence of tribal and non-tribal languages:** In Sikkim, Bihar and W. Bengal, the non-tribal mothertongue identity is claimed between 25-40 per cent, and a majority of the population retains their ancestral languages.

3. **Overwhelming tendency to shift ancestral tribal mothertongue in favour non-tribal language:** In the Central-belt states (Orissa, Madhya Pradesh, Maharashtra, Rajasthan) and in the North (Himachal Pradesh), the non-tribal mothertongue identity is claimed by 40-75 per cent tribal populations and the forces for retaining ancestral language are rather subdued.

4. **Least resistance by tribal languages in favour of dominant language(s):** In most of the southern states (Andhra Pradesh, Tamil Nadu, Kerala), on the west coast (Gujarat, Goa, Deu, Daman), and in the North (Uttar Pradesh), the non-tribal mothertongue identity is claimed by more than 75 per cent tribal population in each state and ancestral language identity gets merged with the dominant language(s).

TABLE 4

Language Retention Ratio among Tribals: 1971-1981

States	Tribal percentage to state population	Tribal population (thousands)	Tribal languages speakers (thousands)	Language retention ratio	Tribal population (thousands)	Tribal languages speakers (thousands)	Language retention ratio
	1981	1981	1981	1981	1971	1971	1971
INDIA	7.9	53,818	22,340	42	38,015	18,420	49
North-East							
Mizoram	93.6	462	412	89	313	NA	—
Nagaland	84.0	651	606	93	458	422	92
Meghalaya	80.6	1,076	1,075	99.9	814	813.6	99.9
Arunachal Pradesh	69.8	441	367	83	369	313	85
Tripura	28.4	584	515	88	451	394	88
Manipur	27.3	388	416	107	335	272	81
Assam	11.0	2,189*	1,836	84	1,607	1,646	86
Centre-East							
Sikkim	23.3	74	55	74	—	41	—
Orissa	22.4	5,915	2,573	44	5,072	1,937	38
A & N Islands (UT)	11.9	22	21.4	99	18	17.96	100
Bihar	8.3	5,811	4,094	70	4,933	3,844	78
W. Bengal	5.6	3,071	1,880	61	2,533	1,765	70

States	Tribal percentage to state population	Tribal population (thousands)	Tribal languages speakers (thousands)	Language retention ratio	Tribal population (thousands)	Tribal languages speakers (thousands)	Language retention ratio
	1981	1981	1981	1981	1971	1971	1971
Centre-West							
Dadra & NH (UT)	78.8	82	70	86	64	62	96
Madhya Pradesh	22.8	11,987	4,031	34	8,387	3,420	41
Gujarat	14.2	4,849	427	9	3,734	756	20
Rajasthan	12.2	4,183	1,586	38	3,126	838	27
Maharashtra	9.2	5,772	1,491	26	2,954	970	33
Goa, Daman and Diu	1.0	11	0.2	2.2	7.7	0.3	3.3
South							
Lakshadweep (UT)	93.8	38	Nil	—	30	Nil	—
Andhra Pradesh	5.9	3,176	391	12	658	377	23
Karnataka	4.9	1,825	0.8	0.04	231	0.5	0.2
Tamil Nadu	1.1	520	2.0	0.4	312	NA	—
Kerala	2.0	261	NA	—	269	NA	—
North							
Himachal Pradesh	4.6	197	76	38	269	NA	—
Uttar Pradesh	0.2	233	1.5	0.6	199	13.5	6.8

5. In Karnataka and Lakshadweep almost all tribals speak a variety of the regional language, i.e. Kannada or Malayalam.

6. The 1981 Census enumerates stray returns (about 1800) of tribal languages from the states which do not come under the purview of Scheduled Tribes: Delhi 774, Haryana 170, Jammu and Kashmir 500, Punjab 255, Chandigarh 43, Pondicherry 1.[5]

Political Response to Linguistic Heterogeneity

Tribal languages of Tibeto-Burman family comprise of eight groups. Among them 9 languages of the Bodo sub-family (Bodo, Garo, Tripuri, Mikir, Rabha, Dimasa, Lalung, Deori, Koch) constitute the largest group, spoken by over half of the tribal population spread in the Brahmaputra valley, N. Cachar Hills in Assam, Meghalaya and Tripura. Languages belonging to other groups are spoken by smaller number of populations: 24 languages of Naga group (19 per cent) in Nagaland, Arunachal and North Manipur Hills; 25 languages of Kuki-Chin group (15 per cent) in Mizoram, Manipur and Tripura (prominent languages Lushai/Mizo, Thado); 55 languages of NEFA group in Arunachal and Northern Assam (12 per cent); 9 languages of Bhotia group (2 per cent), and 14 languages of Himalayan group (2 per cent) are spoken by tribals extending to the central and western sub-Himalayan range (Sikkim, W. Bengal, Uttar Pradesh and Himachal Pradesh).

Bodo group of languages are diffused over a vast area in the Assam plains upto the foothills of Arunachal Pradesh and Bhutan. At one time their use extended till South-East Bengal (now in Bangladesh). The pigdin variety of Bodo and Garo, known as Barish, was used as a contact language among the tribals in Assam plains. "This very extensive Bodo bloc is, however, broken up due to the intrusion of the Aryan Assamese and Bengali" (Chatterji *op. cit.*).

Among the tribes affiliated to the Bodo ancestry, Garo speakers form majority in four districts of Meghalaya (408 thousand), and Tripuri speakers along with their allied communities (Reang, Noatia, Jamatia) are concentrated in Tripura (491 thousand). With the continued exodus of Bengali population from East Pakistan since 1947 (even after the creation of Bangladesh in 1972), the share of Tripuri speaking population in Tripura is now shrunk from 41 percent in

1911, 39 per cent in 1931, to 23 per cent in 1971. During the six decades covering 1901-1961 there was nearly fourfold increase in the tribal population in Tripura, whereas the non-tribal population during the same period increased ninefold (Dutta, 1969).

Two other prominent tribes of the North-East, those belonging to the Naga group and to the Kuki-Chin group (Lushai/Mizo), have after a long-drawn agitation, succeeded in acquiring a degree of autonomy in the federal set up. Nagaland and Mizoram, with much smaller populations have been granted the status of seperate states where they constitute absolute majority, 84 percent in Nagaland, and 94 per cent in Mizoram.

But the most numerous tribe speaking Bodo (estimated 860 thousand in 1981), along with Mikir (230 thousand), and other allied languages—Rabha, Dimasa, Lalung, etc. in the same sub-family—constitute only five to 6 per cent of the total population in the entire Assam state. Bodo-Kachari (Barish) was one time lingua franca among the tribals in the Assam plains. Because of their demographic dispersal in the Brahmaputra valley and their intense interaction with the mainstream culture, most of the Bodos are sucked into the Hindu caste system and are bilingual in Assamese. Till recently they had joined hands with Assamese students in the struggle against "foreigners". Bodos are now left bereft of any autonomy in the new 'homogenized' political set up of the North-East region. Rather late in waking up, they have now become acutely aware of the discrimination in being denied a limited autonomy to the tribal areas (guaranteed in the Constitution). Charged with the feeling of distinct identity, they now assert their share in participating in the political and developmental processes of the region.

The parameters of 'linguistic homogeneity' based on absolute majority as introduced by the States Reorganization Commission in 1956, were later conceded in the cases of granting statehood to the Garos in Meghalaya (combined with the Khasis) and to Mizos in Mizoram. Despite the reorganization of the North-East, the heterogeneous cultural mosaic, called the 'seven sisters', still continues to pose a challenge to those who are striving for solutions based on the strict adherence to the Western model of homogeneity in a region. The truncated

Assam is furious over the demands of further splits under the banners of Udayachal, Bodoland and others.

These struggles pleading the causes of Bodoland, Gorkhaland, Jharkhand should prompt us to re-examine the concept of homogeneity as the sole criteria of organising political units. Instead, we should look for solutions in the composite plurality of traditional *kshetras,* (for a detailed discussion on the concept of *kshetra,* cf. Saraswati 1989; Khubchandani 1989, 1991a).

The Saga of Alliances and Hostilities

In contrast to the distinct identity of many literary languages in the country (such as Bengali, Tamil, Marathi), most of the tribal languages represent oral cultures and are characterized by the flexibility or malleability of its identity. Boundaries between languages on a speech continuum, particularly among those belonging to tribals, are not sharply marked. Dominated by the tribal milieu, different languages in a tradition get identified, not so much by mutual isolation or unintellingibility, but by differentiating proprieties arising out of cultural rivalries in history.

Nagaland represents an area of dialectal confrontation where many small groups have been asserting privileges based on parity for respective languages in education, administration, and public media. Identifying 24 'exclusive' Naga languages (Ao, Konyak, Angami, etc.), claimed together by 810,000 speakers (in 1981), is a characteristic of this phenomenon.

The vast population of the North-Central India, representated by Hindi, Urdu, Panjabi, Pahari and other vernaculars (covering virtually half of the country's total population), is also characterised by such fluid language boundaries, defined on the basis of identity imperatives and *not* on the criteria of historical branching of grammatical features (Khubchandani 1972, 1983). Kloss (1967) distinction of *Abstand* languages (that is, by intrinsic distance) and *Ausbau* languages (that is, by independent development) is quite relevant here.

In such contexts, the illiterate tribals seem to carry the heterogeneity in everyday life communications very lightly on their shoulders, unlike the squabbles over the diversity of language use, visible among the literate cultures in the contemporary milieu (cf. Khubchandani,

1981). One notices among the tribals a greater respect for variation in speech, and consequently, less premium on the values attached to language purism. Many tribals belonging to Austric (Santali, Ho, Munda) or Dravidian (Kurukh, Kui, Kisan) families in the Chotanagpur plateau appear to be at peace with the 'grassroots' grasp of creolised vernaculars of Indo-Aryan origin identified under different labels--Sadri/Sadan, Khortha, Kurmali, or Nagpuria; a large section of tribals have even adopted them as mothertongue. Similar is the case of Halabi—a hybrid of Gondhi (Dravidian) and Chhattisgarhi and Marathi (Indo-Aryan) languages in Madhya Pradesh and Maharashtra.

In the midst of cultural and linguistic heterogeneity in the North-East, it is interesting to note the parallel efforts being made to form new 'alliances' among essthewhile 'hostile' language groups in Nagaland. In recent years a new language acronym, *Zeliangrong,*[6] has emerged by clustering tribes speaking *Zemi* in Nagaland, *Liangmei* in Manipur, and Nruanghmei *(Rongmei)* in the Cacher district of Assam. Tribes identified with *Chokri, Khezha,* and *Sangtam* languages in and around the Kohima district are also welding a common identity under the acronym *Chakesang*. Recently Angamis in the southern part of Nagaland have initiated a movement to bring together all allied and satellite tribes in the region covering Angami, Chakesang, Zeliangrong, and a few other minor tribes namely Rengma, Pome, etc. under one umbrella called *Tenyedia,* the language of 'Tenye people'. A monthly journal *Urauze* is also brought out from Kohima under this banner.

In Arunachal Pradesh, the Tagins had earlier identified with Nissis, later with Adis, and now they claim their identity distinct from either of the two. In Manipur, the Anals, Aimols, and Chirus had earlier identified with the Kuki tribe, but now they prefer affinity with the Nagas.

In the Jharkhand region, covering Chotanagpur plateau and Santhal Parganas in Bihar, along with the southern districts bordering with Orissa and Madhya Pradesh and those adjoining W. Bengal, a distinct identity is emerging around the lingua franca Nagpuria (with an Indo-Aryan base, commonly identified with the caste label Sadan/Sadani) by carving out a regional consensus over and above their Austric/Dravidian mothertongue identities. Such cultural synthesis can be described as 'grassroots-Aryanisation' where the *Jharkhandi* regional identity gets defined around the grasp of Indo-Aryan Sadan/Nagpuria language.

Conclusion

Profiles of tribal cultures provide many insights into probing the questions such as, how to channelise the concerns of ethnic identity of small groups in a positive and sublime manner to enrich the nation's heritage, instead of treating them as underprivileged 'powerless' minorities and allowing the 'small' cultures to submit to the pressure of assimilation within the dominant culture, under the compulsions of joining the mainstream.

NOTES

1. Some sections of the draft study were discussed at 1989 Seminar on Nehru and Evaluation of Tribal Policy, and 1991 Seminar on the Continuity & Change among Tribal Societies, both held at the Nehru Museum and Memorial Library, New Delhi.
2. "Speakers of the Sino-Tibetan languages of Mongoloid origin are considered to have penetrated the Indian frontiers before the advent of the Aryan into India. They have been referred to in the oldest Sanskrit literature as Kirātas"
3. The 1981 Census accords, Halabi an independent status. The 1961 Census regarded Halabi as a dialect of Marathi.
4. Varli, spoken in Dadra N&H and parts of Gujarat (1961: 46 thousand, 1971: 113 thousand), was classified in 1961 as a 'tribal variety of Marathi. But since 1971, it has been clubbed together with Bhili, A tribal language'.
5. At the micro-level a detailed study of language shift among three prominent tribal communities Santals, Mundas, and Oraons in the districts of Bihar is conducted by Ishtiaque (1985). In this study he identifies the areas of linguistic continuity (having more than 75 per cent of tribes retaining their ancestral language), the areas of transition (between 25-75 per cent retention), and the areas of linguistic shift (with less than 25 per cent retention of ancestral language).
6. The word has been derived by juxtaposing the first syllables of three languages.

REFERENCES

Chandra Sekhar, A., 1976. *Census of India, 1971: Social and Cultural Tables*, Pt. II-C (i), New Delhi: Govt. of India.

Chatterji, Suniti Kumar, 1978. "Adivasi and folk literature of India." In: *The Cultural Heritage of India: Languages and Literatures*, Vol. V, ed. by S.K. Chatterji. Calcutta: Institute of Culture, Ramakrishna Mission, pp. 659-676.

Dutta, Alok Kumar, 1969. "Present trend of marriages and its implications among the aboriginal of Tripura". In *Trends of Socio-economic Change in India*, 1871-1961. Shimla: Indian Institute of Advanced Study.

India, Government of 1950. *The Constitution of India*. New Delhi: Ministry of Law.

—, 1954. *The Census of India*, 1951. New Delhi. Registrar General of India.

Ishtiaque, M., 1985. "Language shifts among the tribal communities: A case study of the Santals, Mundas and Oraons in Bihar." *The Geographer* 32:2, pp. 69-78.

Khubchandani, Lachman M., 1972. "Mothertongue in multilingual societies." In: *Economic and Sociocultural Dimensions of Regionalization*. A Chandra Sekhar, gen. ed., Census Centenary Monograph no. 7, New Delhi: Registrar General of India, pp. 427-450.

—, 1981. *Language, Education, Social Justice*. Pune: Centre for Communication Studies.

—, 1983. *Plural Languages, Plural Cultures: Communication Identity, and Sociopolitical Change in Contemporary India*. East-West Center Book. University of Hawaii Press.

—, 1989. "Cultural dynamics among tribals: Issues of social ecology". Seminar on Nehru and the Evaluation of Tribal policy, Nehru Museum and Memorial Library: New Delhi.

—, 1991a. *Language, Culture and Nation-building: Challenges of Modernization*. Shimla: IIAS, and Manohar Publications.

—, 1991b. "Tribal identity in a plurilingual milieu". National Seminar on the Continuity & Change among Tribal Societies. Indian Institute of Advanced Study, New Delhi.

—, 1991c. "Celeberation of diversity: A glimpse of plurilingual communications among tribals in the central belt of India", International seminar on Multilingualism, Bombay University, Bombay.

—, 1992. *Tribal Identity: A Language and Communication perspective*. Shimla Indian Institute of Advanced Study.

Kloss, Hein Z., 1967. "Abstand and Ausbau languages." *Anthropological Linguistics*, 9: 29-41.

Mitra, Ashok, 1964. *Census of India*, 1961: Vol. I, *India: Language Tables*, Pt. 11-C (ii), New Delhi: Govt. of India.

Roy Burman, B.K., 1989. "Tribal and analogous social entities in different countries of the world, and relevance of Gandhi-Nehru framework of socialist humanism". Seminar on Nehru and Evaluation of Tribal Policy. Nehru Museum and Memorial Library, New Delhi.

Saraswati, Baidya Nath, 1988. "Thinking about 'Region". In: *Social Science and Social Concern.* Felicitation Volume in Honour of Professor B.K. Roy Burman, ed. by S.B. Chakrabarti, Delhi: Mittal Publications.

Verma V.S., 1987. *Census of India,* 1981. Series 1, *India: Household Population by Language.* Delhi: Controller of Publications.

CHAPTER 6

LANGUAGE PLANNERS AS ISSUE IDENTIFIERS OR ISSUE EVADERS:

CONFLICTS OF INTEREST IN LANGUAGE PLANNING WITH REFERENCE TO LINGUISTIC MINORITIES

Imtiaz Hasnain

Introduction

It may not be too imprudent and outrageous to describe Indian society and ethos in terms of both pluralism and segmentation. Truly speaking, homogeneity as opposed to heterogeneity and pluralism of speech community are theoretical and/or ideal constructs. Even the West has shed its homogeneity and accepted to render positive outlook towards pluralism. But pluralism and segmentation which are the distinctive features of Indian society and culture have largely been ignored by our language policy makers and planners. Although our Constitution swears to uphold the interest of the divergent ethno-linguistic and cultural groups, the constitutional safeguards provide an ideal ground for the language planners and policy makers to perpetrate their policy of elitism. In the name of constitutional provisions, certain linguistic packages are offered with a view to defer the linguistic outcry of the ethnic group which has been able to raise its voice against the oppressive policies of the dominant language speakers. Instead of looking at the language complexities from a broad and multi-disciplinary perspective, *ad hoc* and patchwork solutions are offered to solve the language problems. This unmindful adhocism and patchwork approach fails to appreciate and is far from providing a semblance of concern for the cultural aspirations and interests of the minority language groups of the pluralistic and segmentative society. Left with Hobson's choice of ethnic awareness and ethnic assertiveness, these linguistic minority groups use ethnicity as language or an idiom for their ethnic assertion. This is evident from the following statements expressed by K.C. Lalvunga, a prominent Mizo intellectual:

> "Our cultural aspirations have clashed in some way with that of the new nation [our new republic]. We are therefore not sure where we stand. If it is a simple tribal deviation time will heal. But if it is something deeper, we have to make some new adjustments without sacrificing our faith, our culture, language and dialects, history and our land, all of which we inherited from our forefathers. We have to settle the fundamental difference amicably and democratically. Our real problems lie near home, in our adjustment with the bigger communities." (Lalvunga cited in John Samuel, 1993: 92)

These sentiments of Lalvunga reflect cultural mood, anxieties and concern, on the one hand, and sociopolitical expediency and understanding, on the other, of a linguistic minority, *vis à vis,* speakers of the dominant language groups. While the former may provide an occasion for ethnic awakening or the resurgence of ethnic consciousness, the latter, if handled judiciously and carefully, may bring about desired integration, with respect ot "organisation" without any loss of faith, language or culture. However, the onerous of the responsibility lies with the institutions, language policy makers, language planners, language strategists and other agents of language implementation.

Nehru as a democrat, an ideologue, a language strategist and a statesman of the newly independent nation was conscious of linguistic complexity and politics of language exploitation. He not only upheld the policy of non-interference with regard to languages, but also vouched for protection of the linguistic minorities irrespective of their strength and location:

> We should have these clear safeguards laid down possibly in the constitution . . . so that a fair deal is given to every language in this country [we should not say that] we are in a majority and therefore our language should prevail. Every language has an equal right to prevail.
>
> (Gopal cited in Mahapatra, 1993: 175)

Thus the Indian Constitution not only provides a fundamental right to the linguistic minorities for the safeguard of their language and culture, but also endeavors to "establish and administer educational institutions of their own choice vide Articles 29(i) and 30(i)". Besides, it also provides "adequate facilities for instruction in the mother tongue . . . to children belonging to linguistic minority groups" through the special directives under Articles 347, 350, 350A and 350B. However, despite all these constitutional safeguards, Nehru still felt that these provisions were not enough. In the light of the then language policy of Soviet Union, he also felt that the Government should not only encourage the tribal and minority languages but these languages also

> "must be given all possible support and the conditions in which they can flourish must be safeguarded . . . In their matter of languages there must be no compulsion whatever".
>
> (Speeches cited in Mahapatra, 1993: 176)

Internal Colonialism and Languages of Minorities

In spite of all these statutory guarantees provided by the Constitution, language of the linguistic minorities continue to lag behind in 'development' pursuits of the nation. This becomes evident if one takes literacy as an indication of development and modernization. The following table shows that the literacy ratio among tribals all over the country is lower than the total literacy ratio in the individual states and Union territories (16.4% as against 36.2% according to 1981 Census).

TABLE 1

*Literacy Growth Among Tribals: 1961-1981**

(Percentages)

States	Total population literacy	Tribal literacy		
	1981	1981	1971	1961
India	36.20	16.35	11.3	8.5
Mizoram	59.88	59.63	53.5	—
Lakshadweep	55.07	53.13	41.4	22.3
Nagaland	42.57	40.32	24.0	—
Manipur	41.35	39.74	28.7	27.3
Sikkim	34.05	33.13	—	—
Kerala	70.42	31.79	25.7	17.3
Meghalaya	34.08	31.55	26.5	—
A & N Islands	51.56	31.11	17.9	11.1
Goa, Daman and Diu	56.66	26.48	12.7	—
Himachal Pradesh	42.48	25.93	15.9	8.6
Tripura	42.12	23.07	15.0	10.0
Maharashtra	47.18	22.29	11.7	7.2
Gujarat	43.70	21.14	14.1	11.7
Tamil Nadu	46.76	20.46	9.0	5.9
Uttar Pradesh	27.16	20.45	14.6	—
Karnataka	38.46	20.14	14	8.2
Dadra and Nagar Haveli	26.67	17.86	8.9	4.4
Bihar	26.20	16.99	11.6	9.2
Arunachal Pradesh	20.79	14.04	5.2	—
Orissa	34.23	13.96	9.5	7.4
West Bengal	40.94	13.21	9.5	6.6
Madhya Pradesh	27.87	10.68	7.6	5.1
Rajasthan	24.38	10.27	6.5	4.0
Andhra Pradesh	22.94	7.82	5.3	4.4

*Source: Raza et al, FIEPA, New Delhi, 1985 qtd. in Khubchandani, 1992.

Why is it that despite Nehruvian policy of non-interference and his favourable disposition towards linguistic minorities, some languages have met their nemesis while others are losing ground and slipping into oblivion? How is it that even these trumpeted rhetorics of linguistic democracy and the concommitant constitutional safeguards have not been able to contain the linguistic genocide and 'internal colonialism' of the dominant language groups and language solutions at both the Union and the State levels continue to elude the nation? In fact these constitutional safeguards or even simply dependence on the constitutional provisions have not only failed to ease the complexities but have even enhanced the complications in the language issue particularly in a democratic set-up like ours. As Khubchandani has pointed out

> "One of the complications in the language issue in India has been rather too much reliance on the constitutional provisions for imposing the switch-over from one language to another, and granting privileges to various languages through legal decrees . . ." (1987: 118)

Certainly these constitutional provisions are not sufficient to provide satisfactory answers to the linguistic problems of the minority groups. The answer may be found in the existing language policy and the kind of language planning processes that we subscribe to. For, it is the immature and myopic language policy and insenstitive and insouciant language planning (LP) that have contributed towards the alienation of linguistic minorities of both scheduled and non-scheduled languages. The vehement protest of the minority-language groups of the North-East in the 50s over the imposition of Assamiya, or the language movements of 1960 and 1972 launched by the Assamiya, or the Manipuri movement for promoting Manipuri or at official level, Konkani movement for the recognition of their language in the VIII-Schedule may all be seen to be emanating as a result of ideologically impregnated and lopsided language policy aimed at differentiation and segregation of linguistic minorities. They have not only brought fission but have even caused the resurgence of ethnic mobilization. The recrudescene of ethnic mobilization is now an ontological reality. Today's political scenario marks the pronounced and gradual increase in peripheral protests in the form of Jharkand Morcha, Naga Movement, Bodo movement, Mizo political movement or Khasi solidarity movement. These protests have not only baffled the liberals, academics and professional ideologues, but have also forced them to believe that science and economic rationalization are now subservient to the ties of language, race and religion even in a secularized and technocractic world. As Greeley puts it:

> "One of the most extraordinary events of our times has been the resurgence of tribals in a supposedly secularised and technocratic world. Science and economic rationalisation had been expected to reduce, if not eliminate, man's attachment to ancient ties of common ancestry, common land and common faith, but suddenly ties of race, nationality and religion seem to have been taken on new importance.
>
> (Greeley cited in Edwards, 1985: 99)

Language and Ethnicity

Fresh awakening emanating from growing awareness of ethnic consciousness has resulted in sudden shift in paradigm from equilibrium to conflict perspective. In the former sense, ethnicity is construed as a group cultural phenomenon in which a group identifies itself with ". . .common bonds such as language, race, and religion" (Edwards, 1985:6) shared within a "culture-population-group frame of reference" (Bennett cited in Paulston 1986: 130) and enjoys an obsequious assimilation. In the latter sense ethnicity holds competitive and confrontationist perspective with an emphasis on the recognition of differentiation and conscious desire to maintain one's identity. This conflict perspective allows the ethnic identities to proceed from the cultural-chosen and not cultural-given of the past. Bennett prefers to call it as 'new ethnicity' whose major function is to evolve "a set of strategies for acquiring the resources one needs to survive and to consume at the desired level" (Bennett cited in Paulston, 1986: 130). It is a conscious, self-chosen ethnicity concerned with power-struggle against the dominant group for social and economic advantages. By laying emphasis on the recognition of differenciation, it strives for maintaining the distinct ethnic identity and forces its members to assert their autonomy—be it linguistic, political, economic etc.

It is generally accepted that ethnicity is a phenomenon that cannot be characterized by any single feature but must be described by cluster of features such as race, religion, nationality, culture, etc. Of the cluster of features, however, a feature of language may not necessarily be an essential criterion of ethnicity. As Haarmann (1986:38) puts it:

> ". . . language—as it is empirically found in concrete settings—is not a necessary criterion of ethnicity and therefore does not play a fundamental role in all processes of ethnic fusion and fission."

Probably it is because of this non-language oriented criteria in the characterisation of ethnicity that language death or language loss had never been a cause of concern for a large number of linguistic minority groups. They readily accepted assimilation as an integral part of composite nationalism without any protest. From this perspective of stable equilibrium, ethnicity ultimately became merely a matter of self-ascription and common cultural beliefs were simply acquired through unconsciously learned behaviour. Language shift was, therefore, a natural outcome of this ethnicity.

However, the history of language movements of both tribal and non-tribal languages in India pointedly established a relation between language and ethnicity. There are innumerable instances showing the movement being spear-headed by leaders exploiting different pools of symbols including language. The most recent being Jharkhand movement in which, interestingly, Santhali (only recently) has emerged as a rallying point. The emergence of conflict perspective from that of stable one marks the struggle of 'us' against 'them' in which different strategies are employed for evoking ethnic consciousness through the exploitation of various symbols, language being one of them. In fact, this sudden spurt in the rise of one's language awareness defies the observations of Haarmann (1986) and vindicates the conflict perspective of new ethnicity in the struggle for linguistic autonomy of the hitherto dominated ethnic groups.

Whether it is an obsequious assimilation leading to homogenisation or a fresh awakening of ethnic consciousness leading to confrontation, there are linguistic consequences in the form of language death, language loss, language shift, language contraction, language maintenance, etc. by the speakers of smaller and weaker languages. This becomes apparent if one looks into mother tongue vacillation phenomenon as recorded during successive censuses of 1961, 1971 and 1981.

TABLE 2

Variation in Mothertongue Claims: 1951-1981

Tribal languagel	Total speakers *1981* *(thousand)*	Variation (increase/decline) *1971-81* *per cent*	*1961-71* *per cent*	*1951-61* *per cent*
1	2	3	4	5
India	22,300	+21.2	+25.0	
Sharp Increase				
Sema	94	+59.4	+37.4	
Change	23	+46.2	+39.6	
Ao	106	+40.1	+30.5	
Yimchungre	27	+39.8	+54.7	
Khezha	16	+39.5	+29.5	
Tangkhul	79	+35.7	+32.1	
Phom	24	+35.0	+34.6	
Vaiphei	16	+33.6	+41.0	
Khasi	632	+32.0	+31.6	+42.9
Mao	57	+62.1	+22.5	
Lushai	385	+41.6	+22.2	
Tripura	491	+31.6	+24.3	
Deori	25*	–	+63.7	+35.9
Bodo	858*	–	+53.8	+118.0
Pawi	–	–	+53.8	+281.4
Lotha	51*	–	+38.9	
Miri	239*	–	+32.3	
Increased checked				
Koch	17	+16.8	+73.3	+58.2
Thado	59	+16.0	+59.7	+147.9
Kinnauri	52	+14.9	+58.8	
Angami	78	+14.5	+60.2	+49.0
Koya	243	+14.4	+50.5	
Paite	33	+20.2	+45.9	
Korku	363	+18.1	+39.6	+28.8
Kabui	53	+4.5	+68.7	+61.8
Khili	4,451	+1.5	+39.3	+103.3
Vacillation				
(a) Jatapu	23	–35.9	+87.1	
Konda	11	–22.6	+174.2	
Lepcha	26	–21.9	+40.7	
Hmar	34	–10.5	+49.7	+92.4
Garo	408	–0.9	+34.1	
(b) Halabi	525	+51.5	+15.5	
Sangtam	29	+44.0	+8.2	
Kuki	46	+42.0	+12.8	
(c) Koda/Kora	22	+88.1	–14.8	–33.1
Juang	19	+53.8	–54.9	

1	2	3	4	5
Kui	508	+51.6	–22.9	+25.4
Gadaba	28	+35.3	–49.3	–25.6
Slow growth				
Lalung	11*		+0.7	
Kurukh	1,265	+2.3	+8.2	
Kharia	198	+3.3	+8.8	
Khond	205	+4.2	+16.8	
Savara	235	+5.8	–16.5	+3.8
Ho	802	+6.8	+15.9	
Santali	4,208	+11.1	+16.6	
Munda	349	+12.8	+18.2	
Gonda	1,955	+15.8	+12.5	
Kolani	79	+17.3	+14.0	
Khiemnungan	17	+18.1	+15.9	
Continuous decline				
(a) Parji	33	–55.2	–32,4	+451.2
Bhumji	47	–9.7	–63.6	+39.2
(b) Bhotia	31	–8.1	+11.0	
Mundari	753	–2.4	+4.6	+26.0
Halam	10	–1.6	+11.3	
Sikkim Bhotia	–	–	–69.6	

Quoted in Khubchandani, 1992. (*1981 figures are based on the estimated projections of the 1971 Census).

The Question of Identity and Language Planning

The signs of sudden spurt of growth or decline in the use of mother-tongue not only indicate vacillation but also mark nexus between language and identity. In fact, whatever may be the form of linguistic consequences, there is an underlying relationship between language and identity i.e. language and the identification of its speakers within a certain speech community. Why a particular language is selected on a particular occasion, what happens if/when a member of one community acquires competence in the language of another community, or loses competence in his own language, or begins/ceases to identify himself as a member of the one or the other community, etc., are the questions which form a language-identity nexus and, therefore, bring us close to looking into the inevitable interaction between LP and language maintenance *vis à vis* smaller and weaker languages. Although the problem of bilingualism and language choice (from very narrowed perspective) have been the main concern of most of the LP activities, any concern for interaction between LP and language maintenance is conspicuously missing in the current state of LP. This is possibly because of the neglect of the languages of the minority groups. As Fishman has rightly observed:

> "Lack of attention to smaller and weaker languages [of the linguistic minorities] led to an almost complete lack of attention to the inevitable interaction between language planning and language maintenance." According to him this interaction is "not only substantial but crucial [and therefore] the entire distinction between primary and secondary institutions of language maintenance (...) must be examined, in terms of *where* language status planning should best be focussed in order to have the greatest payoff for shoring up and strengthening the merger internal vitality of weak speech communities. When we are dealing with severely wounded and weakened speech communities *the functional goals of status planning* (...) and *the specific means (programs, projects) of status planning* must be selected with much more care than is the case in connection with the established language...The former cannot afford the margin of error (and of useless effort) that the latter can take in their strides." (1987: 54-55)

Besides looking into the interaction between LP and language maintenance, the theoretical and methodological issues of language allocation in LP, the ability to address itself to those human sensitivities which may arise as a result of intervention of certain critical variables which are not purely linguistic, and involvement of a common man in the acceptance or rejection of planning provisions are equally important in achieving the desired objectives of LP. But do we have a LP in which smaller and/or weaker linguistic groups are accorded due place in terms of identifying their relation with language? To what extent is the idndividual as a common man allowed to participate in the planning provisions? How far is LP in India (if there is one) sensitive to the issues like functional inequality, ethnic identity, nationalism, interrelationship between language and identity, etc.? How far in the LP activities are the aspirations and interests of the 'have nots' and hitherto dominated groups been taken into cognizance? As mentioned earlier any satisfactory answer to these questions not only require a thorough understanding of language by the language planners but also demand a definite shift in the paradigm of language planning—a shift which has a social science approach where the interest is focussed on the social and not on linguistics. Fishman, while assessing the state of the art in LP study and situating it in the discipline and theory of social science, has succinctly suggested that:

> "It [LP] is primarily the means whereby less fortunate language communities (i.e. those less powerful in their particular confrontation with another ethno-linguistic aggregate) organize their self-defense, as well as their inter-translatability-at least- to-some-extent- and-in-some-functions *vis-à-vis* one or another 'international language'. [Thus] they [language planners] are (or should be) issue definers and consciousness raisers *vis-à-vis* the goal of ethnocultural pluralism and ethnocultural dynamism." (Fishman qtd. in Jernudd, 1991:128)

In the same paper Fishman further commented on the status of 'status planning'. According to him:

"[those interested in LP] have been making up social science theory far too long and, as a result, have benefitted far too little from the theory that has been elaborated by specialists working in other areas of social change and social planning.

But sociolinguistics is also concerned with the exhaustive, multidimensional depiction of the present, with attitude studies, with usage studies, with criterion evaluation studies, in short with quantitative studies of various kinds. We ultimately want to know more about what kinds of populations are more likely, and what kinds are less likely, to adopt the status planning and corpus planning products of language planning authorities and why these differentials exist."

(Fishman quoted in Jernudd, 1991: 129)

This makes LP a *process* rather than a *state of affairs* where both the producers of the planning and the recipients of the planning are constantly involved in the evaluation, as regards the targets of planning. Ideally speaking, LP is an ongoing continuous activity involving regular control of sociolinguistic variables through repeated application of language planning processes under changing societal conditions. However, the processual character of planning has never been on the agenda of LP.

LP in India not only marks the absence of dynamicity and processual character but there are also strong elements of elitism and power structure. By imposing the rationality and dominance of planning activities upon the totality of social body related to speech community the planners in their pursuit of planning have cared least for the consumers of the language, the individual speaker, the smaller and/or weaker linguistic groups and their living language. In the language planning processes "the common man—the 'consumer' of language planning programs—is present only by proxy, carrying the elite 'cross'. It is mainly the custodians of language who loftily decide what is 'good' for the masses, by virtue of their position of power in the sociopolitical and literary scene" (Khubchandani, 1983: 149). In fact, in the eyes of these custodians of language the members of the linguistic minority groups are commonly held to be "low man on the totem pole" (Fishman, 1987: 53) who are not only "expendable [but also] dependent on zeitgeist and ortgeist for any linguistic crumbs that may be thrown their way" (Fishman, 1987: 53). The impersonation of the common man and lack of awareness of individual's crucial role in achieving the desired goals of LP emanates from the belief and general attitudes, shared by both the language planners and sociolinguistic researchers, that planning activities of both the status and the corpus types invariably relate to speech community as a whole and not to the individual speakers. And, insofar as language is a collective means of communication, the goals of language planning will subsequently and automatically fulfil the communicative needs of the individual speakers or "low man on the totem pole". This argument is too simple and far from the truth and existing reality. For, the persisting language problems in India and the conflict perspective of new ethnicity in the struggle for linguistic autonomy are not in tune with the prevailing belief and general attitude.

To achieve the desired goals of LP, particularly, for a country like India which has a multilingual and federal democratic set-up, we not only need to appreciate the dialectic nature of the relationship between the producers and recipients of language planning activities but we also require a multi-disciplinary field of LP where there is a dialectical relationship between subjective and objective factors. Besides looking into "*Who* is engaged in planning *what* language for *whom* and *why*?, [a]nother set of relations must also be taken into consideration, [i.e.]: *Who* accepts *what* planning provisions *from whom* and under *what* conditions?" (Haarmann, 1990: 123) by taking the critical variables like demographic, attitudinal, political, social, developmental, ethnographic, cultural and religious rather than linguistic. Linguistics in its current form does not meet the need of language planning as the concept of language planning involves far more than what could be called 'pure' linguistics. To quote Kavka and Skacel:

> "Language planning (in terms of the aims of LP) is primarily of a semi-linguistic and/or extralinguistic rather than purely linguistic nature, being influenced and effected by many social, political and economic factors. . .LP must be viewed as a multi-disciplinary concept involving economists, sociologists, psychologists, linguists and possibly experts from other fields." (1987: 258)

For a democratic and amicable solution to the language problem and bringing about the cultural aspirations of the marginalised and hitherto dominated ethnic groups, it is important that these critical variables are incorporated in LP. A success in LP is possible only if there is no clash with spontaneous human sensitivities.

REFERENCES

Annamalai, E., 1986. "Linguistic dominance and cultural dominance—A study of tribal bilingualism in India" in D.P. Patanayak (ed.) *Multilingualism in India,* Multilingual Matters, 61.

Dua H.R., 1985. *Language Planning in India,* New Delhi, Harnam Publications.

Dua, H.R., 1987. "Language allocation: Some theoretical and methodological issues in language planning" in U.N. Singh & R.N. Srivastava (eds.) *Perspectives in Language Planning,* Calcutta, Mithila Darshan.

Edwards, J., 1985. *Language, Society and Identity,* Oxford.

Fishman, J.A., 1977. "Language and ethnicity" in H. Giles (ed.) *Language Ethnicity and Intergroup Relations,* New York, Academic Press.

Fishman, J.A., 1987. "Reflections on the current state of langauge planning" in U.N. Singh & R.N. Srivastava (eds.) *Perspectives in Language Planning,* Calcutta, Mithila Darshan.

Govt. of India, 1950. *The Constitution of India,* New Delhi.

Haarmann, H., 1986. *Language in ethnicity: A View of Basic Ecological Relations,* Berlin, New York, Mouton de Gruyter.

Haarmann, H., 1991. "Language planning in the light of a general theory of language: A methodological framework," *International Journal of the Sociology of Language,* 86. 103-126.

Hasnain, S.I., 1991a. "Trends in Indian bilingualism," *Language Sciences,* Vol. 13, No. 2.301-16.

—, 1991b. "Linguistic consequences of social mobilization in a language contact situation," *Indian Journal of Politics,* Vol. XXV, No. 2-3.132-142.

Ishtiaq, M., 1985. "Language shift among the Tribal Communities: A case study of Santals, Mundas and Oraons in Bihar," *The Geographer,* Vol. 32:2.69-78.

Jernudd, B.H., 1990. *Lectures on Language Problems,* New Delhi, Bahri Publications.

—, 1990. "Two approaches to Langauge planning" in Verner Bickley (ed.), *Language use, Language Teaching and the Curriculum,* Hong Kong, Institute of Language in Education.

—, 1991. "Language planning as discipline," *Journal of Multilingual and Multicultural Development,* Vol. 12, Nos. 1 & 2.127-134.

—, and J.V. Neustupny, 1991. "Multi disciplined Language planning," in David F. Marshall (ed.) *Language Planning,* Vol. III, Amsterdam. John Benjamins Publishing Co.

Kavka, S. and J. Skacel, 1986. "Language planning: Implications in a socialist society" in J. Chloupek, J. Nekvapil et al (eds.) *Reader in Czech Sociolinguistics,* Amsterdam, John Benjamins Publishing Company.

Khubchandani, L.M., 1983. *Plural Languages, Plural Cultures: Communication, Identity and Sociopolitical Change in Contemporary India,* Hawaii, University of Hawaii Press.

—, 1987. "Language planning in multilingual communication network: A story of Indian situation" in U.N. Singh & R.N. Srivastava (eds.) *Perspectives in Language Planning,* Calcutta, Mithila Darshan.

—, 1992. *Tribal Identity: A Language and Communication Perspective,* Shimla, Indian Institute of Advanced Study.

—, 1993 (forthcoming). "Planning for whom? Evaluating Language planning in the Indian context", in S.I. Hasnain (ed.) *Language Standardization: Dynamics of Language Planning,* New Delhi, Bahri Publications.

Mahapatra, B.P., 1993. "Individuals as strategists in language planning: Nehru's approach to linguistic minorities," S.I. Hasnain (ed.) *Language Standardization: Dynamics of Language Planning,* New Delhi, Bahri Publications.

Paulston, C.A., 1986. "Linguistic consequences of ethnicity and nationalism in multilingual settings" in B. Spolsky (ed.) *Language and Education in Multilingual Settings,* Multilingual Matters, 25.

Samuel, J., 1993. "Language and nationality in North-East India," *Economic and Political Weekly,* Vol. XXVIII, Nos. 3 and 4, 91-92.

Srivastava R.N., 1987. "Theory of planning and language planning" in U.N. Singh & R.N. Srivastava (eds.) *Perspectives in Language Planning,* Calcutta, Mithila Darshan.

II

CONTACT AND CONVERGENCE

You are eternal as death
The fear of death and your love
As intimate neighbours
They inhabit my dream
And so I play with my life.

(Paraja Song)

'Unending Rhythms'—Sitakant Mahapatra

CHAPTER 7

LOSS OF /O/ IN KUI, SORA, AND ORIYA:

A CLUE FOR A SUB-LINGUISTIC AREA

Panchanan Mohanty

Introduction

Kui, a tribal language belonging to the central branch of the Dravidian family (Krishnamurti, 1969), is spoken mainly in southern Orissa in the districts of Phulbani, Koraput, and Ganjam. Sora, another tribal language belonging to the Koraput Munda group of the Munda branch of the Austro-Asiatic family (Zide, 1969) is spoken mainly in the southern districts of Ganjam, Koraput, and Phulbani in Orissa and in Srikakulam in Andhra Pradesh. Both these languages are reported to possess the half-close rounded back vowel /o/ and its long counterpart /o:/ (Winfield, 1928, 1929; Ramamurti, 1931, 1986). But the Kui data collected from the Daringabadi area in the district of Phulbani and the Sora data collected from the Paniganda area in the district of Ganjam show that both the languages posses the following vowel system, i.e./ i,e,a,ɔ,u/. In other words, there is neither /o/ nor /o:/ in them. In these data /o/ and /o:/ are replaced by either the next lower vowels /ɔ/ and /ɔ:/ or the immediately higher vowels /u/ and /u:/. Here, it is noteworthy that the same kind of change takes place in both the languages even though they belong to two different language families. Again, Oriya, a major Indo-Aryan language, which has the following six vowels-system like /i,e,a,ɔ,o,u/, also shows the same trait. In other words, following Masica (1976:11) these three languages can be said to constitute a *Sprachbund* or 'linguistic area' in this single-feature sense. Emeneau (1956) has identified the whole of India as a 'linguistic area' and the languages under consideration are included in it. That is why, the said *Sprachbund* will be called here a 'sub-linguistic area' under the Indian linguistic area. With these words of introduction, the present paper aims to show how and why /o/ has changed in Kui, Sora, and Oriya and determine the probable source of this change.

Kui

First, let us consider the Kui data. To determine how /o/ and /o:/ get transformed in Daringabadi Kui, it is necessary to compare some data from this variety with those in Winfield (1928, 1929):

Winfield's data	Daringabadi data	Gloss
boka	bɔ:ka	male goat
oli	ɔli	bear
oḍri	ɔri	rat
nahoṛi	nahɔṛi	dog
poṭa	pɔṭa	bird
gossa	gɔsa	forest
joeli	jɔʔeli	maize
beoṭi	beʔɔṭi	behind
seṇḍoni	seṇḍɔ	above
ḍomenju	ḍɔmenju	a man from a scheduled caste
poṭaṛenju	pɔṭaṛenju	a Patthan
ḍo:ṇḍi	ḍɔṇḍi	pumpkin
jo:to	jɔtu	animal
po:te	pɔ:teʔ	necklace
ko:ḍi	kɔ:ḍi	cow
o:ḍa	ɔ:ḍa	goat

Winfield's data	Daringabadi data	Gloss
ko:ru	kɔ:ru	buffalo
bo:ga	bɔ:ga	basket
so:ru	sɔ:ru	hill
jo:ṛi	jɔ:ṛi	stream

It can be noticed that /o/ and /o:/ normally become /ɔ/ and /ɔ:/ respectively in Daringabadi Kui, only in a few cases /o/ changes to /ɔ:/ and /o:/ to /ɔ/. This is also confirmed by the changes that take place in the borrowed words from Oriya:

Standard Oriya	Daringabadi Kui	Gloss
sorisɔ	sɔrsɔ	mustard
godhi	gɔhi	iguana
ghoṛa	gɔ:ṛa	horse
bhoji	bɔ:ji	feast

There are, of course, a couple of words in the data where /o/ is found changing to /u/. For example:

Source Word	Daringabadi Kui	Gloss
oṭɔ	uṭɔ	camel
poṭɔḷɔ	puṭlɔ	a kind of vegetable
jo:to	jɔtu	animal

Out of these three examples, the first two are borrowed from Oriya and the source words given here are from Standard Oriya. But in Southern Oriya that is spoken in Ganjam, Phulbani, and Koraput the /o/ of these words is replaced by /u/ and they become /uṭɔ/ and/ puṭuḷɔ/. As Daringabadi Kui has borrowed them from Southern Oriya, the same forms are retained in it. The third example /jɔtu/ seems to have a drivational relationship with /jɔntu/ 'animal' which is quite frequently used in both the Standard and the Southern varieties of Oriya. Or else the final /u/ of /jɔtu/ may also be a result of the influence of /jɔntu/.

However, from the above discussion it is clear that /o/ and /o:/ have changed to the respective lower vowels, i.e. /ɔ/ and /ɔ:/ in Daringabadi Kui though length variation is noticed in a few cases.

Sora

Let us now compare the Sora data of the Paniganda area with those in Ramamurti (1931, 1986) to determine how /o/ and /o:/ of the latter get transformed in the former:

Ramamurti's data	Paniganda data	Gloss
ontiḍ	ɔntiṭ	bird
rogo:-n	rɔ:gɔ	red gram
togal-an	tɔgal	night
orub	ɔrup	evening
o?o:n	ɔ?ɔn	son
tanonba:	tɔnɔnba	husband
aboi	abɔi	one
molloi	mɔ:lɔi	five
kinso:ḍ-an	kinsɔr	a variety of large deer
ayo:	ayɔ	fish
saro:-n	sɔrɔ	paddy
b?o:b-an	bɔ?ɔp	head
t?o:ḍ-an	tɔ?ɔṭ	mouth
m?o:ḍ	mɔ?ɔṭ	eye
o:n-an	aɔn	child
ansaio:-n	anslɔ	wife
joḍa:-n	jɔ:ṛa	stream
labo:-n	lɔbɔ	earth
to:gi-n	tɔ:gi	fire
biyo:	biɔ	yesterday, tomorrow
ḍo:n	ḍɔn	to

From these examples, it is evident that /o/ and /o:/ change to the next lower vowels /ɔ/ and /ɔ:/ and unlike Kui, length alternation is quite frequent here.

But there are ample data in Ramamurti which show that there is a dialect of Sora in which /o/ is replaced by /u/ and /o:/ by /u:/ at least in some words. The following examples are illustrative:

Ramamurti's data	Paniganda data	Gloss
t?o:ḍ-an	tɔ?ɔṭ	mouth
t?u:ḍ-an		
molloi	mɔ:lɔi	five
munioi		
K?o:-n	ku?u	bottle-gourd
k?u:-n		
jojo:n	jujun	maternal
jujuṅ		grandfather
koḍi	kuṛi	twenty
kuḍi		

The corresponding words for the first two in Paniganda Sora have /ɔ/ and /ɔ:/ in the place of /o/ and /o:/. But the corresponding forms of the last three words have /u/ in the place of /o/ and /o:/. The contention here is that though /o/ and /o:/ get transformed into /ɔ/ and /ɔ:/ in the first two words, in the next three they actually do not change to /u/; rather the dialectal forms with /u/ are used in Paniganda Sora. But the following data pose a problem:

Ramamurti's data	Paniganda data	Gloss
bo:ten	butin	who (relative pronoun)
baḍo:n	baru	hill
ba:o:-n	baũŋ	brother-in-law

However, with these examples, it is very difficult to conclude that /o:/ also changes to /u/ in Paniganda Sora for the reason that /o/ and /o:/ are found to become /ɔ/ and /ɔ:/ in quite similar environments. The following examples are repeated for convenience:

Ramamurti's data	Paniganda data	Gloss
b?o:b-an	bɔ?ɔp	head
labo:-n	lɔbɔ	earth
o?o:n	ɔ?ɔn	son

So it can be argued that /butin/, /baru/, and baũŋ/ are also dialectal forms like /ku?u/, /jujuŋ/, and /kuṛi/ and most probably Ramamurti has not noted them.

On the basis of the above analyses and arguments it can be stated that like Daringabadi Kui, /o/ and /o:/ become /ɔ/ and /o:/ in Paniganda Sora. If it is so, then a question may be raised: what is the cause of this change? To get an answer we will have to see what happens to /o/ in the major language of the area, i.e. Oriya.

Oriya

A careful study of Standard Oriya and its dialects reveals that /o/ has a very restricted occurrence in this language. It does not occur word-finally in any dialect though in Standard Oriya it is found occurring only in a very few monosyllabic verbs like /so/ '(you) sleep', /dho/ '(you) wash', /tho/ '(you) keep' and in a couple of vocatives like /ho/,/lo/ etc. Its use in the word-medial position is also very much constrained. In many cases it changes either to /ɔ/ or to /u/. The following examples are illustrative:

Written Std. Oriya	Spoken Std. Oriya	Gloss
bhugoḷɔ	bhugɔḷɔ	geography
golokɔ	golɔkɔ	heaven
bɔndobɔstɔ	bɔndɔbɔstɔ	arrangement
pɔkoṛi	pɔkuṛi	pakoda
aboriba	aburiba	to surround

Though it occurs more frequently in the initial syllables of words than in the non-initial ones, there are some examples like the following where it is found to be changing to /ɔ/ in the initial syllables in Standard Oriya:

Written Standard Oriya	Spoken Standard Oriya	Gloss
koṇɔ	kɔṇɔ	corner
mote	mɔte	to me
tote	tɔte	to you

It is in the process of disappearing in different dialects. It is not there in the northern dialect at all. It has changed either to /u/ or to /ɔ/ in this dialect (Mohanty, 1987). For example:

Standard Oriya	Northern Oriya	Gloss
ou	ɔu	a vegetable
bou	bɔu	mother
bohu	bɔhu	daughter-in-law
koili	kuili	cockoo
oṭɔ	uṭɔ	camel
oda	uda	wet
corɔ	curɔ	thief
poṛiba	puṛiba	to burn

Though it is retained in the Western and the Southern dialects, the frequency of its occurrence is remarkably less in these varieties than that in Standard Oriya. The following are a few examples to show that /o/ changes to /u/ and /ɔ/ in these dialects:

Standard Oriya	Western Oriya	Southern Oriya	Gloss
goṛɔ	guṛɔ	guṛɔ	leg
corɔ	curɔ	cuṛɔ	thief
oṭɔ	uṭɔ	uṭɔ	camel
oda	uda	uda	wet
soiba	suiba	suiba	to sleep
poṛiba	puṛiba	puṛiba	to burn

The non-occurrence of /o/ in the word-final position in all the varieties including the Standard one and the fact that its occurrence is very much restricted in the medial syllables compared to the initial ones in Standard Oriya makes clear that the disappearance of /o/ has started from the word-final position and it is gradually spreading to other positions.

However, two pertinent questions may be asked here: (i) why does /o/ get eliminated in Oriya and why should this elimination start from the word-final position at all? (ii) why do /o/ and /o:/ change to the lower vowels, i.e. /ɔ/ and /ɔ:/ in Daringabadi Kui and Paniganda Sora whereas they change to both /ɔ/ and /u/ in Oriya? Let us look into these one by one.

Discussion

Oriya is a language that is spoken on the north-eastern border of the Dravidian speaking area and because of its long and close contact with Dravidian languages it has assimilated many features of the latter. It is an established fact that Oriya was first separated from Assamese and Bengali (Chatterji, 1970; Pattanayak, 1966). The main cause of this separation as mentioned in Pattanayak (1966) is the retention of certain characteristic features of Dravidian in Oriya as against the loss of these features in Assamese and Bengali. For example, Oriya still retains the distinction between the retroflex lateral /ḷ/ and the dental lateral /l/, and the retroflex nasal /ṇ/ and the dental nasal /n/; but these distinctions are lost in both Bengali and Assamese. The cause of retention of these features in Oriya is its continuous contact with Dravidian which Assamese and Bengali were deprived of being far away from the Dravidian speaking area.

Out of the four major Dravidian languages, Kannada (Upadhyaya, 1972), Tamil (Rajaram, 1972), and Telugu (Sastry, 1972) each has a ten-vowel system consisting of five short vowels and their long counterparts, e.g. /i, i:, e, e:, a, a:, o, o:, u, u:/. Only Malayalam has an additional short vowel /U/ and thus, it possesses eleven vowel phonemes (Shyamala Kumari, 1972). It is significant to note that none of these languages allows /o/ to occur word-finally. Then Vasanthakumari (1989:16-17) reports that when she calculated the frequency of the vowels /i, e, a, o, u/ in about one thousand words selected randomly from Tamil, the eldest member of the Dravidian family, it was found that /a/ was the most frequent (25.1323 %), followed by /i/ (7.7601 %), /u/ (7.6719 %), /e/ (4.4092 %), and finally /o/ (3.7919 %) which was the least frequent. Again, Zvelebil (1970:61-64) shows that the use of /o/ is also restricted in many non-literary Dravidian languages belonging to all the subgroups like South Dravidian (e.g. Toda), Central Dravidian (e.g. Manda), and North Dravidian (e.g. Brahui). Thus, we can accept the restriction on the use of /o/ including its non-occurrence in the word-final position as a characteristic feature of Dravidian.

Linguists are of the opinion that "Typically, the substratum affects the phonology of the adopted language. . . ." (Lehiste, 1988:60). Since the phonology of Oriya has been shown to have been affected, it can be argued that it has been caused by the Dravidian substratum. In the beginning of the contact, the then Dravidians spoke the Aryan speech, i.e. the then Oriya with interference from their mother-tongue, and in due course adopted it as their primary language. Chatterji (1966:21) also supports this view and remarks:

> The spread of the Aryan language has more or less followed the same pattern all over India. An Aryan-speaking group establishes itself in some part of the country among non-Aryan speakers. It becomes the focus of influence for a new culture and a new civilization, of which this language (both as Sanskrit and as Prakrit) is the vehicle. People round about, particularly the upper class, first pick up the Aryan language while retaining their native speech, and thus become bilingual. The prestige of the Aryan speech has a tremendous influence, and gradually this speech drives to the wall the non-Aryan language of the less exalted masses. In this way the Aryan language carries out a place for itself, which is extending itself as a matter of course at the expense of the earlier non-Aryan language or languages. The same thing can only be expected to have happened in Orissa also.

However, as a result of this contact and adoption of Oriya by the Dravidian substratum, /o/ was first disallowed to occur in the word-final position and then its use is gradually getting restricted in other positions in Oriya.

Regarding the second question, it should be stated here that though the change of /o/ to /ɔ/ is noticed in Standard Oriya, it is more frequently attested in Southern Oriya than in Standard Oriya. There are ample data in which /o/ of Standard Oriya changes to /ɔ/ in Southern Oriya. For example:

Standard Oriya	Southern Oriya	Gloss
soṛa	sɔṛa	soda
gopaḷɔ	gɔpaḷɔ	Gopal (a name)
dokanɔ	dɔkanɔ	shop
koraputḁ	kɔraputḁ	Koraput (a district)

Mohanty (ms.) argues that the back-vowel series is overcrowded in Oriya, and due to the Dravidian substratum influence the functional load of the /o/-/ɔ/ opposition is lower than that of /u/-/o/. As the merger of /o/ with /ɔ/ will create the largest possible margin of security between the remaining vowels, i.e. /i/ and /ɔ/, /o/ changes to /ɔ/ in Standard Oriya and its dialects. As Southern Oriya, unlike Standard Oriya, is very much close to the Dravidian-speaking area where there is a restriction on the use of /o/, this change is more frequently noticed in it. The same trait is also responsible for the change of /o/ and /o:/ into /ɔ/ and /ɔ:/ in Daringabadi Kui and Paniganda Sora.

Conclusion

To sum up, the loss of /o/ in Oriya is a case of the Dravidian substratum influence; because unlike other vowels the use of /o/ is very much restricted in Dravidian. Though only Kui and Sora are chosen in this paper for discussion, changes in the same direction are noticed in the non-literary Dravidian languages like Kurukh, Malto, Kuvi, Toda and Brahui, and interestingly, Manda, a central Dravidian language spoken in Southern Orissa, does not use /o/ at all (Zvelebil, 1970:61-64). The Munda languages spoken in Orissa like Didey, Bonda, Gutob, Juang and Santali also show the same traits (Bhattacharya, 1975:46-49). Thus, the implication of the above discussions is that the whole of the Dravidian speaking area and Orissa together constitute a sub-linguistic area within the Indian linguistic area.

NOTE

* I am thankful to Karunakar Pradhan for the Daringabadi Kui data and to Sanatan Majhi for the Paniganda Sora data.

REFERENCES

Andronov, M., 1977. *Dravidian languages.* Vijayawada: Visalaanandhra Publishing House.

Bhattacharya, S., 1975. *Studies in Comparative Munda Linguistics.* Simla: Indian Institute of Advanced Study.

Chatterji, S.K., 1970. *The Origin and Development of the Bengali Language.* London: George Allen and Unwin (reprint).

—, 1966. *Artavallabha Mahanti Memorial Lectures.* Bhubaneswar: Orissa Sahitya Akademi.

Emeneau, M.B., 1956. 'India as a linguistic area.' *Language* 32.1:3-16.

Grierson, G.A. (comp. and ed.), 1967. *Linguistic Survey of India,* Vol. IV, Delhi, Varanasi, Patna: Motilal Banarsidass (reprint).

Krishnamurti, Bh., 1969. 'Comparative Dravidian Studies.' In Sebeok, ed. *Currents Trends in Linguistics.* Vol. 5.

Lehiste, I., 1988. *Lectures on Language Contact.* Cambridge, Mass: MIT Press.

Martinet, A., 1952. 'Function, structure and sound change.' *Word* 8.1-32.

Masica, Colin P., 1976. *Defining a Linguistic Area: South Asia.* Chicago and London: University of Chicago Press.

Mohanty, P., 1987. 'Where did /o/ go in the northern dialect of Oriya? *Indian Linguistics* 48.76-86.

—, ms. 'Linguistic economy at work: an example from Oriya.'

Pattanayak, D.P., 1966. *A Controlled Historical Reconstruction of Oriya, Assamese, Bengali and Hindi.* The Hague: Mouton.

Rajaram, S., 1972. *Tamil Phonetic Reader.* Mysore: Central Institute of Indian Languages.

Ramamurti, G.V., 1931, *A Manual of the Sora (or Savara) Language.* Madras: Government Press.

—, 1986. *Sora-English Dictionary.* Delhi: Mittal Publications (reprint).

Sastry, J.V., 1972. *Telugu Phonetic Reader.* Mysore: Central Institute of Indian Languages.

Sebeok, T.A. (ed.), 1969. *Current Trends in Linguistics,* Vol. 5. The Hague, Paris: Mouton.

Shyamala Kumari, B., 1972. *Malayalam Phonetic Reader.* Mysore: Central Institute of Indian Languages.

Upadhyaya, U.P., 1972. *Kannada Phonetic Reader.* Mysore: Central Institute of Indian languages.

Vasanthakumari, T., 1989. *Generative Phonology of Tamil.* Delhi: Mittal Publications.

Weinreich, U., 1953. *Languages in Contact.* New York: Linguistic Circle of New York.

Winfield, W.W., 1928. *A Grammar of the Kui Language.* Calcutta: Asiatic Society of Bengal.

—, 1929. *A Vocabulary of the Kui Language (Kui-English).* Calcutta: Asiatic Society of Bengal.

Zide, N.H., 1969. 'Munda and non-Munda Austroasiatic languages.' In Sebeok, ed.

Zvelebil, K.V., 1970. *Comparative Dravidian Phonology.* The Hague, Paris: Mouton.

CHAPTER 8

LANGUAGE SITUATION AND LINGUISTIC CONVERGENCE

(WITH SPECIAL REFERENCE TO KUVI)

M. Israel

Introduction

Koraput District

Koraput is a district in Orissa located in the south-western part of the state, bound by Kalahandi and Phulbani districts in the north and Ganjam district in the east. It also touches the borders of Andhra Pradesh in the south and the east and of Madhya Pradesh in the west.

Population and Languages

According to 1961 Census, the district has a population of 1,561,057, of which as many as 945,338 belong to the scheduled tribes, which alone constitute 61 per cent of the total population. However, it is recorded in the report that Koraput district has 948,766 Oriya speakers. Thus it is evident that a good percentage of tribes has switched over to Oriya and that they would have gradually lost their distinct mothertongues which served as the marker of their ethnic identity.

It is known from the Orissa District Gazetteer published in 1966 that of the 28 languages spoken in the district 11 are modern Indian languages, of which Oriya, Telugu, Hindi, Bengali, Urdu and Tamil have more than 1000 speakers each. Other modern Indian languages include Gujarati, Punjabi, Kannada, Malayalam, Marathi and Nepali. English is the only foreign language spoken in the district. Laria and Halabi are the dialects of Chattisgarh area of Madhya Pradesh. Jharia and Marwari are also other two Indo-Aryan dialects spoken in the region.

The remaining 14 tribal languages can broadly be divided into two groups, viz., the Dravidian group to which belong the languages Kui (162,518), Khond/Kondh (Kuvi-79,034), Konda (Kubi-109,30), Pengo (1,254), Gondi (18,098) and Koya (30,992) and the Austro-Asiatic group which includes Gadaba (31,891), Savara (55,418), Parenga (767) and Santali (7). In 1961 the Dravidian tribal languages Manda and Indi-Awe are not recorded, although they are spoken in the district. Thus in Koraput district, languages of Dravidian family and Austro-Asiatic family (Munda group) and also the members of the Indo-Aryan branch of the Indo-European family are in constant contact. Especially the speakers of the languages of Dravidian group and those of Munda group live adjacently as well as intermixedly in the hill tops and slopes and sporadically in the plains also. They have been in active contact for many years and thereby there has been a continuous interaction among them. Desia Oriya, the dominant spoken language of this multilingual region plays the major role of lingua franca because of its easy accessibility to all the tribal communities despite the fact that the tribals among themselves often communicate in languages of either Dravidian or Munda group.

Bilingualism/Multilingualism

In the Census report of 1961, out of the total population of the district, 264,685 are shown to be speaking a language subsidiary to their mothertongue. These people can speak one or more languages in addition to their mothertongue. Thus there are a good number of speakers who are either bilinguals or multilinguals.

Only a low percentage of women from all the minor linguistic groups speak a language other than their mothertongue, even though a good number of male speakers of various tribal languages are conversant with the local dominant Oriya or some neighbouring minor language for the purpose of trade, sociopolitical activities and also for intercommunication with their neighbours. Intimate as well as constant contact in the physical proximity and also social mobility of the speakers of the varying minor languages have resulted in active bilingualism or multilingualism in the area. This has enabled the carry-over of certain linguistic features across the languages of different genetic groups.

Kuvi

Kuvi was not recognized and identified as one of the languages in the reports of Census until 1971. However, Khond/Kondh and Kui are enumerated separately as two different mothertongues in the Census reports of 1951, 1961 and 1971 and the numerical strength of Kui speakers has always been higher than that of the former. The 1966 Orissa District Gazetteer identifies Kuvi as a dialect of Kui. In the 1971 Census report Kuvi is indicated as an alternate name for Khond/Kondh. Thus Khond/Kondh can evidently be identified with Kuvi. Here a name of the mothertongue is returned after the name of the scheduled tribe. Apparantly Kuvi speaking Konds prefer to return their tribal name as their mothertongue, even though the speakers of the other languages like Kui, Manda, Indi-Awe are also designated as Khonds by their neighbouring Oriyas.

Kuvi is spoken mainly in the Koraput district and also in the adjoining districts, viz., Kalahandi, Ganjam and Phulbani of Orissa state and in the neighbouring border of Andhra Pradesh. As per 1961 Census report, the following are the figures of the distribution of Khonds/Kondhs, i.e., Kuvi speakers:

India	168,027
Orissa	144,923
Andhra Pradesh	22,730
Assam	224
West Bengal	150

As per 1981 Census report, the population of Konds is 204,000. According to the 1966 Orissa District Gazetteer, the population of Kuvi speakers in Koraput District alone is 49,034. Of them 25,638 are recorded as bilinguals. Thus 32 per cent of the entire Kuvi speakers live in Koraput district alone and 50 per cent of them are bilinguals.

Linguistic Convergence

Due to extensive bilingualism, constant interaction, etc., the carry-over of certain linguistic features which are not indigenous to Dravidian has taken place into Kuvi from the contact languages. These features of convergence have been noticed at the phonological, structural and lexical levels. The direction of the convergence in a minor language is largely towards the dominant language. However, in Kuvi certain convergent features have been observed towards the direction of other minority languages also.

An attempt is made here to trace and enumerate a few noteworthy linguistic features at the phonological as well as structural level which Kuvi has adopted from the dominant Oriya language and also from the neighbouring Munda group of languages.

Convergence towards Oriya

A number of features from the dominant Oriya language have been embedded into Kuvi at various levels.

Development of Voiced Stops

Dravidian languages do not have voiced stops in the indigenous phonemic structure. Due to extensive borrowing of vocabulary from, and convergence towards Oriya language, Kuvi has developed some voicing in the stop series:

Dravidian/Proto Dravidian	Kuvi	Gloss
kiṇṇam	gina	'metal cup'
kuṭai	guṛgu	'umbrella'
peruku	bir-	'to grow, multiply'
poŋku	boŋgi-	'to swell'
pey	bō-	'to be spilled'

The phonemic system of Kuvi is converged with that of Oriya by the adoption of a binary opposition of stops, viz., voiceless vs. voiced:

Dravidian/Proto Dravidian		Kuvi	
pālu	'milk'	bālu	'bear'
toya	'fig tree'	doya	'please'
ṭāyu	'place'	ḍāyu	'afterwards'
kata	'matter'	gata	'compost manure'
sopa	'name of a tree'	soba	'wet field'
kutu	'stich'	kudu	'cracked rice'
kāṭa	'tools'	kāḍa	'time of death'
pāka	'large rock'	pāga	'weather'

Initial v-changing into b-

Oriya and other Indo-Aryan languages often prefer word initial b- to v-. In Kuvi the word initial v- has changed into b- in a number of lexical items due to the convergence towards the dominant contact language:

Dravidian/Proto Dravidian	Kuvi	Gloss
vaṭi	baṛga	"a small cane or stick"
vayal	bayalu	"field"
vittu	bica	"seed"
vēṭṭam	bēṭa	"hunting"
vēy	bēcali	"spying"

Noun Derivation

There is a resemblance found between Kuvi and Oriya in the formation of a class of nouns in which the derivative morph indicating the difference in the sex of the persons involved is *-a* or *-i*. This is originally an Indo-Aryan feature which has been embedded into the Kuvi structure:

-a	male	-i	female
kuja	'short man'	kuji	'short woman'
buṛha	old man'	buṛhi	'old woman'
ḍokra	'husband'	ḍokri	'wife'
ḍola	'child' (m)	ḍoli	'child' (f)
kāṇa	'blind man'	kāṇi	'blind woman'

The Use of Enumerator

In the use of enumerator or classifier also Kuvi along with Pengo, Manda and Parji resembles Oriya. The numerals except first two are always construed with the enumerator (classifier) "jaṇa" with the nouns denoting persons and often with "goṭa" with the nouns denoting things:

tīni jaṇa karmagaṭari	'three poor people'
sāri jaṇa gurka	'four gurus'
sāta jaṇa podayā̃	'seven daughters'
sāri goṭa pūṅga	'four flowers'
tīni goṭa ḍokayā̃	'four pots'
sāta goṭa guḍuyā̃	'seven eggs'

This sort of formation is not found in Indo-European other than in Indo-Aryan. However, in Kuvi it is a convergent feature towards the dominant language Oriya which would have internalized such a feature in the remote past possibly from Munda.

Compounds

a. Intensive Compounds:

With regard to the formation of a type of intensive compounds or balanced words in which a free constitutent is followed by an unique constituent which is generally formed by repeating a part of the free constituent and which intensifies its meaning, Kuvi has converged with Oriya:

rāha bāha	'great pleasure'
himbori ḍūki	'clothing of various kinds'
heka ḍuka	'palm fibre'
āsti bāsti	'property, etc.'
lōku bāka	'people of all kind'

b. Fused Compounds:

A type of compound formed by the fusion of the two members adopting the system of sandhi in Indo-Aryan is also found in Kuvi. Here the system of compound-formation and sandhi-formation in Kuvi is due to the convergence towards the dominant language:

Iya	'mother'	+ āba	'father'	>	Iyaba	'parents'
mā	'my'	+ ijo	'in house'	>	mājo	'in my house'
rī	'second'	+ ijo	'in house'	>	rījo	'another house'
mī	'your'	+ āba	'father'	>	mība	'your father'

In Kuvi, there is a series of compounds formed by the addition of -*eka* "one" (full) a borrowing from Indo-Aryan, to the first member of the compound, the usual morphophonemic changes take place and this forms a one word construction:

hēci	'winnow'	+ eka	> hēceka	'one winnow full of'
koṛi	'twenty'	+ eka	> koṛeka	'one score'
garha	'a large measure'	+ eka	> garheka	'one large measure full of'
pomṇa-	'arm'	+ eka	> pomṇeka	'armful'

c. *Verbal Compounds from Adjectives and Adverbs:*
In Kuvi, it is occasionally found that a verbal idea is expressed by the addition of a verbal root to an adjective or an adverb, but the indigenousness of Dravidian is such that the verbalizers are added only to the nouns. This type of compound-formation is also due to convergence towards the dominant language:

Adjective + Verbal Root				
āṭva-ā-	'to become hard'	<	āṭva	'hard'
ūṇa-meh-	'to despise'	<	ūṇa	'small'
Adverb + Verbal Root				
daga-ā-	'to hurry'	<	daga	'quickly'
pṛoke-ā	'to be silent'	<	pṛoke	'silently'

Convergence towards Munda Group of Languages
Certain linguistic features have been embedded into Kuvi due to convergence towards the neighbouring minor Munda group of languages.

Occurrence of Glottal Stop
The glottal stop is not reconstructed as one of the phonemes of the Proto-Dravidian language, even though it is found to occur in Konda, Kui and Kuvi. Glottal stop in Kuvi is definitely a phoneme with numerous occurrences and it is pronounced with much more force than in other languages of the group. In Kuvi it occurs: (1) intervocalically;

(2) between a vowel and certain consonants; (3) between certain consonants and a vowel; and (4) finally, in some verbal roots after vowels:

i?ira	'soil'
ki?eṇi	'castor oil seed'
ha?la	'cow-shed'
kṛa?ni	'tiger'
kā?-	'to watch'

Glottal stop is found to occur frequently in the Munda group of languages. Thus, it may not be wrong to assume that in Kuvi it is a convergent feature towards the Munda group of languages.

Counting in Twenties

In Kuvi beyond twenty is not counted except in multiples of twenty. The word used for twenty is kōṛi/kōṛe:

kōṛi	lābo/kōṛi	roṇḍi	'twenty one'
kōṛi	dūyi/kōṛi	riṇḍi	'twenty two'

For the numerals after two, only Oriya numerals are used:

tīni	'three'
sāri	'four'
pāsa	'five', etc.
rī kōṛi	'forty'
tīni kōṛi	'sixty'
pāsa kōṛi	'one hundred'

This type of counting system is found not only in the Munda group of languages but also in Kuvi, Munda, Gondi, Konda and in Desia Oriya and it is a sign of convergence into Kuvi and other languages towards Munda group of languages.

Echo-Word Formation

Even though the echo-formation is found to occur in all the Dravidian languages, the occurrence of *m-* initially in the second constituent denoting the meaning "and the like, etc.", is peculiar to Kondh languages. In Munda group of languages especially in Savara, *m-* regularly occurs in the initial position of the second member in the echo-formation. Scholars think that the echo-formation in Indian languages had its origin in Munda languages. But the Munda system of echo-formation with the occurrence of the initial *m-* in the second member would have certainly converged into the system of Kuvi, if not the total system of echo-formation:

dara mara	'price, and the like'
kuṭi maṭi	'nail, and the like'
uli muli	'onion, and the like'
āya māya	'woman, and the like'
koyu moyu	'fowl, and the like'
tākihi mākihi	'if walking, etc. ...'

Personal Object Stems

Kui, Kuvi, Pengo and Manda have the two-way distinction of verbal stems, general as well as special throughout the verbal system. The special stem, i.e., known as personal object stem which is used only when the object is first or second person is made by the addition of a derivative suffix */-a/* or its allomorphs */-ta ~ -ya ~ -ja ~ ha/*. It is found that in the Munda group of languages the suffix */-a/* is regularly added to the primary verbal stems to form the personal object stems. In Kuvi all the allomorphs of the personal object suffix have basically */-a-/* in them:

kacitesi	'he bit'	:	kacatesi	'he bit you/me'
hītesi	'he gave'	:	hīyatesi	'he gave you/me'
vecesi	'he heard'	:	venjatesi	'he heard you/me'
kātesi	'he watched'	:	kātatesi	'he watched you/me'
jāphesi	'he taught'	:	jāphatesi	'he taught you/me'

This type of two-way distinction of verbal stems does not occur in the Dravidian languages which are not in contact situation with the Munda languages. This system would have been embedded with Kuvi and neighbouring Dravidian tribal languages through convergence towards Munda.

Plural Action Stem

The plural action stem is formed by adding *-k-* or its allomorph *-p-* to the basic verbal stem to express an action done many times, repeatedly, concentratedly, thoroughly, forcibly or intensively, etc. It is possible that one and the same plural action stem may denote more than one aspect of the action done, i.e., intensively and repeatedly, thoroughly and forcibly, etc.:

kar (i)-	'to chew'	kark-	'to gnaw'
get (i)-	'to jump'	getk-	'to hop'
kat (i)-	'to cut trees'	katk-	'to chop into pieces, repeatedly'
kac (i)-	'to bite'	kask-	'to bite intensively repeatedly'
hūp (i)	'to spit'	hūpk-	'to vomit'
kot-	'to hoe'	kotp-	'to dig'

Such a formation of plural-action-stems is regularly found in the neighbouring Munda group of languages and is not found in the Dravidian languages which are not in contact situation. Thus, this is also a feature in Kuvi converged towards the minority/dominated languages.

Conclusion

An exhaustive analysis of the exact nature and direction of convergence in the languages could only be possible if a thorough study of the descriptive as well as typological structure and history of all the languages involved in the area is completed.

CHAPTER 9

LANGUAGES IN CONTACT IN JHARKHAND

A CASE OF LANGUAGE CONFLATION, LANGUAGE CHANGE AND LANGUAGE CONVERGENCE

Anvita Abbi

Introduction

An area that exists in reality but not in geopolitical maps of the Government of India, an area that contains 55 per cent of tribal population of the country, an area that symbolizes the ancient heritage of India, a centre for cultural and linguistic convergence as it is interwoven by Austro-Asiatic (Munda), Dravidian, and Indo-Aryan speech communities—has always fascinated me. This is the region of Central India, the epicentre of the Indian civilization and culture that encompasses parts of the present Bihar, Orissa, Madhya Pradesh, and Bengal states. Various dialects of Hindi, Bangla, and Oriya dominate the indigenous Munda languages and those of the North Dravidian families such as Kurux/Kurukh (also known as Oraon) and Malto. See Table 1 to get an idea of the distribution of the tribal languages in these four states. The area is known as Jharkhand (see map 1) and is represented by an intense language contact situation unparalleled anywhere else in the

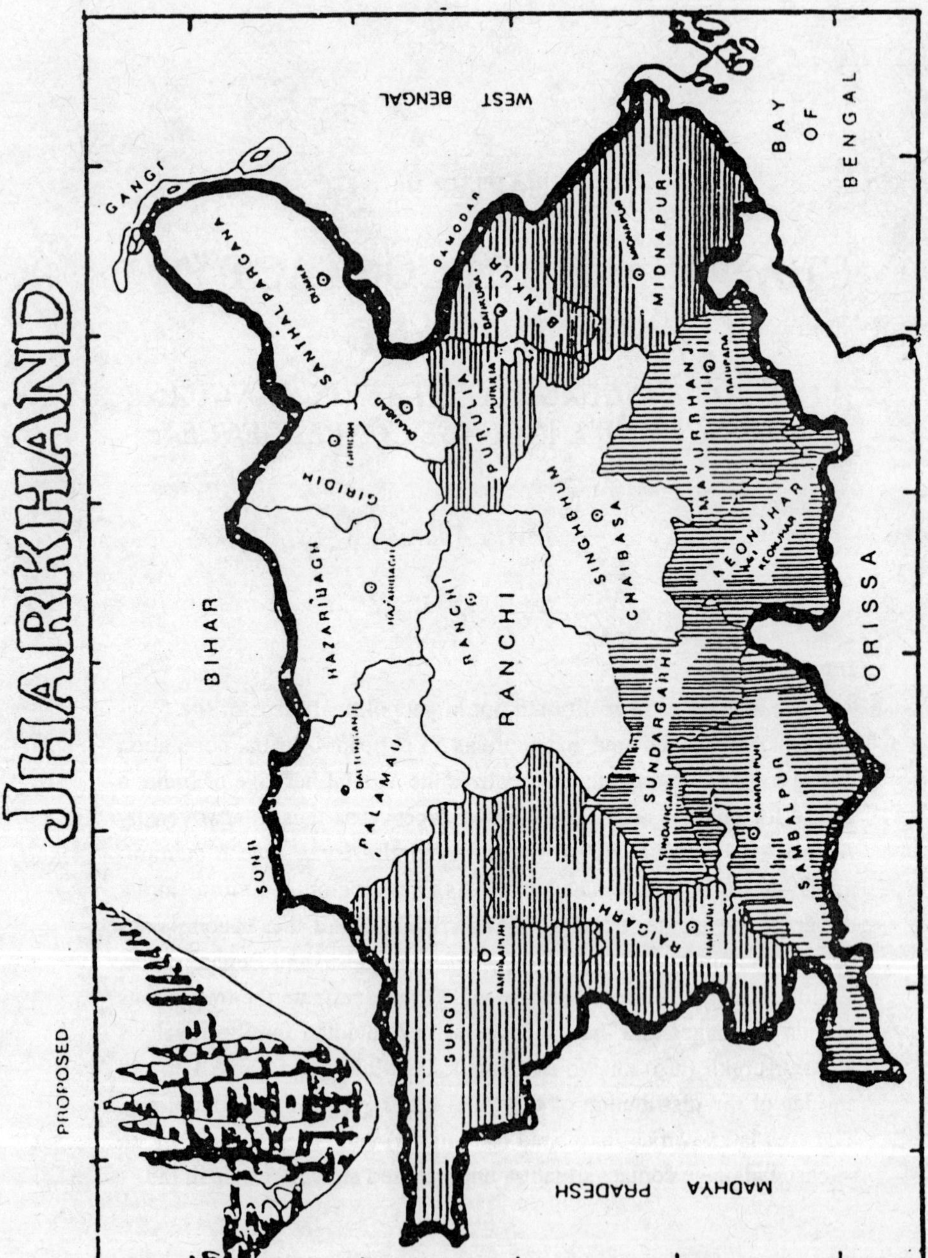
JHARKHAND
PROPOSED
BIHAR
WEST BENGAL
BAY OF BENGAL
ORISSA
MADHYA PRADESH
SANTHAL PARGANA
GIRIDIH
HAZARIBAGH
PALAMAU
RANCHI
PURULIA
MIDNAPUR
SINGHBHUM
CHAIBASA
SUNDARGARH
SAMBALPUR
SURGU
DAMODAR

country. As Ram Dayal Munda, noted Jharkhand Movement propagator and a linguist points out:

> "Culturally this is the only area in the entire country where three major cultural streams—Aryan, Dravidian and Austroasian, represented through various languages—have converged to create a cultural synthesis of its own kind." (1989)

The movement for an autonomous and separate state for Jharkhand is currently being strongly mooted.

Language Contact

The dynamics of language contact is such that the dominant languages are either the Scheduled languages of the Indo-Aryan family or their dialects (non-scheduled), while the dominated ones are those of the Munda and the Dravidian families. Communication within this complex linguistic network has generated bi-/multilingual peoples, with interaction between various indigenous groups such as Kharia (Munda) and Oraon as well as between those of various dominant languages and their dialects such as Hindi and Sadani/Sadari. The resultant scene is of a unique nature where minority community is on higher level at the 'scale of bilingual proficiency' than its dominant majority community/ies. The contact-induced changes in languages such as Kurux and Kharia have led to linguistic typological homogeneity on the one hand, and to a tendency to language attrition, on the other. In the tug of war between language maintenance (retention of mothertongues) and language proficiency in the dominant/contact language/s, the tribal language have begun passing through a transition period of language change and language convergence postponing or avoiding the expected language obsolescence situation. The paradoxical oscillation between language maintenance and language loss or shift is a natural consequence of high rate of bilingualism prevailing in the Jharkhand area (See Table 2 and 3). We must remember that societal bilingualism is frequently mentioned as a prerequisite for language shift. (Fasold, 1984: 216-17)

Bilingualism prevails between intra-tribal and inter-tribal communities. Hence, a typical Kharia speaker might have a working knowledge of Kurux and Sadari or Kurux and Hindi. Fluent monolingual speakers are declining, instead Hindi/Sadari bilingualism has become the rule rather than an exception among the younger generation. Average bilingual intensity in the Jharkhand area runs around 47 per cent. (This is an official figure; in reality the urban Jharkhand area has a bilingual intensity of nearly 85 per cent.) This figure is much higher than the national figure of bilingualism which was 9.7 per cent in 1961. Unfortunately, no data was collected for bilingualism after the 1961 census.

Various mothertongues in an intense language contact situation move from their orbit to engulf the features of the periphery and thus run the risk of resulting in a pidgin-like situation. Fortunately, none of the tribal languages of the area has reached this extreme. However, danger signs of language attrition are visible in the loss of basic vocabulary, borrowings of Indo-Aryan lexicon and morphological processes, as well as in change in word order.

Linguists (Dorian, 1981; Karttunen, 1977; G. Ramat, 1979) working on minority languages and those which are near extinction have identified linguistic features that predict possible language obsolescence. Moungen and Beniak (1989) have isolated such features:

> "Minority language contraction certainly triggers linguistic development that simply do not arise in monolingual settings, such as morphological simplification due to insufficient linguistic input, gratuitious borrowings, nonce or idiosyncratic borrowings, phonological denativization of loan words, interference based innovations etc." (p. 309)

Surprisingly, the same processes which are ear-marked for language death and language obsolescence have saved the languages such as Kurux and Kharia from extinction. This has been possible because of (1) an increase in language-identity consciousness and language-loyalty; and (2) amalgamation or integration of Indo-Aryan morphological structures in the tribal languages. The resultant effect is that languages have conflated themselves so that they may be used in newer contexts. Interestingly, despite the fact that these languages seem to be linguistically converged, they do serve as the identity markers of their respective speech communities. We are going to discuss two such languages in detail in this paper, Kharia and Kurux spoken in the Jharkhand area.[1] The geographical proximity of the two communities almost always exists within this area.

The Ethnolinguistic Status of Kharia and Kurux

The Major Kharia speaking states are Southern Bihar, Northern Orissa, Eastern Madhya Pradesh, and Assam comprising over 3 lakh speakers (1971, Census). (See Nigam, 1972). Kurux, according to the 1981 Census, is spoken by 12,64,548 people out of which 51 per cent reside in Bihar alone. The other states of the area under consideration include Madhya Pradesh, West Bengal, and Orissa (ordered by number of Kurux speakers). The highest percentage of Kuruxs reside in Ranchi and Gumla subdivisions. To facilitate cross linguistic comparison we have restricted our study to Kharia and Kurux spoken in Chotanagpur area, which more or less represents the situation in other areas of Jharkhand as well.

Much of the Kharia-/Kurux-speaking area is ethnically heterogeneous. The coexistence of the two communities with the non-tribal population, which is numerically, socially, and economically dominant, creates a multilingual milieu where these two languages cannot function as socially equal languages.

Another factor determining the sociolinguistic status of the tribal languages in Chotanagpur is the ongoing urbanization and industrialization. There is an inverse correlation between levels of industrialization or urbanization, and the maintenance of tribal language as mothertongues. It is a sad fact that Kurux/Kharia languages are quickly disappearing from most of the urbanized areas of Ranchi district. The trend also indicates that the urban tribals seldom consider it their privilege to speak their mothertongues. On the contrary, ignorance of the tribal languages is regarded as an enhancement of status and prestige. By speaking Hindi they feel superior to other fellow-tribals who cannot speak it.

A low percentage of urban tribals are monolinguals in their ancestral languages. Ethnolinguistic minority status induces a negative attitude toward language loyalty. A gradual adoption of a non-tribal language as mothertongue presents a classic case of language shift. Theoretically, these symptoms are considered diagnostic of potential language death. With this ethnolinguistic background, I will discuss the synchronic grammatical patterns of Kharia and Kurux to see whether these languages are heading towards obsolencence or for a change normally associated with the growth and development of a language in an intense language contact situation and if it is the latter, whether the degree of change is strong enough to identify them as 'converged languages'.

The Journey towards Language Attrition and Loss

Language attrition follows a large scale substitution of existing linguistic structures and processes by those of the dominant languages. The initial stage is that of a gratuitous borrowing of basic vocabulary, a sign of language obsolescence (as widely maintained by various linguists). Let us consider this stage first.

Against the backdrop of the 218 Basic Word list suggested by M. Swadesh (1955) and Gudschinsky (1956) representing a high-frequency use and utmost stability over the years, with these words likely to be most resistant to change, a heavy infiltration of Indo-Aryan loan words is evident.

Numerals

Apart from the lower numerals 'one', 'two', and 'three', the higher numerals are Indo-Aryan (IA) loans in both of the languages. Consider:

IA (Hindi and other dialects)		Kurux	Kharia
ca:r	'four'	ca:ir	cair
pā̃c	'five'	pance:	pā̃c
a:tḥ	'eight'	aṭṭe/axe:	a:ṭ
das	'ten'	dasse/do:y	das
gya:rah	'eleven'	ga:ra	ag:ra:
kuṛi	'twenty'	bisoy/kuṛi	kuṛi
sɔ	'hundred'	sai	se
a:dha:	'half'	adha:	a:da

Kharia and Kurux have the vigesimal number systems and higher numbers are counted in twenties, using the IA base word *kuṛi* 'twenty', e.g. *cair kuṛi* 'eighty'. The alternative direct loans from IA such as *paca:s* 'fifty', *saiṭṭh* 'sixty', *sattar* 'seventy' are also used extensively.

The borrowing of numerals is understandable in view of the extensive commercial transactions between the inter-tribal and non-tribal population, necessitating a common numeral system. The prevailing socio-economic factors justify the total replacement of the indigenous numeral system. Interestingly, the languages have incorporated a new linguistic system within their existing systems; that is, numeral classifiers (see below) have been adopted in adaptation to the new contact situation.

Menninger (1969) predicts that "number words are among the words of a language that most strongly resist change". The Kharia and Kurux data, however, explode this myth. Field investigation in the Ranchi district shows that the speakers have very limited knowledge of their indigenous numeral systems, with the only commonly known terms the numerals 'two'and 'three'. At present even these more resistant low numerals are being replaced by IA vocabulary.

Kinship Terms

Another area known to be least resistant to change has undergone a complete displacement by IA loan words:

IA (Hindi and its dialects)		Kurux	Kharia
bha:i	'brother'	bha:i	bha:i
da:da:	'elder brother'	da:da:	da:da:
di:di:	'elder sister'	di:di:	di:di:
beṭa:	'son'	beṭa:	beṭa:
beṭi:	'daughter'	beṭi:	beṭi:
ka:ka:	'uncle'	kakas	kaka
sasur	'father-in-law	saisras	sasur

Many rural Kharia speakers still maintain the indigenous kinship terms (specially the address forms), and also forms which depict the possessor-possessed relationship. Kurux does not have generic kinship terms, and these are therefore borrowed from Hindi. Reference terminology distinguishing affinal and non-affinal relationships is likewise borrowed from the IA languages of the contact setting.

Apart from the incorporation of lexical loans, the infiltration of Aryan kinship terms into Kurux has brought about a morphological distinction (see Gender Distinction) of gender not known to exist earlier in these languages, with the masculine marked by the terminations *-a:*, *-u:*, *-s* and feminine derivatives by *-i*.

We shall consider this later.

Body Parts

Most of the body parts nomenclatures are indigenous with marginal lexical interference from IA as in Kharia: *gardan* 'neck'; *ṭhoṭho* 'throat'; *camṛaa* 'skin'; and Kurux : *buka:* 'heart', *ke:s* 'hair' etc.

Natural Objects

Not only those objects which are are geographically remote to the area, but also those which belong to the Kurux and Kharia habitats have been replaced by IA words. Consider:

Kharia		Kurux	
ghā̃s	'grass'	ghā̃si	'grass'
dhuri	'dust'	dhu:li	'dust'
pokhra:	'lake'	bada:li	'cloud'
kharom	'ashes'	pū̃:p	'flower'
aṇḍa:	'egg'	kuha:s/dū̃dh	'fog'
mā̃s	'meat'	cando	'moon'

Temporal Organization

The terms used to denote discrete time nouns consist predominantly of Indo-Aryan loans, completely eliminating the indigenous terms. Consider:

IA (Hindi and its dialects)		Kurux	Kharia
din	'day'	din	dinu
mahi:na:	'month'	mahina:	mohina:
varš/baras/sa:l	'year'	bachar	boris/baras/sa:l
pakhva:ṛa:	'fortnight'	pa:kkhe:	—
hafta:	'week'	—	hapta:

These forms have largely displaced the indigenous forms, which exist vestigially mainly in compounded structures.

Adjectives

Though loans in this category are not overwhelmingly large, still we do find a number of adjectives within the basic vocabulary. Consider:

IA (Hindi and its dialects)		Kurux	Kharia
be:s	'good'	be:s	be:s
beka:r	'bad'	begrəṛka	beka:r/bagṛe
ṭhi:k/sahi:	'right'	sahi:	ṭhi:k
khu:b/dḥe:r	'many'	dḥe:r/khob	dḥe:r
moṭa:	'thick'	mo:ṭ	moṭho
patla:	'thin'	patla:	patla:

The colour terminology, barring the one for 'red', is borrowed from Indo-Aryan. The term for 'black' *moxa:ro* is borrowed from Kharia *moghe:r* 'black'. Kharia, in turn, has colour terms for 'pink', 'purple', and 'blue' from Hindi.

Verbs

A large number of Indo-Aryan verbs are incorporated into Kurux lexicon. Recent research (conducted at the Jawaharlal Nehru University) establishes this loan to be around 250 verbs. This is an alarming figure as compared to the Kharia situation, where there has been some resistance to include Indo-Aryan loans in the verb area. However, both languages have witnessed the incorporation of verbs belonging to the basic vocabulary to some extent. For instance, Kharia *socay-na;* Kurux *soc-na* 'to think'; Kharia *khā̃ṛo-na;* Kurux *khaṇḍar-na* 'to cut'; Kurux *laṛ-na* 'to fight', *dhar-na* 'to hold', *gamka:r-na* 'to smell', *ṭuṭur-na* 'to split'are IA loans.

Kharia has borrowed the system of conjunct verb (N + Verb) as in *sā̃:s ḍoḍ-na* 'to breathe', along with the lexical morpheme from Indo-Aryan. The suffix *-na* in both Kharia and Kurux are IA borrowings for infinitive constructions facilitating expansion of the language to incorporate a large number of verbal loans. Kharia also incorporates Hindi *lag-na* 'to attach' as *la?na* to derive experiential verbs as in *betod la?na* 'to feel hungry'.

Conjunction

Three most common conjunctive/disjunctive adverbs belonging to the basic vocabulary such as 'if', 'and', 'because of' are directly borrowed from Hindi and its dialects.

Absolutive/Conjunctive Participle

To denote sequential relationship between two actions or states Kurux replaces the old indigenous *dara:* by Indo-Aryan *-ar* (as in *kar*) or *ki* as in *a:s manne argar ki ḍanḍi: pa:ṛdas* 'he sings after having climbed the tree'. This feature is, however, restricted to urban Kurux speech.

Similar is the case of Kharia *ke, kon* which are of recent origin. Language samples elicited from old informants of 75 years of age and above residing in rural areas, had a negligible occurrence of conjunctive participles in their speech.

The incorporation of IA verbs brought along certain morphological features that are assimilated into tribal languages causing a change in the paradigmatic morphological structure of Kharia and Kurux. The cases in point are passive markers in Kurux such as *kapp-na* 'to touch'; *kapp-r-na* 'to be touched' which is not a typical Dravidian feature (none of the Dravidian dialects possesses any passive particle or suffix), and Kharia causative markers (both single and double) such as *likh-ay-na, like-way-na* 'to get written'. Interestingly, Kharia like other Austro-Asiatic languages has a well developed prefixing and infixing systems of deriving transitives and causatives. The Indo-Aryan loan has produced a redundant complex morphological paradigms at times, e.g. *ob-likh-way-na* 'to get written' (caus-write-caus-inf).

The most interesting aspect of loan verb incorporation is that of copula (see Malhotra 1982 for details). According to her in synchronic Kharia, the verb 'to be' is represented by the existential copula *aij,* the identity copula *heke,* and the inchoative *hoina,* with the suppletive negative forms *umborij* and *na lage* for *aij* and *heke* respectively, and the negative *um* prefixation for *hoina.* A comparative analysis with the South Munda languages shows that there are no cognates for these forms, and their lexical and derivational identities with Sadani forms indicate, quite convincingly, that they are loans.

The predilection of loan words and loan morphology accompanied by decreases in language domain and language use, as well as simultaneous increase in bilingualism are considered sure signs of language attrition in linguistics literature. A recent study conducted at JNU (1991) revealed that out of total number of 15,000 words collected in Kurux, 14 per cent, that is, 2100 words were found to be IA loans. In the noun category, our field data showed 1400 words to be IA loans, i.e. 66 per cent of the total noun vocabulary collected for the present research.

Language Conflation and Language Convergence

Lexical loan component, that has been identified in the basic vocabulary, represents at micro-level, the magnitude of the semantico-cultural interference on the one hand, and sociolinguistic expansion of tribal languages on the other. Contrary to the expectations, gratuitous borrowing, replacement of existing basic vocabulary by Indo-Aryan loan words, and morphemic expansion have helped the languages to conflate. The resulting effect is that Kharia and Kurux have moved towards areal typological consistency at the expense of indigenous lexicon and structures. Paradoxically, this change has been good for the speech communities as it helps in inter-tribal, and tribal/non-tribal communicability.

Incorporation of grammatical features of the neighbouring dominant languages, widening of semantic and cognitive scopes have enabled the tribal languages to enlarge the communicative network across the multilingual Jharkhand. This process of linguistic expansion is known as 'language conflation' (Abbi, 1992). Let us see how Kharia and Kurux have undergone language conflation in their grammatical structures.

Phonological

Aspirates of voiced and voiceless nature have become an integral part of the phonological system of Kurux. Words of the basic lexicon incorporate a large number of aspirates. So is the case of Kharia.

Gender Distinction

Kurux, on the pattern of neighbouring IA dialects, has incorporated gender markers on human nouns. The feminine suffixes are *-i:*, *-in, -a:in, ni:-* such as in *beṭa:* 'son': *beṭi:* 'daughter': *hindu* 'a Hindu man' *hindua:in* 'a Hindu woman'. Kharia follows a similar pattern of marking gender hitherto unknown to a typical morphological pattern of Kharia. Thus masculine is marked by *-a/-u* and feminie by *-i,* e.g. *caŋgna* 'rooster': *caŋgni* 'hen': *ma:ma:* 'mother's brother' and *ma:mi* 'mother's brother's wife'.

The distinction in gender is carried over to modifiers also. Hence, on the pattern of Hindi, Kurux adjectives are marked for masculine and feminine nominals, e.g. *kaṇḍa: a:las* 'blind (one-eyed) man'; *kaṇḍi: a:li:* 'blind (one-eyed) woman.

Classifiers

Alien to Dravidian and Austro-Asiatic languages in general, Kharia and Kurux have developed numeral classifiers in accordance to Indo-Aryan languages of the Jharkhand region. Kharia *jhan* (< IA *jan~jɔn*) with human nouns, *goṭ/tḥong (IA tḥo)* with inanimate nouns are typical examples. Kurux also has *jhan* as in *pãce: jhan a:lar* 'five men'; *goṭa* as in *mu:ṇḍ goṭa xa:lba:r* 'three thieves'.

Morphological Expansion

As considered earlier, the infinitive *-na* with verb, conjunctive participles such as *-ar* or *-ki,* gender distinction in nouns that none existed before, transitive and causative as well as passive markings on the root form of verbs (see above), creation of conjunct verbs for experiential verbs and a large number of IA nominal suffixes to create agentive nouns and abstract nouns in Kurux and Kharia have certainly restructured and expanded the morphological domians of these tribal languages. A few examples from Kurux will validate our point.

Suffix

-ai	moṭh 'obstinate'	>	moṭhai 'obstinacy'
-ait	ḍonga: 'boat'	>	ḍongait 'boat man'
-ba:n	gaṛi: 'cart'	>	gari:ba:n 'cart man'
-har/har	kamna: 'to work'	>	Kamhar 'tool'
-ya:	muṭhi 'fist'	>	muṭhiya: 'bangle'

Semantic Expansion

There has been almost an explosion of new words in the two languages under consideration, specially in the realm of cultural/material artifacts. The industrialization and urbanization of Chotanagpur, the advent of Christian missionaries and the introduction of formal education brought about a radical change in the social structure and the cognitive world. Introduction of material artifacts not indigenous to the Kharia or Kurux habitat, along with religious discourse and educational experience, introduced abstract nouns and words pertaining to reason. This is one area where the languages have conflated most.

The advent of Christianity has brought an elaborate terminology pertaining to Christian doctrines and institutions such as, *pa:pi:* 'sinner', *dharm* 'religion', *mukti* 'salvation', *ji:sas* 'Jesus', *girja:* 'church' etc. in Kurukh as well as in Kharia.

Similarly, there has been an extensive borrowing of words related to mental faculty such as *sambhar* 'ability', *bipat* 'adversity', *chema:* 'apology', *hunar* 'art/dexterity', *calan* 'behaviour', *subha:o* 'nature', *akbaki:* 'confusion', *ma:ya:* charity, *akil* 'talent', *parpanc* 'fuss' etc. in Kurux.

Language conflation is not restricted to words and word-formation processes alone. The syntactic realm of languages are also expanded to fit into the areally uniform linguistic scene.

Syntactic Expansion

The incorporation of relative pronouns, and the relative clause structure, presumably from the IA languages has resulted in the re-ordering[2] of syntacic structure of complex constructions. Extensive contact with Aryan languages has gradually displaced the unreduced, unembedded phrasal juxtaposition for the expression of restrictive modification by relative clauses on the IA patterning in Kharia. It must be noted that although restrictive relative clause appears to be borrowed from IA, its syntactic ordering diverges significantly from dominant relative clauses found in indo-Aryan languages. Hence, the phrasal juxtappsitional structure of SOV + SOV or with identical subject/object deletion, depending on the nominal constituent relativized—SOV + OV, SO + SV has resulted in embedded restrictive relative clauses of the S (Rel. Cl.) OV or SO (Rel. C1.) V type. Consider:

1. *konsel-ḍu ber inya-ghaḍ merom song-ka:y-o? bes aij*
   women who me for sheep buy -ben- pst good is
   'The women who bought the sheep for me is good.'
2. *aning sob maš-te ɲo-kho?-ning (aje?) iḍa? song-si-kho-ma:y*
   we all meat acc eat pst we that yesterday bought had
   'we ate all the meat that we bought yesterday'.

Due to heavy Aryanization the simplistic nature of Kharia bound morphology is giving way to complex syntactic structure of inflecting type. It is a common-knowledge to linguists that verb stem alone may serve as a full phrase in Munda. This mot-phrase[3] characteristic of archaic Kharia/Munda formations are becoming rare. For instance, following type of sentences are becoming extinct:

3. *kol-ob-no-ḍa:m—dha:bna:la:?- ki-ya:r*
   rec caus eat pass quick inf. pst cont dual
   'you were being fed by each other quickly'.

Language contact situation forces the language to adopt complex structures—a contradiction to the theory of language attrition. It is maintained that language obsolescence or death is always preceded by simplistic or reduced linguistic structures which are not foreseen in the case of Kharia and Kurux. Contrary to Karttunen (1977) and Ramat (1979)'s investigation of the phenomenon of structural simplification in dying languages, we witness complexity of structures in minority tribal languages under consideration. We can either conclude that these are NOT dying languages or propose that multilingual contact-induced morphosyntactic restructuring in monority languages serves a facilitating device for inter-group communication. I would prefer to believe the latter. The linguistic structures of these minority tribal 'languages give us excellent examples of linguistic accommodation.

Conclusion

An interesting linguistic scene emerges in the Jharkahand area. The dominated languages undergo a drastic change towards a typological homogeneity of the area under the Sprachbund pressure. The speakers find their mothertongues not much of functional use hence the tendency towards bilingualism increases. this leads to gratuitous borrowing of lexicon and linguistic structures at the expense of syntactic simplicity and grammatical economy. The striking feature is that these languages also expand in their linguistic structures as seen earlier in the paper. The dominated tribal languages, thus, both shrink and conflate at the same time. This oscillation between the two processes give them new lease of life and saves them from the dangers of extinction. Semantic expansion coterminous with the morphological and syntactic expansions make the languages befitting the multilingual scene of intense language contact.

On the basis of this strong evidence offered by Jharkhand area, we can safely conclude that the contact-induced changes may not necessarily be detrimental and fatal to language growth. Jharkhand offers and ample opportunity for disparate and diverge speech communities to interact with each other. The tribal languages of the area have begun utilising this opportunity by changing and converging themselves to the mainstream linguistic structures.

TABLE 1

Interstate distribution of selected tribal languages in Jharkhand area

Languages	**Speakers (thousands)**	**Percentage of speakers in states**
Munda		
Santali	4208	Bihar 50, W. Bengal 37, Orissa 13
Ho	802	Bihar 67, Orissa 33
Mundari	753	Bihar 84, Orissa 14, W. Bengal 1.4
Kharia	198	Bihar 50, Orissa 39, Madhya Pradesh 6, W. Bengal 4
Bhumij	47	Bihar 15, Orissa 28, W. Bengal 6
Korwa	28	Madhya Pradesh 90, Orissa 6, Bihar 4
Dravidian		
Kurux	1265	Bihar 51, Madhya Pradesh 28, W. Bengal 13, Orissa 7
Parji	33	Madhya Pradesh 86, Orissa 14

Adapted from Khubchandani, 1992.

TABLE 2

Bilingualism among few selected tribal speech communites of Jharkhand, 1971

Mothertongue groups	Total speakers (thousands)	Bilinguals (thousands)	Percentage
Munda			
Santali	3787	1201	31.7
Mundari	771	280	36.3
Ho	751	167	22.3
Munda	309	149	48.1
Kharia	191	98	51.7
Kisan	74	35	47.4
Bhumij	52	21	40.9
Dravidian			
Kurux	1236	571	46.7

Adapted from Khubchandani, 1992.

TABLE 3

Percentage of Kurux maintenance or shift

State	Maintained	Shifted to other language
Bihar	72.4	27.6
Madhya Pradesh	89.2	10.8
West Bengal	33.9	66.1
Orissa	44.7	55.3

Adapted from Ekka, 1980.

NOTES

1. The study is based on extensive fieldwork done by Veena Malhotra on Kharia during 1978-1982 and by Awadhesh K. Mishra on Kurux during 1985-1990 under the supervision of the author. The author is grateful to Nancy Dorian for her comments and suggestions on the earlier version of this paper which was published in *International Journal of Sociology of Language,* 1995.116, pp. 175-185.
2. Synchronic Kharia has SOV instead of the archaic structure of SVO presumably under the pressure generated by language contact situation.

3. One word equivalent to one phrase, as the dichotomy between morphology and syntax is rather weak in Munda languages.

REFERENCES

Abbi, Anvita (edited), 1986. *Studies in Bilingualism.* New Delhi, Bahri Publications.

—, 1992. Language death and language conflation. A paradoxical oscillation. *South Asian Language Review.* Vol. 11, No. 2.39-49.

Allardts, Erik, 1984. What constitutes a language minority? *Journal of Multilingual and Multicultural Development,* Vol. 5 No. 3, 4.195-205.

Blount, B.G. & M. Sanches (eds.), 1977, *Sociocultural Dimensions of Language Change.* New York. Academic Press.

Dorian, Nancy C., 1981. *Language Death: The Life Cycle of a Scottish Gaelic Dialect.* Philadelphia. University of Pennsylvania Press.

—, 1989. *Investigating Obsolescene: Studies in Language Contraction and Death.* Cambridge, Cambridge University Press.

Ekka, Francis, 1972. Men's and Women's speech in Kurux. *Linguistics.* 81.25-31.

—, 1980. *Language Maintenance and Shift among Tribes in India.* Paper presented at the III-International Conference on South Asian languages and linguistics. Osmania University, Hyderabad.

Gal, Susan, 1989. Lexical innovation and loss: the use and value of restricted Hungarian. In Nancy Dorian, 1989.

Gudschinsky, Sarah C., 1956. The ABCs of lexicostatistics (glottochronology), *Word* 12.175-210

Giacalone Ramat, A., 1979. Language function and language change in minority languages. *Journal of Italian Linguistics.* Vol. 4.142-62.

Haugen, Einar, 1989. The rise and fall of an immigrant language: Norwegian in America. In Nancy Dorian, 1989.

Karttunen, F., 1977. Finnish in America: A case study in monogenerational language change. In Blount & Sanches, 1977.

Khubchandani, Lachman M., 1992. *Tribal Identity. A Language and Communication Perspective,* Shimla, Indian Institute of Advanced Study.

Lehiste, Ilse, 1988. *Lectures on Language Contact.* Massachusettes, MIT Press.

Malhotra, Veena, 1982. *The Structure of Kharia. A Study of Linguistic Typology and Change.* Ph.D Dissertation, JNU. Unpublished.

Mougeon, Raymond and Edouard Beniak, 1989. Language contraction and linguistic change: The case of Welland French. In Nancy Dorian, 1989.

Mishra, Awadhesh K., 1991. *Word Formation in Kurux. A Study of Linguistic Typology and Language Change.* Ph.D. Dissertation. JNU. Unpublished.

Munda, Ram Dayal, 1989. In search of tribal homeland. *The Statesman.* New Delhi. February 4.

Muntzel, M.C. & Lyle Campbell, 1989. The structural consequence of language death. In Nancy Dorian, 1989.

Nigam, R.C., 1972. *Language Handbook on Mothertongues in Census.* Census Centenary Monograph No. 10.

Seliger, Herber W. and Robert M. Vago, 1990. *First Language Attrition.* Cambridge. Cambridge University Press.

III

INDO-ARYAN

The tree looks beautiful
With the red bird on its bough
If the bird is caught in a net and taken away
The tree will look desolate, sad.

(A Jatara song of Mundas)

'The Awakened Wind'—Sitakant Mahapatra

CHAPTER 10

THE GRAMMAR OF POETICS: ON SOME LINGUISTIC TECHNIQUES IN AN ORAL EPIC FROM THE GARHWAL HIMALAYAS

Claus Peter Zoller

Introduction

In 1987 and 1989 I taped two oral versions of the Mahābhārata in the Garhwal Himalayas. The language of the epic is Baṅgāṇi, which belongs to the Western Pahāṛī subgroup of Indo-Aryan. The word also designates the speakers of this language. The region Baṅgāṇ is located at the border to Himachal Pradesh. It comprises a long ridge from south to north, which is enclosed by the rivers Tons and Pabar. There are several dozen villages in Baṅgāṇ, but the exact size of the population is unknown.[1]

The dominant group are the Rajputs,[2] followed by the low-caste Koltas. There are only few Brahmans and members of artisan-castes. Most of my linguistic data I collected from Rajputs, Koltas and so-called Devals. Devals *(deuāḷ)* are low-caste specialists for the transmission of much of Baṅgāṇi oral literature.[3] There exists no written Baṅgāṇi literature.

The Baṅgāṇi version of the Mahābhārata is called *pɔ̃ḍuaṇ*. Both recorded versions have an approximate length of eight hours on the tape recorder. Though they were taped from different singers in different villages, they show a very high degree of conformity in their contents.[4] Traditionally the *pɔḍuaṇ* is sung in February during a festive time. Every day the Devals go into another village on a prescribed route, and sing every evening on the village ground a section of the epic. Such a section is called *śaṭi* 'twig'.[5]

Salient Features of Baṅgāṇi

Before I start to describe some of the linguistic techniques used by the bards in order to 'create' poetic texts,[6] I would like to present some of the most characteristic features of Baṅgāṇi. This will help to understand some of the techniques used by the bards.

As a member of Western Pahāṛī, Baṅgāṇi shows the following salient features in its phonology with regard to OIA:[7]

1. Preservation of two voiceless sibilants: *s* (dental) and *ś* (postpalatal). In *ś* both OIA sibilants *ś* and *ṣ* have merged.
2. Preservation of old consonant clusters, e.g. *rś, rk, br, pr, tr, dr, gr, st, ṣṭ*.[8] These are traces of r-metathesis, but they do not seem to be typical for Baṅgāṇi (they are rather found in borrowed words). The old consonant clusters are especially well preserved inside words (and not initially, what normally is to be expected). In word-initial position there is a strong tendency for *svarabhakti*.
3. Preservation of medial *m*. Preservation of other single consonants in medial position is difficult to judge (in any case, there would be only a few examples).
4. Preservation of geminates together with preceding short vowel.[9]
5. There is no *h* and there are no aspirated voiced occlusives.
6. The class of occlusives and affricated comprises six articulatory positions:[10] *p, t, ṭ, k, ć,*[11] *c*.

Many of the above-mentioned features are also found in other NIA languages outside the northwestern group. But taken all together, they separate fairly clearly Western Pahāṛī from the other languages. On the other hand, Western Pahāṛī has many affinities with the Dardic group of languages, and both share a common vocabulary. With regard to the points 1 and 6, a number of Dardic languages have preserved three voiceless sibilants and seven articulatory positions (because of the phonemes *ṣ* and *ć*). Thus, Western Pahāṛī stands more or less between Dardic and 'standard' NIA languages.

Point 4 is specially interesting. Though all Western Pahāṛī dialects show a more or less pronounced tendency to either delete the aspiration of voiced occlusives or shift it within the sememe to another position, all of them nevertheless have a fourfold pattern of oppositions, e.g. *p, ph, b, bh.* The only exception seems to be Baṅgāṇi, which has *p, ph, b.* Baṅgāṇi shares this structural feature with Dardic dialects, especially the western ones.

This loss of aspiration has led to the development of tonemes. There are four tones, one 'high-level' and three 'high-falling'. The three 'high-flling' tones differ from each other by the 'steepness' or extension of their 'falling contours'. Furthei analysis has to show, whether or not they can be reduced, at an emic level, to less than four tonemes.

Regarding its vocabulary, Baṅgāṇi shows some peculiarities which still await a satisfactory explanation. Both in colloquial speech and in oral litterature Sanskritic words are used, but the circumstances of their origin are unclear.[12] Additionally, there are several dozen words whose etymologies seem to be Indo-European but non-Indo-Aryan.[13] In comparison with the entire vocabulary, however, these two 'layers' make up only a few per cent. The problems posed by the Sanskritic words have to do with historical phonology and morphology.

There are, for instance, several Baṅgāṇi words which seem to have preserved OIA stops and certain consonant clusters in medial position. These words cannot easily be explained as (recent) borrowings. The following examples are only given to illustrate the problems, and not to offer definite solutions:

jotṇɔ 'to look, stare.'[14] Related to OIA *dyotate* 'shines'.

utkār 'sunrise'. Probably related to OIA **utkāla* 'going up or out.'[15]

In the first case the *-t-* is unusual; compare Hindī *johnā* 'to await, look for'. In the second example it is the cluster *-tk-*. If treated as a borrowing, it would be a borrowing of a reconstructed word![16]

The following preservations of medial consonant clusters are also fairly rare:

bipru 'foreign'. Related to OIA *vipriya* 'estranged'.[17]

barja[1] 'bride.' Related to OIA *bhāryā* 'wife'.[18]

Two more words from the *pɔ̃ḍuaṇ* may suffice to illustrate some of the problems of this Sanskritic 'layer': *patra* means 'foot (print)', and derives from untestified OIA **padara* 'foot'.[19] It has not only not lost the media but rather strengthened it into a tenuis.[20] The expression *mɔdiṣṭa* means 'one's own sight', and apparently reflects OIA *maddṛṣṭa.* How could one explain the origin of this old compound in Baṅgāṇi?

Concerning the words of possible Indo-European and non-Indo-Aryan etymology, I want to mention just two.[21] Consider *kir* 'head', which may derive from PIE *ḱer, ḱerə* 'head' (cp. OIA *śiras*);[22] *suni raja* 'sun king' (PIE *sun-* 'sun').

Archaic Words and Poetic Techniques

There is, of course, only a very indirect connection between archaic words and poetic techniques in an oral epic like the *pɔ̃ḍuaṇ.* The connection consists in the fact that the bards 'work' with the distinction between everyday (or common) and rare words.[23] There are also archaic words used in everyday speech, but their archaic nature is not known to the speakers. But words like *mɔdiṣṭa* or *tirpəto* 'the three worlds' (related to OIA tripatha), or *nirlāṭ* 'a pure forehead' (a word composed of OIA *nīraja* 'free from dust' and OIA *lalāṭa* 'forehead')[24] are rarely, if ever, used in colloquial speech.

This first artistic technique, the use of rare words, serves, like all other techniques introduced below, to create poeticity.[25] The distribution of such words in the epic corresponds to some extent to the dichotomy of prose pasages (containing less rare words, being less poetic) and the songs (more unusual words, greater poeticity).

Both prose and song passages of the *pɔ̃ḍuaṇ* differ phonologically, morphologically, and syntactically from colloquial speech. Deviation and transgression are the (perhaps universal) means in creating poetic language. Some forms of morphological and syntactical deviations I shall take up later. Regarding the phonological system of Baṅgāṇi, the bards use (among others) following techniques: I mentioned above that Baṅgāṇi has no phoneme *h*. In the *pɔ̄ḍuaṇ*, however, *h* is used quite extensively, thereby increasing the 'expressiveness' of the text. The bards often do not distinguish whether the words originally contained such a consonant or not, e.g. *hā* 'a magical power of the Koltas' < OIA *āpad* 'distress'; *hum* 'the syllable om'; *ghəṇeś* 'the god Ganeśa', etc. Sometimes this leads to a breach of a Baṅgāṇi syllable-structure rule, according to which a Baṅgāṇi word cannot contain more than one aspiration. e.g. in *ćhɔṭhuɔ* 'sixth' (standard pronunciation *ćhɔṭuɔ*). Another way of 'colouring' the text is a frequent pronunciation of ə instead of 'normal' ɔ, or of *s* instead of *ś*. This, I was told, gives a 'touch of Hindi' to the sound of the epic.

Reduced 'Semanticity'

Now I would like to present another widespread principle, appearing in a number of different forms. It may be circumscribed as 'a reduction in 'semanticity" in exchange for an increase in sound-pattern expression.' This reduced semanticity, created through elliptic syntax, through the use of rare or obscure words, or through various forms of echo-formations and alliterations may make it fairly difficult to understand a song.[26] But what is gained, on the other hand, is an incantation-like quality of such passages. Thus, the 'reduction in 'semanticity" is compensated by an 'increase in "spellboundness" (and an 'increase in poetic expressiveness'). This may be illustrated with some lines of a song sung by a magic iron rod. This powerful rod is first in the posession of a giant and then captured by the Pāndavas. In this moment the rod, which is somehow a living being, sings the following song:

> *ār na tirpəto*
> *ṭhār*[4] *na tirpəto*
> *ār na tirpəto*
> *ṭhār*[4] *na tirpəto*
> *gəja nam nā tirpəto*
> *eḱ mile ki eki ek*
> *śɔti mile ki śɔti śɔt*

ai pur ki aũ sɔ̃khia na manu

dai baiũ ki aũ sɔ̃khia na manu.

The word-by-word translation would be:

On this side are the three worlds
on the footing are the three worlds
the name of the rod is but three worlds
meet one, then only one
meet hundred, then only hundred
I do not count the number of the magical *ai* and *pur* powers
I do not count the number of cousins[27] and brothers.

Indeed, these lines are also not easily comprehensible for the Baṅgāṇis as well. Their meaning is the following:

'The three worlds are engraved in the point of the rod, they are also engraved in its footing;[28] the name of the rod is but three worlds.[29] When my owner encounters one enemy, then I shall be one enemy against him; when he meets hundred enemies, then I myself shall be hundred enemies against them. I do not differentiate between Koltas and Rajputs,[30] I do not differentiate between Pāṇḍavas and Kauravas.

These utterances of the rod, expressed in a highly elliptic and obscure manner, stress her impartiality. As she contains everything she need not be biased, whether she is in the hand of a giant or a god.

Many other songs display a similarly reduced semanticity, sometimes to a lesser degree, but sometimes so markedly that they are hardly understood anymore by the locals. This holds especially true for the set of refrains and some songs which are regularly repeated with very little variation.

Echo-Formations or Reduplications

The phenomenon of echo-formation with its great variety of repetition mechanisms over a wide range of morphemes and other syntactic units is extremely widespread in the languages of the subcontinent. Consequently, they involve a whole gamut of grammatical and semantic functions and changes. I shall therefore only quote a few examples where the primacy of the poetic is clearly present.

Some examples of 'symmetrical' reduplications—synonym, antonym, gradual, etc.—and their syntactic surroundings:

a) *jiũdɛ-jiaḷɛ* 'they live-wake up,' i.e. 'they are fit as a fiddle' (< OIA *jīvanta-***jīvāla*).[31] As in the following sentence: *se jiũdɛ-jiaḷɛ koiki, mũɛ na goɛ koiki* 'they are fit as a fiddle somewhere; on no account they are dead or killed'. Here the echo-formation creates an allusive meaning which is 'more' than just the meanings of the two words added up.

b) *boiri-śətər* 'enemy-enemy', i.e. 'enemy' (< OIA *vairin-śatru*). Almost at the end of the epic comes a description of the funeral for Karṇa: *kɔriero amarɛ tumarɛ boiri-śətər khi śukɔ hɔrɔ čəntən* 'prepared were for our and your enemy dry and green sandalwood'. This example is more complicated than the preceding one, because here the duplication of 'enemy' is merely a semantic one, although carried-out 100%. *boiri* and *śətər* are semantically equal, but morphologically they are unequal. An additional aesthetic effect results from the emerging parallels: *amarɔ boiri, tumarɔ śətər* 'my enemy, your enemy'. The construction of these symmetrical pairs is further strengthened through the following word pair *śukɔ hɔrɔ* 'dry-green'. Thus, we have here a sequence of reduplications: pronoun-noun-adjective. Semantically, the adjectives *śukɔ* and *hɔrɔ* are antonyms, and the nouns are synonyms. The pronouns, on the other hand, are opposing elements within a grammatical paradigm.

c) *nɔḷɛ-śɔḷɛ* 'tubular bones/non-tubular bones,' i.e. 'all sorts of bones' (< OIA *naḍa-śɔḷɛ*), As in the following sentence: *okɛ pɔ̃ḍɔũ dekhɛ: nɔḷɛ-śɔḷɛ guṭɛ*[1] *durbɔ̃śa* '(when the other Pāṇḍavas look at her, she, (the fire-goddess) Durbansha, swallows down all sorts of bones'. In this example the reduplication is interweaved in several other sorts of relations. The preceding sentence of the one quoted here reads *jɔtɛ biũsɔṇ dekhɛ tɔ čičoṛi kɛ̃ kha haṛgɛ*. 'When she looks at Bhīmsen, she properly gnaws off the bones'. The context of these two sentences is this: The fire-goddess Durbansha, who is invited by the Pāṇḍavas for dinner, is actually demon-natured and thus very fond of eating bones. Only Bhīma is suspicious—which she realizes. Consequently, when she and Bhīma look at each other she gnaws at the bones, and when she and the other Pāṇḍavas look at each other, she indecently swallows them down. We thus discover in these two small and inconspicious sentences a whole series of oppositional pairs, in which the *nɔḷɛ-śɔḷɛ* forms just one functional unit within this aesthetical design. The two sentences convey: Bhīma knows (her nature), but cannot see anything suspicious in her behaviour; the other Pāṇḍavas see her swallowing bones but do not comprehend the act. Durbansha looks at Bhīma; the other Pāṇḍavas look at her. In front of the one Bhīma she gnaws at *haṛgɛ* 'bones' (one noun); in front of the four other Pāṇḍavas she swallows down *nɔḷɛ-śɔḷɛ* (two nouns), not just bones, but tubular bones and non-tubular bones.

Some examples of 'asymmetrical' reduplications:[33] In the expression *rɔiṇɔ rat* 'night' (< OIA *rātra* 'night') the word *rɔiṇɔ* is a sort of drawn-forth 'echo' without a meaning of its own. But at least a minimal echo-like character is recognizable here in the alliteration. There are cases, however, where there is neither a semantic nor a morphological repetition of whatever sort, but where a word is added to another one which has neither a meaning of its own nor a phonetic resemblance with the basic one. Examples are *ɔgən bai* 'fire', *ḍaki mɔ̃gta* 'drummer.' In the first example *ɔgən* 'fire' is related to OIA *agni* 'fire' but *bai* has no meaning; in the second example *ḍaki* 'drummer' derives from OIA* *ḍākka* 'goblin'[34] but *mɔ̃gta* has no meaning.[35]

In another interesting example from the epic we can observe two counter-moving tendencies: on the semantic level towards asymmetry, and simultaneously on the morphological level towards symmetry: There is the expression *sərəth, - bərəth,* which still is known to the locals to mean 'Śatrūghna and Bhārata,' the brothers of Rāma. Also here the first element is a drawn-forth reduplication of the second one. Thus, the first brother's name Śatrūghna has almost lost its independent character and become a mere copy of the morphologically dominant *bərəth.* But the loss of semantic independence is compensated by an increase in morphological symmetry.

In the following two examples from songs of the epic there is both alliteration and echoing, with both techniques distorting the 'basic semantics' of the sentences:

ċaduri baduri ċauri ċɛ̃ṭaḷi.

'(You are a) cunning cobbler-daughter of glittering apperarance'.

And:

ǰɔtra ǰɔka-ǰɔ̃r nɔśɛli ḍɔi dɛa hər hai hərdi bəḷe.

'When (fire) will break out (in the place named) Jaka-Jar, let it burn, hey, in this difficult moment.'

In a short prose passage there is a description of how god Nārāyaṇa brews poison for certain purposes. The passage has several echo-formations, but this time the duplication of the words is not done through synonyms or antonyms, but through the change of concrete words into abstracts. The effect again is an increase in sound-pattern expression and an obscuring of meaning:

naraiṇ debta ne kia kəra ki: ɛ sɔǰɔ̃r mɔǰɔ̃r ɔr rāt kɛ ǰorɛ dusɛ kɛ ǰorɛ, ċotha-ċōthiɛ, hɔṇka-hɔṇkiɛ, ṭhɔṇka-ṭhɔṇkiɛ, kĩdra-kĩdriɛ sāt beṭa ɔǰpaḷ kɛ sā̃jierɛ.[1]

'What did god Nārāyaṇa do: (out of the poisons named) Sazdār and Madzār, and with the help of the night, with the help of the day, (with the help) of the fourness of the fourth, (with the help) of the momentariness of a moment, (with the help of) the noise of rattling, (with the help) of the intelligence of the intellect, the seven sons of (the god of poison) Ajpal were brewed.'

Breaking of the Normal Order

Like other Indian languages, Baṅgāṇi also uses the possibility of deviation from a normal or basic word order in order to express specific meanings. There exists a 'permitted' range of such deviations in colloquial speech,[36] which are usually motivated by communication needs. And there exist other, sometimes, more drastic deviations, which are motivated by aesthetic 'considerations'. In the following prose sentence from the *pɔ̃ḍuaṇ* the normal word order is heavily altered, and thereby transgresses the limits set by the rules for colloquial speech:

pā̃c pā̃ḍɔ̃,[1] *bulɛ tiũ giṇɔ khūb nā̃j baṇi, jeśɔ pā̃c daunie*[1] *mɔṇchaḷi rɔ nā̃j giṇɛ baṇiɔ.*[37]

'The five Pāṇḍavas, these simple ones, prepared fine food and brought it along; they prepare and bring along in five baskets such food that is suitable for human beings.'

It is possible to distinguish in this sentence milder forms of deviation from more severe ones. A mild deviation (but still possible in colloquial speech) is the reversal in the order of the verbal expression in *giṇɔ ... baṇi* resp. *giṇɛ baṇiɔ.* Both expressions are similar to Hindi constructions involving an 'absolutive'[38] verbal form and a second predicate. Frequently, these constructions express two verbal actions with the 'absolutive' action preceding the other one. In these Baṅgāṇi examples the normal order has been altered, and in the first one the main verb not just precedes the 'absolutive', but is separated from it through two more words (*khūb nā̃j*). A more severe deviation is in the second part of the sentence, where *pā̃c dauniɛ* 'five baskets' should have appeared between *nā̃j* and *giṇɛ.* Such a deviation in word order would be considered as completely wrong in colloquial speech. But here, in the epic, the audience will appreciate it as the artistic talents of the bard.

This opposite evaluation holds also true for another linguistic phenomenon which, because of its unwieldiness, can only be described here without illustrative evidence. The case of anacoluthons. They are a natural phenomenon of all colloquial speech, and if they attract any attention at all, they are generally marked as mistakes. Not so in the *pɔ̃ḍuaṇ* where its able use proves the ability of the singer. Able use here means that he cuts short a sentence, continues with several other sentences, and then takes up the first sentence again.

There are other forms of breaking 'compounds', which can be illustrated more easily. In the first example—a line from a song—a noun is pushed between the normally unseparable bond between noun and postposition:

eki athe[4] *gəṭi ma, e eki athe*[4] *kā̃p*

'In the one hand a small bell, hey, (in) the other hand a bowl.'

This is a quite severe case of lingual transgression, perpetrated through the insertion of *gəṭi* 'small bell' between the normally unseparable *athe ma* 'in the hand'. This poetic technique is driven even further in those cases in the epic where the bard has broken open the integrity of a sememe, or the normally unseparable unity of sememe and grammeme.

An example for the first case would be the name *doṇatārǰi* 'Droṇācārya'. This form is occasionally changed by the bard into *tarǰi duṇa,* a change which cannot at all be explained by etymology or word-formation rules. The 'action' of the bard rather has to be characterized as 'creative violence.'

There are several cases where the gammeme expressing future tense has been 'broken off' its sememe and reloacted somewhere else in the sentence. Consider the following example:

ǰɔ eskɛ nā lɛ bɔḷiɛ[1] *tɔ aũ bi mɔdəth kɔrulɛ kuč̌h.*

'If he will not manage it, then I could help him a little bit.'

The normal way would have been to say *na bɔṭiɛlɛ*[1] 'he will not manage it.' Moreover, the replacing of the future grammeme before its sememe affects the vowel length in the negation particle, which changes from short to long.

Conclusion

In conclusion I would like to quote a prose sentence, selected by me completely at random. I do this with the following intention. I think it is possible to compare the whole *pɔ̃ḍuaṇ* metaphorically with a net, whose threads (the *pɔ̃ḍuaṇ*) are 'spun' more or less poetically. This net (the text as a whole) displays a continuous change and variation in the density of its texture, its poeticity, where it is often difficult to decide where 'normal' speech ends and lyric starts. Consider the following sentence:

khā ǰieṇ marāǰ, arām kɔi rɔeṇ sare, rõś na, ǰīd na, mīś na, kuč̌h na, eki gɔḷɛ paṇi jā.

Translation: 'They eat and just enjoy life, they all live in peace; (there is) neither anger nor jealousy, neither hostility nor greed, nothing; through just one throat runs the water.'[39] This prose sentence almost asks for a graphical representation in the form of a poem. For instance like this:

khā j̃ieṇ marā̃j̃
arā̃m kɔi rɔeṇ sare
rō̃ś na, rī̃ś na
j̃ī̃d na, mī̃ś na
kuc̃h na
eki gɔḷɛ paṇi jā

Abbreviations

IA	=	Indo-Aryan
MIA	=	Middle Indo-Aryan
NIA	=	New Indo-Aryan
OIA	=	Old Indo-Aryan
PIE	=	Proto Indo-Aryan
<	=	deriving historically from

NOTES

1. According to a rough estimate the number of speakers should be somewhere between ten and twenty thousand.
2. On the Garhwali Rajputs and their relation to ritual performances of the Mahābhārata, called Pāṇḍava Līlā. See Sax 1991 and 1992.
3. All following transcriptions, written in italics, are based on the system used by TURNER. Additionally, tones are written with the exponents 1 to 4. The word *deuāḷ* probably derives from OIA *devapāla* in the sense of 'someone who controls the gods'. It belongs to a group of semantically cognate words found in the Central and Western Himalayas, all with the meaning of 'bard' or 'shaman.' In the Khashali dialect of Himachal Pradesh there is *diala* 'oracular priest' (Varma, p. 51), probably deriving from OIA* *devipāla*, Schina has *ḍaydl* 'priest of fairies', which derives from OIA* *ḍākinī pāla*, and Garhwali has *paṃwāḷ* 'reciter of the Mahābhārata' (Sax, p. 278), which derives from OIA **pāṇḍavapāla*.
4. The contents, which will not occupy us further here, are very different from the story of the Sanskrit Mahābhārata. Although there are also the Pāṇḍavas and the Kauravas and their final battle in Kurukṣetra, most of the plots of the pɔ̃ḍuaṇ are not found in the classical version.

5. I recorded both versions en bloc at other times of the year. The making of the records was extremely strenuous, as my informants and I felt never sure whether the singers would complete the whole epic or not. Moreover, I had to convince one of the singers through intricate arguments that I had not come from the underworld, and that it was not my intention to cut down the world-tree.
6. According to local understanding, the bards are neither the authors nor the interpreters of the epics they perform. The 'creative subjects' are rather the epics themselves, which use the bards as media for their 'incarnation'. The detailed implications of such an attitude will be described by me somewhere else.
7. For abbreviations see the end of the article.
8. The sound ṣ here is an allophone of phonemic *ś*.
9. This is, of course, the preservation of a MIA feature, and is also found in Punjabi and Lahnda.
10. Six positions are also found in Marathi and Konkani.
11. This is a voiceless dental affricate, its voiced counterpart is graphically represented as a *j̈*.
12. Similar observations have been made by D.D. Sharma in two dialects in the Central and Western Himalayas, namely in Chinali and Kinnauri (see References). It is interesting to see that these dialects are located at the northern fringe of the Indo-Aryan language area.
13. See my articles in MSS 42 and 50.
14. The word is not used in this epic but in colloquial speech and other oral texts.
15. See Turner 1720.
16. The change from *-l-* to *-r* is plausible, because this leads to the common form of a Baṅgāṇi 'agent'-suffix *kār*.
17. The regular development of *-pr-* is to become *-pp-* (Masica, p.175).
18. "The sequences *-yy-* and *-ry-* become *-jj-* in any case." (Masica, p.169).
19. See Turner 7756.
20. There exist more words in Baṅgāṇi showing such phonetic strengthening.
21. For various reasons there are not many of them in this epic anyway.
22. The accent on the *k* in *ḱer, ḱerɔ* indicates a palatalized voiceless stop. In OIA (but not in the so-called Kentum languages) the stop became a sibilant.
23. This does not mean that the bards would deliberately choose between various alternatives at their disposal. On the contrary, they are very faithful towards the traditional 'correct' form of the text. Moreover, they do not have such choices. As illiterate members of a low caste, they never encounter people with a knowledge in Sanskrit literature. But I want to say that the distinction between everyday (or common) and rare words coincides to a certain extent with the distinction between various styles of the epic.
24. It is very difficult to judge the 'archaicness' of this Baṅgāṇi word. From the point of historical phonology the whole expression is 'normal', except the unvoiced *-ṭ*. The loss of one *-l-* is the result of haplology. But again, the whole expression is a 'rare compound.'
25. I shall not try to define this expression, but I would like to say here that the concept of poeticity in the *pɔ̃duaṇ* is not only associated with aesthetic qualities, but also with notions like 'purification', 'rapture', 'the other world', 'presence of the divine', etc.

In order to keep this article within a reasonable length, I shall also not describe the more common forms of rhyming. Seminal work in the field of poetic techniques in oral shamanic texts has been done by Strickland. His articles contain also further literature on this topic. For a more general discussion of the relations between grammar and poetics see Jakobson.

26. The word 'understand' becomes a very complicated affair in this connection. But instead of long discussion I would prefer to say simply the following: During the performance my informants were able in most cases to explain to me any word or passage I asked for. When they heard the epic later on the tape recorder, they had much more difficulties in understanding. And when they got read out the transcribed text, they often could not make any sense of whole passages. The situation is different, of course, with my native collaborator of long standing. But even for him some of the songs were difficult to understand.
27. The Baṅgāṇi word *dai* means more exactly 'sons of the fatherbrothers'.
28. These lines are sung twice.
29. This means that it represents or encompasses the three worlds, that is the whole universe. The rod (regarded as a female being) obviously represents a sort of world axis. Now 'she' starts to talk about 'her' owner.
30. Who are the respective possessors of the magical *ai* and *pur* powers.
31. Turner 5247.
32. For the sake of clarity I have given here the non-oblique forms of the possessive pronouns.
33. 'Symmetrical' reduplications mean, that there is some sort of similarity between 'origin' and 'copy'; 'asymmetrical' reduplications means the opposite: no or hardly any similarity between the two. This distinction, however, is perhaps too gross for the rather gradual 'estrangement' (be it morphological, semantical, conceptual, etc.) which can be observed in the relation between origin and copy in many examples. Moreover, the greater the 'estrangement' between the two, the more pointless it is to speak of reduplication or echo.
34. Turner 5541.
35. It is likely, however, that both *bai* and *mɔ̃gta* originally had a meaning. But they are no more recognizable for the locals.
36. Speech errors are left out of consideration here.
37. Word-by-word: 'The five Pāṇḍavas, these simple ones, they brought much food after preparation, like five baskets human beings for food they bring after preparation.'
38. Usually formed through adding *kar* or *ke* to the verb stem.
39. This is a metaphorical way of expressing complete harmony and unity.

REFERENCES

Jackobson, Roman and Pomorska, Krystyna, 1980. *'Dialogues'*. Paris.

Kluge, Friedrich, 1989. *'Etymologisches Wöterbuch der deutschen Sprache'*. De Gruyter.

Masica, Colin P., 1991. *'The Indo-Aryan Languages'*. Cambridge University Press.

Mayrhofer, Manfred, 1986-91. *'Etymologisches Wörterbuch des Altindoarischen.'* Heidelberg.

—, 1986. *'Indogermanische Grammatik.'* Heidelberg.

Pokorny, Julius, 1959. *'Indogermanische etymologisches Wörterbuch.'* Bern.

Sax, William S., 1991. 'Ritual and Performance in the Pāṇḍavalīlā of Garhwal.' In: *Essays on the Mahābhārata.* Edited by Arvind Sharma. Leiden.

Sharma, D.D., 1985. 'Preservation of Old Indo-Aryan Dialects in the Mid-Himalayas'. In: *Ganganatha Jha Kendriya Sanskrit Vidyapeetha.* Allahabad.

—, 'Old Indo-Aryan Element in Kinnauri'. *IJDL,* XIII, No. 2, 1984.

—, 1991. *'A Descriptive Grammar & Vocabulary of Chinali.* Himachal Academy of Arts, Culture and Languages. Shimla.

Strickland, S.S., 1983. 'The Gurung Priest as Bard.' *Kailash,* X, Number 1-2.

—, 1987. 'Notes on the language of Gurung *Pe*'. *JRAS* 1.

Turner, R.L. 'A Comparative Dictionary of the Indo-Aryan languages.' London, 1966.

—, *'Addenda and Corrigenda.'* London, 1985.

Varma, Siddheshwar, 1938. 'The Dialects of the Khaśālī Group'. *JRASB,* IV.

Zoller, Claus Peter, 1988. 'Bericht über besondere Archaismem im Bangani, einer Western Pahari-Sprache.' *Münchener Studien Zur Sprachwissenschaft* 49.

—, 1989. 'Bericht über grammatische Archaismen im Bangani,' *Münchener Studien Zur Sprachwissenschaft* 50.

IV

DRAVIDIAN

The village of Sosore—Jaranga
Is at the heart
Of a deep, dense, forest,
O my elder brother
Tell me if I should stay there?
I had gone tc fetch water
And my binda was transformed
Into a snake.

O my elder brother, how will I stay there,
I had gone to fetch firewood
And my axe became a tiger,
O my elder brother
Tell me how to stay there.

(A Jatara song of Mundas)

'The Awakened Wind'—Sitakant Mahapatra

CHAPTER 11

TWO REMARKS ON DRAVIDIAN HISTORICAL MORPHOLOGY:

FIRST PERSON PRONOUN IN BRAHUI AND TENSE FORMS IN GONDI

M.S. Andronov

Brahui

Pronouns of the First Person

The Brahui pronouns of the 1st person have a peculiar and intricate history, which, despite several attempts to clarify their etymology, remains obsure for many decades. It is significant that Caldwell failed to recognize the Dravidian elements found in the Brahui language: both *ī* 'I' and *nan* 'we' (as distinct from pronouns of the 2nd person) were dropped from the table of Dravidian personal pronouns[1] as well as from the list of the Brahui Dravidian features drawn elsewhere in his book.[2]

On the contrary, Ramaswami Aiyar resolutely connected both the Brahui pronouns with the respective forms in other Dravidian languages, i.e., *ī* with *ēn* 'I', as in Malto and Kurukh (which he regarded as proto-Dravidian), and *nan* with such inclusive pronouns as *nām*, 'we' in Tamil.[3] Yet in the absence of convincing genetic arguments his resolution seems to have been based on purely semantic identity of these words and, in the case of *nan* 'we', their obvious phonetic similarity.

No wonder that nearly 17 years later Bloch returned to Caldwell's view of the singular pronoun and, in an attempt to find out the source of borrowing, believed it to be a loan from Baluchi.[4]

This etymology is a puzzle: the Baluchi demonstraive pronoun *ē* 'this' and its enclitic forms *-ē/ -ī* are used with reference to the 3rd person and cannot serve as a source of a personal pronoun of the 1st person in another language. Bloch seems to have felt the weakness of this etymology himself and offered an alternative one: *ī* < **ē* < *ēn* (cf. *ēn* 'I' in Malto and Kurukh) where **ē* was, as Bloch put it, assimilated with *nī* 'you' (sg.).[5]

Later Emeneau accepted Bloch's etymology having reworded it in the following way:

> We cannot explain on the basis of regular correspondences either the loss of *-n* in Br. *ī*, or the vowel quality. A solution which will explain both points is analogy with the 2 sg. pronoun *nī*... . This would seem to be the simplest explanation.[6]

It is evident that on the grounds of this statement the Brahui pronoun *ī* 'I' was included DED 4234/DEDR 5160 together with Ta. *yān* 'I', etc.[7]

In a number of publications that followed the Bloch-Emeneau etymology of Br. *ī* 'I' was repeated without any essential amendments.[8]

Meanwhile the validity of such an etymology can look questionable from the very outset: Bloch himself put it forward as one of the tentative hypotheses in the absence of a better explanation and did not insist on it as the only possible one. With his experience in historical linguistics, he knew the main theoretical defect of this etymology: there could not be any reason for the development by analogy in the case of *ī* in Brahui. Analogy is a means of morphological levelling of differing language units within one paradigm and operates on the principle of proportion, i.e., equation of two ratios.[9] None of these conditions is found in the case of Br. *ī* 'I' and *nī* 'you' (sg.).

As no etymology is better than a wrong etymology, Bloch made it clear that his remarks on the genetic ties of this pronoun were a scientific guess, liable to discussion and revision, rather than a final dictum. And at least in two cases criticism and dissent were expressed in the most unambiguous manner. "In the comparative plane, it was stated, the common Dravidian parallels of the pronoun of the 1st person singular *ī* 'I' are the least obvious (cf. *yān* in Old Tamil, *ēn* in Malto and Kurukh, *ēnu* in Old Telugu, *ān* in Gadaba, Parji, Naiki, Kolami, Old Kannada and Kota, *ānu* in Kui, *anā* in Gondi), for in them neither the quality of the vowel nor the loss of the final consonant in the nominative form have as yet been convincingly explained."[10] As regards the crucial question of the analogy with *nī* 'you' (sg.), the doubtfulness of such an explanation was specifically stressed elsewhere: *ī* can be derived from **yān* only if an indemonstrable influence of the pronoun *nī* 'you' were admitted.[11]

Once the obsessive desire to establish genetic ties between Br. *ī* 'I' and pronouns of the 1st person singular in other Dravidian languages at all costs is overcome, the problem may be viewed in a broader context of correlations which exist in this language between personal and demonstrative pronouns, on the one hand, and singular and plural forms of the verb, on the other.

It is remarkable, for instance, that the Brahui formants of the singular and the plural in the 1st person of the verb are distributed in the reverse order as compared with what is found in other Dravidian languages: the Brahui singular suffixes *-v* (< **-m*) / *-ṭ* (as in *barēv* 'I can come', *maxāṭ* 'I laughed') historically correspond to similar plural suffixes in other Dravidian languages [as in Mal. *bandim* (excl.) / *bandit* (incl.) 'we drag', Go. *guhtām* (excl.) / *guhtāṭ* (incl.) 'we caught', O.Ka. *Kēḷdem* / *kēḷdevu* 'we heard'], whereas the Brahui plural suffix *-n* (as in *barēn* 'we can come', *maxān* 'we laughed') has regular correspondences in singular forms (as in Mal. *bandin* 'I drag', Go. *guhtān* 'I caught', O.ka. *kēḷden* 'I heard'). Historically the Brahui singular suffixes are plural in origin and vice versa.

There are reasons to suspect that the Brahui plural pronoun of the 1st person *nan* 'we' is a result of a similar evolution. Although the change of the final *-m* into *-n* is not unknown in Dravidian (e.g. O.Ta. *nilam* / *nilan* 'ground', *palam* > *palan* 'result' from Skt. *phalam,* Kol. *am* 'he' < **an*), it does not occur in pronouns of the 1st and 2nd person in any of the Dravidian languages as the *-n* / *-m* contrast in such forms is grammatical in origin, *-n* forms denoting singular pronouns and *-m* forms plural [as in *yān* / *nān* 'I' *yām* (excl.) / *nām* (incl.) 'we' in Tamil, *ām* 'we' in Kota, Old Kannada, Kolami, Naiki, Parji, Gadaba and Manda, *ēn* 'I'—*ēm* 'we' in Kurukh and Malto, *(n)ānu* 'I'—*(m)āmu* 'we' (excl.) in Kui, *nānu* 'I'—*māmbu* 'we' (excl.) in Kuvi, *an(n)ā* 'I'—*ammaṭ* 'we' (excl.) in Gondi, *(n)ēnu* 'I'—*(m)ēnu* 'we' (excl.) in Telugu, *ōn* 'I'—*em* (excl.) / *om* (incl.) 'we' in Toda, *ñān* 'I'—*ñaṅṅāḷ* (< *ñām-kaḷ*) 'we' (excl.) in Malyalam, *nīn* 'thou'—*nīm* 'you' in Old Kannada, Kurukh and Malto, *īn* 'thou'—*īm* 'you' in Parji, Gadaba and Manda, *(n)īnu* 'thou'—*nīm* 'you' in Kui, *nī* 'thou'—*num* 'you' in Brahui, etc.]. It is extremely significant that in reflexive pronouns, where the same *-n* / *-m* contrast is regularly employed for the sigular-plural opposition (e.g. *tān* 'onself'—*tām* 'themselves' in Tamil, Malyalam, Kota, Kannada, Parji, Gadaba, Kurukh, Malto, etc.), the Brahui *-m* form is similarly lost in the plural and the singular form in *-n* is used istead; e.g. *nājōr karē tēne* 'He pretended (lit. made himself) to be ill', but *dā kārēme tēnaṭ xalās karēr* 'They finished this work by themselves'. The process is the same as in the case of the pronoun *nan* 'we' with the difference that the reflexive pronoun, unlike *nan,* has retained its original meaning of the singular form as well.

As regards the pronoun *ī,* which filled the vacant position of the Brahui singular pronoun of the 1st person, Bloch was the first to compare it with the demonstrative pronoun *ī* 'this' found elsewhere in Dravidian. True, he rejected any genetic relationship between them on the ground that the Dravidian demonstrative pronoun *ī* 'this' was missing from the Brahui system.[12] It is clear, that originally Br. *ī* could have been a deomstrative pronoun which later became a personal pronoun and, consequently, ceased to be used as a demonstrative. In this case the absence of the demonstrative *ī* in Brahui should be regarded, contrary to Bloch's interpretation, as an argument in favour of the development of Br. *ī* 'I' from *ī* 'this'.

Another descendant of this demonstrative in Brahui is a peculiar indefinite-personal pronoun. *ī-*,[13] which possesses only oblique case-forms and is never used without objective-possessive particles (as in *īki-ka ant hēsur*? 'What have they brought for me?', *sardār harrifē īān-ta* 'The sardar asked him', *masiṛ hinā ītō-tā* 'The girl went away with them', etc.). The lack of oblique case-forms in Br. *ī* 'I' and the lack of the nominative, genitive and objective case-forms in the

Brahui indefinite-personal pronoun *ī* can be qualified as an indication of their common origin from **ī* 'this' which split into two: the nominative form turned into a personal pronoun, while the oblique case-forms gave rise to an indefinite-personal pronoun.

The loss of the original demonstrative pronoun *ī* 'this' was compensated by borrowing *dā* 'this' from Pushtu. Its similarly with the ordinary Dravidian remote demonstrative *ā* 'that'[14] may have been a decisive factor in its selection, which, however, became fatal for *ā* ousted from Brahui altogether.

If the origin of the personal pronoun *ī* 'I' from the lost demonstrative **ī* 'this' is accepted, the suppletive nature of its oblique base *kan-* (as in *kane antey pāsa*? 'Why are you telling me that?', *kanā matlab dād ē* 'This is my opinion', *kantō bā* 'Come with me', *kanēṯī nume kārēm e?* 'Have you any business with me?') becomes self-evident, whether this form can be traced to the proto-Dravidian **yan-* (the oblique base of PDr. **yān* 'I') or not. As the form *an-* is a possible reflex of PDr. **yan-* in Brahui, *kan-* is generally analysed in several ways. Thus, Sten Konow (in the Linguistic Survey of India, Vol. IV) suggests that it may have been taken from the *-k-* of the dative case (through metathesis of the case suffix in the form similar to Ta. *enakku* 'to me'). Although metathesis of this type is not attested anywhere in Dravidian, this etymology, dispite its doubtfulness, has become popular with some authors and is constantly repeated, with minor modifications, up to the present.[15] However, displacement of sounds, whenever it occurs in personal pronouns (e.g. Brahm.Ta. *nēkku* < *enakku* 'to me', Te., Go., Kui *nā-* < **an-a-*, etc.), generally affects only vowels of the pronominal bases (apheresis, assimilation, compensatory elongation) and does not spread to consonants of inflectional suffixes.

Ramaswami Aiyar admits, as one of the possible hypothesis, that *k-* in *kan-* could be borrowed by Brahui from the Austric (= Munda) languages in a pre-historic age. But, he adds, "the influence of Austric on Dravidian...has yet to be investigated, and therefore nothing definite could be said at present".[16] In these circumstances, Ramaswami Aiyar continues, "the only explanation now possible is that, as a spontaneous velar aspirate *h* is common in prothetic positions before vowels (p. 32 of Bray's Grammar), a fricative, from which the aspirate was evolved, may have given rise to a full plosive surd initially in *kan-* and in instances with a similar initial *k-*".[17]

Unfortunately for Ramaswami Aiyar's etymology, the change of *h-* [?-] into *k-* seems to be properly attested neither in Brahui itself[18] nor anywhere in Dravidian.[19] Five of six such instances, which he adduced, were later discarded as erroneous,[20] and only Br. *kun-* 'to eat, drink' traced to the common Dravidian **uṇ-* (as in Ta. *uṇ-* 'to eat, drink') may be considered. Contamination with the Sindhi synonym *khā-*, which is sometimes believed to be responsible for the initial *k-* in Br. *kun-* (as in DEDR 600), is not indisputable: Emeneau's main argument that the initial *k-* in *kun-* "can hardly be Dravidian **k-* since in Brahui this should become *x-*"[21] is wide of the mark as *k-* in Br. *kun-* is traced to an innovated *h-* [?-] rather than Dr. **k-*. Nevertheless it is clear that, even if Emeneau's criticism of this etymology is ignored, the link between *kan-* and **(y)an-* cannot be regarded as established convincingly enough.

Emeneau's suggestion is to attribute the development of the initial *k-* in *kan-* to the process of morphological redistribution on the boundary of **an-* (> *kan-*) and its antecedent: when the latter ends in *-k* with a preceding short vowel, this consonant may be reduplicated before *a-* of **an-*, one of the *k*'s being shifted to the beginning of the following word "by 'wrong' word-division",[22] as, e.g., in *dā kucak kanā e* 'This dog is mine' with *kucak kanā* < **kucakk* **anā* < *kucak* **anā*.

Such 'wrong word-division' is a well-known process in languages of the world, e.g., *an apron* < *a napron* in English or *mamie* < *m'amie* in French. In Russian it is even responsible for the development of *n-* forms is oblique cases of pronouns of the 3rd person (as in *on* 'he' & *ono* 'it'—gen. *ego / nego*, dat. *emu / nemu*, instr. *im / nim*, *ona* 'she'—gen. *eyo / neyo*, dat. *ey / ney*, instr. *eyu / neyu*, *oni* 'they'—gen. *iḥ / niḥ*, dat. *im / nim*, instr. *imi / nimi*, etc.), which borrowed their initial *n-* from the end of the old prepostitions *v°n* 'in', *s°n* 'with', *k°n* 'towards' after they lost it and turned into *v* 'in', *s* 'with', *k* 'towards', respectively (i.e., *k nemu* 'to him' < *k°n emu*, *s nim* 'with him' < *s°n im*, *v niḥ* 'in them' < *v°n iḥ*, etc.).[23]

However, such development, by no means frequent in the history of languages, can occur only within set phrases which become equal to an integral word phonetically and semantically. The situation in Brahui is different. Two examples, which could be collected by Emeneau from Bray's book, represent free combinations of words, in which *kanā* and the preceding word can even belong to different syntagmas. The number of such examples is equally disappointing. In addition to those above, only one more is available: *ilāj asujjik kane* 'I can think of a remedy'. The third example, in which a *k-* ending word precedes *kane* 'me', disproves Emeneau's theory rather than corroborates it: as there is no short vowel before *-k* in the word *xalk* 'it struck', no reduplication of this consonant can take place in the phrase *xaṛ ṭakkar xalk kane* 'The ram butted (lit. butting struck) against me'.

As several attempts to explain the development of Br. *kan-* from PDr. **yan-* have ended in failure, the very existence of genetic relationship between *kan-* and **yan-* becomes doubtful. Indeed, if the nominative form of the singular pronoun left its original place in the paradigm and occupied the position of the plural pronoun, it would be natural to except that the oblique base would follow suit. And the form of the base *nan-* with the formant of the singular number *-n* (instead of the ordinary *-m* denoting plurality elsewhere in Dravidian and in the pronoun of the 2nd person in Brahui itself) makes it evident that such a shift did actually occur. As distinct from a similar process in verb forms of the 1st person, the original plural pronoun did not take the place of the singular one but, in all appearance, was assimilated by the latter. This means that *kan-* has no etymological relationship neither with ī 'I' nor with PDr. **yan* (**yan-*). Its story must be similar with that of ī 'I' with the difference that the source of its origin still remains unknown. Its obvious phonetic resemblance both to *nan-* and **yan-* has no bearing on its original meaning and etymology, though it could have played its part when *kan-* was selected for its present role.

Some Tense Forms in Gondi

Among several structural types of tense forms which are attested in Dravidian the commonest and apparently the oldest one is that which is found in the indicative past and future of Tamil. It is based on combinations of verbal participles, historically differentiated into past and present-future,[24] with personal suffixes traceable to reconstructed finite forms of the verb *'be'*:

		Singular		Plural	
1st person		**ĕ̄n* / **ă̄n*	'I am'	**ă̄m* / **ĕ̄m*	'we are'
2nd person		**ă̄y*	'thou art'	**ĭ̄m*	'you are'
3rd person	masc.	**ă̄n*	'he is'	**ă̄r*	'they (epic.) are'
	fem.	**ă̄ḷ*	'she is'		
	neu.	**tu*	'it is'	**a(v)*	they (neu.) are'

In the course of time such constructions got morphologized and turned into ordinary tense forms; e.g. **ceytu* **ēn* 'having done I am' Ta. *ceytēn* 'I did', **vantu* **āy* 'having come thou art' > Ta. *vantāy* 'you (sg.) came', **pāṭuku* **am* 'intending to sing we are' > Ta. *pāṭukam* 'we shall sing', etc.[25]

After the primary forms of the verb 'be' had got morphologized and turned into personal suffixes, this proto-Dravidian principle of tense formation persisted, and new predicative constructions combined of verbal participles and finite verbs denoting being, becoming or remaining continued to develop in descendant languages. Instances of such development are well-known practically in all languages of the Dravidian stock; e.g.

Ta. *vant-irukkiṟēn* 'I have come' (lit. 'having come I am'),

Ma. *etti-y-irunnu* '(one) had come' (lit. 'having come one was'),

Ka. *māḍutt-iruvanu* 'he will be doing' (lit. 'in the act of doing he will be'),

māḍ(i)-iruttēne 'I have done' (lit. 'having done I am'),

Kod. *māḍiyaṇḍ-uḷḷe* 'I am doing' (lit. 'in the act of doing I am'),

māḍiyaṇḍ-iññe 'I was doing' (lit. in the act of doing I was'),

māḍit-uḷḷiya 'you (sg.) have done' (lit. in the act of doing you are),

Kuvi *tō̆ssi-macc'e* 'I was showing' (lit. in the act of showing I was'),

tō̆ssa-ma'i 'I have shown' (lit. 'having shown I am'), etc.

In many cases such constructions evolve into synthetic tense forms; e.g. Betul Go. *guhcītōnā* 'I had seized' < *guhcī mattōnā* 'having seized I was', Ka. *māḍuttēne* 'I do' < *māḍutta ahene* 'in the act of doing I am', Te. *cēsinānu* 'I did' < *cēsi unnānu* 'having done I am', Pa. *cūṛen* < *cūṛeten* 'I saw' < *cūṛi metten* 'having seen I was', etc. This mode of developing tense forms is predominant in the Dravidian languages and can be regarded as one of the distinctive features of their morphology traceable to the proto-Dravidian stage.[26]

Another type of tense formation, which is exclusively Dravidian in structure, is attested in dialects of Gondi. One of the clearest examples of this kind is the present tense in Betul Gondi with the tense suffixes *-t(ōn)- / -t(ōṛ)-* (as in the paradigm of *doh- / doht-* 'to bind' and hūṛ- 'to see, look'):

		Singular	
1st person		*dohtātōnā*	*hūṛītōnā*
2nd person		*dohtātōnī*	*hūṛītōnī*
3rd person	masc.	*dohtātōl*	*hūṛītōl*
	non-masc.	*dohtātā*	*hūṛītā*
		Plural	
1st person		*dohtātōṛām*	*hūṛītōṛām*
2nd person		*dohtātōṛīṭ*	*hūṛītōṛīṭ*
3rd person	masc.	*dohtātōṛ*	*hūṛītōṛ*
	non-masc.	*dohtātaṅg*	*hūṛītaṅg*

The whole form is a recent contraction of a periphrastic conjugation with the auxiliary *āitōnā* 'I am', *āitōnī* 'you (sg.) are', etc. (< *āy-* 'to be'), joined to the supine in *-ā / -ī* of the conjugated verb.

A peculiar feature of this paradigm is the alternation *-n- / -ṛ-*, *-l / -ṛ* in the tense suffix in all forms other than those of the 3rd person non-masculine, as in *dohtātōnā* 'I bind': *dohtātōṛām* 'we bind'. The comparison of singular and plural forms makes it evident that this alternation is directly connected with the expression of number, the suffixes in *-n- / -l* and *-ṛ-* appearing in singular and plural forms respectively.

As in Dravidian tense forms number and person are usually expressed in personal suffixes which follow the suffix of tense, the consonants *-n- / -l* and *-ṛ-* could not be an integral part of the temporal suffixes from the very beginning but originally must have had a function similar to that of personal suffixes. As *-n-* can be shown to be an alternant of *-l* in intervocalic position, the problem comes to the original nature of the forms of the 3rd person masculine and the nature of personal suffixes these forms take in the 1st and 2nd person.

The similarity of the suffixes *-ōl* / *-ōn-* and *-ōṛ* in the 3rd person masculine with the personal pronouns *ōl (ōn-)* 'he' *ōṛ* 'they' (masc.) can be indicative of their origin and explain their number meaning: structurally forms of the type *dohtātōl, dohtātōṛ* may be compared with participial nouns widely used in many Dravidian languages, where they are commonly received by joining pronouns of the 3rd person to tense suffixes (e.g. Ta. *ceytavan* < *ceyt-avan* 'he who did' or relative participles (e.g. Te. *ceppinawāru* < *ceppina-wāru* 'they who spoke').[27] Forms of the 1st and 2nd person, then, have to be interpreted as ordinary personal nouns which add personal suffixes to nominal bases[28] and in this case are produced from historical participial nouns, i.e., *dohtātōl* 'he binds' < 'he who binds', *-dohtātōnā* 'I bind' < 'I am he who binds', *dohtātōṛ* 'they bind' < 'they who bind' *-dohtātōṛīṭ* 'you bind' < 'you are they who bind', etc. The non-masculine form of the 3rd person singular is a relative participle incorporated into the tense paradigm, whereas the corresponding plural form is the same participle with the plural suffix attached.

Tense forms constructed in a similar way are widely used both in the Betul dialect and in other dialects of Gondi. The tense suffixes *-(tō)n-* / *-(tō)ṛ-* (with the ordinary phonetic variations), traced to the present or the past forms of the auxiliaries *āy-* / *man(d)-* 'to be, remain' (like *āitōnā* 'I am', *mattōnā* 'I was'), are their distinctive feature; e.g. Betul.Go. *guhtōnā* 'I have seized' *-guhtōṛām* 'we have seized', *guhēnā* 'I should have seized' *-guhēṛōm* 'we should have seized'. Mard.Go. *undīntōnān* 'I drink' *-undīntōrōm* 'we drink', Mur.Go. *hīyintona* 'I give' *-hīyintorom* 'we give', *hīyinton* (sg.) *-hīyintoriṭ* (pl.) 'you give'. Ab.Mar.Go. *tindākintonān* 'I shall be eating' *-tindākintorōm* 'we shall be eating', *wattintonān* 'I was coming' *-wattintorōm* 'we were coming', etc.

In the Abujhmaria imperfect tense the 3rd person also has the same structure; e.g. *kītintonōr* 'he was doing' *-kītintorōr* 'they (masc.) were doing'. On the contrary, there are cases when the basic suffixes have been lost in the 3rd person and the system can be traced in a residual form only in the 1st and/or the 2nd person, as in Mur.Go. *tinen* (sg.) -*tineṛiṭ* 'you would have eaten' [but *tinuṛ* 'he / they (masc.) would have eaten'].

An intermediate stage in the process of erosion of the element -*ōn*-/ -*ōr*- in the suffix -*tōn*- / -*tōr*- is attested in the Mardia dialect: in the Mardia present tense both alternants are used in free variation; e.g. *undīntōnān* > *undīntān* 'I drink', *undīntōrōm* > *undīntōm* 'we drink', etc. Several stages in the evolution of this system coexist in Muria. In the present tense -*on*- / -*or*- are retained in the 1st and the 2nd person of verbs which take the suffix -*int(on)*- / -*int(or)*- (like hī- 'to give'). But in verbs which end in -*latona* in the 1st person singular (as *hūṛlatona* 'I look' < *hūṛ*- 'to look') the element -*on*-, as a result of metanalysis, has been incorporated into the personal suffix, i.e., *hūṛ-la-ton-a* > *hūṛ-lat-ona,* and the suffix -*oma,* innovated by analogy with -*ona* of the singular form, replaced the original -*or-om* in the plural: *hūṛlatoma* 'we look'. In the 2nd person the element -*on*- has been lost altogether: *hūṛlati* (sg.) - *hūṛlatīṭ* (pl.) 'you look'. In verbs which take -*ind*- as a tense suffix neither -*on*- nor -*or*- can be traced anywhere; e.g. *kēyinda* 'I call' - *kēyindom* 'we call', *kēyindi* (sg.) -*kēyindaṭ* (pl.) 'you call', *kēyinduṛ* 'he calls', they (masc.) call', *kēyind(u)* 'she / it calls' - *kēyinduṅg* 'they (non-masc.) call'. In the Muria perfect tense the situation is the same as in the -*latona* verbs of the present; e.g. *vidtona* 'I have crossed' - *vidtoma* 'we have crossed', *vidti* (sg.) - *vidtiṭ* (pl.) 'you have crossed', etc.

In certain cases the eroded system can be restored from one or two residual forms, as in the Maria subjunctive mood [e.g. *pōyēr* 'one/they would have seized' -*pōyērōm* 'we should have seized', but *pōyēn* 'I should have seized', *pōyīn* 'you (sg., pl.) would have seized'].

Outside Gondi a full set of forms, based on the same principle, can only be found in what may be regarded as the subjunctive mood of Telugu. As distinct from Gondi, parallel masculine and non-masculine forms are used there throughout the singular number (as, e.g., in the paradigm of the verb *cey-cēy-/cēs*- 'to do'):[29]

	Singular		Plural	
	Classical	Modern	Classical	Modern
1st person	*cēsēvāḍanu*	*cēsēvāṇṇi*	*cēsēvāramu*	*cēsēvāḷḷamu*
	cēsēdānanu	*cēsēdānni*		
2nd person	*cēsēvāḍavu*	*cēsēvāḍivi*	*cēsēvāru*	*cēsēvāḷḷu*
	cēsēdānavu	*cēsēdānivi*		
3rd person	*cēsēvāḍu*	*cēsēvāḍu*	*cēsēvāru*	*cēsēvāḷḷu*
	cēsēdi	*cēsēdi*	*cēsēvi*	*cēsēvi*

In Classical Tamil isolated forms of this kind are used sporadically in old texts (e.g. *nīyē aṟantuñ cuṟantaip porunanai* 'It is you who are the ruler of Uraiyur, the abode of virtue', *porāap porunarēm* 'We are warriors which are not going to fight'). They have no developed system in that language and are produced from substantivized participial nouns (as *prounan* 'warrior' 'king' < *por-* 'to fight'). The existence of the participial nouns, differentiated for person, (e.g. *aṟiyunan* 'we who will know', *aṟinai* 'thou who wilt know', *aṟiyunan* he 'he who will know', etc.)[30] would have made such a system redundant.

It is evident that the finite forms, based on participial nouns, could appear after the primary suffixes of person had developed from the reconstructed verb *'be'*. Yet in spite of its secondary nature, the system of such forms, reflected at least in three different branches of the Dravidian languages, should be regarded as a heritage of the proto-Dravidian stage.

Abbreviations

Ab.Mar.Go.	Abujhmaria Gondi	Mard.Go.	Mardia Gondi
Bet.Go.	Betul Gondi	Mur.Go.	Muria Gondi
Br.	Brahui	O.Ka.	Old Kannada
Brahm.Ta.	Brahmin Tamil	O.Ta.	Old Tamil
Go.	Gondi	Pa.	Parji
Ka.	Kannada	PDr.	proto-Dravidian
Kod.	Kodagu	Pe.	Pengo
Kol.	Kolami	Skt.	Sanskrit
Kur.	Kurukh	Ta.	Tamil
Ma.	Malyalam	Te.	Telugu
Mal.	Malto		

dat.	dative	masc.	masculine
epic.	epicene	neu.	neuter
fem.	feminine	non-masc.	non-masculine
gen.	genitive	pl.	plural
instr.	instrumental	sg.	singular
lit.	literally		

NOTES

1. R. Caldwell, *A Comparative Grammar of the Dravidian or South-Indian Family of Languages,* 3rd ed., L., 1913, p. 416.
2. *Ibid.,* p. 633.
3. L.V. Ramaswami Aiyar, *Brahui Forms and Dravidian Origins,* "Educational Review," Madras, 1929. Reprinted in Collected Papers of *L.V. Ramaswami Aiyar,* Vol. 2, Annamalai University, n.d., pp. 85-86.
4. J. Bloch, *Structure Grammaticale des Languages Dravidiennes,* P., 1946, p. 24. As regards the plural pronoun, Bloch followed Ramaswami Aiyar.
5. "Il est également possible que **ēn,* passé à *ē, ait été assimilé à *nī* de la 2e personne" (*ibid.,* p. 24).
6. M.B. Emeneau, *Brahui and Dravidian Comparative Grammar,* Berkeley and Los Angeles, 1962, p. 15.
7. T. Burrow & M.B. Emeneau, *A Dravidian Etymological Dictionary,* Oxford, 1961, p. 353; 2nd ed., 1984, p. 468.
8. Bh. Krishnamurti, *Dravidian Personal Pronouns,* Studies in Indian Linguistics (Professor M.B.Emeneau ṣaṣṭipūrti Volume), Poona, 1968 p. 196; S.V. Shanmugam, *Dravidian Nouns: A Comparative Study,* Annamalainagar, 1971, pp. 178, 183; P.S. Subrahmanyam, *The Personal Pronouns in Dravidian,* "Bulletin of the Deccan College Research Institute," Vol. 28, Poona, 1968, p. 203.
9. *Linguistic Encyclopaedia,* Moscow, 1990, p. 31, [In Russian].
10. M.S. Andronov, *The Brahui Language,* Moscow, 1980, p. 48.
11. M.S. Andronov, *Dravidian Pronouns: A comparative study,* "Journal of Tamil Studies," Vol. 7, Madras, 1975, p. 16.
12. "On y reconnaîtrait volontiers le démonstratif rapproché, généralement *i* en dravidian, si précisément *i* ne manquait à la série des démonstratifs en brahui" (J.Bloch, *Structure Grammaticale des Languages Dravidiennes,* p. 24).
13. D. Bray, *The Brahui Language,* Vols. 2-3, Delhi, 1934, p. 143.
14. Sometimes it was even suggested, erroneously as it is admitted today, that *dā* was related to ā 'that' (e.g. M.B. Emeneau, *Dravidian and Indian Linguistics,* Berkeley, 1962, p. 95). It seems that Tuttle was the first to identify a Pushtu borrowing in Br. *dā* 'this' (*ibid.,* p. 91).

15. E. Tuttle, *Dravidian 'I', 'we' and 'you'*, "American Journal of Philology," Vol. 49, 1928, p. 335; id., *Some Dravidian Prefixes*, "Bulletin of the School of Oriental Studies," Vol. 8, L., 1936, p. 813; P.S. Subrahmanyam, *The Personal Pronouns in Dravidian*, p. 203; i.e., *Dravidian Verb Morphology (A Comparative Study)*, Annamalainagar, 1971, p. 527; S.V. Shanmugam, *Dravidian Nouns: A Comparative Study*, p. 180.
16. L.V. Ramaswami Aiyar, *Collected Papers*, Vol. 2, p. 86.
17. *Ibid.* It must be added that *h* in Brahui commonly denotes a glottal stop rather than an aspirate. Cf.: "Phonetically it turns out that Bray's *h* in all positions is a glottal stop, with very few exceptions (all non-Dravidian) in which *h* is the voiceless aspirate" (M.B. Emeneau, *Dravidian and Indian Linguistics*, p. 103).
18. At least two cases of Br. *-h-* [-?-] < **-k-* in intervocalic position are known, i.e., Br. *tahō* / Mal. *tāke*, Kur. *tākā* 'wind' and Br. *brāhūī* 'Brahui' < **vaṭa-kō-ī* 'northern mountaineers', 'people of the northern mountains' (M.S. Andronov, *The Brahui Language*, pp. 16-17).
19. The initial glottal stop seems to be unstable in languages of the world and has a tendency to disappear rather than be strengthened into *k-*. Even in Arabic dialects it is regularly dropped (cf. Y.N. Zawadowsky, *Arabic Dialects of the Maghreb*, Moscow, 1962, p. 45 [In Russian]).
20. M.B. Emeneau, *Brahui Personal Pronouns: First Singular and Reflexive*, "Studies in Dravidian and General Linguistics: a Festschrift for Bh. Krishnamurti," Hyderabad, 1994, p. 2.
21. M.B. Emeneau, *Brahui and Dravidian Comparative Grammar*, p. 55.
22. M.B. Emeneau, *Brahui Personal Pronouns*, p. 3.
23. *A Grammar of the Russian Language*, Volume 1, Moscow: USSR Academy of Sciences, 1952, pp. 390-391. [In Russian]
24. A few rare examples of such present-future participles employed in classical texts can be found in M.S. Andronov, *A Grammar of the Tamil Language*, 2nd ed., Moscow, 1987, 191, p. 151. [In Russian] For those who cannot read Russian the English translation of the book is available: M.S. Andronov, *A Grammar of Modern and Classical Tamil*, 2nd ed., Madras: New Century Book House, 1989, 191, pp. 189-190. However, the readers of the English version must be warned against numerous misprints, as the author's corrections made at the proof-reading stage have not been put right.
25. For details cf. M.S. Andronov, *Notes on the Genesis of Finite Forms of the Verb in Dravidian*, "Indian Journal of Linguistics," Vol. 14, Calcutta, 1987, pp. 56-63. Constructions with nominal components developed in a similar way; e.g. **nāy* **ēn* 'I am a dog' > Ta. *nāyēn* 'dog-like I', **vān* **āy* 'thou art the heaven' > Ta. *vānāy* 'Thou who art the firmament', etc.
26. Exceptions to this rule, when some of tense forms in Kurukh, Malto and Brahui are based on relative participles, are evident innovations (cf. M.S. Andronov, *A Comparative Grammar of the Dravidian Languages*, Moscow, 1978, pp. 320, 341-342, 377 [In Russian].
27. The only Betul Gondi example of this kind, *sātalōṛ* 'they who died', is a fossilism. The loss of participial nouns in this language is probably the result of their transformation into finite forms of the 3rd person.

28. Cf. *kaṭai* 'meanness' -*kaṭaiyān* 'he who is mean' -*kaṭaiyānēn* 'I who am he who is mean' in Classical Tamil.
29. K. Mahadeva Sastri, *Historical Grammar of Telugu,* Anantapur, 1969, p. 233.
30. M.S. Andronov, *A Grammar of the Tamil Language,* 216-217, pp. 166-168.

CHAPTER 12

THE USE AND SEMANTIC VALUES OF VERBAL STEMS IN BADAGA

Christiane Pilot-Raichoor

Introduction

Among the tribal languages spoken in the Nilgiri Hills area (Tamil Nadu), viz. Toda, Kota, Kurumba and Irula, Badaga holds a special status. Due to its historical background it has been considered for long as a dialect of Kannada.[1] Not only the name itself "baḍaga" meaning "north(ener)", but also linguistic features specific to Kannada,[2] support this view. Nevertheless, whatever may have been the varieties of speech of the people who originally formed the Badaga community, their long stay in the Nilgiri hills (which were fairly isolated till the beginning of 19th century) and their close connection, economically and culturally, with the other inhabitants of the hills made their speech evolve in a very peculiar way, so much so that the present speech forms of the Badagas[3] have been deeply influenced by the neighbouring languages and cannot any more be said to be dialects of Kannada. The differences with modern Kannada extend throughout the language from phonology to lexicon, but are particularly evident in the morphology of both nominal and verbal systems.

Some aspects of the verbal system, namely structural similarities which belong exclusively to the Nilgiri languages or are shared by them but not by Kannada, will be taken as examples of the influence of these tribal languages on Badaga. Among features present in the Nilgiri languages and in other languages of the Tamil-Kodagu group, but not shared by Kannada, are: (1) the distribution of verbs in different morphological classes according to their S2 stem (usually called "past stem"); (2) the use of the variants of these stem suffixes to carry a transitive/intransitive distinction as it is usually aknowledged, or more accurately an affective/effective opposition as Paramasivam (1979) put it. Among features exclusively present in the Nilgiri languages are (3) the distinction between an exclusive and inclusive first person plural in verbal paradigms; and (4) the specific use of the S2 stem in the formation of past as well as non-past paradigms of the positive declarative mood. This feature which was pointed out as being unique to the Nilgiri languages by M.B. Emeneau (1967: 366) concerns not only Toda and Kota but also Alu Kurumba (Kapp, 1982:122) and Badaga.

The consequence of this use of stem S2 for both tenses is that the stem suffixes cannot be taken as having purely temporal semantic values (past vs. non-past) in these languages. In the last part of this paper I shall attempt to bring out some elements of the semantics of these stem formatives in Badaga, through their distribution in different verb formations.

Let us start with a brief presentation of the basic elements of verb formation.

The Morphological Classes of Verbs

The analysis of Badaga verb forms leads to identification of fundamental elements: a basic stem, called S1 and two derived stems made by the adjunct of two different sets of suffixes, S2 suffix and S3 suffix,[4] more or less directly corresponding to what is commonly called past (S2) and non past (S3) suffixes in South Dravidian languages (cf. Subrahmanyam, 1971).

The basic S1 stem[5] is an abstract form obtained by segmentation of the infinitive form of the verb built on S1+ a, the suffix of infinitive, ex. INF. nooḍ.a, S1 nooḍ- "to see".

The variants of the S2 suffix (mainly characterized by a dental phoneme) determines the classification of the verbs. On this basis, four main classes may be distinguished, which are subsquently subdivided by the variants of the S3 suffixes (characterized by a labial phoneme):

	S2 suffix	S3 suffix
class I	-i (d)-	-uv-
class II	-d-	-v-/-b (b)-
class III	-t-	-uv-/-p (p)-
class IV	-nd-	-mb-

Class I is the most regular and the most numerous. Classes II and III contain both a few dozens of items. Class IV contains less than twenty verbs, but some of them with high frequency.

For the verbs of classes II, III and IV the identification of the stem suffix is frequently obscured by morphophonemics phenomena which will not be stated in detail here.[6]

This classification can be illustrated by the following items:

Class I suffixes: S2: -i (d)- , S3 -uv-

Some monosyllabic S1 stems ending in a consonant and all plurisyllabic S1 stems ending in a consonant (derived or not) belong to this class:

	S1	S2	S3
ettu "to take"	ett-	etti (d)-	ettuv-
a:ru "to jump"	a:r-	a:ri (d)-	a:ruv-
oragu "to sleep"	orag-	oragi (d)-	oraguv-
to:ricu "to show"	to:ric-	to:rici (d)-	to:ricuv-

Class II suffixes: -(d)- -v-/-b (b)-

(1a) Some monosyllabic or disyllabic S1 stems ending in a vowel:

gi: "to do, make"	gi:-	gi:d-	gi:v-
naḍe "to walk"	naḍe-	naḍed-	naḍev-
ari "to know"	ari-	arid-	ariv-

including lexical items ending in a vocalic group:

ae "to measure"	a:-	a:d -	a:v-
kui "to pluck"	ku:-	ku:d-	ku:v-

in a few cases, the length is applied either to the vowel or to the consonant:

bui "to fall"	bu:-/bu-	budd-	bu:v-

(1b) Some monosyllablic S1 stem of (C) V:C- structure whose last consonant fuses with the suffix:

te:du "to melt"	te:d-	te:d-	te:v-
se:ru "to join"	se:r-	se:d-	se:v-

(2) Some S1 stems ending in a ling lateral which fuses with the suffix:

ellu "to get up"	ell-	edd-	ebb-
kollu "to kill"	koll-	kodd-	kobb-
nillu "to stand up"	nill-	nidd-	nibb-

(this last verb sometimes adheres to class IV: nind-, nimb-).

Class III suffixes: -t- -uv-/-p-

(1) To the first subgroup with -p- as S3 suffix belong—some monosyllabic or disyllabic S1 stems ending in a vowel:

ke: "to hear, listen"	ke:-	ke:t-	ke:p-
bi: "to keep"	bi:-	bi:t-	bi:p-

some lexical items ending in a vocalic group which lost their final vowel before the suffix:

u:i "to bury"	u:-	u:t-	u:p-
ka:i "to protect"	ka:-	ka:t-	ka:p-

usually when the first vowel of the vocalic group is short it is lengthened: *soe* "to be tired" or "to be defeated" have S2 stems *so:t-* and S3 stems *so:p-*. But for the verb *ui* "to plough" the length is applied to the consonant: *utt-*, *upp-*.

Disyllabic stems 1 ending in vowel:

kudi "to boil"	kudi-	kudit-	kudip-
bare "to fry"	bare-	baret-	barep-
iḍi "to break"	iḍi-	iḍit-	iḍip-

(2) The second subgroup with -uv- S3 suffix contains S1 stems of (C)VC-structure:

(h)oru "to carry"	(h)or-	(h)ott-	(h)oruv-
koḍu "to give"	koḍ-	koṭṭ-	koduv-
iḍu "to throw"	iḍ-	iṭṭ-	iḍuv-

Class IV suffixes: -nd- -mb-

(1) This subgroup contains some S1 stems ending in a vowel of (C)V:- or (C)VCV-structure to which the suffixes are added:

me: "to graze"	me:-	me:nd-	me:mb-
mede "to float"	mede-	medend-	medemb-

(2) The second subgroup contains some S1 stems ending in a consonant which is assimilated to the following suffix:

tinnu "to eat"	tinn-	tind-	timb-
ennu "to say"	enn-	end-	emb-

but retroflexion of the final consonant of S1 is maintained in the S2 suffix:

aḷu "to rule"	a:ḷ-	a:ṇḍ-	a:mb-
koḷḷu "to have"	koḷḷ-	koṇḍ-	komb-
ka:ṇu "to see"	ka:ṇ-	kaṇḍ-	ka:mb-

(this last verb has an irregular short vowel in S2 which appears also in other languages).

Some verbs do not fit completely in this classification and must be added as irregular. So are *sae* "to die" and *au* "to cry" with S2 suffix of class III (*satt-, att-*), but an irregular S3 suffix (*sa:v-, av-/avuv-*). For some other verbs, the varieties of their formations cannot be reduced to the three basic stems; consider:

Lexical Item	S1	S2	S3	Other Bases
a:gu "to become"	a:g-	a:d-/a:i	a:p-	a:-, a:n-
(h) o:gu "to go"	(h) o:g-	(h) o:d- / (h) o:i	(h) o:p-	(h) o:-, (h) o:n-
ta: "to give"	tar-	tand-	tapp-	tan-
ba: "to come"	bar-	band-	bapp-	ban-

This verb classification is reminiscent of the general pattern set up for Proto-South-Dravidian with four S2 stem formatives: -i-, -d-, -t-, -nd- (cf. Emeneau 1967:387), but it does not agree with it in its details. Two classes, the first (cl. I) and the last (cl. IV) do not strictly follow the usual pattern. For class I, the S2 suffix has two variants, -i- and -id-, and this last variant must be paralled to the same formative in Kannada which appeared due to the spread of -d- formative to most of the verbs in this language. In class IV, unlike the purely labial formatives of the other classes (-p-, -v-, -b- etc.), the nasalized S3 suffix *-mb-* does not seem to be a primitive South-Dravidian one but must be taken as an innovation (probably under the stimulus of verbs having a S1 ending in a nasal consonant like *tinnu* "to eat" and has a parallel only in Alu Kurumba (cf. class 5 in Kapp 1982:126).

In support of the historical link between Badaga and Kannada, we can account for the importance and productivity of class I in both languages. But to confirm the originality of Badaga—despite some disagreement in details[7]—we must take into account the functional use of class II and class III suffixes to carry the opposition between affective (cl. II) and effective (cl. III) meaning, ex.: *oḍe* (*oḍed-*. *oḍev-*) "to break (/be broken)" vs. *oḍe* (*oḍet- oḍep-*) "to break something", *basi* (*basid, basiv-*) "to get filtered" vs. *basi* (*basit-, basip-*) "to filter".[8]

The Present-Future and Past Paradigms

As pointed out one of the main structural feature which links Badaga to the surrounding tribal languages is the building of the tense paradigms—roughly speaking the present-future (T1) as well as the past (T2) on the S2 stems of the verbs.

The paradigms of the positive declarative mood are distributed into two types according to the variants of the present-future tense (T1) affixes. Type A, illustrated by the *ma:ḍu* "to do" concerns the verbs of class I. Type B, illustrated by the verb *gi:* "to make" concerns the verbs of class II, III and IV.

Type A			T1 (present/future)		T2 (past)	
			S2 + T1 + p.e		*S2* + p.e.	
1°	(na:)	:	maaḍi-n-e	"I do"	maaḍid-e	"I did"
2°	(ni:)	:	maaḍi-r-e	"you do"	maaḍid-e	"you did"
3°M	(ama)	:	maaḍi-n-a	"he does"	maaḍid-a	"he did"
3°F	(ava)	:	maaḍi-y-a	"she does"	maaḍid-a	"she did"
3°N	(adu)	:	maaḍi-r-a	"it does"	maaḍid-tu	"it did"
I°ex.	(enga)	:	maaḍi-n-eyo	"we do"	maaḍid-eyo	"we did"
I°inc.	(nanga)	:	maaḍi-n-o	"we do"	maaḍid-o	"we did"
II°	(ninga)	:	maaḍi-°-aari	"you do"	maaḍid-i	"you did"
III°M/F	(avaka)	:	maaḍi-°-aara	"they do"	maaḍid-aru	"they did"
III°N	(ave)	:	maaḍi-r-o	"they do"	maaḍid-o	"they did"
Type B						
1°	(na:)	:	giid-an-e	"I make"	giid-e	"I made"
2°	(ni:)	:	giid-ar-e		giid-e	
3°M	(ama)	:	giid-an-a		giid-a	
3°F	(ava)	:	giid-iy-a		giid-a	
3°N	(adu)	:	giid-ar-a		giid-a (/-atu)	
I°ex.	(enga)	:	giid-an-eyo		giid-eyo	
I°inc.	(nanga)	:	giid-an-o		giid-o	
II°	(ninga)	:	giid-° -aari		giid-i	
III°M/F	(avaka)	:	giid-° -aara		giid-aru	
III°N	(ave)	:	giid-ar-o		giid-o	

The proposed synchronic analysis stresses the structural parallel between types A and B, both being formed on the same pattern:

S2 stem + tense affix (T1) + personal endings (p.e.) in present-future and direct affixation of personal endings to S2 in past. In this analysis, the variants of the S2 affix in type A (*ma:ḍ i- / ma:ḍ id-*) can be accounted for by a specific morphonemic rule: *-i-* variant in front of a consonant initial affix (ex. *ma:ḍ i-n-e, ma:ḍ i-tu...*) and *-id-* variant in front of a vowel initial affix (ex. *ma:ḍ id-e, ma:d. id-aru...*).[9] In the II° and III°M/F person plurals of the present-future paradigm, the application of the rule is blocked by the presence of a double juncture and a null T1 segmental unit (-°-). In these two persons (II° and III° M/F), the tense and person/- gender/number distincition is amalgamated in the personal endings which is the only case where personal endings significantly differ in present-future and past (*-aari* vs. *-aara* vs. *-aru*).

As pointed out before, the use of S2 stem as the basis of both present-future and past tenses is a distinctive areal feature of the Nilgiris, but interestingly there are signigicant differences in the flexional elements of the paradigms and it cannot be said that Badaga has actually imitated any of the other languages.

In Toda and Kota,[10] it is in the past paradigm that a temporal affix (a sibilant) is added: ex. To. *po:r* "to come", (S2 *pod*), present-future *pod-pen* "I come" vs. *pod-s-pen* "I came", exactly the reverse of what is observed in Badaga. In Kurumba,[11] besides the fact that there is no exclusive/inclusive distinction in the verbal paradigms, the tense opposition between present and preterite is carried out through the variants of the S2 suffix and two different sets of personal endings: ex. AKu. *ma:ḍ-* "to do", pres.-fut. *ma:ḍ-in-e:nu* "I do", *ma:ḍ-id-o* "they do" vs. preterite *ma:ḍ-in-e* "I did", *ma:ḍ-id-aru* "they did".

Modern Kannada has a different system: there are three paradigms using three different sets of pronominal endings and two bases. Present-future is based on S1 stem and a specific suffix (*-tt-*), past and future-contingent are formed on S2 stem with different sets of personal endings, cp. Ka. pres. -fut. *ma:ḍutt-e:ne* "I do" vs. past *ma:ḍ id.e:nu* "I may do".

This last form is of particular importance as it is the modern representative of an old periphrastic present tense form mentioned by the grammarians[12] in old and medieval Kannada as being formed of past adverb (=S2) + future tense forms of *a:gu* "to become" (cf. Subrahmanyam, 1971:255) giving forms like OKa. *ke:ḷ.d+ap.eM* and MKa. *ke:ḷ.d+ah.eM/ke:ḷ.d+ah.enu* "I hear". Though it raises unsolved historical problems,[13] this type of formation: # S2 + affixal material derived from *a:gu* + personal endings # would be a tempting ancestor for the structural as well as the phonetic material[14] observed in the present-future formations in Badaga.

Whatever is the actual history of the present-future forms of Badaga, two points must be stressed. First, the fact that the present day Badaga verbal paradigms do not have any direct parallel with any other language is an important point to confirm its status as an independent language. Secondly, comparison with Kannada points out that the use of S2 in non-past formations, characteristic of the Nilgiri languages, may not be as isolated and as erratic as it seems at first.

Some Aspects of the Semantics of Verb Stems in Badaga

From the fact that present-future and pase paradigms are both based on S2 in Badaga, we can say that, at least in this case, the S2 suffix does not carry tense distinction. But it is necessary to examine what semantic value(s) it can carry.

Without entering in too much details and discussion, let us call a few basic facts about the syntactic structure of Badaga and the relation between predication and assertion. There are several syntactic patterns of both verbal and non-verbal sentences, which with few exceptions, conform to the logical pattern of associating a "term" and a "predicate".

The simplest of the non-verbal syntactic structure is the apposition of two nominals: (1) *ra:ma buddi*[15] "Rama [is] intelligent" or as in the two sentences of this proverb (2) *haṇa hage; hiṭṭu naṭṭu* (Prv. 812b)[16] "Money [is] enmity; food [is] friendship". Without any specific marker, they are all declarative assertive sentences. If we treat each element as an independent set respectively labelled for the simplicity of exposition as subjectal set (S) and predicate set (P), assertion means the adequation of both sets. But, by addition of clitics, this adequation may be challenged: (3) *ra:ma buddi. (y)a:?* "Is Rama intelligent?" or put in doubt (4) *ondu kaṇṇu kaṇṇ. o:?* (Prv.157b) "A single eye is it really an eye?". Agreement, question and doubt about the adequation of P and S are then the three basic values of assertion at the sentential level. If we want to negate a non-verbal sentence we have to modify the structural schema and introduce a verbal element. Two different verbs are used, one (*alla*) for the negation of an essential property (5) *adu enna tamma alla* "It is not my younger brother", (6) *ama ra:ja alla* "he is not a king", the other one (*ille*) for an accidental property (7) *i: si:le sudda ille* "This sari is not clean".

The simplest verbal sentence follows a similar pattern (8) *karaḍi banda* "the bear came", but here the subjectal logical set (S) is formed of two elements the nominal (*karaḍi*) and the personal ending (*-a*) included in the verb form, so that the nominal can be suppressed, the verb form itself remains a full assertive sentence: *banda* "he came". With the same clitics, a verbal sentence can be put in question (9) *(ni:) bandari. (y)a:*? "Will/do you come?" or in doubt (10) *hetta makkella makka(n)a:ra. (v)o:*? "Will all begotten children be [real] children?" (Prv.19). To negate a verbal sentence, different morphological devices can be used, but the negative meaning is always carried by a verb form (11) *ama ninne bappile* "he did not come yesterday". Negative morpheme, as well as other categorial morphemes (tense, mood, aspect), can be attached only to an element belonging to the morphosyntactic category of verb in Badaga.

To attempt to determine the semantic value of the basic stems, stated as S1, S2 and S3 in § 3, we shall back up our analysis on a limited subset of simple verbal forms called "finite verb forms"[17] which, roughly speaking, always act as the main predicate of a sentence.

Stem 1	Stem 2	Stem 3
Imperative	Past declar.mood	Prospective mood
Optative	Pres.-Fut. decl.mood	Hortative
Negative mood		

First, two subsets of forms must be distinguished. The "modal forms" which differ in their morphology: the modal value and subjectal reference are amalgamated in the verb form and, in the case of imperative singular, merely indicated by intonation. Some of these modal forms are specific of a particular person (imperative (2nd sg.): *tinnu!* "eat!" or pl.: *ke:.vi!* "listen!" and hortative, 1st sg. or pl.: (12)

nanga erada gelasa ke:p.a! "Let us both ask for work!"), while others are unspecified for person, optative: (13) *kunnave.yella illi.ga barali!* "Let all the children come here!", (14) *siva ma:ti, ni: ail[u]eccili!* "Son of Shiva, may you increase your misericordia!"). In these forms, the subjectal referent (S) does not necessarily appear as a phonetic segment and may remain undeterminated in "person" variations, but it is always logically present and can always be expressed by an external coreferent nominal (cf. (12), (13) and (14)). They also differ from the declarative verb forms we have previously seen in that the predicative relation between the verb and the subject is not stated but only proposed through what is usually called a "speech act". The remaining forms: negative, prospective and indicative (past and present-future), which are inflected with a full set of personal endings and do not carry any specific modal value, can be called declarative "moods".

Out of these, three forms are of special interest in that they are built on a identical pattern: stem + personal endings. The negative mood is based on S1+p.e., the past indicative forms, as previously stated, on S2+p.e. and the prospective mood, on S3+p.e. They offer the ideal conditions to test the contrast between the three stems, but—natural language never being ideal—it must be acknowledged that two of them, the negative and the prospective, are not very frequent and tend to be substituted by more complex formations. Nevertheless, their spontaneous occurrence in different texts is enough to attest that they remain actual parts of modern Badaga grammar. The following sentences illustrate their common uses:

Past Declarative Mood (T2): S2 + personal endings

Tales usually begin with this tense:

(15) *ondu aṭṭi.yo:ge...ondu jena... aid'a:ra...o:daru*
village.LOC one day five six go+T2+III°
"One day, in a village, five or six people went away"
it also refers to past events, distant (16) or not (17)-(18).

(16) *baḍugaru munde maisu:ru:nda bandaru (atte endu ondu kade aḍade).*
"(There is a story telling that:) 'Badagas', in the past, came from Mysore"

(17) *ninne.ya ku:ṭa.no:ge e: emm:ti kade e:gida*
yesterday.GEN meeting.LOC which woman song tell+T2+3°
"Which woman sang in yesterday's meeting?

(18) *ni:illi,ga ette bandi?*
you here,DAT how come+T2+2°
"How did you come here?"

Present-Future Declarative Mood (T1): S2 + Pres.-Fut. sfx. + p.e.

In narratives, T1 frequently alternates freely with T2:

(19) *a:ga, e:na ma:ḍidaru, a:kunnaveႉ?*
then what do+T2+III° that children
"Then, what did they do, those children?
a: maṇeya ma:ti a:kiya:ra
"They change the board."
that board.ACC change+CP put+T1+III°

but, this can be taken, as in many other languages, as stylistic.

In discourse, T1 usually refers to a present event (punctual (20), (21) or usual (22)).

(20) *avve, satakana ba:! amme attiya!*
mother quickly come+IMP sister cry+T1+3°F
"Mother, come quickly! (younger) sister is crying!"

(21) *ni: i:ga e:na ma:ḍire?*
you now what do+T1+2°
"What do you do now?"

(22) *avaka e:gua enna no:ḍileyu: korici (h)iṭṭu tanda:ra.*
they when I+ACC see+HYP+"ever" call+CP food give+T1+III°
"Whenever they see me they call me and give me food"

The same T1 forms can as well refer to a future event:

(23) *na:iga na:ku maṇi.ga munda:ḍu enga illi.ga banneyo.*
tommorow four hour.DAT before we here.DAT come+T1+I°ex
"We will arrive here before four o'clock tomorrow".

(24) *na: e:gida ma:ke ma:ḍire.ya:? —ha:, na: ma:ḍine*
I tell+P2ADJ as do+T1+2°.INTERR yes I do+T1+1°
"Will you do as I told you?" "yes, I shall do it"

Prospective Mood: S3 + personal endings

(25) *nii enga mane.yoo aaḍu ka:pe*
you our house.LOC goat keep.PROSP.2°
"You will (/can) keep the goats for us"

(26) *nanga ganji ma:ḍi kuḍipo*
we gruel do+CP drink+PROSP+I°
"We shall/can prepare gruel and drink it"

(27) *ninga o:gi kappa ke:tu bappi*
you go+CP tax ask+CP come+PROSP+II°
"You will go [there], ask him tax and come back [here]"

Negative Declarative Mood (Neg): S1+personal endings

This verb form, which tends to be replaced by other negative formations, is well attested in negative modal auxiliaries (uninflected for "person") such as *muḍiya* "cannot" *be:ḍa* "must not" and in the fossilized form *ka:ṇe* (lit. "I do not see") frequently used in the meaning "(somebody) has disappeared". In some sentences, inflected forms occur as the main predicate. For instance:

(28) *ama illi.ga bar.a*
he here.DAT come [Neg].3°
"He won't come here"

(29) *ama.na aṇṇa kuḷabane geṭṭa ama kuḷi.y-a*
he.GEN elder brother sit+P1ADV until ama sit [Neg].3°
"He does not sit until his elder brother sits"

(30) *a: kunnave tanna appa endu ari.y-o*
those children their father <that> know[Neg]. III° Npl.
"Those children did not know that he was their own father"

and very frequently as an answer to:

(31) *....endu ni: aridi.ya:?—ille, na: ariye*
"Do you know that/if....?" "No, I don't know"

(N.B: -y- is a phonetic sandhi in all these negative forms).

First, let us compare sentences (25)-(27) in the prospective mood and the sentences (23)-(24) in the present-future form. It can be noticed that they all refer to a "future situation", therefore, here again, the distinction cannot be accounted for as pertaining only to tense. As the translations indicate, sentences in the prospective forms are less assertive: most of them express a possibility (as (25) and (26), but even in (27), which, in the context, is actually a kind of order, the execution of the process is not asserted. The process is presented as executable but no commitment is made about its achievement. On the contrary, in the sentences where present-future forms are used (23)-(24), the achievement of the process does not seem to be doubtful. See for example (24) where the subject firmly committed himself to some precise achievement. In a future situation, the choice between prospective and present-future forms seems therefore to be dependent on the "achievement" value of the process: prospective mood carrying a value of unachievement while present-future forms carry a value of achievement.

But this seems to be contradictory with two other important facts:

(a) Despite the oppostition we have noticed between prospective and present future forms, we must acknowledge that they both actually refer to a situation of non achievement, where the process is yet to be carried on (a "future").

(b) If we now consider sentences (15) to (22), in which T1 (present-future) forms are used to refer to a "present situation" in opposition to T2 (past) forms which are used to refer to a "past situation", it seems, there too, that the opposition bears on the achievement versus non-achievement of the process, but, in these cases, it is to T2 (past) forms that the value of achievement is to be given while the T1 (present-future) forms refer to a non achieved process. T1 (present-future) forms would then been carrying two opposite values: achievement in opposition to prospective mood and non achievement in opposition to T2 (past) forms.

One way to get out of this apparent contradiction is to recognize two distinct sets of categorial values:

(1) A set of categorial "mood"(?) values concerning the achievement of the process and opposing the use of stem 3 (S3) suffixes for non achievement to the use of stem 2 (S2) suffixes for achievement.

(2) An evalutation of this mood value at a specific temporal reference point (given by the speech situation or its substitute). This can be acknowledged as a categorial tense value.[18] This evaluation can be made in different ways, either tacitly by simply suffixing the personal endings to the stem. In this case, the personal ending which links the predicate to the referential coordinates of the speech situation directly

validate the mood value of the stem: non achievement for the prospective mood (S3+p.e.: *(na:) ma:ḍuv.-e* "I shall/can do (it)", *enga sa:.v.-o* "We shall/can die") and achievement for the past forms (S2+p.e.: *ma:ḍd.-e* "I did (it)", *sa.tt.-a* "he died"). Otherwise, the evaluation can be made explicitly, through a tense suffix: the T1 (present-future) suffix then indicates that the achievement value of the predicate, which is validated by the perosnal ending, is not yet reached at the given referential (speech) time.[19]

	mood value		tense value
S3 suffix:	non achievement		—
	vs.		
S2 suffix:	achievement	T1 sufffix:	"future" (= "not yet reached")
		vs.	
		(T2)	: " actual" (= "reached")

In support of the distinction introduced just above we find some apparent counter examples to the uses of past and present-future tenses with verbs expressing a state—typically *iru* "to be" and in a few other specific uses of some verbs. With such non-processive uses, "achievement" can only mean "to be in a certain state" and non-achievement "not (yet) to be in a certain state" at a definite moment: there is no intermediate value. Actualization of a state becomes then identical with its achievement. Thus, it is not so surprising to see that with a verb like *iru* "to be", when the choice is only[20] between T1 and T2 forms, the T2 (past) forms are used to refer to a present situation:

(32) *ni: i:ga elli iddi?—na: i:ga bangalu:ru.no: idde*
you now where be+T2+2° I now Bangalore.LOC be+T2+1°
"Where are you now?"—"Now I am in Bangalore"

(compare with (21) above), whereas, as usual, the T1 (present-future) forms are used to refer to a future situation (33) or to a general statement (34):

(33) *na:iga orakadu mane. o:ge iddari.ya:?—ha:, iddane*
tomorrow morning house.LOC be+T1+2°.INTERR yes be+T1 +1°
"Will you be at home tomorrow morning?"—"Yes, I shall be there"

(34) *eggu ama eṭṭu maṇi.ga mane.yooge idda:na.*
always he eight hour.DAT house.LOC be+T1+3°M
"He is always at home at 8 o'clock."

The same use of T2 (past) forms in a "present" speech situation can occur with the verb *ari* "to know" (35) and in some occurrences of the verb "to come" (*bande*! "I am coming right now"!).

(35) *ni: ra:ma.na aride.ya:?—ha:, na: amana aride*
you Rama.ACC know+T2+2°.INTERR yes, I he+ACC know+T2+1°
"Do you know Rama?"—"Yes, I know him"

We turn our attention to the negative mood, illustrated in sentences (28)-(31) above. The formation of this negative by direct addition of the personal endings to the bare verb stem (S1), can be considered in the general linguistics field, as a curiosity.[21] There is no segmental unit to which the negative meaning can be attributed: the S1 stem is, in numerous instances, equivalent to the verb root itself and the suffix—often formed of a single vowel—is clearly equivalent to personal endings in other formations. Even if, for the purpose of analysis, we introduce a null morpheme between the stem and the personal ending—as it is usually done in the linguistic description of similar formation—it is puzzling that a null element can carry a clear negative meaning, and in any case will remain an oddity whatever explanation one may suggest.

From the precedent comparative analysis of the uses of the prospective mood and of the present-future and past forms in Badaga, it has been concluded that the distinction introduced by the stem suffixes crucially concern the achievement of the process: S2 suffix brings the value "achieved", S3 suffix, the value "unachieved". If we integrate the negative mood into an oppositive system with the other parallel formations, we can admit, at a first step, that compared to S2 stem and S3 stem, which has no suffix, it is left undetermined for the value of achievement.

To go beyond, let us recall the specificity of the predicate verb forms. In the beginning at a certain level of logical analysis, it can be considered that a predicative verb form can be roughly likened to the validation of a "predicate" by a "term". Briefly, a verb form built on S2+p.e. can them be read as "(p.e.) validates S2(=process+achieved)", and a verb form S3+p.e. as: "(p.e.) validates S3 (=process+unachieved)". What this presentation intends to enlighten is that the validation does not bear on the process alone, but bears on a process to which an achievement value has already been given, whether it is achieved or unachieved. The opposition of the two values of achievement—in the sense of bringing a process to its end or not—implicitly implies some validation of its execution, a positive or negative statement can be made only on something which pre-exists. Therefore, the presence of S2 and S3 suffixes minimally assumes that the process is "executable"—a value which is frequently apparent in the prospective mood (cf. (25)-(26) above). Now, if we extend this analysis to the negative verb forms, S1+p.e. can then be read "(p.e.) validates S1 (=process [unspecified for achievement]). Taking into account the double contribution of the stem (S2 or S3) suffixes to the specification of the process, it follows, from the absence of any stem suffix, that not only the achievement value is left unspecified, but that, consequently, the execution value of the process—which was only assumed indirectly through the achievement value of the stem suffixes—is also left unspecified. The process then remains "virtual", neither its execution, nor its non execution is assumed. Many modal forms illustrate this specific feature of stem S1: the value of execution of the process is left open not only with the Imperatives and Optative forms mentioned above, but also with all the modal forms built on the infinitive, i.e. stem, 1+*a*+ auxiliary, such as potential (INF+*a:ku* "may do"), and negative injunctive forms, (INF+-*ku:ḍa:du* "should not do", INF+*be:ḍa* "don't do!").

Regarding the negative verb mood, it seems that it can be said that it is precisely from the strong positive validation of the virtuality of the process that the resultant negative meaning may be derived. In the preceding modal forms the execution of the process is not asserted but only proposed through varied modal devices, its value is then really open. But asserting that, at some given time, the execution of a process remains virtual, cannot be accounted for in any other way but by assuming that, at that precise time, the process is not executed.

This analysis of the negative mood follows the path opened long ago by illustrious grammarians of Kannada such as Kesava for the verb formation ("a verb's theme *dhātu* appears when one removes the termination *vibhakti* of the conjugated negative *pratishēdhakriye*" sutra 216 in Kittel, 1903:160), or as Kittel for the meaning[22] ("*no:ḍem* therefore, signifies "a yet to see-I", i.e. "my seeing (is or was) yet to be" [....], or "my seeing (is) not actually existing", whence we arrive at the meaning "I do not see", Kittel, 1903:161) but what the Badaga data show clearly is that, in that language, the stem suffixes do not carry a proper tense value, but that an "achievement" value bearing more fundamentally on the execution of the process itself.

Conclusion

It is then possible to establish, at least, two distinct levels of assertion in Badaga: the sentential level, presented in the beginning (with agreement, challenge (*-a:*) and doubt (*-o:*) values), and the verb stem level concerning the execution of the process for which we have so far identified the values:

unspecified	(specified)	
S1 stem	unachieved	achieved
(no morpheme)	S3 stem	S2 stem
"virtual"	"executable"	"executed"

to which must be added a true "negative" value brought by the suffixation to the verb stem 1 of the negative marker *-a(:)d-*, which occurs in all non predicative forms (such as the negative adjectival participle *tinn.a:.da* "who do(/did/will) not eat" and in some derived predicative forms (INF+*kuḍa:d.u* "should not do..."). The other negative declarative predicative forms, more usual than the negative mood, are all formed with the addition of *ille* "is not" more or less morphologicaly integrated (often using a S3 stem base, for example past negative *bi:p.ile* "has not kept", future negative *timb.adu.g.ille* "will not eat").

If our analysis of the negative mood is correct, this type of verb formation would then be interesting for general linguistics as, in this type of languages, it would make a morphosyntactic unit of the "verb" category much closer than in most of the languages to what is precisely called in logics a "predicate" or an "operator": the verb being an "abstract" notion which can be used syntactically only when it is validated in some way. The minimal validation is seen in the infinitive form (stem S1+*a*) giving the verb a kind of "abstract noun" value (with no specification concerning the execution of the process) and in the negative mood as proposed above. All the other formations derived from a verb stem require the addition of a positive (S2 or S3) suffix or negative (*-a:-d-*) suffix to establish the process. In opposition to a noun bare stem which syntactically can function indifferently as a subject (or any other nominal functions) or as a predicate, a bare verb stem cannot function independently. Either it must be inserted in predicative relation—where it is attributed minimally a modal category (cf. imperative sg.) or a personal ending (cf. negative mood)—to form a finite predicate, or, it must be asserted minimally be a stem suffix (S2, S3 or negative) to form a "referential unit" whatever will be its final syntactic category, nominal, adjectival or adverbial phrase. Even the less specified verb form, the "compound participle" (cp.) (cf. (26), (27) above) is formed with a S2 stem suffix, though its value is essentially dependent of the values of the main predicate.

Therefore, the role of the stem suffixes appears to be primordial in Badaga verb formation. On one hand, the study of their uses in verb forms occurring in actual sentences allowed us to establish that they carry categorial values linked to the achievement of the process which significantly differ from the tense category. On the other hand, the study of the differential values of stem S1, stem S2 and stem S3 in a close oppositive system led us to identify the essentially "abstract" nature of the verb bare stem (S1) and to indicate briefly its consequences on the word formation of predicative as well as non predicative verbal forms.

The careful study of deviant facts observed in minor languages—such as the use of "past" stem for present-future tense in Badaga—should not be neglected as it is often a good indicator of archaisms or of potential grammatical properties which have remained unexpressed or have disappeared from the main languages of the group.

NOTES

Originally, most of the Badaga speakers could have been immigrants from the Mysore plains (probably mainly in the 16th/17th centuries).

1. Cf. Hockings, 1980.
2. Cf. Emeneau 1967 lists some of the features supporting the diachronical link between Kannada and Badaga, among them the evolution from PDr. initial **p-* to *h-* (and its subsquent deletion in Badaga) which is found only in the Kannada branch of South Dravidian languages.
3. The expression "speech forms" refer to the fact that there are dialectal varieties in a population of about 1,50,000 Badagas.
4. This labelling of the stems is slightly different from what I used in my other publications (where S^3 suffix = TH1 and S^2 suffix = TH2), but it follows from M.B. Emeneau's fundamental article (1967) and the notation adopted by D. Kapp in his description of Alu Kurumba (1982) to facilitate the comparison.
5. It differs from the "citation form" of a verb (= Imperative singular form) for verbs ending in the "enunciative" *-u* (cf. Bright 1972), for verbs ending in a vocalic group and for some verbs like *ba:* "to come", *ta:* "to give (to 1st or 2nd person)" whose S1 is respectively *bar-* and *tar-*. It also differs from the verb root in that it may contain derivative suffixes (transitive, causative, etc.).
6. Cf. Pilot-Raichoor, 1991 for a more detailed presentation.
7. Some verbs do not belong to the same class in Badaga and Kannada, see for ex.: K. *hiḍi (hiḍi/hiḍidu)* "to catch" vs. B. *(h) iḍi ((h) iḍit-)*, K. *ke:ḷ (ke:ḷd-/) ke:ḷu (ke:ḷi)* "to hear, ask" vs. B. *ke. (ke:t-)*, K. *pol (polt-)* "to sew" vs. B. *(h)ollu ((h) odd-)*, etc.
8. A first list of these "paired" verbs has been given in Emeneau (1967:392-393) and another, slightly modified by my own data, in Pilot-Raichoor (1991:338-339).
9. Similarly, the /a/ occurring in the variant of the T1 affix of type B paradigm (*-an-*, *ar-*...) can be accounted for synchronically as a linking vowel to prevent a cluster of two consonants.
10. Cf. Emeneau (1984:130-131) for the details of Toda verb morphology or Subrahmanyam (1971:116-127 and 252-254) for a brief account of Toda and Kota.
11. Cf. Kapp (1982:127-130) for the details of verbal flexion,
12. Cf. Kittel (1903:126-133) about Old and Medieval formations of present tense and contingent present-future tense.
13. There is a gap of several centuries between the mention of these present tense forms, already archaic, in the old grammars of Kannada (12th-13th centuries, cf. Kittel 1903:3) and the probable date of the arrival of the Badagas in the Nilgiris (in 1603 Father Fenicio mentioned only four villages, which may be taken as an indication of a fairly recent settlement). Have these forms survived in some unrecorded dialectal varieties of Kannada? Have they been re-created in Badaga?
14. See particularly the T1+p.e. suffixes of type B paradigm which show (minus 3 renewed forms) striking similarities even with the modern present-future paradigm of *a:gu:a:ne, a:re, a:ra, (a:diya), a:ra, a:neyo, a:no, (a:da:ri), (a:da:ra)*.
15. Despite the translation, *buddi* is a categorial nominal in Badaga, meaning "wisdom, intelligence" as well as "wise, intelligent"; There are less than ten categorial adjectives such as *doḍḍa* "big", *oḷḷiya* "good" etc.
16. Cf. Hockings, 1988.
17. For a thorough discussion of "finiteness" in Dravidian languages, see Steever (1987:2-5).

18. The opposition between what we call in Badaga "tenses" and "aspects" (another set of verb forms, not discussed here, using auxiliaries, such as *uḷ-* for progressive or *buḍ-* for perfective) is that in one case, i.e. tense, the reference point is linked to the speech event while in the other, i.e. aspect, it is linked to the process itself.
19. Note that, if the same value of achievement can be given to S2 stems in Toda and Kota, it seems that a reverse system to express this evaluation has been adopted: it is the positive value "already achieved" at a given referential time which is explicitly expressed [cf. (Sib.) affix for "past" in Toda] while the opposite tense value is left unexpressed morphologically.
20. In the first and second person, the verb *iru* has, as any other verbs, only past and present-future forms, while in third person it has three distinct forms a past *idd* (sg.), a present *idda:ne* (3°M) and a present-future *idda:na* (3°M), [N.B. in Kannada, the three paradigms are fully developped (cf. Schiffman, 1979:64)].
21. Among Dravidian languages it is found only in the Kannada-Tamil group, cf. Subrahmanyam, 1971:385-386.
22. See also Kushalappa Gowda (1972:267, n. 6) for different grammarians' point of view concerning the "negative" verbs *il-* and *al-*.

REFERENCES

Emeneau, M.B., 1967. The South Dravidian Languages. *Journal of the American Oriental Society,* 87/4:365-413.

Emeneau, M.B., 1984. *Toda Grammar and Texts.* Philadelphia American Philosophical Society (Memoirs 155).

Hockings, P., 1980. *Ancient Hindu Refugees. Badaga Social History,* 1550-1975. The Hague, Mouton Publishers; New Delhi, Vikas Publishing House.

Hockings, P., 1988. *Counsel from the Ancients. A study of Badaga Proverbs, Prayers, Omens and Curses.* Berlin- New York-Amsterdam, Mouton de Gruyter.

Kapp, D.B., 1982. *Ālu-Kuṟumbaru Nāyan: Die Sprache der Ālu-Kuṟumbas. Grammatik, Texte, Wörtebuch.* ¯5Wiesbaden, Otto Harrassowitz.

Kittel, F., 1903. *A Grammar of Kannada Language in English Comprising the Three Dialects of the Language (ancient, medieval and modern).* Mangalore, Basel Mission Book and Tract Depository.

Kushalappa Gowda, K., 1972. *A Grammar of Kannada. (Based on the inscriptions of Coorg. South Canara and North Canara)* Dts. 1000 to 1400 A.D. Annamalainagar, Annamalai University.

Paramasivam, K., 1979. *Effectivity and Causativity in Tamil.* Trivandrum, Dravidian Linguistics Association.

Pilot-Raichoor, C., 1991. *Le Badaga: Langue Dravidienne (Inde.) Description et Analyse.* (ms. Ph.D Thesis, Paris III).

Schiffman, H., 1979. *A Reference Grammar of Spoken Kannada.* Seattle University of Washington, Department of Asian Languages.

Steever, B.S., 1987. *The Serial Verb Formation in the Dravidian Languages.* Delhi, Motilal Banarsidass.

Subramahnyam P.S., 1971. *Dravidian Verb Morphology (a Comparative Study).* Annamalai University. Department of Ling., Publ. n°24. Annamalainagar (Tamil Nadu), Annamalai University.

CHAPTER 13

MALTO NUMERAL CLASSIFIERS

B.P. Mahapatra

Introduction

Numeral classifiers are found throughout South-East Asia, in languages of all genetic affiliations—Thai, Mon Khmer, Tibeto-Burmese, Malayo-Polynesian, Chinese, and they are even found in a number of Indo-Aryan languages like, Oriya and Bengali (Emeneau, p. 647 ff., Burling, p. 244). These peculiar processes of categorizing the nouns along certain semantic dimensions, reveal highly differentiated perceptual and conceptual referents although do not seem like characteristic of the major Dravidian languages of India, Malto, the northern most Dravidian language of India, being clearly an exception.[1]

Numeral Classifiers

With regards to the numeral classifiers, Malto enjoys certain special position for having the 'most complex' system of all among languages of this area (Emeneau, p. 649). The morpheme structure of the numeral phrase in Malto is number + classifier + noun, when the number is 'three' or above and the number is not a 'group' such as: *ko: ṛi* 'a score'. For example:

tini jan maler— three + classifier + noun (men)
tini maq o:yd̲u— three + classifier + noun (cows)
tini kaṛsa amd̲u— three + classifier + noun (water)

The other variant structure is classifier + number + noun, when the numbers are, 'one' or 'two' and the noun is 'non-human'. For example:

maq-ond o:yd̲u— classifier-number (one) noun (cow)
maq-s o:yd̲u— classifier-number (two) + noun (cow)
tep-ond pu:pd̲u— classifier-number (one) + noun (flower)
top-s pu:pd̲u— classifier-number (two) + noun (flower)

when the noun is 'human' portmanteau forms *ort-* 'one human' and *jo:ṛ- nd* or *irw-* 'two humans' occur.

The Malto numeral classifiers fall into two distinct functional groups: subject classifiers and action classifiers. The later classifiers, such as *ke-pond* - 'one time', *rik-ond-* 'a little' *pahr-ond-* 'a while', etc. do not occur in a noun phrase and are of little interest for our present purpose. The object classifiers fall into three major groups:

1. Classifiers which specify the status of an object
2. Classifiers which specify the state of an object
3. Classifiers which specify the quantity of an object as measured along some dimension.

Status Classifiers

All nouns which co-occur with the 'dimensional' and 'unique' classifiers are discrete individual entities. The domain of discrete individual objects are marked by a set of mutually exclusive morphemes: classifiers with 'live' and 'shaped' referents and classifiers with 'unique' referents (See, Table I).

Dimensional Classifiers

The forms which occur in the numeral phrase structure number + classifier + noun are treated as basic and other forms are treated as variants. Morphophonemically, all classifiers of this sub-class of phonemic structure CV(C)CV alternate with CV(C)C when followed by the morphemes *-ond-* 'one' and *-s-* 'two'. The classifiers are listed in their basic forms.

Classifier with 'live' referents

jan—'human': man, woman, brother, thief, watchman, witch, etc.

tini jan maler— three + classifier + men
tini jan qa:pur— three + classifier + watchman
tini jan ceṛer— three + classifier + witches

maq—'non-human': horse, frog, snake, fish, fly, earthworm, divinities, etc.

tini maq go:ṛo— three + classifier + horses
tini maq tiléṛḍu— three + classifier + files
tini maq bu:te— three + classifier + ghosts

Classifiers with 'shaped' referents

ḍaṛa—'long', large objects': bamboo, branch, gun, leg, penis, horn, river, etc.

tini ḍaṛa ma:sḏu— three + classifier + bamboos
tini ḍaṛa qeḍḏu— three + classifier + legs
tini ḍaṛa nadi— three + classifier + rivers

kaṭi—'long, small objects': needle, pen, arrow, grass, hair, thorn, 'biri', etc.

tini kaṭi te:qṛi— three + classifier + needles
tini kaṭi ta:li— three + classifier + hair
tini kaṭi cabi— three + classifier + keys

panda—'long, flexible objects': rope, necklace, ribbon, tail, road, song, 'mantra', etc.

tini panda dawṛa— three + classifier + ropes
tini panda pa:wḏu—three + classifier + roads
tini panda ca:me— three + classifier + songs

paṛa—'long pods/fruits': banana, beans, snake gourd, pod beans, string beans, 'drumsticks', etc.

tini paṛa kaldi— three + classifier + bananas
tini paṛa simbi— three + classifier + beans
tini paṛa jiṅga— three + classifier + gourds

paṭa—'flat, broad, objects': cloud, axe, comb, cake, dish, bed, tongue, vagina, etc.

tini paṭa badli— three + classifier + clouds
tini paṭa kake— three + classifier + combs
tini paṭa taṛte— three + classifier + tongues

pata—'flat, broad, thin objects': leaf, paper, letter, paper, money, etc.

tini pata a:ṭṛe— three + classifier + leaves
tini pata lo:ṭe— three + classifier + notes
tini pata kagte— three + classifier + papers

kanḍa—'flat, broad, cotton objects': pants, blanket, rag, 'sheet' socks, etc.

tini kanḍa pente— three + classifier + pants
tini kanḍa komle— three + classifier + blankets
tini kanḍa keta— three + classifier + rags

goṭ—'round, heavy objects and miscellaneous objects': head, eye, pot, basket, well, wheel, house, bottle, stone, seed, rice, egg, fruit, berry, star, moon, dream, etc.

tini goṭ pa:nḏu— three + classifier + fruits
tini goṭ bin:nke— three + classifier + stars
tini goṭ tumglḏu— three + classifier + dreams

The variant forms are *pa:n*—which occurs only before *-ond-* 'one' and *panḍ* - which occurs only before *-s-* 'two'.

pula—'round, light objects': flower, cooked rice, pop-corn, popped rice, etc.

tini pula pu:pḏu— three + classifier + flowers
tini pula ja:gu— three + classifier + rice (cooked)
tini pula lawa— three + classifier + pop corn

Unique Classifiers

These 'echo' classifiers as Burling calls them, are applicable only to a narrowly restricted sets of nouns, and mostly to a single noun only (Burling, p. 250). Invariably, the classifier is identical in form to the noun it classifies. The list is exhaustive according to my data, but a few more forms are not ruled out.

qep— 'village': qepond qepd̲u— classifier + number + village
man— 'treȩ': manond mand̲u— classifier + number + tree
kiṛ— 'small plant': kiṛond kiṛd̲u— classifier + number + plant
kaṛi— 'hole/cave': kaṛiond kaṛi— classifier + number + hole
kuji— 'shadow/reflection': kujiond—classifier + number + kuji shadow.

Given this paradigm 'discrete individual objects', and rough semantic definitions of the individual terms belonging to this set, it is now possible to identify the dimensions of meaning underlying this field and to map the values or the distinctive features of meaning on these dimensions on to the set of terms (See, Lounsbury, Berlin). The aim of this analysis is to isolate in most economical and non-redundant terms the relevant components, what one must know in order to categorise objects correctly.

Componential Definitions of Numeral Classifiers and Semantic Domain

'Discrete Individual Object'

Dimensions		Values
'membership' (A)	:	unique (a^1), dimensional (a^2)
'dimension' (B)	:	animate (b^1), inanimate (b^2)
'shape' (C)	:	long (c^1), broad (c^2), round (c^3)
'saliency' (D)	:	high (d^1), low (d^2)
'specification' (E)	:	specific (e^1), general (e^2)

To this dimensional analysis of the field, and components that constitute it, the following rewriting rules may be introduced to account for the extensional meaning of some of the basic components. This formulation is necessary to explain the variables at realization level, in different contexts. The rules are,

(i) 'low'	a	'non-human' in the context 'animate'
	b	'flexible' in the context 'long'
	c	'thin' in the context 'broad'
	d	'light' in the context 'round'
(ii) 'specific'	a	'fruit' in the context 'long'
	b	'cotton' in the context 'broad'

Componential definitions:

jan	:	a^2	b^1		d^1	
maq	:	a^2	b^1		d^2	
daṛa	:	a^2	b^2	c^1	d^1	
kaṭi	:	a^2	b^2	c^1	d^2	
panda	:	a^2	b^2	c^1	d^2	e^2
paṛa	:	a^2	b^2	c^1	d^2	e^1
paṭa	:	a^2	b^2	c^2	d^1	
pata	:	a^2	b^2	c^2	d^2	
kanḍa	:	a^2	b^2	c^2	d^3	e^1
goṭ	:	a^2	b^2	c^2	d^1	
pula	:	a^2	b^2	c^3	d^2	
qep	:	a^1				
man	:	a^1				
kaṛi	:	a^1				
kuji	:	a^1				

To sum up, the status classifiers of Malto divide the nouns into two sub-sets: discrete individual objects and non-discrete objects. The individual objects are also of two types: unique objects and live and shaped objects. The live objects are further subdivided into two sub-sets: human objects (*+jan*) and non-human (*+maq*). The shaped objects are also subdivided into three subsets: one-dimensional or characteristically long objects, two-dimensional or characteristically broad objects and three-dimensional or characteristically round objects. Each of these sub-sets of shaped nouns are further sub-classified into two or more classes: (+ *ḍaṛa*, + *kaṭi*, + *panda*, + *paṛa*), (+ *paṭa*, + *pata*, + *kanḍa*), and (+ *goṭ*, + *pula*).

State Classifiers

These classifiers are but a few in Malto and are generally neutral to the basic discrete/non-discrete opposition of the nouns. The classifiers are as follows:

baha —area: field, market place, etc

ṭaḍa —small area: as is usually occupied by spit, wound, or primary vaccination mark etc.

ḍika —puddle: cow-dung, excreta, etc.

ḍe:la —clod: earth, mud, etc.

topa —cluster: flower, fruit, crop, etc.
ṭopa —drop: water, blood, soup, etc.
ba:gi —share, portion.
pobi —portion, cross-sectional.
cowḍa —piece

Classifiers of Quantity

These classifiers are generally neutral to the discrete/non-discrete opposition and are organized under dimension along which the objects are measured.

(i) Depth:

capṭ —foot
bagḍ —ankle
qosa —thigh
kaṛm —waist
buki —chest
qasr —neck
toro —mouth

(ii) Length:

bilas —span
muḍr —length of the forearm from the elbow to the fist
muk —cubit

(iii) Volume:

muṭ —fist-full
pohl —as much as one hand will contain
pasi —as much as two hands put together will contain, and various standard containers:
kaṛs —pitcher
gilas —glass
patli —pot, etc.

(iv) Weight:

boj —one head-load etc.

(v) Girth:

muṭ —circumference around which the index finger and the thumb can reach, etc.

(vi) Time:

din —day
mehn —month
bacr —year, etc.

(vii) Groups of number:

ko:ṛi —a score, etc.

Semantic Relationship

After this somewhat detailed analysis of the numeral classifiers, we can now look for the semantic relationship among the terms within the total structure of the system. From a structural point of view, any further ordering of the state classifiers, and the classifiers of quantity seem less promising, but the 'status classifiers' can genuinely be called a microsystem with high degree of semantic structuring.

Malto Object Systems

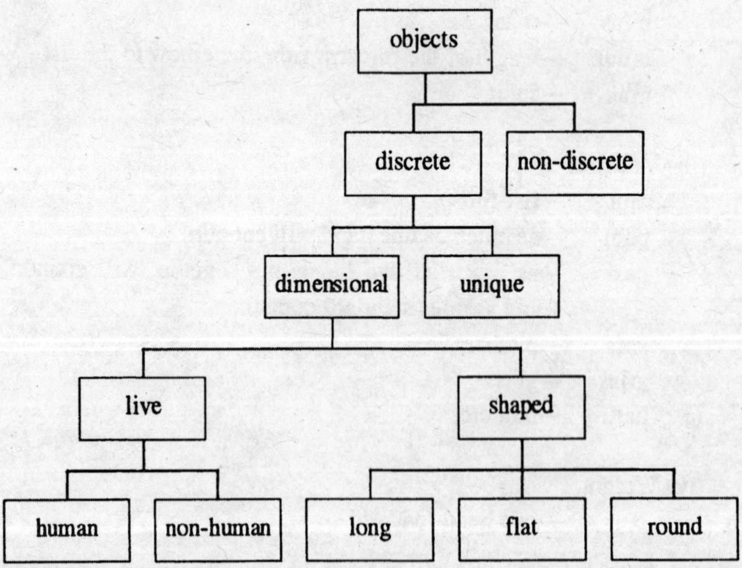

The peculiarity of the Malto system is the lack of overt distinction between discreteness and non-discreteness of objects, and it has to be postulated on the basis of inclusion and exclusion relationships, operating among lower level taxonomy. Secondarily, the semantic domain 'descrete objects' is divided into two sub-sets: unique objects and dimensional objects. The dimensional objects are divided along dimensions of 'life' and 'shape'. The former is realised as 'human' and 'non-human' and the latter as one-dimensional, two dimensional, and three-dimensional, or characteristically, long, broad and round. The one-dimensionality is the property of four kinds of objects: large, small, flexible and fruit; two-dimensionality is of: large, thin and cotton, and three-dimensionality is of: large and light.

Origin: Retention and Borrowing

Now, we can speculate about the evolution of these complicated classificatory system. For Malto, Emeneau assumes that, it "began borrowing numerals and classifiers from a neighbouring Magadhan language, and subsequently elaborated the system independently, chiefly on the basis of inherited material" (Emeneau, p. 649, see note 3). It is of course doubtful what this "inherited material" is, but it is a necessary prerequisite for keeping the hypothesis from falling into utter disrepute of a fallacy. What is indeed there in a 'nest' other than the little bird's picking up knick-knack from the nearest garbage dump? Malto barring the unique classifiers, has a total number of eleven classifiers of which only *maq-* and the variant *pa:n-* may be said as truely indigenous. All other forms are generally borrowed from neighbouring languages like hundreds of other forms. Furthermore, only three of these words, *jan-*, *goṭ-* and *kanḍ-* might be said as true classifiers in the Magadhan Languages. Others have no such function, and have general meanings like:

Malto		**Oriya**	
ḍoṛa	:	dhɔḍa	—bamboo pole
		ḍaḷɔ	—branch
kaṭi	:	kaṭhi	—stick, twigs
panda	:	phandɔ	—net-work of ropes, rope-trap

paṛa	:	phoḷɔ	—fruit
		phɔṛa	—silver
paṭa	:	pɔṭa	—board
pata	:	pɔta	—leaf, eye-lid
pula	:	phulɔ	—flower

Therefore, linguistic borrowing, no matter how extensive, is too sterile a process to explain the development and diffusion of conceptual system either within or across genetic boundaries. The true significance of a numeral classifier lies not in its independent existence as an individual item, but rather in its occupying a particular categoric position within the totality of a classificatory scheme.

A probable explanation may also be found in Durkheimian "sociocentrism", which posits the centre of the first schemes of nature in society itself. For him, all logical hierarchies are only different aspects of social hierarchy, "and the unity of knowledge is nothing else than the very unity of the collectivity extended to the universe" (Durkheim, pp. 83-84). Although Durkheim sees all other classificatory systems in relation to and as a consequence of the cardinal system of totemic classification, which no doubt is untenable, for all societies with or without totemic systems do classify humans and objects according to their form, character or utility. However, the crux of his argument lies not in explaining the nature or the elements of classification but in providing a model for the development to systems of hierarchaized notions.

Human Cognition and Relativity

The third possibility lies in assuming certain probable universal concepts which are present in the semantic substructure of all languages (See Mathiot, p. 17). It proposes that while each culture has its own way of viewing reality, there are certain characteristics of the real world for which there is a high likelihood that every culture has linguistic means of expression. For, in no other way can we explain the similarities between Tarascan and Malto object systems except by chance.

The tarascan system is, according to Friedrich:

(i) a dimensionless set lacking both shape and mass,

(ii) a dimensional set of masses, classified by 'container' and of shapes, saliently one-dimensional, two-dimensional and three-dimensional,

(iii) a speech-capable and approximately 'human' set.

The Malto system is, according to this paper:

(i) a dimensionless set lacking both life and shape,

(ii) a dimensional set of life, saliently human and non-human, and of shapes, saliently one-dimensional, two-dimensional and three-dimensional.

Now, we can raise the question of relevance this kind of a study. What does it prove? It probably proves nothing other than what Chomsky would say that "the mind attempts tc impse some organization on the physical world—that humans classify, if they perform any mentional acts at all" (Chomsky, 1968: p. 65). But, why should it classify? The main function of a classificatory schema, like any other, is to simplify the huge mass of information, and to render it easily understandable. It separates the likes from the dislikes and makes the distinguishing features clear which help in organising a system of significances in which every part has a significant function. It is one form of thought bearing properties common to all thought, whether of a higher or lower order, of technological or philosophical nature, of practical or speculative value. It reveals that the classificatory system is not merely an arbitary or ad hoc collection of phenomena, but the result of a sustained intellectual preoccupation with the environment towards formulating a conception of relaity and beyond it, a natural philosophy of ethnometaphysical speculation.

NOTES

1. The data presented here are based on my field work on the Malpaharia dialect of Malto which differs from the Sawria dialect in some aspects. Apparently, Ernest Droese's 'Introduction to the Malto Language' is based on the latter dialect to a large extent. Therefore, some discrepancy between these materials may be considered natural.
2. ḏ is dental fricative which contrasts with d in Malto.

3. The 'neighbouring' Magadhan language for Malto was Bengali until Bihari replaced it in very recent times. Secondly, all my observations on the Magadhan languages are based on my findings on Oriya and to some extent Bengali only.

REFERENCES

Berlin, B., 1968. *Tzeltal Numeral Classifiers. A Study in Ethnographic Semantics*, Mouton.

Burling, R., 1965. How to Choose a Burmese Numeral Classifier. In M.E. Spiro (ed.) *Context and Meaning in Cultural Anthropology.* The Free Press.

Chomsky, N., 1968. *Language and Mind*, Harcourt. Brace & World. Inc.

Droese, E., 1884. *Introduction to the Malto Language*, Agra.

Durkheim, E., M. Mauss., 1903. *Primitive Classification*, translated by Rodney Needham, Cohen West Ltd.

Emeneau, M.B., 1956. India as a Linguistic Area, Reprinted in; Dell Hymes (ed.), *Language in Culture and Society.*

Friedrich, P., 1970. Shape in Grammar, *Language* Vol. 46, No. 2 (Part I).

Lounsnbury, F., 1964. The Structural Analysis of Kinship Semantics in *Proceedings of the Ninth International Congress of Linguists.* Mouton, pp. 1073-1090.

Mathiot, M., 1968. *An Approach to the Cognitive Study of Language.* Indiana University, Bloomington, Mouton.

V

AUSTRO-ASIATIC

O my dear dad
Don't get me married to an old man

O my dear father
Don't get an old man for me
If you get me married to him
I will soon be widow

My dear dad
Don't give me to a servant
He will be obedient to his master
And I will have to get up early
Don't send me away my father
Don't give me to an old man

Well, if you find a suitor for me
You may find a shepherd
But again to say
The shepherd should be tough and healthy
He should not be an ill man
Please do not get me married to an old man
Otherwise I will be a widow soon.

I would prefer a Pohal (a sheep rearer)
As he can provide me
Enough meat to eat
Enough wool for a chola.

(A Gaddi song)

CHAPTER 14

NOUN-VERB DISTINCTION IN MUNDA LANGUAGES

D.N.S. Bhat

Introduction

One of the fascinating characteristics of Munda languages is their ability to use "any word for any concept" (Pinnow, 1966:101). Part of speech distinctions like nouns, verbs, adjectives and adverbs are vague or lacking in these languages. Hoffmann (1903:xix) suggests that parts of speech are a kind of "crystal" which offers to the mind readymade signs for every kind of abstract thought that it is capable of; words in Mundari, according to him, are of great functional elasticity; they generally do not by themselves connote the manner in which the mind conceives the thing signified; that connotation is usually left to the context of the proposition or the circumstances under which it is uttered.

Santali (Bodding, 1929) and Ho (Deeney, 1975), show a similar absence of parts of speech distinctions, and according to Pinnow (1966:101), this phenomenon of using any word for any concept goes back to ancient times and can probably be accepted as Proto-Munda. Unfortunately, Pinnow does not consider it necessary to regard this characteristic as distinctive of these languages because, there are "innumerable other language families in which the situation is the same". He concludes that "the matter thus deserves only a brief consideration". Konow (1906) and Bhattacharya (1975:104) also refer to this interesting characteristic of Munda languages but the latter expresses his desire of not elaborating upon it because "enough has already been said on this point by previous writers".

This has also been the view of most of the later grammarians of Munda languages. Some, like Cook (1965) and Osada (1992) on Mundari, Deeney (1975) on Ho, and Suryakumari (1991) on Santali do concede the possibility of freely using any word as a noun or verb in the language that they are describing, but their grammars are mainly based upon the traditional word class distinctions like nouns, verbs, adjectives and adverbs and do not in any way reflect the former point; Cook (1965:109) bases his parts of speech distinctions on "statistical" grounds, i.e. by assigning primary and secondary functions to forms on the basis of their frequency of occurrence in the relevant form classes; others provide certain minor morphological criteria for differentiation, but it is generally conceded that only the frequency of occurrence can form the primary basis of this differentiation.

Other grammarians like Ramaswami (1992) on Bhumij, do not even make any reference to this interesting Munda characteristic. They simply use the traditional parts of speech distinctions as the basis of their descriptions without providing any justification as such. This latter tendency has had the effect of completely masking this most interesting typological characteristic of Munda languages in the current studies of this language family.

Universality of Noun-Verb Distinction

The question, whether there can be any language that does not make a distinction between nouns, verbs, adjectives and adverbs has been a controversy among linguists. As I have pointed out elsewhere (Bhat), linguists are generally willing to concede that the categories of adjectives and adverbs may be missing in some languages, with the adjectival bases being grouped with nouns or verbs, and the adverbial ones with verbs or particles. But this is not considered to be possible in the case of the distinction between nouns and verbs, which is generally regarded as relevant for all languages. This latter claim apparently derives from a fundamental assumption about the structuring of sentences that has been stated by Sapir (1921:121) in the following terms:

> There must be something to talk about and something must be said about this subject of discourse...No language wholly fails to distinguish noun and verb, though in particular cases the nature of the distinction may be an elusive one. It is different with other parts of speech. None of these is imperatively required for the life of language.

However, the need to have something to talk about and be said about it need not necessarily lead to a noun-verb distinction in the case of all languages. There is a possibility of expressing both these types of notions in the predicate itsetlf, as has been pointed out be some linguists. That is, the nuclear element in the predicate can denote the various participants that are involved in the event (and also their relationship with the event). In the case of such languages, constituents other than the predicate in a sentence would only have the function of modifying one of these elements of the predicate.

For example, the following statement of Hoffmann (1903:1) concerning the sentence-structure of Mundari:

> ....all the purely logical relations, viz., those between subject and predicate as well as those between the predicate and its objects, are welded together into one polysyllabic word, and this word constitutes the whole proposition as such. Additional words which may be met with are mere explanations of either the pronominal subject, or the predicate, or the pronominal direct and indirect objects.

A similar view has been expressed by Boas (1911:673) regarding Chinook (an American language). All the syntactic relations between the verb and the nouns of a sentence, according to him, must be expressed in this language by means of pronominal and adverbial elements incorporated in the verb, so that the verb is the skeleton of the sentence, while the nouns or noun-groups held together by the possessive pronouns are mere appositions.

Kinkade (1983:32) also points out that in Salishan languages, the predicate itself contains affixes which fully denote the subject and object, and the complements which follow the predicate and which can be "translated" as subjects and objects (some Salishan languages allow only one of these to be expressed in a sentence) are in appositive relation with those affixes. He considers it more appropriate to regard these complements as embedded predicates that characterize the pronominal affixes. He also points out that, in view of the above-mentioned situation, there is no basis, in these languages, for establishing a distinction between nominal and verbal expressions.

Van Valin (1985) also suggests the possibility of providing a similar description for the clause structure of Lakhota, a Siouan language. He writes:

> "The agreement suffixes on the verb function like pronominals, and their reference is minimally specified, with only person, number and animacy being given. A verb like *wayaka* has the meaning *'3sg animate saw 3sg animate'* and the function of NPs is to *specify* which 3sg animate is being referred to. They thus function as what Keenan calls 'reference restricting operator'. They force the pronoun to refer to a specific person in the case where the full NP is e.g. a proper noun, or they constrain the pronoun to take its reference within a certain class in the case of a common noun. The NPs are attributes of the pronominal elements in so far as they serve as reference-restricting modifiers."

Dispute and its Resolution

The status of the noun-verb distinction in some of the native languages of America, such as those of Salishan, Wakashan and Chimakuan languages has given rise to a long-standing dispute among the concerned lunguists. Some like Swadesh (1939), Kuipers (1968), Thompson (1979) and Kinkade (1983) have argued that the distinction is missing in one or the other of these languages, whereas others like Jacobson (1979), Hébert (1983) and Van Eijk and Hess (1986) have argued that the concerned languages do possess sufficient basis to establish the distinction. The consensus among linguists in general is apparently that the former claim still remains unsubstantiated and also probably unsubstantiable (see Dixon, 1982:2; Hopper and Thompson, 1984:747; Schachter, 1985:7; Dik, 1989:162; Croft, 1991:130).

I would like to argue, however, that this dispute cannot be resolved by merely adducing data from different languages in support of one or the other of these two opposing claims. There are two interesting points that need to be recognized in this context. First of all, as pointed out by Croft (1991:45), the real problem in these cases is to decide as to what kind of grammatical evidence would justify our distinguishing two different sets of lexical items as constituting two major categories, and what kind of evidence would merely support the claim that they are only subgroups of a single major category. Croft points out, in this connection, that grammatical evidence can distinguish count nouns from mass nouns (or stative verbs from processual verbs), in English, but no grammarian treats these as major categories.

Secondly, a bland yes/no answer to the question as to whether or not a particular categorial distinction exists in a given language would not be a satisfying one. As pointed out by Lyons (1989:158), there is a need to determine the "relative importance" of that categorial distinction for the language under consideration. This relative importance can be measured, according to Lyons, on the basis of the number of criteria that are satisfied, or the linguists' ease or difficulty in applying them. The distinction between nouns and verbs is clearly less important in the structures of Munda and Salishan languages than it is in the structures of, say, English or Kannada.

Languages appear to fall into a gradation with some showing several differentiating characteristics between nouns and verbs and others showing very few such differences. The division of lexical items into nouns and verbs is also rather rigid in some languages and very fluid in others. Linguists who consider the noun-verb distinction to be a language-universal one would have no explanation for this cross-linguistic variation as well. They merely have to assume that the variation represents different degrees of lexicalization of the concerned functional distinction.

However, I believe, that the dispute can be resolved with the help of a different approach to this situation; instead of directly answering the question as to whether there can be languages that do not make any distinction between nouns and verbs, we may merely postulate an idealized language type which does not make any distinction. The function of reference (or participant identification) would be carried out in that abstract language type with the help of the person-number-gender markers that occur in the predicate, and the argument-like structures that occur in the sentence would only have the function of modifying either the nuclear part of the predicate or the elements which occur with it, such as the personal affixes, and also the affixes that denote time, place, manner, etc. These latter structures would differ from predicates proper only by the fact that they would be presupposing the relevant events or properties rather than asserting them or questioning them.

Individual languages can then be regarded as being more or less close to this idealized language type. The advantage of such a postulation is that it can provide an explanation for the occurrence of variations in the amount of differences that languages show between nouns and verbs. That is, the occurrence of very little difference between nouns and verbs in the case of some languages can now be accounted for on the basis of the assumption that they are very close to the idealized language type, and make use of an entirely different strategy of sentence structure.

Characterizing Properties

In the case of familiar languages like English, in which nouns and verbs form distinct categories, verbs are used primarily for representing actions and events, whereas nouns are used primarily for representing the various types of participants that are involved in those actions or events. Most of the differentiating characteristics which occur between nouns and verbs in these languages derive from this basic functional difference between the two.

We can postulate that the idealized language type mentioned above will not be using any of these differentiating characteristics as the basis of a major categorial distinction (like the one between nouns and verbs) because, the function of participant identification is not being carried out by a major class of lexical items in that language type. I propose to exemplify this point in the following sub-sections with the help of data from two different Munda languages, namely Mundari and Santali, because these languages are found to be close to this idealized language type.

Difference in the Temporal Status

In the case of languages in which nouns and verbs are distinct, nouns denote entities that have continuous identity over time, whereas verbs denote ephemeral and unique entities. Du Bois (1980:220) suggests that reference to a new entity by a noun involves opening of a "cognitive file" for that entity; subsequent references to it add information to update that file. Verbs, on the other hand, do not establish any such entities on their own; rather, they provide information about an entity that has been established earlier by a noun. Du Bois points out in this connection that successive verbs ordinarily do not refer back repeatedly to a single event, and are therefore very different from nouns on this point.

This difference between nouns and verbs gets reflected, in the case of languages in which the two form distinct categories, in the fact that they take two entirely different sets of inflectional affixes. Nouns typically show number-gender distinctions and take determiners. They also show distinctions for case and for pragmatic factors like topic and focus. As pointed out by Croft (1991:117), the given-new taxonomy is applied essentially to noun phrases and not to verbs or predicates.

Verbs, typically show tense, aspect and mood distinctions; they may be affirmed or negated, and are typically transient in nature; they also get differentiated on the basis of the number and type of complements (arguments) that occur with them, and show distinctions for voice, such as reflexive, reciprocal, passive, transitive-intransitive, and causative.

There would generally be a tendency, in these languages, to maintain this distinction between nouns and verbs even when prototypical verbs are nominalized, and prototypical nouns are verbalized. For example, Comrie and Thompson (1985:397) point out that nouns formed from verbs for naming one of the arguments of the latter, such as the agent, object, instrument, location, etc., behave very much like other nouns, bearing only morphological and (often unpredictable and idiosyncratic) semantic relations to the associated verbs; nouns formed for naming an activity or state (called "action nominals") also show several properties of nouns, but unlike the former, these tend to retain some of the properties of the verbs to which they are related.

Similarly, when prototypical nouns are verbalized, they behave like verbs externally (i.e. in their function in a clause), but internally they reatin several of their nominal characteristics. They may denote a participant in addition to the action or event in which it participates, and may show number, gender and other inflectional markers that are related to that participant.

This interesting distinction between nouns and verbs in their temporal status arises because the two have to perform very distinct functions in the languages concerned. We can assume that this difference is absent between the corresponding sets of lexical items in the idealized language type under consideration on the basis of our assumption that the relevant functional distinction is lacking in that language type.

As pointed out earlier, one of the striking characteristics of Munda languages like Mundari and Santali is the ease with which any given lexical item can be used as a predicate. Unlike languages in which nouns are quite distinct from verbs, these languages allow words which translate as nouns (i.e., as denoting concrete objects), personal names, pronouns, numerals, prepositions, clitics, etc. to be freely used as "verbs" without any need to undergo verbalizing processes and without requiring the support of an auxiliary verb. The various verbal inflections like tense, aspect and mood, agreement markers, voice markers, etc. can be directly attached to these words.

In Mundari, for example, there is apparently no restriction as to the type of lexical item that can directly take the verbal inflections and thereby function as a predicate. Hoffmann (1903:xxi, 112) points out that concrete nouns denoting living beings or inanimate objects, pronouns, numerals, post-positions, adverbs, interjections—all these can be used as verbs for denoting states or actions in this language. Examples:

(1) sim-ked-ko-a-le
fowl-past-DO (3pl)-cop-Subj (1pl)
'We have (acquired) fowls'

(2) duṛa-tan-a-ing
dust-passive-pres-cop-Subj(1sg)
'I am getting covered with dust'

(3) kented-ja-iñ-a-ko
many-ind.past-DO (1sg)-cop-Subj (3pl)
'They outnumbered us'

(4) mid-jan-ge-a-le
one-ind.past-emph-cop-Subj (1pl)
'We are equal (in a game)'

(5) dal-ked-ko-a-e
strike-past-DO (3pl)-cop-Subj (3sg)
'He struck them'

Notice that tense, aspect, voice and other such affixes and also the markers of subject and object are directly added to these bases. Hoffmann (1930) considers these predicates to be containing a copula *a*, but notice that it occurs in the case of all these bases, including the ones which translate as verbs (5); Cook (1965) considers this *a* to be an indicative mood marker, whereas Osada (1992) regards it as a predicator.

Similar use of lexical items has been reoprted in Santali, a language which is closely related to Mundari. According to Suryakumari (1991:156), any word or any concept can function as a verb root or a base in this language. Bodding (1929:5) points out that even borrowed words are freely used as verbs in Santali, whatever may be their status in the language to which the words originally belonged. There is no need to attach any "verbalizing" affix or an auxiliary for using such words as finite verbs.

Lexical items also show a similar kind of freedom in their occurrence in nominal functions like being subjects, objects, or other types of complements, in these languages. There would be no need to attach any "nominalizing" markers for that purpose. However, as pointed out earlier, the reason why there is such a freedom of usage in these languages is that the items do not have a distinct nominal function in these usages, but only that of modifying the referential elements occurring in the predicate; they are different from predicates proper only in representing presupposed predications.

For example, Mundari allows any of its content words (i.e. words which translate as nouns, adjectives, verbs, adverbs, etc.) to occur as arguments in a sentence without undergoing any morphological changes (see Hoffmann, 1903:120; Cook, 1965; Osada, 1991:41). Examples verbs *ote* 'to share' and *ol* 'to write':

(6) ote-ra haṭingem
share-gen land
'share of land'

(7) ol-tea
write-instr
'writing materials like pencil, pen, paper, etc.'

It has been reported that the morphological process of inserting the affix *n* or *p* can be used in this language for deriving nominal bases from verbal bases (Hoffmann, 1903:108; Sinha, 1975; Osada, 1992:62); Hoffmann considers these affixes to be indicating the "beginning" that is being made by the language to differentiate between nouns and verbs. Examples:

(8a)	dub	'to sit'	dunub	'a meeting'
	haṭing	'to divide'	hanaṭing	'a division'
	kumṛu	'to steal'	kunumṛu	'a theft'
(8b)	om	'to give'	opom	'a gift'
	erang	'to fight'	eperang	'a fight'

Notice, however, that the relevant bases can function as nouns without the addition of such affixes as well. For example, *haṭing* can also be used in the sense of 'a division or part', and *kumṛu* in the sense of 'a theft or a thief'. Further, the affix *n* is relatable to the reflexive affix *en* and the affix *p* with the reciprocal affix *p.* Examples:

(8c)	dal	'to strike'	dal-en	'to strike oneself'
	tusing	'to put'	tusing-en	'to put on oneself'
	ur	'skin'	ur-in	'to shed one's own skin'
(8d)	om	'to give'	o-p-om	'to give to one another'
	dal	'to strike'	da-p-al	'to strike one another'
	ti	'hand'	ti-p-i	'to take one another's hand'

According to Bodding (1929:46), Santali comes near to forming nouns by infixing an *n* or *t* after the first vowel of a word and repeating the vowel after the infixing consonant. Examples (Suryakumari, 1991:133):

(9)	bet'	'to stop'	be-n-et'	'lid, stopper'
	bak'	'to hook'	ba-n-ak'	'a hook'

(10)	ehop'	'to begin'	e-t-ohop	'beginning'
	jelen	'long'	je-t-len	'length'

Bodding points out, however, that this formation is not frequent in Santali. Further, this kind of word-formation is not restricted to nouns; any of the forms derived in this fashion may be used as adjectives or even as verbs; there are some, like *unum* 'submerge' (from *um* 'wash' and *otor* 'to pull down' from *or* 'beginning'), which are especially used as verbs; but, on the whole, these are mostly used as nouns.

When predicates are used in the "nominal" position, they retain all their tense, aspect and mood affixes in Mundari (Hoffmann, 1903:xxv). They may be denoting concrete or abstract entities or may be functioning as adverbial or adjectival modifiers; there is no neutralization or loss of verbal inflections when they are used in these latter positions. Examples:

(11a) om-ked-a-ing
give-past-cop-subj (1sg)
'I gave to (to someone)'

(11b) om-ked-*á*
give-past-it
'the thing that (I) gave'

(11c) om-ked-tare
give-past-there
'the place where (I) gave (something)'

(11d) om-ked hoṛo
give-past man
'the man who gave (something)'

(12a) ol-ked-ra gonong
write-past-gen price
'the price for a piece of past writing'

(12b) ol-ked-i
write-past-3sg
'the one who wrote'

(12c) ol-o-ra hukum
write-passive (future)-gen order
'the order of having (ones name) written'

(13) dal-ko-tan-king
beat-DO (3pl)-present-3du
'the two who beat them now'

Lexical items in Mundari can also retain their case markers like genitive and locative (there are no case markers for core arguments in this language—see below) when they are used as predicates; further, pronouns, demonstratives and spatial adpositions can also occur as predicates in this language. Examples:

(14) oṛa-re-ko-a
house-in-DO (3pl)- cop
'They are in the house'

(15) bir-te-i-jan-a
forest-to-DO (3sg)-ind.past-cop
'He went to the forest'

(16) apan-ked-ko-a-e
self-past-DO (3pl)-cop-subj (3sg)
'He made ('self ed) it his own'

(17) hente-ko-jan-a
there-DO (3pl)-ind.past-cop
'They went that way'

That is, the languages under consideration do not appear to show any special characteristics in their predicate or argument-expressions which are indicative of a temporal distinction between nominal and verbal expressions as seen in the case of familiar languages.

Difference in Relationality

In the case of languages in which nouns and verbs constitute distinct categories, there is a clear-cut ditinction between the two in their relationality; verbs show the characteristics of being inherently relational, whereas nouns show characteristics of being inherently non-relational. For example, the former require one or more arguments (or "complements") to occur with them to complete the sense that they denote, whereas the latter require, prototypically, no such complements; they provide a complete sense (and thereby denote a referent) by themselves. When these latter type of expressions are used in functions for which a relation needs to be specified, as for example, in predication or modification (where the expressions need to be related with a subject or head noun), there would be a need to coerce or construe some kind of relation (see Langacker, 1987; Croft, 1991:69) through the use of an auxiliary or the genitive affix.

Notions like transitve-intransitive, reflexive, reciprocal, passive, etc. are typically verbal notions in these languages because, they invlove the number and relatedness of the arguments that occur with verbs; on the other hand, notions like identity, possession, existence, etc. are typically nominal notions because, they are connected with the referents or participants that the nouns (or noun phrases) introduce.

This relationality distinction between nouns and verbs also results from the fact that nouns have the function of identifying participants whereas verbs have the function of expressing actions or events in which the former have different roles to play. We can assume that the idealized language type under consideration does not show any such relationality distinction between the two corresponding sets of lexical items, on the basis of the eariler assumption that identification of participants is not a function of those sets of lexical items in this language type.

This is true of Mundari and Santali; any given lexical item can take complements (or arguments) without undergoing any change in these languages. There is no basis for differentiating between relational and non-relational lexical items in these languages. Further, in the case of Mundari, Hoffmann (1903:155) points out that one may use any and every root with a transitive or an intransitive function.

There are two different ways in which intransitive and transitive forms of predicates are differentiated from one another in this language: (i) in the case of tense suffixes like *ken, ked* 'past', *len, led* 'anterior past', *tan, jad* 'present' and *akan, akad* 'perfect', the forms ending in *n* are intransitive and the ones ending in *d* are transitive (here, these affixes have been split into tense and transitivity affixes by Osada, 1992); and (ii) markers for direct and indirect objects occur only in the case of transitive predicates and not in that of intransitive predicates. Examples:

(18a) dal-ked-ko-a-e
strike-past-DO (3pl)-cop-subj (3sg)
'He struck them'

(18b) uri-ked-ko-a-e
bullock-past-DO (3pl)-cop-subj (3sg)
'He acquired (some) bullocks'

(19a) lel-akad-ko-a-le
see-perfect-DO (3pl)-cop-subj (1pl)
'We have seen them'

(19b) mahara-akad-ko-a-le
cowherd-perfect-DO (3pl)-cop-subj (1pl)
'We have engaged them as cowherds'

(20a) lel-o-tan-a-ing
see-passive-present-cop-subj (1sg)
'I am visible'

(20b) dura-o-tan-a-ing
dust-passive-present-cop-subj (1sg)
'I am getting covered with dust'

Notice that the two types of structures occur with words which translate as verbs and also the ones which translate as nouns. Expressions occurring as arguments can also show this distinction. Examples:

(21a) ol-ken-te-*á*
write-past-instr-it
'that with which this (letter) was written'

(21b) dal-ked-ko-ni
strike-past-DO (3pl)-he
'the one who struck him'

(22a) ol-*á*
write-it
'that which is written'

(22b) ol-ked-*á*
write-past-it
'that which someone has written'

Related voice distinctions like reflexive and reciprocal can also be used with both types of bases in Mundari. Examples:

(23a) dal 'to strike' dal-en 'to strike oneself'

(23b) dasi 'servant' dasi-n 'to make oneself a servant'

(24a) nel 'to look' ne-p-el 'to look at one another'
(24b) ti 'hand' ti-p-i 'to take one another's hand'

Bodding (1929:177) points out that in Santali, the reciprocal is not principally a verbal formation, but a regular word-formation. In the case of predicates it denotes "reciprocality, doing the same to one another, meeting in performing similar action", whereas in that of words which do not principally function as verbs, the meaning conveyed is that of "a collection, a company, or even a class of such people as are designated by the simple word". He points out that the idea of reciprocality, i.e. meeting or coming together, is apparent in this latter usage; the word gives the result of a collective action of the single base-word. The form is also used, according to him, to denote the place where a collective action occurs.

Santali also has a suffix *n* or *ok'* which can be used to denote intransitivity; it has a passive connotation when used with transitive verbs, and that of 'becoming' when used with adjectives (see Suryakumari, 1991:181). Examples:

(25) ale do sen-e-n-a-le
we subj go-asp-intr-ind-ind-pl
'We went'

(26) uni do kaḍa ţhene rok -e-n-a-e
he subj buffalo by gorge-asp-intr-ind-3sg
'He was gorged by the buffalo'

(27) ponḍ 'white' ponḍ-ok' 'to become white'

In the case of familiar languages, nouns require the addition of a possessive or genitive marker to get related with other lexical items (nouns). Croft (1991:72) points out that such affixes help to construe a relation for nouns, i.e. expressions which are inherently non-relational. However, there is no need to have such suffixes in the case of languages in which words are not divided into relational and non-relational items.

For example, Mundari does not have a general genitive or possessive suffix; it treats most of the possessive relations that are represented by the genitive affix in familiar languages as merely local relations; it uses different locative postpositions for denoting them (Hoffmann, 1903:86). Examples:

(28a) hatu-re-n hoṛo
village-in-that (anim) man
'the man of the village'

(28b) oṛ*á*-ré*á* duar
house-in-it door
'the door of the house'

(29a) samron-r-*á* mundam
gold-in-it ring
'a ring of gold'

(29b) ol-r-*á* gonong
write-in-it price
'the price for an act of writing'

(29c) ol-ked-r-*á* gonong
write-past-in-it price
'the price for a piece of past writing'

(30) paku-tare-n-dasi
Paku-near-that (anim) servant
'Paku's servant'

These locative suffixes can also occur in predicates. There is an additional suffix *á* which is attached to animate words only to denote possession; Hoffmann considers this suffix to be relatable to the suffix *a* 'to' which denotes an indirect object in predicates. Examples:

(31) paku-*á* oṛa
Paku-to house
'Paku's house'

(32) om-a-me-tan-a-ing
give-to-IO (2sg)-pres-cop-subj (1sg)
'I am giving (it) to you'

Differences in Semantic Prototypes

Nouns and verbs differ from one another in familiar languages as they represent distinct semantic prototypes. Nouns denote prototypically a thing or an object, whereas verbs denote prototypically an action or process, i.e. a notion that involves change. We can regard this differntiating characteristic also as deriving from their basic functional difference, namely that nouns have to identify participants whereas verbs have to express actions or events in which the participants are involved in one way or the other.

We may assume that the idealized language type under consideration would not show any semantic prototype distinction of this nature among its lexical items. This point can be exemplified with the help of data from Mundari. Consider, for example, the following predicative uses of Mundari words which translate as prototypical nouns:

(33) sim-ked-ko-a-le
fowl-past-DO (3pl)-cop-subj (1pl)
'We have acquired (some) fowls'

(34) raja-akan-a-e
king-perfect-cop-subj (3sg)
'He is a king (He has been kinged)'

(35) dasi-akan-a-e
servant-perfect-cop-subj (3sg)
'He is a-serving'

The use of the word *sim* 'fowl' as a predicate in (33) appears to resemble the "extended" use of a noun, like *blanket* as a verb (as in *She blanketed the bed*—see 7.2.1) in English, but there are certain important differences between the two. The usage, in the case of English, is restricted to certain specific relations like instrument, location and agent, and the nouns function as covert arguments in addition to being the predicates of the relevant sentences. That is, the relation that the verbalized nouns indicate in these English sentences is highly constrained by the nouns occurring in their extended uses as predicates.

In Mundari, there is apparently no such restriction on the use of these words as predicates; (33), for example, can imply several of the possible connotations, such as that of acquiring or possessing some fowls, existence of fowls in a certain place, killing some fowls for one's meal, calling something or someone a fowl, representing or making someone represent a fowl, and so on (Hoffmann, 1903:112, 1930). That is, these specific connotations are deteremined by the context, and not by the sentence itself. The meaning of the sentence is more general as in the case of other verbal (as against nominal) sentences of English.

Hoffmann (1903:xix) considers Mundari words to be of great functional elasticity, having very vague signifying power. He establishes this elasticity of Mundari words, rather convincingly, in his twelve-volume Mundari Encyclopedia (Hoffmann, 1930), in which almost every word is shown, with copious examples, to be occurring as a substantive, adjective, and also as a transitive and intransitive verb. I find it difficult to see how we can claim, if such is the nature of Mundari words, that they can be arranged "semantically" into nouns, verbs and adjectives; the only basis for such a grouping would be their translation equivalents in languages such as English, and also probably a statistical study of the most frequent uses of lexical items in the relevant sentential positions (see Cook, 1965:109). However, neither of these can form the basis for establishing the relevant "semantic" prototypes distinctions for that language.

Another semantic criteria that can be used for establishing a categorial distinction between nouns and verbs concerns the notion of overlap. Dixon points out that there is very little overlap between nouns and adjectives in Dyirbal, but a great amount of overlap (far more than in English) between verbs and adjectives. There are distinct lexical items of the following type in the latter case:

(36)	jalgi	'to cook'	mundan	'cooked'
	nanda	'to tie'	jagu	'tied'
	munja	'to be hungry'	ngamir	'hungry'

Nouns and adjectives form a single category whereas verbs and adjectives form very distinct categories in Dyirbal, as has been pointed out by Dixon. That is, the occurrence of an overlap between the connotations of lexical items can be regarded as a property of categorially distinct groups of words, and hence, its absence in a given situation can be used as a criterion for postulating categorial identity between two sets of lexical items.

An examination of Mundari dictionary reveals that there is no overlap of connotations between "verbal" and "nominal" bases; instead, there is an extensive "homophony" between the two which, once again, appears to indicate that the distinction is being imposed upon them by the language of translation. The following examples illustrate this point (Hoffmann, 1930):

(37)	buru	'a mountain, to heap up'
	gapa	'tomorrow, to procrastinate'
	haṭing	'a part, to divide'

kumṛu	'a thief, to steal'
kali	'a language, to speak'
lel	'good eyesight, to see'
lutur	'ear, to listen'

The Place of Referential Function

I had suggested earlier that the idealized language type under consideration can be regarded as carrying out the function of identifying the participants with the help of personal affixes occurring in the predicate and not by the arguments or complements which occur separately in the sentence along with the predicate. That is, the personal markers are not to be regarded as agreement markers or anaphoric elements as in familiar languages, but rather as entities that carry out the function of identifying the relevant participants on their own. Such a postulation has been helpful in providing the basis for another assumption namely that the idealized language type does not make any categorial distinction between nouns and verbs. That is, the assumption that nouns do not function as participant introducers in this language type has been helpful in accounting for the absence of any differentiating characteristics which derive from the functional distinction between identifying a participant and expressing action or event among its major lexical categories.

There are also certain additional factors which support this assumption that the function of participant identification is to be assigned to personal affixes that occur in the predicate in this language type. In Mundari, for example, the use of personal markers for denoting the subject, direct object and indirect object is obligatory, whereas the use of independent arguments for denoting the same is non-obligatory. That is, the latter are like other modifiers in the sentence whose presence is required only for providing additional information about the participants which are introduced by personal markers in the predicate.

Another interesting point is that in Mundari there are no "case markers" that can be attached to the arguments themselves for denoting the three major relations mentioned above; nor is there any strict word order distinction among the arguments to represent these distinctions. The distinctions are, instead, indicated by the fact that the subject marker in the predicate occurs after the copula *a* (it may also be shifted to the end of the word which immediately precedes the verb), whereas the object marker occurs before the copula; an indirect object marker can also be differentiated from a direct object marker through the use the affix *a* 'to' before that marker (Hoffmann, 1902:14, 118; Osada, 1991:46). This latter distinction can be exemplified with the help of the following pairs of sentences:

(38a) kul-me-a-e
send-DO (2sg)-cop-subj (3sg)
'He will send you'

(38b) kul-a-me-a-e
send-to-IO (2sg)-cop-subj (3sg)
'He will send (something) to you'

(39a) om-ked-ko-a-ing
give-past-DO (3pl)-cop-subj (1sg)
'I gave them (to someone)'

(39b) om-a-d-ko-a-ing
give--to-past-IO (3pl)-cop-subj (1sg)
'I gave (something) to them'

Another point which supports the above-mentioned claim is that personal markers which occur in the predicate in these languages show a greater number of distinctions than is generally found to occur in other languages. In Mundari, for example, the elements show a threefold person distinction, a threefold number distinction (singular, dual and plural), a twofold inclusive-exclusive distinction in the first person dual and plural, and a twofold animate-inanimate distinction in the third person. Added to this, is the distinction between direct and indirect object markers brought about by the use of the suffix *a* 'to' mentioned above.

Santali allows a possessive suffix *t* to be attached to the object marker occurring in the predicate in order to indicate that the object is one which is in possessive relation with the referent of that marker (Suryakumari, 1991:149). Examples:

(40) hopon-e nel-e-t-iñ-e
son-3sg see-poss-1sg-active
'He will see my son'

(41) oṛak'-ko-e nel-ke-t'-ta-m-a
house-pl-3sg see-past-trans-poss-2sg-indicative
'He saw your house'

(42) seta-e dal-e-t-iñ-a
dog-3sg beat-poss-1sg-indicative
'He will beat my dog'

According to Bodding (1929:166), such possessive suffixes generally indicate a possessed object in the case of active verbs, and possessed subject in the case of medium and passive verbs, and also in the case of active verbs. He refers to the posibility of two different genitive affixes occurring in a single predicate, with the first one referring to the possessed object and the second one to the possessed subject.

Differentiating Characteristics

As mentioned earlier, the postulation of an idealized language type allows us to regard different natural languages as being more or less close to such an idealized language type. There would be no need to find languages that are identical in all respects with the idealized one. That is, the usually raised question as to whether there can be any language that does not make any distinction between nouns and verbs becomes irrelevant. Further, the discovery of additional differentiating characteristics (between nouns and verbs) in any given language would not make it necessary to discard the original assumption; it would only make it necessary to reassign that language to a less closer position. The crucial point here is that the absence of several of the functionally motivated differentiating characteristics between nouns and verbs in the languages under consideration receives an explanation through the postulation of this abstract language type.

As pointed out so far in this paper, Mundari and Santali appear to be quite close to this idealized language type, as they show several of its characterizing properties. However, a closer examination might reveal morphosyntactic properties that can be used to differentiate between verbal and nominal expressions in these languages as well. In the case of Mundari, for example, there are what are called "nominal" sentences that are said to be formed either by juxtaposing two different "nominal" expressions or by using equational copula *tan*.

Hoffmann (1930:xxxviii, 1930) suggests that the latter can occur as a link word only when the predicate is a noun or a personal name. Examples:

(43a) niku hoṛo-ko
these Munda-pl
'These are Mundas'

(43b) niku hoṛo-ko tan-ko
these Munda-pl equative-Subj (3pl)
'These are Mundas'

Hoffmann (1930:6) suggests that this equative copula is related to the verb *ta* 'to remain' and the consonant *n* occurring in it is a contracted form of the reflexive in ('to remain oneself'). It denotes stability in space and permanence in time, and can be contrasted with the copula *a* as in the following examples:

(44a) raja tạn-í
king equative-Subj (3sg)
'He is the king'

(44b) raja-akan-a-e
king-perfect-cop-Subj (3sg)
'He is a king'

It is not clear, however, whether this construction can help us to establish a division of words into nominals and verbals in this language; because, it is quite possible that the notion of being a "nominal" in this case has been based upon the nature of the translation equivalents of the concerned forms.

As pointed out earlier in Mundari, subject and direct object are differentiated from one another by the relative position of personal markers that occur in the predicate and the latter is differentiated from indirect object by the use of a case marker in the predicate itself. I had suggested that this property supports my claim that the relevant participants are introduced by the predicate itself, Osada (1992:46) points out that there has been a recent development in Mundari, namely that of adding the suffix *ke* to the argument concerned for denoting the direct object. He suggests that this is a borrowing from the neighbouring Indo-Aryan languages, notably Sadani.

Bhumij, which is closely related to Mundari, appears to use this suffix more consistently than Mundari for denoting the direct object. According to Ramaswami (1992:78), the suffix is used to differentiate between animate and inanimate direct objects; the former occurs regularly with this suffix, whereas the latter occurs without it. Examples:

(45a) aʔe sadəm-ko-ke aulia
he horse-pl-acc bought
'He bought the horses'

(45b) ako baba-ko irla
they paddy-pl reaped
'They reaped the paddy'

The exact position of other Munda languages concerning this noun-verb distinction is not very clear because, as I have pointed out, the concerned grammarians generally fail to say anything interesting about this topic. Further, their grammars deal primarily with prototypical nouns, verbs, adjectives and adverbs under those headings, and because of this, the type of data that can determine the closeness or otherwise of these languages to the idealized language type that I have postulated here are generally missing in those grammars. There is clearly a need to reexamine these languages from this particular point of view especially because of its typological importance.

REFERENCES

Bhat, D.N.S., 1994. *The Adjectival Category: Criteria for Differentiation and Identification.* Amsterdam: John Benjamins Publishing Company.

Bhattacharya, S., 1975. *Studies in Comparative Munda Linguistics.* Simla: Indian Institute of Advanced Study.

Boas, F., 1911. Chinook. In Boas, F. (ed.). *Handbook of American Indian Languages.* Part I and II. Oosterhoot, N.B., The Netherlands: Anthropological Publications. (559-677).

Bodding, P.O., 1929. *Materials for a Santali Grammar.* Benagaria: Santal Mission Press.

Comrie, B. and Thompson, S.A., 1985. Lexical nominalizations. In Shopen (ed.) Vol. III Grammatical Categories and the Lexicon. Cambridge: Cambridge University Press (349-398).

Cook, W.A., 1965. *A Descriptive Analysis of Mundari.* Unpublished Georgetown University dissertation.

Croft, W., 1991. *Syntactic Categories and Grammatical Relations: The Cognitive Organization of Information.* Chicago: The University of Chicago Press.

Deeney, S.J.J., 1975. *Ho Grammar and Vocabulary.* Chaibasa: Xavier Publications.

Dik, S.C., 1978. *Functional Grammar.* Amsterdam: North Holland.

Dixon, R.M.W. 1982. *Where Have All the Adjectives Gone?* Berlin: Mouton Publishers.

Dixon, R.M.W. Forthcoming. Adjectives. To appear in *The Encyclopedia of Language and Linguistics.* Pergamon Press/Aberdeen University Press.

Du Bois, J.W., 1980. Beyond definiteness: the trace of identity in discourse. In Chafe, W.L. (ed.). *The Pear Stories: Cognitive, Cultural and Linguistic Aspects of Narrative Production.* New Jersey: Ablex publishing Corporation (203:274).

Hébart, Y.M., 1983. Noun and Verb in a Salishan Language. *Kansas Working Papers in Linguistics* 8.2:31-81.

Hoffmann, J., 1903. *Mundari Grammar.* Calcutta: Bengal Secretariat Press.

Hoffmann, F., 1930. *Encyclopedia Mundarica* (in 12 volumes). In collaboration with A. van Emelen. Patna: Government Printing Press.

Hopper, P.L. and S.A. Thompson, 1984. The discourse basis for lexical categories in universal grammar. *Language* 60: 703-752.

Jacobson, W.H.Jr., 1979. Noun and verb in Nootkan. In Erfat, B.S. (ed.). *The Victoria Conference on Northwestern Languages.* Victoria: British Columbia Provincial Museum: 83-153.

Kinkade, M.D., 1983. Salish evidence against the universality of 'noun' and 'verb' *Lingua* 60 (25-40).

Konow, S., 1906. *Linguistic Survey of India,* Vol. IV (Edited by G.A. Grierson). Reprinted by Motilal Banarsidass, Delhi.

Kuipers, A.H., 1968. The categories verb-noun and transitive-intransitive in English and Squamish. *Lingua* 21 (610-626).

Langacker, R.W., 1987. *Foundations of Cognitive Grammar,* Vol. I: *Theoretical Prerequisties.* Stanford: Stanford University Press.

Lyons, J., 1989. Syntactic ascent: a neglected aspect of syntactic typology. In Arnold, D. et al (eds.). *Essays on Grammatical Theory and Universal Grammar.* Oxford: Clarendon Press (153-186).

Osada, T., 1992. *A Reference Grammar of Mundari.* Tokyo: Institute for the Study of Languages and Cultures of Asia and Africa, Tokyo University of Foreign Studies.

Pinnow, H.J., 1966. A comparative study of the verb in the Munda languages. In Zide, N.H. (ed.). *Studies in Comparative Austroasiatic Linguistics.* The Hague: Mouton: 96-193.

Ramaswami, N., 1992. *Bhumij Grammar.* Mysore: Central Institute of Indian Languages.

Sapir, E., 1921. *Language.* New York: Harcourt Brace.

Schachter, P., 1985. Parts-of-speech systems. In Shopen, T. (ed.). *Language Typology and Syntactic Description.* London: Cambridge University Press: 3-61.

Sinha, N.K., 1975. *Mundari Grammar.* Mysore: Central Institute of Indian Languages.

Suryakumari, 1991. *A Descriptive Study of Santali.* Unpublished doctoral dissertation, Central Institute of Indian Languages, Mysore.

Swadesh, M., 1938. Nootka internal syntax. *International Journal of American Linguistics* 9 (77-102).

Thompson, L.C., 1979. Salishan and the Northwest. In Campbell, L. and Mithun, M. (eds.). *The Language of North America: Historical and Comparative Assessment.* Austin: University of Texas Press.

Van Eijk, J.P. and Hess, T., 1986. Noun and verb in Salish. *Lingua* 69 (319-331).

Van Valin, R.D.Jr. 1985. Case marking and the structure of Lakota case. In Nichols, J. and Woodbury, A. (eds.). *Grammar Inside and Outside the Clause.* Cambridge: Cambridge University Press: 363-413.

CHAPTER 15

PRONOMINAL AND NOMINAL INCORPORATION IN GORUM

Arlene R.K. Zide

Introduction

Gorum, an Austroasiatic language of Orissa and Andhra Pradesh, displays a full range of subject (nominative) and object (accusative) pronominal incorporation in the verb. This system apparently reflects the otherwise largely archaic historical situation of Proto-Munda (and possibly Proto-Austroasiatic).

This pronominal incorporation, as a method of agreement, is in addition to (and separate from) a coexistent now-vestigial system of nominal incorporation in verb stems which has correlations with subject- and object-affectedness in the verb morphology.

This paper is primarily intended to present significant sigle-language data and will simply describe the semi-independent systems in some detail. The nominal combining forms of Sora and Gorum have been analysed in detail in an earlier paper.[1] Some attempt will be made to present some cohesive overall picture of the way in which the language effects agreement.

Pronominal Incorporation

Since the verb /taj-/, meaning 'to give', will be used as the focal point in our discussion of the incorporation of pronouns within Gorum verb stems, it is useful to begin with a discussion of certain morphophonemic behaviour patterns which bear on the characterization of the final segment in the root. Morpheme-final / b, d, g / are realized phonetically as glottalized, devoiced [b̥^{1} d̥^{1} g̊^{1}]; in this same position, /j/ is realized phonetically as [y].[2]

At a morpheme boundary, and before a vowel-initiated following morpheme, [b̥^{1}, d̥^{1}, g̊^{1}] become [?b, ?d, ?g], respectively:

$$\text{-}C_i\ \#\ \longrightarrow \left\{ \begin{array}{l} \text{-}C_i\ \#\ C\ \ldots. \\ \text{-}C^{i}_{1}\ (N_i)\ \#\ V \\ \text{-}?\ N_i\ \#\ N \end{array} \right.$$

Similarly, [y^{1}] becomes [?y]:[3]

Hence:

$$\text{-j}\ \longrightarrow \left\{ \begin{array}{l} \text{-y}^{1}\ \#\ C \\ \text{-y}^{1}\ \#\ N \\ \text{-?y}\ \#\ V \end{array} \right.$$

Thus, given a morphophonemic transcription for the root form of the verb, 'to give', {taJ-}, i.e., phonetically [tay^{1}], the infinitive[4] form of the verb, {taJ- u} is [ta?yu] (~ [tay^{1}yu]).[5]

Verbal Classifications

Gorum verbs fall into two major categories (which may be roughly characterized by the designations "transitive" and "intransitive", respectively permitting (or not permitting) pronominal object-incorporation within the verb stem as the ordinary method of indicating more than one participant, rather than e.g., employing elaborate syntactic circumlocution.) There is a further divison into [±affectedness],[6] where there is some reason to associate [+affectedness] with focus or emphasis on the subject NP of a verbal construction, in terms of volition or internal motivation of the subject. While generally, [affectedness] appears to be concomitant with transitivity, we find that certain 'intransitive' verbs, i.e. objectless verb phrases can take either [±affected] affixes and clitics.[7]

All verbs in the language, regardless of their class, have root forms to which are added prefixes (of "actor", causation, and what, for the present may be termed "verbalization" for lack of a better term), and suffixes (of tense, aspect, and Bloomfieldian "goal" and "referent", i.e., accusative and dative object respectively).

The Pronominals

The pronominals in the language take varied forms; there exist free (i.e., unbound) "lexemes" which correspond to "I, you (sg.), he/she/it, we, you (pl.) and they"; however, there is probably reason to consider the increased use of these forms to be a result of contact with Indo-Aryan (and possibly Dravidian) syntax and not indicative of the situation historically:

Singular:	"Actor"	"Non-Actor"
1st person	/miŋ/ 'I'	/eniŋ/ 'me, to me'
2nd person	/maŋ/ 'you'	/enom/ 'you, to you'
3rd person	/nod/ 'he, she, it'	/enod/ 'him, her, it/ to him, to her, to it'
Plural:		
1st person	/bileŋ/ 'we'	/enleŋ/ 'us, to us'
2nd person	/babiŋ/ 'you'	/enbeŋ/ 'you, to you'
3rd person	/nod-gi/[8] 'they'	/enod-gi/ 'them, to them'

What is of interest to us here is the existence as well of presumably historical, incorporated pronominal affixes for both 'subject' and 'object'.[9] There are also a set of possessive suffixes with close ties to the objective pronominals.

Possessive Suffixes:

	Singular	Plural
1st person	/-niŋ/ 'my'	/-leŋ/ 'our'
2nd person	/-nom/ 'your'	/-beŋ/ 'your'
3rd person	/-ḍɔy/ 'his, her, its'	/-ḍɔy-gi/ 'their'[10]

Aside from the unbound pronominal lexeme series of "actor" and "non-actor" which may be designated {P_a and P_n} and the related noun-adjuncts indicating possessor {-Nu}, there are two main series of pronominal affixes to the verb which bear examination. {Obj}:

"Non-Actor" (Object Pronominal), Suffixes:

	Singular	Plural
1st person	/-iŋ/	/-ileŋ/
2nd person	/-om/	/-ibeŋ/
3rd person	/-u/	/-u/

and {Subj-}, the subjective prefixes to the verb of which there are two subclasses, $\{S_1\text{-}\}$ and $\{S_2\}$. $\{S_1\text{-}\}$ is a discontinuous morpheme which is affixed to a primary verb; $\{S_2\text{-}\}$ is a partially discontinuous morpheme which is affixed to a co-occurrent verbal component, {Aux-}.

$S_{i:}$

"Actor" (Subject Pronominal), Prefixes:

	Singular	Plural
1st person	/ne- ... u/	/le- ... u/
2nd person	/mo- ... u/	/be- ... u/
3rd person	/ø- ... u/	/ø- ... ei/

So that, you may contrast the following uses:

/miŋ nega?aru/, i.e.,	{miŋ	ne-	ga?-	r-	u}
'I ate'	$\{P_a\}_i$	$\{S_1\}_i$	√ Vb.	Tense	{Obj}

(agreement between $\{P_a\}_i$ and $\{S_1\}_i$)

agreement

/miŋ nega?aumeru/, i.e.,	{miŋ	ne-	ga?-	u	ne-	r-	u}
'I am eating (it)'	$\{P_a\}_i$	$\{S_1\}_i$	√ Vb.	infin.	$\{S_2\}_i$	Tense	{Obj}

(agreement between $\{P_a\}_i$, $\{S_1\}_i$ and $\{S_2\}_i$)

agreement

/nod-gi taj-u-luromgi1/, i.e.,	{nod-gi	ø-	taj-	u	-lu-	r-	om	-gi}
'they are giving you'	$\{P_a\}_i$	$\{S_1\}_i$	√ Vb.	infin.	$\{S_2\}_i$	Tense	{Obj}	$\{...S_1\}_i$

(agreement between $\{P_a\}_i$, $\{S_1\}_i$, $\{S_2\}_i$ and $\{...S_1\}_i$)

agreement

/miŋ ne-ga?a-tu/ 'I will eat',

/maŋ mo-ga?a-t-iŋ/ 'you will eat me'

/babiŋ bo-ga?a-tu/ 'you (pl.) will eat (it)'

/bileŋ le-ga?a-t-ibeŋ/ 'we shall eat you (plu.)'

/kula-di ga?a-t-iŋ/

'tiger-foc. eat - non-past-me'
'the tiger will eat me'
/taj-t-iŋ/

{ø}-	{taj}	-{t}	-{iŋ}
{S1}-	{√Vb.}	{-Tense}	-{Obj}

'he will give me'
/taj-t-iŋ-gi/

{ø}-	{taj}	-{t}	-{iŋ}	-{gi}
$\{S_1\}_i$-	{√Vb.}	{-Tense}	-{Obj}	-$\{...S_1\}_i$

'they will give me'

/bo-	taj-	u—bo	-r	-iŋ/
$\{S_1\}_i$-	{√Vb.}	-inf.—$\{S_1\}$	-Tense-	{-Obj}

'you (pl.) are giving me'

/ø	-taj	-u—lu	-r	-ei/
$\{S_1\}_i$-	{√Vb.}	-Inf.—$\{S_2\}$	-Tense-	$\{...S_1$ + Obj$\}$

'they are giving him'[11]
/taj- u/ *'he gave him'*, but
/taj- ei/ *'they gave him'*, i.e.,

{ø}-	{taj}-	{u}	-{gi}.
$\{S_1\}_i$-	{√Vb.}	-{Obj}	-$\{S_1\}_i$
/bo-	taj-	u-	ni/[12]
$\{S_1\}_i$-	{√Vb.}	-{Obj}	-$\{S_1\}_i$

'you (pl.) are giving him (or them), you (pl.) keep on giving him (them)'

It needs to be noted that while this system is found throughout Gorum speech, with and without corresponding unbound pronouns, the syntax has been greatly influenced by the syntax of Koṭia Desia, a dialect of the local dominant Indo-Aryan language, Oriya. There is some indication that a good percentage of the traditional Munda vocabulary and perhaps some pronominal subject-incorporation is being lost in the speech of younger generation speakers who generally speak as much Desia as they do Gorum. Cf., the following example of a story as told in the speech of a younger Gorum speaker, where both vocabulary and forms bear the evidence of dominant IA language influence:

Sample text:

/surudusuru	jeljellei suru	jelleinu belke	tilej-di	jellu
[lit. again-again	conversed- they again	conversed- gen. time-at	old man- foc.	say past

suru:	miŋ	uitaj[13]	kuila?a	guni-nen- entur	oŋtai-dontal
again	I	shall go	old woman	girl-this-to	sell-shall-bring- shall
iŋgai	juaī	-entur	taj-tai-du,	ua?atai;	surudu ... /
some	son-in- law	-to	give-shall- completive	come-will;	again- completive...

Afterwards, they conversed and while they talked the old man said: I'll go, old woman and bring this girl to 'sell' to some son-in-law; having given (her to him) he will come; this done.....(then)....

Nominal Combining Forms

This topic has been dealt with in detail in an earlier paper in conjuction with similar, and more elaborate forms in Sora, the sister language of Gorum.[14] As is Gta?, another Koraput Munda language, we find in Sora and Gorum an old set of syntactic-semantic structures, presumably reconstructable for South Munda, which use, in a variety of constructions, combining forms (CFs) or compositional "short forms" of longer full form (FF) nouns, Truncated or otherwise shortened bound morphemes, these CFs are derived from underlying FF nominals. They are frequently attached to verb roots as their object forming complex verb stems which can be inflected for tense, aspect, and so on.[15] Sora preserves these phenomena in a relatively active state; Gorum, however, has not preserved the derivational process to any extent, but we nevertheless find forms which can be shown to have been derived in a similar fashion of some earlier period. The following are examples of such forms:

Sora:

doŋ-gəl 'to shoot forth' (of an ear of corn) < FF gəle 'ear of corn' > CF -gal.

Gorum:

gal-ba?a- 'to tie a turban' (lit. 'tie-head'), < FF bab 'head' > CF -ba?a.

CF. Sora FF bɔ?ɔb > CF -bəb probably < SJG *bɔ?ɔb.

Monosyllabic Cfs of FF nominals compounded with verb roots are exemplified by the following sentences:

Sora:

/kəṛib-ñen mal-jom-j. -mər-te/

2 1 3 5 4

'My sword longs to eat human flesh.'

1 2 3 4 5

Here /-mər/ is the CF of /mənra/ 'man' while /-j. l/ is the CF of /j. lu./ 'meat, flesh'. In the following sentence /- bɔŋ/, the CF of /-bɔŋt. l/ 'buffalo', is used in the same way:

/gəd -bɔŋ -te -ji/

3 4 2 1

'They are cutting (=slaughtering) the buffalo.'[16]

1 2 3 2 4

Gorum sentences which illustrate the incorporation of CFs in verbal forms are:

/miŋ kitun-ḍi-ɛ̃tur ne-soy-jaŋ-uH-ni/

1 2 1 3 4 6

'I am offering rice on a jackfruit leaf to the god.'

1 6 3 6 4 2

/maŋ mo-aH -jiŋ-tu/

1 1 2 2_1 3 4

'you will wash your (own) feet'

1 4 2 2_1 3

'you will wash your feet'

NOTES

1. Zide, Arlene R.K. (1973) Nominal Combining Forms in Sora and Gorum, in Austroasiatic Studies, Part II. *Oceanic Linguistics Special Publications*, No.13, eds., Jenner, Thompson, and Starosta. University Press of Hawaii: Honolulu. 1259-1294.

2. /j/ has a variety of allophones including (dz) and (z) initially and intervocaliy as well, but this is not in contrast to morpheme-final [y'] or [ʔy].
3. (The notation on the right is phonetic.) "/y/" as a separate entity (i.e., phoneme) does not occur; (y) is a member of the phoneme /i/ in complementary distribution with /i/ and /I/.
4. Infinitive morphemes are {-u}, and {ai}, translocative and cislocative resepectively. For a detailed discussion of these forms cf. Zide, A. (1990).
5. "-" indicates morpheme boundary, "~" indicates variation. ***/taʔi-u /** would, however, be an unacceptable transcription since a phonemic contrast between (i) and (y) is undesirable, in view of e.g. the following phonetic pair, **[ji ʔiu]** vs. **[taʔyu]**, the infinite forms, respectively, for **{jiʔ -u}** 'to tie, bind', and **{taj -u}** 'to give', where **/Iʔ/** is realized phonetically as **[iʔi]** with regular "nachklang" of the root vowel.
6. Cf. earlier detailed discussions of this feature in Zide (1972, 1984, 1990.)
7. Those taking the [+affected] affixes connote deliberation or volition, i.e., internal motivation which affects the subject. In the [-affected] forms, the subject is not directly affected by the action, but is considered to be merely a performer.
8. {-gi} is a pluralizing suffix used with certain classes of nouns as well as with pronouns.
9. Generally, dative objects are expressed in full nominal form, not pronominally. There are no examples in my corpus of material which include prefixed pronominal subject, and suffixed accusative as well as dative objects. In case of three-place verbs such as 'to give', e.g. I give it to him, the 'it' is usually expressed in its nominal form, i.e., 'book', 'mango' etc. and not pronominally (e.g. as **/nŏd/** '3p.sg.').
10. These suffixes are added to nouns, not verbs: e.g., **/aHsuŋ-niŋ/** 'my house'; there is also a genitive suffix which attaches to the 'actor' lexemes: thus, **/miŋ-nu aHsuŋ/** 'my house' it is useful to note that geminate consonants, though they do occur, are comparatively rare in the language, especially in the nasals. (Note: H stands for creaky voice, e.g. [v̰] where v is a vowel.)
11. By a morphophonemic rule, the sequence {lu} + {gi} → /ei/, just as sequence {u} + {gi} → /ei/, e.g. {ø-taj-u '*he* gave him', but {ø-taj-e '*they* gave him'.
12. There are a number of aspects which, like **{-ni}** are affixed at the ends of verb stems:
    {-ni} '(present) durative aspect'
    {olku} 'conditional durative, repetitive, (past) durative aspect'
    {-ḍu} 'completive, perfective aspect'
    Tense is **{Past}** = **/-r-/** in the env. **/V$_f$—** or in the env./ʔ—/; **/-ḍr/** in the env./ **Nasals—**, or **/-ø/** in the env. **/C$_f$—** and **/ai-**, or **/-l/** in the env. **/ l—**; or alternately, **{Non-past}** = **/-t-/**.
13. 'go' and 'come', as in most languages is highly irregular.
14. Sora and Gorum are sister languages sopken in various parts of southern Orissa and Andhra Pradesh. Together with Juray they form a subbranch of the Koraput Munda branch of the South Munda family.
15. Also found are complex nominal forms consisting of a series of Cfs or created by the additon of a CF to a FF or by the addition of one or more Cfs to a verb root with an appropriate nominalizing infix. However, these do not concern us here in the discussion of types of agreement.

16. In Sora, subject pronominals are suffixed rather than prefixed as is the case in Gorum.

REFERENCES

Mahapatra, Khageswar, and Norman H. Zide., 1972. Gta? Nominal Combining Forms, *Indian Linguistics,* 33, 3: 179-202.

Ramamurti, Rao Sahib G.V., 1931. "Sora Contracted Forms," excerpted from *A Manual of the Sora (or Savara) Language,* Madras.

Zide, Arlene R. K(irschenbaum), 1963. *Pronomnal Incorporation In Parengi.* University of Pennsylvania. unpub. ms.

Zide, Arlene R.K., 1990. Cislocative, affectiveness, and experiencer subject in Gorum. In *Experiencer Subjects in South Asian Languages,* eds. M.K. Verma and K.P. Mohanan. Menlo Park: The Stanford Linguistics Association.

—, 1984. Who's doing what to whom or is someone always doing something: participant roles and the semantics of causatives. In Proceedings of the Conference on *Participant Roles: South Asia and Adjacent Areas,* ed. by Arlene R.K. Zide, David Magier, and Eric Schiller, 189-210. Bloomington: IU Linguistics Club.

—, 1976 "Nominal combining forms in Sora and Gorum," in *Austroasiatic Studies,* Part II, eds. Philip N. Jenner, L.C. Thompson, and S. Starosta. (Oceanic Linguistics Special Publication No. 13) The University Press of Hawaii, Honolulu.

—, 1972. Transitive and causative in Gorum. *Journal of Linguistics* 8. 201-357.

CHAPTER 16

SORA NOUN INFLECTION[1]

Stanley Starosta

Introduction

This paper is a lexicase description of the inflectional categories of Sora nouns, especially as connected with possession and attribution. It attempts to go beyond Ramamurti's analysis of these forms in the area of accounting for their external syntactic consequences. It is also intended as a contribution to general linguistic theory, in that it provides a formal word-and-paradigm mechanism for describing the internal and external characteristics of a noun-possession system of a type that is found not only in Sora but in such diverse and unrelated languages as Hopi, Hungarian, Yup's ik Eskimo, and Austronesian language such as Palauan.

Sora

The Sora language is a member of the Southern Munda subgroup of the Munda branch of the Austroasiatic language family. It is spoken by about 3,00,000 people in the border districts of Andhra Pradesh and Orissa in India. The first linguistic description of Sora was G.V. Ramamurti's "A manual of the Sora (or Savara) Language", published in 1931. Subsequent work includes "Sora syntax: a generative approach to a Munda language" (Starosta 1967), and more restricted studies of verbs (Biligiri 1965), nominal combining forms (A. Zide 1976), case marking (Starosta 1976), and phonology (Stampe 1963).

The present paper is designed to do for Sora nouns what Bilgiri did for Sora verbs: provide a reasonably detailed and exhaustive description of their classification and inflectional properties. It will review and update previous work by Ramamurti and Starosta, and will discuss some of the theoretical consequences that follow from the attempt to describe the Sora nominal system within the lexicase framework of grammatical description.

Lexicase

Lexicase is a generative but non-transformational grammatical model which was developed at the University of Hawaii, and has been applied in the description of a number of primarily Asian and Pacific languages since 1970. In its current conception (cf. Starosta 1978, 1979a, 1982), it is composed of the following components:

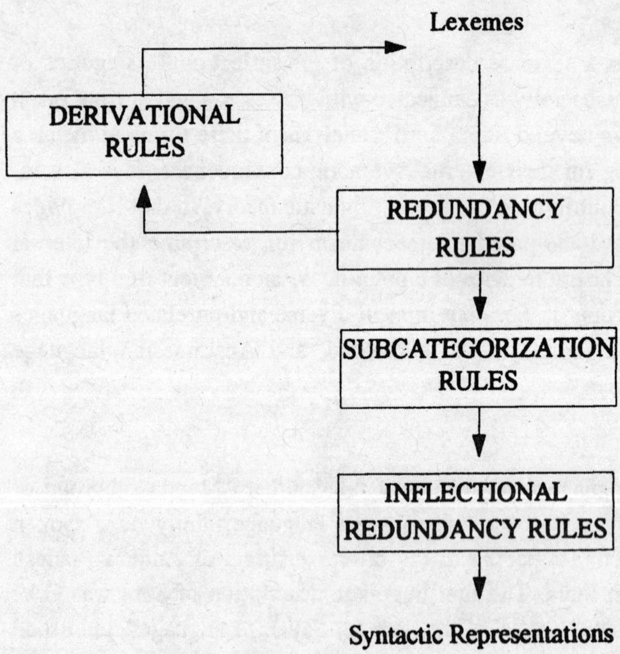

Figure 1. Lexicase Flow Chart.

In the lexicase framework, words are pivotal. Morphology is the study of the internal structure of words, and syntax is an account of the distribution of words in sentences. Grammar is the set of all general statements that can be made about the internal structure and external distribution of words in sentences, and the lexicon is a list of lexemes, words which have been stripped of all aspects of their sound-meaning-form correspondences which can be predicated by general rules.

Redundancy Rules predict one or more features of a lexeme from other features marked on that same lexeme, thus allowing the predictable feature(s) to be omitted from the lexical representations. For example, the feature [+N] ('plus noun') is predictable from the presence of the feature [+prnn] ('plus pronoun'), so pronoun lexemes need not be marked for the feature [+N]; instead, this feature can be supplied prior to lexical insertion by means of a redundancy rule:

1-1. RR-O [+prnn] → [+N]

Subcategorization rules characterize the way the lexicon is partitioned into syntactic and semantic sets, e.g.

1-2.	SR-A	[+anmt]	→	[±humn]
	SR-B	[+N]	→	[±prnn]
	SR-C	[-prnn]	→	[±plrl]

Formally, all subcategorization rules in a lexicase grammar have the same basic form: a class of lexical items characterized by the features on the left side of the rule is composed of two (or a power of two) subcategories. However, two subtypes of SR can be distinguished on the basis of their function: lexical subcategorization rules such as SR-A and SR-B, which characterize lexical classes in terms of features permanently marked on lexical entries, and inflectional subcategorization rules such as SR-C, which generate the set of inflected forms represented by a given lexeme. As an illustration, consider the following lexemes (given in the form in which they would appear after the operation of the redundancy rules):

1-3. house dog woman we

$$\begin{bmatrix}+\text{N}\\ -\text{prnn}\\ -\text{anmt}\end{bmatrix}\quad\begin{bmatrix}+\text{N}\\ -\text{prnn}\\ +\text{anmt}\\ -\text{humn}\end{bmatrix}\quad\begin{bmatrix}+\text{N}\\ -\text{prnn}\\ +\text{anmt}\\ +\text{humn}\end{bmatrix}\quad\begin{bmatrix}+\text{N}\\ +\text{prnn}\\ +\text{plrl}\\ -\text{spkr}\end{bmatrix}$$

Features of animateness, humanness, and (pro-) nominality are permanent and unalterable parts of the lexical specifications of these entities; any change in these features would result in a matrix which belonged to a different word, or possibly to no word at all. On the other hand, SR-C states that the feature of plurality is freely variable for almost all common noun in English; the entry for *house* given above is really an abbreviation for two words, *house* (singular) and *houses,* which jointly constitute the inflectional paradigm of the lexeme *house* in English.

Inflectional redundancy rules add those features of an inflected lexical item which are predictable from its inflectional features, e.g.

1-4. IRR-O [+plrl] → [-[-plrl] ____]

This rule states that a plural constituent head (a noun here) can not follow a singular attribute in the same constituent, thus accounting for the ungrammaticality of collocations such as **this houses.* The rules which make changes in the phonological form of a lexical entry depending on its inflectional features also satisfy the definition of inflectional redundancy rules, although they will be referred to as *'Morphological Rules'* here for the sake of convenience of reference; for example:

1-5. MR-O] → z] / [+plrl]

which can be read as 'add a /z/ suffix at the end of a stem if it is positively marked for the feature of plurality'.

Derivational Rules are the patterns by which a language adds new words to its lexicon based on analogies with words already present. These rules differ from those already presented in that they represent words which are potentially present in the lexicon, rather than those which already constitute part of a speaker's linguistic inventory. Thus

1-6. DR-O $\begin{bmatrix} +\text{Adj} \\ \alpha F_i \end{bmatrix} \rightarrow \begin{bmatrix} +\text{Adv} \\ +\text{manr} \\ \alpha F_i \end{bmatrix}$

$$] \rightarrow \text{ly}]$$

is a derivational rule of English that states that manner adverbs can be formed from adjectives by adding the suffix *ly*. However, the only way we can tell that *freshly* is an English manner adverb but that **stalely* is not (but could be), is by looking in the lexicon and finding that *freshly* is listed there but that *stalely* is not.

So far, nothing has been said about Phrase Structure Rules. This is because a lexicase grammar doesn't need any (cf. Starosta 1979a). Instead, it is sufficient to impose a requirement that contextual features can only refer to heads of sister categories (the 'sisterhead hypothesis'), and add a universal rule to the grammar that no lexical item can have any sisters, e.g.

1.7 IRR-Ω $[\ ] \rightarrow \begin{bmatrix} -\underline{\quad\quad}[+\text{N}] \\ -[+\text{N}]\underline{\quad\quad} \\ -\underline{\quad\quad}[+\text{Det}] \\ -[+\text{Det}]\underline{\quad\quad} \end{bmatrix}$

For a given language, particular subcategories of lexical items will be marked as exceptions to this general 'omega-rule', e.g.

1-8. IRR-A [-prpr] → [+([+Det])___]

that is, common nouns in English as allowed to occur after determiners. The feature [+([+Det])___] blocks the assignment of the feature [-[+Det]___] by IRR-Ω, though this does not affect the assignment of [-___[+Det]], [-[+N]___], etc. The parallels with Natural Phonology (Stampe 1973) should be obvious.

By presenting my analysis of Sora nouns within the lexicase framework outlined above, I hope to accomplish two mutually reinforcing goals:

(1) to elucidate the properties of Sora nouns by placing them within a framework designed to accommodate all and only the characteristics of Natural languages; and

(2) to text the ability of a proposed universal grammatical framework, lexicase, to accommodate and account for some of the properties of a natural language.

Nouns and Noun Phrases

In Starosta 1967, the following Phrase Structure rules were given for Sora Prepostitional Phrases and Noun Phrases:

2-1.

$$\text{Adverb} \rightarrow \text{Adv} \quad \text{(Adv)} \quad \text{(Adv)} \qquad \text{(p. 165)}$$

$$\text{Adv} \rightarrow \left\{ \begin{array}{ll} \text{NP} & \text{Post} \\ \text{(adv} & \text{adv} \end{array} \right\} \qquad \text{(p. 165)}$$

$$\text{NP} \rightarrow \left\{ \begin{array}{ll} \text{S} & \\ \text{(Det)} & \text{N} \end{array} \right\} \quad \text{(Interj)} \qquad \text{(p. 214)}$$

If I were asked to produce PS rules for these same constructions now, given the benefit of some eleven years of hindsight, I would present something more like the following:

2-2.

$$\text{PP} \rightarrow \left\{ \begin{array}{l} \text{S} \\ \text{NP} \end{array} \right\} \text{P}$$

$$\text{NP} \rightarrow \left\{ \begin{array}{l} \text{Det} \\ \text{(NP)}^{n}\,\text{(Adv)} \end{array} \right\} \text{N}$$

The differences are prompted by a number of considerations. The most important is that the major goal of linguistic theory is to construct a universal descriptive framework which maximally constrains the number of lexical categories and syntactic constructions that can be present in a natural language. Any descriptive linguist who is interested in advancing the cause of linguistic theory is thereby placed under the obligation of trying to fit his observations and description into some proposed universal system of categories, and of thoroughly documenting and justifying any deviation from these categories, since any such deviation is in effect a claim that the proposed metatheory is invalid. That is, the burden of proof for any proposed deviation from a descriptive system claiming to be universal is on the deviator.

It now appears that the facts of Sora do not justify the earlier set of within the second system of two rules, rules which with minor differences are the same as those that have been proposed for a number of other languages being treated within the lexicase framework. The adverb category proposed in the earlier set now appears unmotivated, since there is little evidence that a series of two or more non-subject nominal constituents constitutes a single constituent, and since the lexicase requirements on sisterhead subcategorization predict that such a construction should be impossible. *Adv* was originally proposed to account for the fact *NP's, PP's,* and *adv's* could be regarded as interchangeable functional equivalents in terms of their ability to satisfy a verb's selectional requirements. However, lexicase can provide for this equivalence in terms of lexical case relation features, so this motivation is lost. *Adv* was also needed to reflect the fact that degree adverbs modified adverbs which followed them. However, this can be handled instead by independently necessary semantic interpretation rules which account for scope phenomena via surface structure sequential order rather than constituency. Constituent structure defines the domain and the direction of modification, but any further clustering within a constituent depends on sequence, scope, and a principle of semantic assimilation, similar to a principle of phonological assimilation proposed by Greg Lee (personal communication): a word which is not the head of a construction can be modified by another non-head provided that the two words are semantically similar.[2]

The category *Adv* in the Sora Phrase Structure rules above also obscures the fact that Sora, like every other language I am familiar with, has an endocentric construction composed of a Noun Phrase and a member of a closed set of relation-marking words which we can justifiably consider to be members of a single universal category *P* ('preposition' or 'postposition', depending on the language typology).

The earlier set of rules allowed for a sentence *S* to be an attribute of a noun. This was necessary to account for relative clauses and nominalized clausal modifiers of nouns. However, this approach required transformations to derive the correct surface structure. Since lexicase contains no transformations, however, such structures have to be generated directly in the base, and I hope to demonstrate in this paper that this is possible for Sora, at least for the nominalized modifiers. A consequence of allowing nominalized constructions to be generated directly is of course that an Adv node must be provided directly in the NP rule.

No *Interj* or *Adj* slots are provided in the revised rules. The reason is that 'interjections' in this position, e.g. *po* 'question', derivational affixes (cf. section 3.4). Adjectives are not included in the NP rewrite rule above because the Sora counterparts of English noun-adjective combinations are compound nouns (cf. Starosta 1979b). There are a very limited number of what might be called 'predicate adjectives' in Sora, identifiable by the absence of the usual verbal and nominal affixation; however, syntactically they are by definition members of the class of verbs, since they are heads of endocentric sentences (cf. Starosta 1977). In terms of their behaviour in sentential negation and compounding, these words are more similar to nouns than to adjectives are syntactically and morphologically nouns.

Determiners (Det) in Sora include attributive numbers, e.g.

2-3. *bagu mənra* 'two people'
1 2 1 2
aboj kəmbon-ən 'one pig'
1 2 1 2

and articles derived from numbers and demonstrative pronouns, e.g.

2-4. *bɔ kəmbon-ən* 'a pig' cf. abɔj 'one'
1 2 1 2
kun aŋgaj-ən 'the moon' cf. kuni 'that'
1 2 1 2

However, demonstratives modifying nouns occur much much more frequently as pronoun 'possessors' of possessed nouns (see section 4.3), e.g.

kən ə-mənra 'this man'
1 2 3 1 3

Sora Noun Classes

3.1 Major classes

This following rules characterize the major syntactic, semantic, and morphological categories of Sora nouns (cf. Stampe, 1965b):

3-1.	SR-1	[+N]	→	[±prnn]
	SR-2	[+prnn]	→	[±prsn]
	SR-3	[+prsn]	→	[±spkr ±plrl]

SR-4	[-spkr]	→	[±adrs]
SR-5	[-prsn]	→	[±dmns ±ntrg]
SR-6	[+dmns −ntrg]	→	[±prxt]
SR-7	[-dmns]	→	[±bstr]
SR-8	[-bstr]	→	[±anmt]
SR-9	[+bstr]	→	[±lctn]
SR-10	[-prnn]	→	[±nrml]
SR-11	[-nrml]	→	[±dgre]
SR-12	[+dgre]	→	[±ntns]
SR-13	[-dgre]	→	[±ctvt]
SR-14	[+ctvt]	→	[±prps]
SR-15	[+nrml]	→	[±anmt ±prpr]
SR-16	[-prpr]	→	[±dfnt ±dlmt ±nlps]
SR-17	[±dfnt −prpr]	→	[±pssd]
SR-18	[+dfnt −dlmt −nlps]	→	[±plrl]
SR-19	[+pssd]	→	[−[±plrl] −[±spkr]]
SR-20	[- [+spkr]]	→	[- [adrs]]
SR-21	[- [+adrs]]	→	[± [+N] ___]
SR-22	[−pssd +dfnt +NM]	→	[±VC]
SR-23	[-NM]	→	[±L]
SR-24	[+L]	→	[±drcn]

SR-25 $\begin{bmatrix} +\text{N} \\ -\text{drcn} \end{bmatrix} \rightarrow [\pm\text{trmn}]$

SR-26 $\begin{bmatrix} +\text{N} \\ -\text{drcn} \\ +\text{trmn} \end{bmatrix} \rightarrow [\pm\text{ntrr}]$

SR-27 $\begin{bmatrix} +\text{N} \\ +\text{drcn} \end{bmatrix} \rightarrow [\pm\text{goal}]$

SR-28 $\begin{bmatrix} +\text{N} \\ -\text{goal} \end{bmatrix} \rightarrow [\pm\text{sorc}]$

3.2 Pronouns

The following lexical rules are relevant to the subcategorization and description of Sora pronouns (cf. Stampe 1965a):

3-2. SR-1 [+N] → [±prnn]

Sora nouns are divided into two primary classes, pronouns and non-pronouns, on the basis of their syntactic morphological and semantic properties.

3-3. SR-2 [+prnn] → [±prsn] prsn = person

The basic division within the pronouns is between personal pronouns ([+prsn]) and all the rest. Personal pronouns constitute a separate class because they are lexically subcategorized by person but not interrogative, whereas all the rest of the nouns are redundantly third person, and because they act as a single class in terms of the limitations on their ability to occur as attributes in possessed noun constructions (see section 4.3).

3-4. SR-3 $[+\text{prsn}] \rightarrow \begin{bmatrix} \pm\text{plrl} \\ \pm\text{spkr} \end{bmatrix}$ plrl = plural; spkr = speaker

SR-4 [-spkr] → [±adrs] adrs = addressee

Personal pronouns are subcategorized for plurality; personal pronouns are either first person ([+spkr]) or non-first, and non-first person pronouns are either second person ([+adrs]) or third person ([-adrs]):

3-5. SR-5 $[-\text{prsn}] \rightarrow \begin{bmatrix} \pm\text{dmns} \\ \pm\text{ntrg} \end{bmatrix}$

Non-personal pronouns are cross-classified in terms of their membership in the demonstrative or interrogative subsets:

3-6. SR-6 $\begin{bmatrix}+\text{dmns}\\ -\text{ntrg}\end{bmatrix} \rightarrow \pm\text{prxt}$ prxt = proximate

Non-interrogative demonstratives are either proximate *kən, kəni* 'this') or distal *kun, kuni* 'that'). The single interrogative demonstrative is *əyɛŋən* 'which?':

3-7.						
SR-7	[-dmns]	→	[±bstr]	bstr	=	abstract
SR-8	[-bstr]	→	[±anmt]	anmt	=	animate
SR-9	[+bstr]	→	[±lctn]	lctn	=	location

Non-demonstrative pronouns are divided up into abstract and concrete varieties, with each subgroup further divided according to animateness and location respectively:

3-8.

			Interrogative		Declarative	
-dmns	-bstr	+anmt	*bote-n*	'who'	*bote-n-te*	'whoever'
		-anmt	*ete-n*	'what'	*ete-n-te*	'whatever'
	+bstr	+lctn	*oa-n*	'where'	*oa-n-te*	'wherever'
		-lctn	*aŋa-n*	'when'	*aŋa-n-te*	'wherever'

The parallelism in the two sets is the result of a derivation rule which produces indefinite pronouns from interrogatives. Other members of the declarative set, however, are not derived in this way, e.g. *tetne* 'here' and *tette* 'there', which like *kən* and *kun* are distinguished by the feature [±prxt]:

3-9. RR-19 $[+\text{prsn}] \rightarrow \begin{bmatrix}+\text{dfnt}\\ +\text{anmt}\end{bmatrix}$

RR-22 $[+\text{dmns}] \rightarrow [+\text{dfnt}]$

RR-23 $\begin{bmatrix}-\text{dmns}\\ \alpha\text{ntrg}\end{bmatrix} \rightarrow [\alpha\text{dfnt}]$

(For the complete list of redundancy rules, see Appendix A).

Although definiteness is an inflectional category for non-pronouns, it is a permanently specified though non-distinctive lexical feature for pronouns. Personal pronouns and demonstratives are definite (this is presumably universal), and interrogative pronouns are definite, in the sense that the existence of their referents is presupposed and recoverable by the hearer (see section 4.1, Definiteness), while the matching declarative class is indefinite.

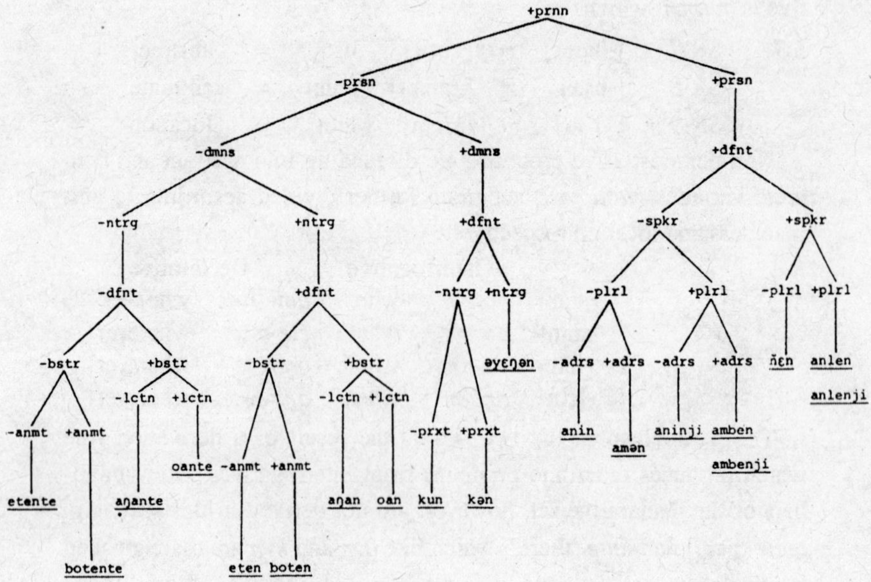

Figure 2. Sora Pronouns.

Non-Pronominal Nouns

3-10. SR-1 [+N] → [±prnn]

As indicated by this rule, Sora nouns are divided into two basic types, pronouns and others. This division is based on differences in syntactic, morphological, and semantic properties. Syntactically, pronouns never take attributes of any kind, and never occur as attributes of other nouns; morphologically, they never occur in compounds in either the head or the attribute position (although there are possessive inflectional affixes on nouns that are etymologically related to pronouns); and semantically, pronouns are subcategorized by features such as proximity and person, which are not relevant to the subcategorization of other Sora noun classes:

3-11.	SR-10	[-prnn]	→	[±nrml]
	SR-11	[-nrml]	→	[±dgre]
	SR-12	[+dgre]	→	[±ntns]

Non-pronouns are divided into 'normal' nouns, those which constitute the bulk of the nominal vocabulary and have the broadest distribution in terms of possible constructions and inflectional categories, and a few other minor classes with more restricted ranges of occurrence. Among the minor classes are the degree nouns, words often translatable by adjectives in English, e.g.

3-12.	əsu-n	'sickness'
	pəlu-n	'white (ness)'

but syntactically close to nouns in their morphological properties (cf. Ramamurti, 1931:24). These nouns normally occur as predicate nominatives, and since in such constructions they are normally indefinite and thus unaffixed, they are difficult to distinguish from true stative verbs such as *suṛa* 'big' or *bəŋsa* 'good'. Both classes are negated by a suffix *-ted* when occurring as predicates, both can be modified by degree adverbs such as *boyboy* 'very', and both form compounds with combining forms of nouns (cf. Starosta, 1979b), e.g.

3-13.	pəlu-mər	'white man' (cf. *mənra-n, -mər* 'man')
	əsu-poŋ	'stomach-ache, pains of childbirth' (cf. *kəmpoŋ, -poŋ* 'stomach').

Compare stative verb formations such as:

suṛa-mər	'big man'
suṛa-poŋ	'big stomach'

Alternatively, it might be better to consider words such as *pəlu* 'white' to be stative verbs in their predicative functions, but derivable as nouns by a rule such as:

3-14. DR-1 $\begin{bmatrix} +V \\ +sttv \\ +dgre \\ \alpha F_i \end{bmatrix} \rightarrow \begin{bmatrix} +N \\ +dgre \\ \alpha F_i \end{bmatrix}$

This rule states that for every stative degree verb ('predicate adjective' in traditional terms) which has an array of semantic features [αF_i], there can be a corresponding (non-stative) degree noun with the same semantic features. One argument against treating *pəlu* and *soṛa* 'big' as being in the same class is that when 'true adjectives' like *soṛa* are derived as nouns, they require an *a-* prefix[3], while *pəlu, əsu* 'sick', *laŋgi* 'beautiful', etc., don't take a special prefix. The final answer to this question will require further investigation.

Both noun and 'adjectives' degree words are subject to the following derivation rule:

3-15. DR-2 $\begin{bmatrix} +dgre \\ -ntns \end{bmatrix} \rightarrow \begin{bmatrix} +dgre \\ +ntns \end{bmatrix}$

] → *dəm*]

This rule states that an intensified degree word of any syntactic class can be derived from a corresponding non-intense word. The second part of the rule states that the resulting form is marked by the addition of a *dəm* affix at the end (]) of the word. The result is the cleavage of non-intense subclasses, with many members of both classes having intense and non-intense forms, e.g.

3-16.	pəlu	'white' [+N]
	pəlu-dəm	'very white' [+N]
	kora	'angry, pugnacious; to be angry' [+V]
	kora-dəm	'cruel, wicked, rude' [+V]

Because of the very close match in grammatical behaviour between the nominal and verbal degree classes, it is likely that speakers are not always consistent in identifying degree words as members of the noun or stative verb classes, and that for most speakers, many of these words are members of both classes. This would help to account for the otherwise unexplained variability in the presence of the definite noun suffix *-(ə)n* with these forms:

3-17.	SR-13	[-dgre]	→	[±ctvt]
	SR-14	[+ctvt]	→	[±prps]

Two further classes of Sora nominals are the action nominalizations [+ctvt, -prps], e.g. *ga-ga-n* [+N] 'eating' (cf. *ga-* [+V] 'eat (semi-liquid food)', *ga-ga-n* [+V] 'eat' (intransitive)) and the purpose nominalizations [+ctvt, +prps, -pssd], e.g. *-paŋ-be* [+N] 'in order for someone (the possessor) to carry' (cf. *paŋ-* [+V] 'carry, take'). Action nominalization also includes perfective nominalizations, e.g.

3-18.	ə?-ti-lɛ-n asən	'because he/she hasn't given'
	ɛr-t-ən-i-ən asən	'because of not having given'

(cf. *ti-* [+V] 'give', *asən* 'because'; *ə?-* and *-lɛ* are verbal negative and perfective inflectional affixes respectively, and negative *ɛr-* occurs only in this class of negative action nominalizations.

Sora

3-19.	RR-18	[-ctvt]	→	[+time]

Time nouns such as *gonta* 'hour' and *dinna* 'day' are morphologically and syntactically distinguishable from other nouns in not having a possessed form, in not allowing syntactic attributes other than determiners, especially numerral determiners such as *bagu* 'two', and in not entering into attribution compounds as either the head or the modifier.

Normal Nouns

3-20.	SR-10	[-prnn]	→	[±nrml]

The ramaining set of Sora nouns may be referred to for convenience as the 'normal' nouns. This set includes all Sora nouns except pronouns, degree, activity, and time nouns:

3-21. SR-15 $[+\text{nrml}] \rightarrow \begin{bmatrix} \pm\text{anmt} \\ \pm\text{prpr} \end{bmatrix}$ anmt = animate
prpr = proper

Normal nouns are subcategorized into animates and inanimates, and cross-classified into proper and common nouns. The animacy distinction in Sora is important grammatically, since verbs do not accept non-nominative ([-NM], i.e. non-subject) animate nouns as heads of sister constitutents:

3-22. IRR-11 $[+\text{V}] \rightarrow \left[\_ \begin{bmatrix} -\text{NM} \\ +\text{anmt} \end{bmatrix} \right]$

This means that animate nouns can appear as non-subjects only when they are dominated by inanimate possessed relator nouns like -*dɔʔɔŋ* 'to; object', or when psuedo-compounded with bound relator nouns such as *-ba-n* 'place' (cf. 4-30; Starosta 1976, 1979b). This preference for animate subjects is referred to by Fillmore as 'saliency' (Fillmore 1977:75). Proper nouns are distinguished from common nouns in not taking the definite *-(ə)n* inflection, in not having possessed or combining forms, and in not allowing any kind of syntactic attribute:

3-23. SR-16 $[-\text{prpr}] \rightarrow \begin{bmatrix} \pm\text{dfnt} \\ \pm\text{dlmt} \\ \pm\text{nlps} \end{bmatrix}$ dfnt = definite
dlmt = delimited
nlps = inalienabldy posessed

Definiteness is discussed in section 4.1. The feature 'delimited' is based on a similar distinction made in Korean (Yang 1972: 59-76; Yang 1973). The members of the [+dlmt] class are all derived from the [-dlmt] class by a rule which adds a suffixed 'particle' such as *-po* 'interrogative' or *-jə* 'some', any' ([+rbtr] 'arbitrary'), e.g.

3-24. DR-3 $\begin{bmatrix} +\text{N} \\ -\text{dlmt} \\ +\text{dfnt} \end{bmatrix} \rightarrow \begin{bmatrix} +\text{N} \\ +\text{dlmt} \\ +\text{ntrg} \\ +\text{dfnt} \end{bmatrix}$ Example: *raʔan-po* 'elephants'

] → *po*]

$$\text{DR-4}\quad \begin{bmatrix}+\text{N}\\ -\text{dlmt}\\ +\text{dfnt}\end{bmatrix} \rightarrow \begin{bmatrix}+\text{N}\\ +\text{dlmt}\\ +\text{rbtr}\\ +\text{dfnt}\end{bmatrix}\qquad \text{Example: } \textit{kekəmər-jə} \text{ ‘some lunatic’}$$

$$]\ \rightarrow\ \textit{jə}]$$

DR-3 is actually more general, and can also be used to derive interrogative finite verbs, thereby making a question out of the clause of which the verb is the head. By RR-30, delimited nouns cannot be subjects:

$$\text{3-25.}\quad \text{RR-30}\quad \begin{Bmatrix}[-\text{dmns}]\\ [+\text{dlmt}]\\ [+\text{P}]\end{Bmatrix} \rightarrow [\text{-NM}]$$

So a clause with a derived interrogative main verb can be interpreted as questioning either the subject or the sentence as a whole by this analysis. *-jə* seems to be connected with the postposition *jənaŋ* ‘also’, even’, and is presumably to be identified with the suffix *-jə* which derives indefinite pronouns such as *bute-jə* ‘someone, anyone’ and *ete-jə* ‘something, anything’ from interrogative pronouns (cf. *bute-n* ‘who?’, *ete-n* ‘what?’). Common nouns may belong to either the class of obligatorily possessed or non-obligatorily possessed nouns. If they are obligatory possessed, then by RR-1 and RR-2 they must be definite:

$$\text{3-26.}\quad \text{RR-1}\quad [+\text{nlps}] \rightarrow [+\text{pssd}]$$

$$\text{RR-2}\quad [+\text{pssd}] \rightarrow \begin{bmatrix}-\text{prpr}\\ +\text{dfnt}\end{bmatrix}$$

Obligatorily possessed nouns have to be possessed by something to which they bear an intrinsic relationship, usually part-whole. Members of this class are either certain kinship terms, e.g. *ə-yəŋ* ‘(his/her/its) mother’, body parts, e.g. *ə-r-ən-eŋ-ən* ‘(its) wing’ (cf. *-rəŋ* ‘wing’ as a combining form), relator nouns, e.g. *ə-luŋ* ‘(its) inside’, or words which can be looked at either way, e.g. *ə-sambi-n* ‘the rectum, the bottom, buttock; at the foot of, at the bottom of, under’:

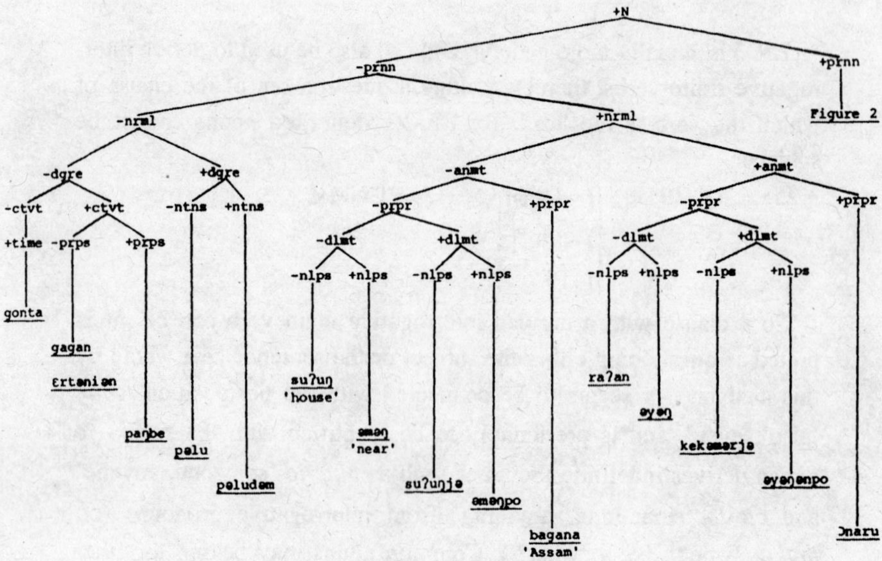

Figure 3. Major Sora Noun Classes

Inflectional Categories

4.1 Definiteness

4-1. RR-19 [+prsn] $\rightarrow \begin{bmatrix} +\text{dfnt} \\ +\text{anmt} \end{bmatrix}$

RR-20 [+prpr] $\rightarrow \begin{bmatrix} +\text{dfnt} \\ -\text{plrl} \end{bmatrix}$

RR-22 [+dmns] $\rightarrow$ [dfnt]

RR-23 $\begin{bmatrix} +\text{dmns} \\ -\alpha\text{ntrg} \end{bmatrix} \rightarrow$ [αdfnt]

SR-16 [-prpr] $\rightarrow \begin{bmatrix} \pm\text{dfnt} \\ \pm\text{dlmt} \\ \pm\text{nlps} \end{bmatrix}$

Sora nouns are inflected for definiteness. For proper nouns, and within the pronoun class, this is a lexical rather than an inflectional subcategorization feature, since every proper noun is by definition definite, and every pronoun entry is permanently specified as [+dfnt] (personal, interrogative, and demonstrative pronouns) or [-dfnt] (indefinites). Degree nouns only occur as predicates, and since these are almost always indefinite. Among activity nouns, purpose nominalizations (Ramamurti's 'infinitives', Ramamurti 1931: 29) are always definite, since they are obligatorily possessed, and possessed nouns in Sora (and in other languages such as English as well) are necessarily definite:

4-2. RR-2 [+pssd] $\rightarrow \begin{bmatrix} -\text{prpr} \\ +\text{dfnt} \end{bmatrix}$

Other activity nominalisations also appear normally in the definite inflected form, though this may be due to situational rather than grammatical factors. Time nouns, on the other hand, don't appear in definite form, at least when realizing the Time case relation:

4-3. MR-6

$$] \rightarrow n] \; / \; \left\{ \begin{bmatrix} +\text{dfnt} \\ -\text{pssd} \\ \left\{ \begin{matrix} -\text{prpr} \\ +\text{ctvt} \end{matrix} \right\} \end{bmatrix} \begin{bmatrix} -[+\text{adrs}] \\ -[\text{N}]\_\_ \end{bmatrix} \right\}$$

The phonological exponent of definiteness in non-proper and activity nouns in the suffix *-n,* realized after consonants as *-ən.* See Appendix B for a list of all the noun-related MR's.

Two examples of a minimal contrast between the presence and absence of *-n* occur in my data:

4-4.

a-soṛa-n	bagu	'two	big	ones'		
1	2	2	1-	-1		
a-soṛa-n	bagu-n	'the	two	big	ones'	
1	2	2-	-2	1-	-1	
kekə-boñaŋ	yɛr-lay	'(My)	crazy	brother	has	come.'
1 2	3 4		1	2	4	3
kekə-boñaŋ-ən	yɛr-lay	'(My)	crazy	brother	has	come.'
1 2	3 4		1	2	4	3

The first two have a syntactic structure indicated by the following dependency diagrams. (Because of the sisterhead hypothesis and the restrictions on possible domanis of subcategorization, the node labels are predictable from the syntactic category of the head of the construction and thus don't need to be marked explicitly.)

4.5.

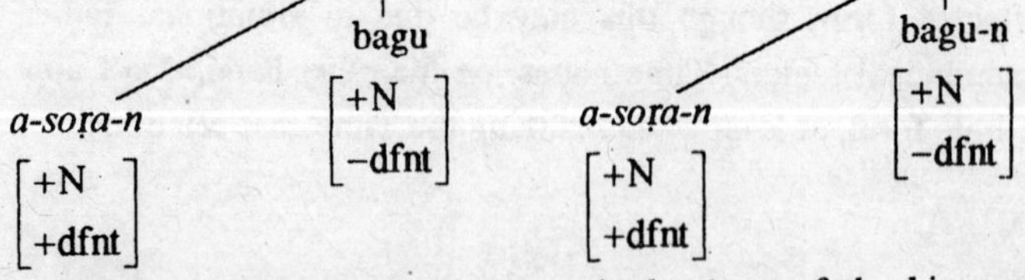

Literal translations would be, respectively, 'two of the big ones' and 'the two of the big ones'.

The difference between the second pair of examples is not as transparent. According to my consultant, the first would be said only to oneself, while the second would be spoken to other people. This may mean that when one is speaking to oneself, there is no need to add a suffix that serves to signal the hearer that the identity of the referent of the noun so marked is shared information. Possibly this represents a Sora counterpart of 'headline style' or telegraphic style in written languages. It could also be that, as in many other languages, kinship terms are used as proper nouns. Certainly, terms such as *boñaŋ* 'younger brother' are very common terms of address. For this reason, *keka-boñaŋ* in the third example might be better glossed as "Crazy Brother."

An interesting and somewhat unexpected fact about the distribution of the definite suffix *-n* is that it occurs on interrogative pronouns, e.g.

4-6.	bote-n	'who?'
	ete-n	'what?'
	oa-n	'where?'
	aŋa-n	'when?'
	ete-n asən	'why?'; literally 'for what?'

It seems strange at first that a word intended to elicit unknown information should be marked to indicate shared information. However, it does not seem quite as strange if we remember that definite marking indicates that the existence and identity of the referent of a noun is shared information which the speaker assumes the hearer can recover from context, and this is of course entirely appropriate in the use of these pronouns. That is, a speaker would not ask:

4-7.	kən-ate ete-n?	'What is this?'
	1 2 3	3 1-2

unless both she and the hearer had a particular entity in mind about which the information was to be supplied.

Accounting for the exact distribution of the *-n* suffix has long been a difficult problem in Sora grammar. As long ago as 1966, David Stampe (personal communication) suggested that *-n* marked definiteness, but the present author was unable to adopt that suggestion because there were too many exceptions and counterexamples.

An alternate hypothesis proposed by Ramamurti (1931: 16) was that *-n* marked the nominative case. However, he found it necessary to list a number of classes of exceptions where *-n* couldn't occur although it should have if it actually did mark the Nominative. His list (my own paraphrase) included the following:

Sora nouns do not have an *-n* suffix:

a) when modified
b) when marked for first or second person possession
c) when occurring as predicate
d) in the vocative case form
e) when occurring as an adjunct in a compound (e.g. *sindi-sal-ən* 'palm wine', where *sindi-* 'palm' cannot be suffixed by *-n*, although it could if occurring independently)
f) when occurring in copulative compounds such as *təmba-tɔgəl* 'day and night'
g) when occurring as the first member of a 'descriptive compound' such as *ɔŋgɛr-sij-ən* 'male child' (cf. *ɔŋgɛr-en* 'the male' and *pəsij-ɛn* 'the child'
h) when followed by certain 'form-words and particles'
i) when they appear (in their Combining Forms) as included objects of verbs

Starosta 1967 was also not able to do more than indicate general tendencies (255-7):

-n is frequently or always omitted

j) in VP's
k) in conventional fixed phrases such as

bɔ dinna	'one day'
bɔ mənra	'one person; by oneself'

1) with certain 'relator nouns' (see sections on possession and compounding), though it is retained with others

I think I am now in a position to do a little better than list exceptions, though the final word is still not in. It now seems that most of the occurrences of *-n* can be explained if we assume Stampe's hypothesis to be essentially correct: *-n* marks definiteness. Ramamurti's and Starosta's observations about the tendency for this suffix to occur on subjects and but not in VP's can then be viewed as a result of the fact that in Sora, as in many other languages, subjects must be definite. That is, in more traditional terms, the subject is old information shared by the speaker and hearer, while the rest of the sentence, the 'predicate' (I use the term here to refer to information structure, not constituent structure) provides new information about the subject, information which may or may not include definite nouns but tends not to.

Ramamurti's observations e), g), and i) are explained by the fact that a noun which is part of a compound is no longer a noun; it is a morpheme which is part of another word which may or may not itself be a noun. The *-n* suffix is attached to nouns, words with their own independent syntactic status, not to their constituent morphemes. Note that this means that the second elements of noun- noun-compounds also have no *-n* suffix. The -n of *sindi-sal-ən* 'palm wine' and *ɔŋgər-sij-ən* 'male child' is a suffix on the word as a whole, not on the second element of the compound as such, which in fact is formally not a noun at all, but an affix (see Starosta 1979b).

The absence of *-n* on non-third person possessed nouns is the result of a historical streamlining process; since a possessive suffix such as *-ñən* 'my' in *su?uŋ-ñən* 'my house' unambiguously marks *su?uŋ* 'house' as possessed and therefore definite, the *-n* suffix would provide no new information. That this suffix did appear on these nouns historically is suggested by a comparison of pronouns and related possessive suffixes and incorporated objects:

4-8.

	Pronoun	Possessor	Incorporated Object
1 sing	ñɛn	- ñɛn	-iñ
2 sing	amən	-nəm	-əm
3 sing	anin	(ə-)	—
1 plur	anlen	-len	-len
2 plur	amben	-ben	-ben
3 plur	aninji	-ji	-ji

The first and second singular possessor forms indicate the presence of an extra *-n* which could be explained as a retention from an earlier stage when possessor suffixes were added to definite nouns already inflected for definiteness. The evolution may have proceeded in something like the following stages:

4-9.

Stage I:	N-n-iñ	N-n-am
Stage II:	N-ñ-iñ	—
Stage III:	N-ñ-ɛñ	N-n-əm

(Stage IV: N-ñɛ-n?)
Stage V: N-ñɛn N-nəm

The new suffux *ñən* then analogically replaced the original independent **iñ*, which is the form retained in incoporated object derivation and reflected in corresponding morphemes in related languages, such as *añ*, *-ñ* 'my' (Juang, Matson 1964) and *-iŋ* 'my' (Mundari, Langendoen 1966), while an *-ən* suffix was added to the original *am*, possibly by analogy with the other *n*- final pronouns and with the final *-n* suffix of definite common nouns.

When a noun has a syntactically independent attribute, it frequently does not have an *-n* suffix (cf. Ramamurti's *a*)). This again appears to be a matter of elimination of redundancy: the attributes are restrictive, and therefore have the function of making the noun's referent identifiable by the hearer, that is, definite. Since the attribute's presence is sufficient to mark the noun as definite, the *-n* suffix is redundant. Although I have incoporated this characteristic of *-n* as an integral part of my grammatical description (cf. the second part of MR-6 and SR-21 in the Possession section), this phenomenon is still subject to variation, and my consultant accepted modified nouns with or without the *-n* suffix. This probably indicates a grammatical change in progress, with some of the dust not yet settled.

Ramamurti's observation c) that predicate nominatives are not marked with *-n* is easily explained in light of the fact that almost all predicate nominatives in Sora and other languages are descriptive rather than referential; that is, in sentences such as:

4-10. anin kristu-mər 'She is a Christian' (-mər = 'person')
1 2 3 1 2-3

the word *kristu-mər* is a description of *anin*, not a noun naming a particular individual whose identity is part of the shared knowledge of the speaker and the hearer. Since it is not part of the shared knowledge, the predicate noun is by definition not definite, and thus will not be assigned a definite suffix by Morphophonemic Rule 7.

The absence of the definite *-n* on vocative nouns (Ramamurti's d)) provides a very convenient means of determining the division between the stem of the noun and its suffix. This fact has provided endless hours of amusement for Sora consultants, who have been called upon to summon by name hordes of snakes, tigers, scorpions, rocks, clouds, mountains, etc., all in the interests of linguistic science. This omission of *-n* seems to be another case of streamlining the noun morphology. If a speaker utters a sentence such as:

4-11. ja?ad! yɛray! 'Snake! Come here!'

(and I have personally heard speakers utter many such sentences in the course of my research on Sora), then the speaker assumes that his addressee can identify the referent of the vocative noun; that is, the vocative noun is definite. Since the syntactic properties of the noun and the intonation it carries identify it as vocative and thus definite, the *-n* suffix becomes potentially expendable. This of course doesn't automatically mean that the suffix *will* be expended, but provides a post hoc explanation of why it *was.*

If vocative nouns are assigned the feature [+adrs] "addressee" (second person), then we can prevent them from taking the definite *-n* suffix by adding the feature [-adrs] to the upper matrix of MR-7, that is, by marking vocatives as second person. This will limit the rule to applying only to third person possessed common nouns. Alternatively, we can say that only proper nouns can be vocative, and that any common noun being used as a vocative (such as *ja?ad* in 4-11) must have been first derived as a proper noun. This is fairly plausible, and would be compatible with consultants' reactions to sentences with vocative common nouns. It wouldn't account, however, for the fact that proper nouns can't be plural (RR-20), whereas vocatives can—unless Sora, like English, allows some marked plural proper nouns, e.g. the Packers, the Maple Leafs, and the Lions, which can be used as vocatives.

The 'form-words and particles' listed in Ramamurti's observation h) constitute a mixed bag. 'Particles' such as *-jə* and *-po* have been analyzed in my paper (section 3.4) as suffixes that mark the derivation of indefinite (arbitrary and interrogative respectively) nouns. Since the output of the *-jə* and *-po* derivation rules are lexically indefinite, they will of course never be marked with a definite inflectional suffix. Similarly, 'particles' marking contrary-to-fact conditionals would not be expected to occur on definite nouns, since it would be contradictory for a speaker to mark a noun's referent as simultaneously shared knowledge and non-existent.

Derivation also accounts for some observations under f) and k). The reduction of the determiner *aboj* 'one' to *bɔ* in fixed expressions such as *bɔ mənra* 'one person; by oneself' and the use of such expressions as syntactic equivalents of underived adverbs suggests that these are derived single-word adverbs, which means of course that they cannot carry noun inflections. The same explanation probably applies to 'copulative compounds' such as *təmba-tɔgəl* 'day and night'; this form has the distribution of an adverb rather than a noun, and so should not be expected to be inflected as a noun.

The list under h) includes some but not all 'relator nouns'. As noted under l), individual relator nouns differ in this respect. In section 4.3 and in Starosta 1979b, I attempt to show how this can be accounted for by grouping relator nouns into sets; one set are really noun Combining Forms, affixes appearing only in pseudo-compounds. Their partners in these compounds are thus not independent nouns, and therefore can't carry their own inflections. The relator nouns listed by Ramamurti, such as *-ba-n* 'place of' and *leŋ (-ən)* 'inside of', are members of this class. Other relator nouns, such as *məŋ* 'vicinity of', are syntactically independent nouns allowing definite inflected nominal attributes.

One of the defining characteristics of inflection is that each inflectional choice within a syntactic category has its own external syntactic consequences. The syntactic correlates of definiteness in Sora are specified by the following rules:

4-12. SR-17 $\begin{bmatrix} +\text{dfnt} \\ -\text{prpr} \end{bmatrix} \rightarrow [\pm\text{pssd}]$

IRR-4 $\begin{Bmatrix} [-\text{pssd}] \\ [-\text{dfnt}] \end{Bmatrix} \rightarrow [+([+\text{Det}])\underline{\quad}]$

IRR-5 $\begin{bmatrix} +\text{N} \\ -\alpha\text{dfnt} \end{bmatrix} \rightarrow \begin{bmatrix} \begin{bmatrix} +\text{Det} \\ -\alpha\text{dfnt} \end{bmatrix} \\ - \end{bmatrix}$

$$\text{IRR-}\Omega \qquad [+\text{N}] \qquad \rightarrow \qquad \begin{bmatrix} -[+\text{N}] \\ -[+\text{Det}] \\ -[+\text{V}] \\ -[+\text{Adv}] \\ -[+\text{AGT}] \\ -[+\text{PAT}] \\ -[+\text{INS}] \\ -[+\text{LOC}] \\ -[+\text{COR}] \\ -[+\text{PLC}] \\ -[+\text{REF}] \\ -[+\text{RSN}] \\ -[+\text{MAN}] \end{bmatrix}$$

The full list of IRR's is given as Appendix C.

Non-possessed common nouns and indefinite nouns are allowed to with a determiner to the left of the noun (IRR-4). By itself, this rule doesn't mean much. It allows correct combinations, but doesn't exclude bad ones. Its real significance becomes apparent, however, when considered together with IRR-Ω, the 'Omega-rule'. This rule states, very simply, that nothing can co-occur with anything. Each of the features introduced by this rule can be considered an abbreviation for two rules, e.g.

4-13. [- [+N]]

is equivalent to the two features.

4-14. $$\begin{bmatrix} - \underline{\qquad} [+\text{N}] \\ -[+\text{N}] \underline{\qquad} \end{bmatrix}$$

and marking, say, a verb with the feature [+([+N])____] indicates that the verb is an exception to part of the Omega-rule in allowing a left sister constituent whose head is a noun. As in natural phonology, the assumption I make here is that a child starting to learn his first language starts off with nothing but a universal Omega-rule, an assumption that only one-word utterances are possible. Then, after sufficient exposure to the language around him, he begins to learn the exceptions to this rule that constitute the syntax of his language.

In the case of a child learning Sora, among the things he must learn is the rule IRR-4; determiners may occur before definite common nouns if they are not possessed, but (by the Omega-rule) may not occur as sisters of any other category. In performance terms, these rules can be thought of as Phrase-marker construction instructions: a word from the category-marked by [+Det] may be associated with a noun as its left sister attribute if the noun satisfies certain requirements. IRR-5 states the agreement relation obtaining between a noun and any Determiner attributes: a Det occurring as the sister of a noun cannot disagree with it in definiteness.

4.2 Number

4-15.

$$\text{RR-20} \quad [+\text{prpr}] \rightarrow \begin{bmatrix} +\text{dfnt} \\ -\text{plrl} \end{bmatrix}$$

$$\text{RR-21} \quad [-\text{nrml}] \rightarrow [-\text{plrl}]$$

$$\text{SR-18} \quad \begin{bmatrix} +\text{dfnt} \\ -\text{dlmt} \\ -\text{nlps} \end{bmatrix} \rightarrow [\pm\text{plrl}]$$

$$\text{IRR-9} \quad [-\text{dfnt}] \rightarrow [-\text{plrl}]$$

$$\text{IRR-10} \quad \begin{bmatrix} +\text{N} \\ \alpha\text{plrl} \end{bmatrix} \rightarrow \left[\_ \begin{bmatrix} +\text{Det} \\ -\alpha\text{plrl} \end{bmatrix} \right]$$

$$\text{MR-7} \quad] \rightarrow \textit{ji} \ / \ \left\{ \begin{matrix} \begin{bmatrix} +\text{plrl} \\ -\text{spkr} \\ -\text{adrs} \end{bmatrix} \\ \begin{bmatrix} +\text{VC} \\ +\text{plrl} \end{bmatrix} \\ \begin{bmatrix} -[+\text{adrs}] \\ -[-\text{plrl}] \\ -\text{plrl} \end{bmatrix} \end{matrix} \right\}$$

All Sora nouns are grammatically either singular or plural. Words such as *bagu-len* 'we two' and *bagu-ben* 'you two' (cf. *bagu* 'two', *an-len* 'we' and *amben* 'you (plural)') might appear to be dual, but grammatically they are identical to their corresponding pronominal sources, and should be considered derived pronouns.

For pronouns, plurality is a lexical feature: every pronoun is permanently marked as plus or minus plural, and pairs of pronouns such as *nən* 'I' and *anlen* 'we' which differ semantically only in the feature of plurality are unrelated morphologically. For non-normal, indefinite, and proper nouns ([-nrml], [-dfnt], and [+prpr]), the feature [-plrl] is added by RR-20, RR-21, and IRR-9; this feature varies freely for all other nouns, that is, undelimited definite nouns. All nouns must agree in number with determiners in the same constituent if any (IRR-10).

The feature of plurality is realized by a suffix *-ji* on all nouns which are either a) third person plural unpossessed, b) vocative plural, or c) marked for third person plural possession (MR-9):

4.3 Possession

4-16. SR-17 $\begin{bmatrix} \text{+dfnt} \\ \text{−prpr} \end{bmatrix} \rightarrow$ [±pssd]

Definite common nouns are either possessed or unpossessed. Indefinite nouns are not marked for possession. In Sora as in English, possession implies definiteness, that is, both *su?uŋ-ñən* and its English translation, 'my house', refer to an entity whose referent is part of the knowledge shared by the speaker and the hearer. 'Possession' as it is used in this paper is not meant in the limited sense of legal ownership or physical proximity and control over an object. Rather, it refers to a grammatically marked relation between a noun phrase and the noun it modifies. The relation may be one of kinship, part to whole, patient to activity, or any other kind of correspondence a speaker wants to indicate between a head noun and its nominal modifier in order to aid in the identification of the referent of the head noun.

In Sora, as in many other languages such as Hungarian (Mel'chuk 1972), Yup'ik Eskimo (Reed et al 1977), and Palauan (Josephs 1975), possession is marked morphologically by pronoun-like markers on the head noun, rather than on the attribute as it is in English. A possessive affix on a noun indicates that the range of reference of the noun is restricted by the implied modifier, but the implied modifier itself need not be overtly present in the noun phrase.

It seemss likely that the present Sora system is a streamlined version of an earlier system in which pronominal attributes were syntactically indistinguishable from non-pronominal ones. This is reflected in the ability of third person pronouns in related languages such as Juang and Mundari to take non-third pronouns as syntactic attributes, e.g.

4-17.	añ-a-iña	'my mother'	(Juang, Matson 1964)
	1 2 3	1 3	
	a-ben aq oḍaq	'your (plural) house'	(Mundari
	1 2 3	1 3	Lagendoen 1966)

cf. Sora

4-18.	yəŋ-ñɛn	'my mother'	cf. *ñɛn a-yəŋ
	1 2	2 1	
	su?uŋ-ben	'your (plural) house'	cf. *amben a-
	1 2	2 1	u?uŋ

In a subsequent stage, nouns began to lose this ability. This probably began with kinship terms, the only class of Mundari nouns restricted in this way, e.g.

4-19. apu-iŋ 'my father' (Langendoen, op. cit.)

and spread in Sora to include the rest of the possessed nouns.

4-20. SR-19 [+pssd] $\rightarrow \begin{bmatrix} -[\pm\text{plrl}] \\ -[\pm\text{spkr}] \end{bmatrix}$ plrl = 'plural', spkr = 'speaker'

SR-20 [– [+spkr]] → [– [±adrs]] adrs = 'addressee'

Since possessed nouns imply but do not require the presence of a 'possessor', agreement features introduced in SR-19 and SR-20 are stated negatively. That is, [– [–plrl]] can be read as 'implies a plural possessor', since if a possessor does appear overtly, it cannot be marked as singular. Similarly, [– [+plrl]] implies a singular possessor, [– [–spkr]] a first-person possessor, and [– [+spkr]] a non-first person one. If the implied possessor is not first person, it is either second person [– [–adrs]] or third person [– [+adrs]].

4-21. MR-1] → *ñɛn*] / $\begin{bmatrix} -[-\text{spkr}] \\ -[+\text{plrl}] \end{bmatrix}$ (first person singular)

MR-2] → *nəm*] / $\begin{bmatrix} -[-\text{adrs}] \\ -[+\text{plrl}] \end{bmatrix}$ (second person singular)

MR-3] → *len*] / $\begin{bmatrix} -[-\text{spkr}] \\ -[-\text{plrl}] \end{bmatrix}$ (first person singular)

$$\text{MR-4}\quad] \rightarrow \textit{ben}] \;/\; \begin{bmatrix} -[-\text{adrs}] \\ -[-\text{plrl}] \end{bmatrix} \quad \text{(second person singular)}$$

$$\text{MR-5}\quad [\rightarrow [\text{ə} \;/\; \begin{bmatrix} +\text{pssd} \\ -[+\text{adrs}] \end{bmatrix} \quad \text{(third person)}$$

4-22.

$$\text{MR-7}\quad] \rightarrow \textit{ji}] \;/\; \left\{ \begin{matrix} \begin{bmatrix} +\text{plrl} \\ -\text{spkr} \\ -\text{adrs} \end{bmatrix} \\ \begin{bmatrix} +\text{VC} \\ +\text{plrl} \end{bmatrix} \\ \begin{bmatrix} -[+\text{adrs}] \\ -[-\text{plrl}] \\ -\text{plrl} \end{bmatrix} \end{matrix} \right\}$$

Non-third person possessors are marked by a single pronoun-related suffix for each person-number combination. Third person possession is marked by a prefix *ə-* in singular and plural, with an additional *-ji* suffix added in the case of a plural possessor. It should be noted that there are a number of *ə-* prefixes operating in Sora word formation, and that so far, not all of them can be identified with the third person possession marker, though many of them can. Note also that unlike previous treatments of noun phrase structure by Ramamurti 1931 and Starosta 1967, the possesive ə is treated here as a prefix on the following noun instead of as an attribute marker on the previous attribute. This change in the analysis is due to the fact that the ə remains even when no overt possessor is present, and a lexicase grammar provides no means for positing an underlying possessor which gets deleted on the way to the surface. It is also motivated by the fact that the ə prefix is paradigmatically related to first and second person possessor markers, which are clearly suffixes, and because this brings the Sora noun possession system into line with the widely attested systems of unrelated languages such as Hungarian, Eskimo, and most if not all Austronesian languages.

As can be seen from MR-7, the suffix *-ji* is ambiguous. For the first two environments listed, it marks plurality of the head noun, that is, a situation in which the referent of the head noun itself is viewed as composed of more than one element, e.g.

4-23.	pəsij-	ən-	ji	yɛr-	lay-	ji	'The	children	came.'
	1	2	3	4	5	6	2	1-3	4-5-6

	jaba,	geriŋ-	ji	'Come	on,	friends!'
	1	2	3	1-	-1	2-3

For the third environment, however, *-ji,* marks possession by a third person plural noun, irrespective of the inherent number of the possessed noun itself, e.g.

4-24. ə-su?uŋ-ən-ji 'their house'

Given this situation, we might except that a) example 4-24 above should be ambiguous, since it would also look this way if it meant 'his houses', and b) that a plural noun with a third person plural possessor should have two *-ji* suffixes. In this respect, our first expectation would be satisfied but the second would not: Sora does not allow two *-ji*'s on the same noun. Instead, only one appears, and example 4-24 is thus actually three ways ambiguous, the third reading being 'their houses'. This fact is incorporated into the grammar by rather arbitrarily cutting up the pie so that *-ji* marks a plural possessor only on nouns with singular reference, and all other *-ji's* mark plurality of reference regardless of the possessed status of the affixed noun. Thus in example 4-24, if the suffix *-ji* is introduced in the first environment, the word could mean 'his house' or 'their houses', whereas a *-ji* introduced in the third environment would reflect a meaning of 'their house':

4-25. SR-21 [- [+adrs]] → [± [+N] ___]

SR-22 states that third person possessed nouns either must take an attribute or cannot take one. An alternative formulation would be to simply introduce the feature [+([+N]) ___] in IRR-3, making attributes optional for third person possessed nouns. However, it turns out that the presence or absence of an attribute has morphological consequences:

$$\text{4-26.}\quad \text{MR-6}\quad] \rightarrow \text{n}] \;/\; \left\{ \begin{matrix} \begin{bmatrix} +\text{dfnt} \\ -\text{pssd} \\ \left\{\begin{matrix} -\text{prpr} \\ +\text{ctvt} \end{matrix}\right\} \end{bmatrix} \\ \begin{bmatrix} -[+\text{adrs}] \\ -[+\text{N}]\ \underline{\qquad} \end{bmatrix} \end{matrix} \right\}$$

As indicated by the second part of this rule, the definite suffix *-n* is added to third person possessed nouns with no overt syntactic attribute, but not to those that have one:

4-27. əsuʔuŋ-ən soṛa 'Her house is big'
1 2 3 — 1 2 3

ə-məŋ-ən dəko It's near him (in his vicinity)
1 2 3 — 3- -3 1 2

ənsɛlɔ-n ə-məŋ dəko It's near the woman (in the woman's vicinity)
1 2 3 4 — 4- -4 1 2 3

This may be a case where it is necessary to recognize unconditioned variation in Sora, since at least in some sentence, the *-n* suffix is optional when an overt attribute is present, e.g.

4-28. eten ə-j-ən-omjom (ən) ñaŋtɛji (1, 210.10)
1 2 3 4
'What food do they get?'
1 3 4- -4

This can't be a matter of a contrast between definite and indefinite according to the present analysis, since it is claimed here that possessed nouns are definite, and since *əjənomjom* is marked as a possessed nominalization (cf. *jom-* 'eat'). If this is in fact a case of free variation, a lexicase analysis will reflect this by essentially positing two different grammars for Sora, one containing the second part of MR-7 and one without it. In choosing to recognize this as a regular exception to *-n* suffixation or to ignore it, speakers are choosing between these two grammars. The choice probably depends on the formality of the situation, who the speaker talked to last, etc., but this would be a matter of usage, and not something the grammar per se need concern itself with.

For the alternative grammar in which *-n* is excluded by the presence of an overt syntactic attribute, the feature [– [+N]____] is required to condition the rule of *-n* suffixation. Its positive counterpart, [+ [+N]____], is also needed, as a lexical exception marker on the animate oblique third person possessed relator noun dɔʔɔŋ 'to; object'. This word, unlike other syntactically independent relator nouns such as məŋ, can't occur without an overt syntactic attribute:

4-29. *ə-dɔʔɔŋ-ən gij-lɛ 'He saw her (body)'

1 2 3 3- -3 1 2

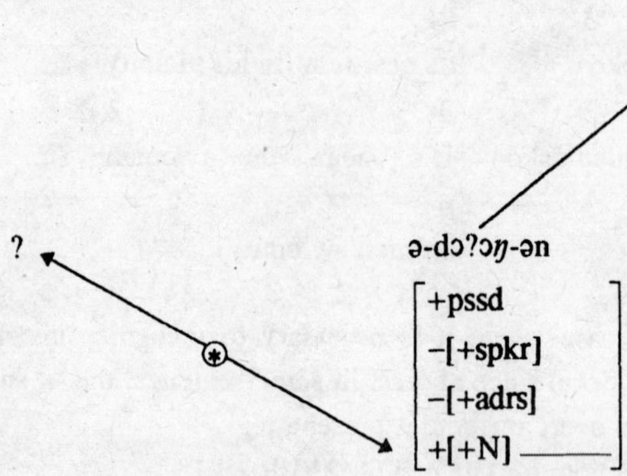

4-30. ənsɛlɔ-n ə-dɔʔɔŋ gij-lɛ 'He saw the woman ('s body)'

1 2 3 4 4- -4 1 2 3

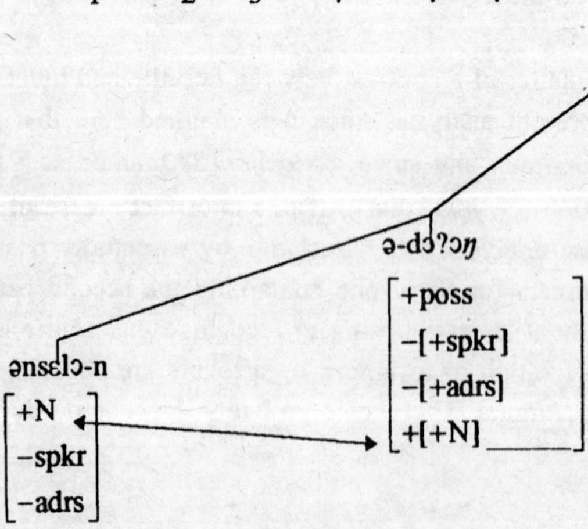

4-31. IRR-3 $\begin{bmatrix} \text{+pssd} \\ \text{–[+adrs]} \\ \text{–[+spkr]} \\ \text{–[+plrl]} \end{bmatrix} \rightarrow$ [+ ([+COR])]

IRR-Ω (see 4-12)

The feature [+ ([+COR])] assigned by IRR-3 states the case relation of nominal attributes in Sora: all nominal attribute 'possessors' bear the Correspondent Case relation to their head nouns. 'Correspondent' is simply the relation of association (cf. Starosta 1978: 498-500), found in verbal sentences such as the following:

4-32. Stan has a long history of lexicosis.
[+COR] [+PAT]
Morris ascribed the hypothesis to Busky.
[+AGT] [+PAT] [+COR]

Since all nouns will be marked with some case relation, and since the Omega-rule plus IRR-3 state that no case relation other than Correspondent can cooccur with a noun, IRR-3 has the effect of marking all possessed nouns as implying a Correspondent attribute.

4-33. RR-17 [+ctvt] $\rightarrow \begin{bmatrix} \text{–plrl} \\ \text{+pssd} \\ \text{–[+adrs]} \\ \text{– + plrl]} \\ \text{–[+spkr]} \\ \text{+([+N] [+N]) \_\_\_\_} \end{bmatrix}$

IRR-9 [+ [+N] ____] $\rightarrow \begin{bmatrix} \text{– [+N] [+N] \_\_\_\_} \\ \text{–} \begin{bmatrix} \text{+prnn} \\ \text{+prsn} \end{bmatrix} \text{\_\_\_\_} \end{bmatrix}$

The first of the two features [– [+N] [+N] ____] and [– [+prnn, +prsn] ____] in IRR-9 states that a possessed noun with an overt possessor cannot have more than one syntactic attribute. The feature [– [+prnn, +prsn] ____] excludes personal pronouns from being syntactic attributes of nouns. This necessarily refers to third person pronouns, since 1) the Omega-rule prevents nouns in general from cooccurring with any nominal attributes at all, 2) SR-21 optionally marks third person possessed nouns as exceptions to this general prohibition, and 3) the feature [– [+adrs]] and the feature [– [+spkr]] implied by it would prevent first [– [+adrs]] and the feature [– [+spkr]] implied by it would prevent first and second person pronouns from occurring as attributes of third person possessed nouns. Again, *dɔʔɔŋ* is a lexical exception to this feature:

4-34.	*anin ə-pəsij	'his child'
4-35.	ə-pəsij-ən	'his child'
4-36.	anin ə-dɔʔɔŋ	'(to) him'
4-37.	*ə-dɔʔɔŋ-ən	'(to) him'

Nominalizations ([+ctvt]) are an exception to the feature [– [+N] [+N] ____]. The range of attributes that occur with a nominalized word is controlled by the contextual features of the source verb, which carry over onto the noun in derivation. Both purpose ([+prps], suffixed by *-be-*) and non-purpose nominalizations are obligatorily possessed, with implied possessors corresponding to the grammatical subjects of the corresponding verbs. This characteristic of Sora nominalized constructions is parallelled in other languages, including Korean, Japanese, Manchu, and English, e.g.

4-38. (John's) kicking his grand-aunt down the cellar stairs
John kicked his grand-aunt down the cellar stairs.

It may be the case that nominalizations can't be marked by non-third person possessive suffixes, but this needs to be checked out with a native speaker.

As mentioned above, 'possession' as used in this section refers to any kind of restrictive noun attribution, not just to legal or local possession. Thus the modifiers signalled by the third person possessive marker ə- are not limited to animate nouns. In fact, the most common modifiers seem to be demonstrative and interrogative or indefinite pronouns, e.g.

4-39.	kən ə-mənra	'this man'
	ete-n ə-bara-n	'what work?'
	ete-n-te ə-bara-n	'whatever work?'

Corresponding to the demonstrative pronouns *kən, kəni, kun,* and *kuni* are the definite determiners *kən* 'this' *kun* 'the, that'. These are obviously derived from the corresponding demonstrative pronouns. They can be distinguished from their pronoun counterparts, however, by the fact that 1) they don't occur with the possessed form of the noun, and that 2) the *i-* final forms don't appear in this construction, e.g.

4-40.	kun aŋgaj-ən	'that moon'
	*kuni aŋgaj-ən	'that moon'

The derivation of determiners from demonstratives is of course very common in languages, with English *the* and Mandarin Chinese *.neige* being well-known examples.

In this paper, I have tried to describe the classification and inflection of Sora nouns in a compact and hopefully insightful way, stating the analysis in explicit rules and finding no need to resort to powerful mechanisms such as transformations. The approach seems to be potentially capable of being applied to other languages of various typological classes as well. If so, the paper represents a potential contribution to universal linguistic theory as well as, hopefully, our knowledge of Munda grammar.

NOTES

1. The final version of this paper was written under a fellowship from the Alexander von Humboldt Foundation, while I was a guest researcher at the Institut für deutsche Sprache in Mannheim, Germany.
2. A similar principle of semantic similarity was proposed by Steinberg (1970: 50) to account for the fact that a high degree of semantic similarity is necessary before two words can be perceived as opposites.
3. In Khmer, the prefix *qaa-*[ʔa:] corresponds almost exactly to this prefix; "It has a pronominalizing function before adjectival verbs or adjectives" (Huffman 1970: 314), e.g.

touc	'small'
qaa-touc	'the small one (s)'

REFERENCES

Abraham, Werner (ed.), 1978. Valence, semantic case and grammatical relations, *Studies in Language*. Companion Series, Volume 1, Amsterdam: John Benjamins.

Biligiri, H.S., 1965. The Sora verb, a restricted study. In G.B. Miner and Eugénie J.A. Henderson (eds.), 231-50.

Cole, Peter and Jerrold M. Sadock (eds.), 1977. Grammatical Relations. *Syntax and Semantics*, Volume 8, New York: Academic Press.

Fillmore, Charles J., 1977. The case for case reopened. In Peter Cole and Jerrold M. Sadock (eds.), 59-82.

Huffman, Franklin E., 1970. *Modern Spoken Cambodian*. Yale Linguistic Series, New Haven: Yale University Press.

Jenner, Philip, Laurence C. Thompson and Stanley Starosta (eds.), 1976. Austroasiatic studies. *Oceanic Linguistics*, Special Publication No. 13, Parts I and II. Honolulu: University Press of Hawaii.

Josephs, Lewis S., 1975. *Palauan Reference Grammar*. Pali Language Texts: Micronesia. Honolulu: University Press of Hawaii.

Kiefer, Ferenc and Nicolas Ruwet (eds.), 1972. *Generative Grammar in Europe*. Dordrecht: D. Reidel.

Langendoen, D. Terence, 1967. The copula in Mundari. *The Verb 'be' and Its Synonyms*, Volume 1, ed. by John W.M. Verhaar, 75-100. (Foundations of language supplementary series 1: philosophical and grammatical studies.) Dordrecht: D. Reidel.

Matson, Dan M., 1964. *A Grammatical Sketch of Juang, a Munda Language*. Ph.D. dissertation, University of Wisconsin at Madison.

Mel'čuk, I.A., 1972. On the possessive forms of the Hungarian noun. In Ferenc Kiefer and Nicolas Ruwet (eds.), 315-32.

Milner, G.B. and Eugénie J.A. Henderson, 1965. *Indo-Pacific Linguistic Studies*, Part II: *Descriptive Linguistics*. Amsterdam: North-Holland Publishing Co.

Ramamurti, G.V., 1931. *A Manual of the Sora (*or *Savara) Language*. Madras: Government Press.

—, 1933. *English-Sora Dictionary*. Madras: Government Press.

—, 1938. *Sora-English Dictionary*. Madras: Government Press.

Reed, Irene, Osahito Miyaoka, Steven Jacobson, Paschal Afcan and Michael Krauss, 1977. *Yup'ik Eskimo Grammar*. Alaska Native Language Center and Yup'ik Language Workshop. Fairbanks: University of Alaska.

Stampe, David L., 1963. *Proto-Sora-Parengi Phonology*. Master's Thesis, University of Chicago.

—, 1965a. Categories of the Sora pronoun. Abstracted in *IJAL* 31.4: 335-6.

—, 1965b. On the Sora noun. Unpublished Ms, Chicago. Abstracted in *IJAL* 31.4: 336.

—, 1973. *A Dissertation on Natural Phonology*. Ph.D. dissertation, University of Chicago.

Starosta, Stanley, 1967. Sora Syntax: A Generative Apprach to a Munda Language. Ph.D. dissertation, University of Wisconsin.

—, 1971. Derivation and case in Sora verbs. *Indian Linguistics* 32.3: 194-206.

—, 1976. Case forms and case relations in Sora. In Philip N. Jenner, Laurence C. Thompson and Stanley Starosta (eds.), 1069-108.

—, 1977. Affix hobbling. University of Hawaii. *Working Papers in Linguistics* 9.1: 61-158.

—, 1978. The one per Sent solution. In Werner Abraham (ed.), 459-576.

—, 1979a. The end of Phrase Structure as we know it. University of Hawaii, *Working Papers in Linguistics* 11.1: 59-76.

—, 1979b. *The Derivation of Combining Forms and Nominal Pseudocompounds in Sora.* Symposium on Austroasiatic Languages, Helsingr, 24-26 October, 1979.

—, 1982. "Lexicase: an attempt at a generative reformation." *Kiswahili* 49/2. 62-79.

Steinberg, Danny D., 1970. "Analyticity, amphigory and the semantic interpretation of sentences." *Journal of Verbal Learning and Verbal Behaviour* 9: 37-51.

Yang, In-seok, 1972. *Korean Syntax.* Seoul. Paek Hap Sa.

—, 1973. Semantics of delimiters. *Language Research* 9.2. Seoul: Seoul National University.

Zide, Arlene K., 1976. Nominal Combining Forms in Sora and Gorum. In Philip N. Jenner, Laurence C. Thompson and Stanley Starosta (eds.), 1259-94.

APPENDIX A

Lexical Redundancy Rules for Sora Nouns

RR-1.	[+nlps]	→	[+pssd]
RR-2.	[+pssd]	→	$\begin{bmatrix} -\text{prpr} \\ +\text{dfnt} \end{bmatrix}$
RR-3.	[±adrs]	→	[−spkr]
RR-4.	[+prxt]	→	$\begin{bmatrix} -\text{dmns} \\ +\text{ntrg} \end{bmatrix}$
RR-5.	[±dmns]	→	[−prsn]
RR-6.	[±spkr]	→	[±prsn]
RR-7.	[±prsn]	→	[+prnn]
RR-8.	$\begin{bmatrix} -\text{prnn} \\ +\text{lctn} \end{bmatrix}$	→	[−anmt]
RR-9.	[-nlps]	→	[−prpr]
RR-10.	[±prpr]	→	[+nrml]
RR-11.	[±ntns]	→	[+dgre]
RR-12.	[±prps]	→	[+ctvt]
RR-13.	[±ctvt]	→	[−dgre]
RR-14.	[±dgre]	→	[−nrml]

RR-15. [±nrml] → [−prnn]

RR-16. [±prnn] → [+N]

RR-17. [+ctvt] → $\begin{bmatrix} -\text{plrl} \\ +\text{pssd} \\ -[+\text{adrs}] \\ -[+\text{plrl}] \\ -[+\text{spkr}] \\ +([+\text{N}]\,[+\text{N}])\_\_\_ \end{bmatrix}$

RR-18. [−ctvt] → [+time]

RR-19. [+prsn] → $\begin{bmatrix} +\text{dfnt} \\ +\text{anmt} \end{bmatrix}$

RR-20. [+prpr] → $\begin{bmatrix} +\text{dfnt} \\ -\text{plrl} \end{bmatrix}$

RR-21. [−nrml] → [−plrl]

RR-22. [+dmns] → [+dfnt]

RR-23. $\begin{bmatrix} -\text{dmns} \\ \alpha\text{ntrg} \end{bmatrix}$ → [αdfnt]

RR-24. [±ntrr] → [+trmn]

RR-25. [±trmn] → [−goal]

RR-26. [±sorc] → [−drcn]

RR-27. [±goal] → [+drcn]

RR-28. [±drcn] → $\begin{bmatrix} +\text{L} \\ -\text{NM} \end{bmatrix}$

RR-29. [+N] → [−L]

RR-30. $\begin{Bmatrix} [-\text{dmns}] \\ [+\text{dlmt}] \\ [+\text{P}] \end{Bmatrix}$ → [−NM]

RR-31. [+dmns] → [−VC]

RR-32. [−drcn] → [−trmn]

RR-33. [−NM] → [−L]

APPENDIX B

Sora Morphological Rules

MR-1 $] \rightarrow$ *ñɛn*] / $\begin{bmatrix} -[-\text{spkr}] \\ -[+\text{plrl}] \end{bmatrix}$ (first person singular)

MR-2 $] \rightarrow$ *nəm*] / $\begin{bmatrix} -[-\text{adrs}] \\ -[+\text{plrl}] \end{bmatrix}$ (second person singular)

MR-3 $] \rightarrow$ *len*] / $\begin{bmatrix} -[-\text{spkr}] \\ -[-\text{plrl}] \end{bmatrix}$ (first person singular)

MR-4 $] \rightarrow$ *ben*] / $\begin{bmatrix} -[-\text{adrs}] \\ -[-\text{plrl}] \end{bmatrix}$ (second person singular)

MR-5 $[\rightarrow$ [ə / $\begin{bmatrix} +\text{pssd} \\ -[+\text{adrs}] \end{bmatrix}$ (third person)

MR-6 $] \rightarrow$ *n*] /
$$\left\{ \begin{matrix} \begin{bmatrix} \\ +\text{dfnt} \\ -\text{pssd} \\ \begin{Bmatrix} -\text{prpr} \\ +\text{ctvt} \end{Bmatrix} \end{bmatrix} \\ \begin{bmatrix} -[+\text{adrs}] \\ -[+\text{N}] \;\underline{\qquad} \end{bmatrix} \end{matrix} \right\}$$

MR-7 $] \rightarrow$ *ji*] /
$$\left\{ \begin{matrix} \begin{bmatrix} +\text{plrl} \\ -\text{spkr} \\ -\text{adrs} \end{bmatrix} \\ \begin{bmatrix} +\text{VC} \\ +\text{plrl} \end{bmatrix} \\ \begin{bmatrix} -[+\text{adrs}] \\ -[-\text{plrl}] \\ -\text{plrl} \end{bmatrix} \end{matrix} \right\}$$

APPENDIX C

Inflectional Redundancy Rules

IRR-1. $$[+\text{VC}] \rightarrow \begin{bmatrix} +\text{adrs} \\ -\text{spkr} \\ -[+\text{Det}]\_\_\_ \end{bmatrix}$$

IRR-2. $$[+\text{N}] \rightarrow [-\text{NM}]$$

IRR-3. $$\begin{bmatrix} +\text{pssd} \\ -[+\text{adrs}] \\ -[+\text{spkr}] \\ -[+\text{plrl}] \end{bmatrix} \rightarrow [+\ ([+\text{COR}])]$$

IRR-4. $$\begin{Bmatrix} [-\text{pssd}] \\ [-\text{dfnt}] \end{Bmatrix} \rightarrow [+\ ([+\text{Det}])\_\_\_]$$

IRR-5. $$\begin{bmatrix} +\text{N} \\ \alpha\text{dfnt} \end{bmatrix} \rightarrow \left[-\begin{bmatrix} +\text{Det} \\ -\alpha\text{dfnt} \end{bmatrix}\right]$$

IRR-6. $$\begin{bmatrix} +\text{N} \\ +\text{dfnt} \end{bmatrix} \rightarrow \left[-\begin{bmatrix} +\text{N} \\ -\text{dfnt} \end{bmatrix}\right]$$

IRR-7. $$[-\text{dfnt}] \rightarrow [-\text{plrl}]$$

IRR-8. $$\begin{bmatrix} +\text{N} \\ \alpha\text{plrl} \end{bmatrix} \rightarrow \left[-\begin{bmatrix} +\text{Det} \\ -\alpha\text{plrl} \end{bmatrix}\right]$$

IRR-9. $$[+\ [+\text{N}]\_\_\_] \rightarrow \begin{bmatrix} -[+\text{N}]\,[+\text{N}]\_\_\_ \\ -[+\text{prnn}]\ \_\_\_ \end{bmatrix}$$

IRR-10. $$[+\text{N}] \rightarrow \begin{bmatrix} -\text{adrs} \\ -\text{spkr} \end{bmatrix}$$

IRR-11. $$[+\text{V}] \rightarrow \left[-\begin{bmatrix} -\text{NM} \\ +\text{anmt} \end{bmatrix}\right]$$

$$\text{IRR-}\Omega \qquad [\,] \qquad \rightarrow \qquad \begin{bmatrix} -[+\text{N}] \\ -[+\text{Det}] \\ -[+\text{V}] \\ -[+\text{Adv}] \\ -[+\text{AGT}] \\ -[+\text{PAT}] \\ -[+\text{INS}] \\ -[+\text{LOC}] \\ -[+\text{COR}] \\ -[+\text{PLC}] \\ -[+\text{REF}] \\ -[+\text{RSN}] \\ -[+\text{MAN}] \end{bmatrix}$$

CHAPTER 17

GUTOB PRONOMINAL CLITICS AND RELATED PHENOMENA ELSEWHERE IN GUTOB-REMO-GTA?

Norman Zide

Introduction

In trying to reconstruct the verb morphology and something of the syntax of Proto-South Munda (SM), and then of Proto-Munda (PM), we deal with two topics of some current interest: clitics and nominal incorporation. Both of these are innovations in Munda: the incorporation of monosyllabic 'combining forms' of nouns (usually objects or instruments) into verb stems goes back to SM, and subject-marking enclitic constructions of several kinds (presumably independently innovated) are found in some of the Munda languages, both North and South. These are probably of comparatively recent origin. We reconstruct subject (verb) prefixes for SM, and probably for PM as well. The Munda languages (Western Austroasiatic), like the other language families of non-peripheral India, Indo-Aryan and Dravidian, are SOV languages, but, for Munda, with evidence of the earlier SVO pattern common in Mon-Khmer (Eastern Austroasiatic), and perhaps Proto-Austroasiatic. Object suffixes on the verb probably go back to PM.

This paper gives data for languages of one branch of Koraput Munda (KM). Gutob-Remo-Gta (GRG). Koraput Munda is one branch of South Munda, the other being Kharia-Juang (KJ). There are four languages in GRG: Gutob (Gad(a)ba)—Gu, Remo (Boṇḍa)—Re, Plains Gta? (Ḍiḍayi)—GaP, and Hill Riverside Gta? (Ḍiḍayi) GaH. The data come from text collections—from Gutob, by Bimal P. Das, Richard DeArmond and Norman Zide, and from Plains Gta?, by Khageshwar Mahapatra and Norman Zide. There are a few pages of text at the back of Sudhibhushan Bhattacharya's Boṇḍa (Remo) Dictionary, and this is all the Remo text material I have access to. A sizable collection of Remo Texts was made by scholars at Osmania University, but I haven't seen it. There are no texts recorded for Hill/Riverside Gta?, or for Hill Remo, or for Andhra Gutob dialects. (All four languages are spoken in the Koraput District of Orissa, and Gutob and Hill/Riverside Gta? in the adjacent areas of Andhra as well.)

Gutob

Gutob-Remo has lost both sets of SM verb affixes, the subject prefixes (preserved in Gta? and, therefore, GRG), and the object suffixes, lost in GRG, GR has developed a set of enclitic subject markers, and it is the placement of these that we discuss. Most of the data come from Gutob, but what there is of Remo material shows much the same grammar (see the short note on Remo following the Gutob section). The distribution of enclitic subject pronouns (-PR) in Gutob is more complex, and open to variation than the parallel data in Gta? taken up at the end of this paper.

-PR in Gutob is commonly attached to some verb in the complex verb piece of the verb phrase, which verb and what determines that we take up shortly. Where there is only one (finite) verb form in the verb phrase there is no choice in -PR-attachment. Where there are two or more there are choices to be made. There are a few cases of -PR-attachment to an adverb (that precedes the verb) in the verb phrase, and, at least for one informant, a movement to the end of the sentence, where it is no longer enclitic, but looks like a kind of vocative, and, it was thought, a very few cases of -PR-attachment in the (sentence-initial) subject noun phrase. These -PR types will be taken up in the order listed below. The enclitic pronoun is obligatory (there are a very few exceptions), but the free subject pronoun in the initial noun phrase is commonly deleted in informal styles. Examples of deletion of both -PR and the free pronoun in a few narrative texts are found, as well as double enclitic marking within a verb phrase. There is a considerable variation - PR use in non-finite verb phrases. One informant (Muroli) uses them infrquently in certain *-su* constructions. Others use them fairly regularly with either one or both clausal clitics (*-su* and *-na*). *-su* and *-na* are clause-final clitics, called by some perfective and imperfective: *-su* translates 'after having V-ed', 'after V-ing', 'and'—the subject of the non-finite pre-clausal clitic verb is usually identical with that of the finite verb. *-na* translates most commonly 'if' or 'when'. Both follow a V-Past- form (which, in that position, contrasts with nothing), which looks like a borrowing from (on one interpretation) of the Oriya *V-i,* although I think *-su* and *-na* constructions of this sort are old.

It is clear that discourse contexts are crucial for making judgments and rules about -PR placement, deletion, meaning, and that the kind of fine-grained discourse analysis (building on a full syntactic analysis of Gutob, a pragmatic analysis, etc.) and the knowledge of the Gutob language to base it on do not exist, here or anywhere else. I present and analyse the data—with notes and comments, some of them on superficial discourse structure, in the following order:

2.1 *Double Verbs*

Examples of double verb and paired verb phrase constructions:

A) sentences with -PR attachment in the verb complex, and sentences without -PR

1. Sentences with neither PR nor -PR
2. Sentences with PR but no -PR
3. Sentences with both PR and -PR
4. Sentences with -PR but no PR

for 3. and 4. sentences with two finite verb forms in the verb complex:

X: where V2 is VAuxA
Y: where V2 is VauxB
Z: where V2 is neither
K) where neither V1 or V2 take -PR
KH) where V1 takes -PR
G) where V2 takes -PR
(GH where both take -PR is rare. See 6 GH, and 11 on multiple attachment.)

5. X (where V2 is VAuxA) 5K, 5KH, 5G
6. Y (where V2 is VAuxB) 6K, 6KH, 6G, 6GH
7. Z where V2 is not Aux, or an Aux other than AuxA or AuxB
   a. Discourse notes on a V1 V2 construction, with V1 as *bug-*, V2 *piŋ-* in one text (the Barogaṭia/Jom story)
   b. sentences with -PR attachment outside the verb complex
8. Sentences whmere -PR attaches to an adverb (preceding the verb) in the verb phrase
9. Sentences where -PR attaches to something in the initial, subject, NP
10. Sentences where -PR a decliticized -PR, occurs after the VP as a quasi-vocative (in Duaru's speech)
11. Sentences with multiple -PR attachment (with or without PR).

Double verbs, those with +V2 as a phonological echo, and those with +V2 as a frozen paired verb which may or may not occur independently, are common in the GRG languages. Both take the same -PR (and tense) markings. A similar construction where verb phrases are paired—not two verb forms separated by plus juncture in a single word—has been noted:

a. maj-nen rone+bone ḍeŋ-gu buron-gu-NEN+a?so-gu-NEN
   they happy become—Past 1 live-Pst 1-PR+echo-Pst 1-PR
   They, having become happy, lived (on that way); i.e. They lived happily ever after.

b. tirgig-NEI+juju-NEI pi-loŋ- ki- na
   follow-WE+ see-WE (piŋ-) come-PrFu1- 'or not'
   Shall we follow (you) and see, or not?

c. (it is not necessary that...) ('you' refers to the tiger)
o-niŋ nom ṭia gil (-ei)-tu-NOM, ṭia ag(-)ei-tu-NOM
acc-I you(sg) standing standing defecate-PrFu2-PR
swallow-Pres-Fu-PR
you, standing, swallow me (up) and, standing, defecate (me) (out)

The words (*ṭia, gil-ei-, ag-ei*) and the idiom are borrowed from Desia/Oriya:

d. (this is an example of two separate actions, not 'conjoined', both marked with -PR).
apaŋ, ite keroŋ, irig, sa?mel etek-maṛ NOM mono?
father this paddy millet sp ragi this much you where millet
suŋmol-nu mila-?-NOM-ḍu-gu-su ri-o?-su biṛ-o?-NOM,
seed -gen. oobtain-Pst2-PR-AuxA-Pst1-su bring-Pst2-PR
on-o?-NOM?
plant-Pst2-PR
'Father, where did you get so much paddy and millet seed and bring it and sow it, and (then) (trans)plant it?

2.1.

a. irig oi-oj-ḍu-tu?
millet sp Redup-harvest/reap/cut-VAuxA(progressive)-PRFu2
Are you harvesting the irig millet? (ḍu-)

The subject, 'you' (nom) was last mentioned in the text—conversation—two sentences back *ui-loŋ-NOM ḍej?* 'Will you go, then?', answered 'Yes'. (*hũ*), followed by the sentence in la:

b. iḍa? iṛ-o?-su ui-ḍe=loŋ ?
millet gruel drink-Pst2-su go-AuxA(ḍem-)PrFu1
ḍem- is a borrowed wide-spectrum modal: can/may/should/ must
The subject understood is pen, you pl; the reply also lacks a (-) PR, which would, in that sentence, be NEI, 'we'.
Will/must you go after eating (lit. drinking) millet gruel?

2.2.

a. hã, kete lok NOM ai-o? ri-loŋ, be?
Yes, how many people you call/invite-Pst2
bring-PrFul, Voc
Yes, how many people will you call and bring?

b. MAJ-NEN ũbo? kuruŋ ai=o? ri-loŋ, be

they where road/way/area call-Pst2 bring-PrFu, Voc

Where will they call and bring (you)?

All the sentences in 1. and 2. can occur with both PR and -PR, e.g. for la *'NOM irig oioj-NOM-ḍutu?'*. Sentences of type 2. with PR but not -PR are comparatively rare, not nearly as common as type 4. sentences. What sort of stylistic effects -PR-deletion gives I cannot say.

2.3

a. NIŋ-o-maj-toŋ-nen ob-gir-o?-NIŋ-su

I acc-3rd Sg-nom-Plu caus-learn-Pst2-PR-su

MAJ-NEN gir-gu-NEN (Mur)

they learn-Pst1-PR

I taught them and they learned.

-su is a clausal clitic—'conjunctive participle', that can translate 'and', '(after) having V-ed'; the non-finite verb form ob-gir-o?-nen-su, if the sentence ended here would be replaced by the finite form ob-gir-o?-NEN:

b. su MAJ-NEN boji+bat som-o?-NEN (Du)

Then they vegetables+rice eat-Pst2-PR

Then they ate rice and vegetables.

Here, Duaru uses the clausal *su* (not the full verb form, recapitulated from the previous sentence, *ḍem-o?-NEN-su* 'after they did that', which is what Muroli would use) as a free word. For Muroli, *-su* occurs only after a past verb form. Sentences with both sentences, those with -PR only.

2.4

a. so din-bo? ḍi-e?-su maṭi kam ḍẽ-ḍem-NEI-ḍugu

six day-Loc Quotative earth work Redup-do-PR-VAuxA-Pst1

For six days we were doing road work.

b. an-o?-su mo?ṛ-gu piŋ-gi-NIŋ

pull -Pst2-su rise-Pst1 come(back)-Pst1-PR

(I) pulled (it) out, got up and came (back home).

This is the most common (-)PR usage.

2.5

The VAuxA are *ḍu-*, with which perfective and progressive tense forms are made, perfective on a past stem, progressive on an infinitival present, and *ḍem-* a modal meaning can/should/may/must, which attaches to the infinitive. There are a very few examples of 5G forms, i.e. where -PR attaches to the auxiliary, and these only with the auxiliary *-ḍu* The verb form has—what is usual— -PR on V1, or no -PR at all (5K). PR may or may not occur. The negative copulae, *ura?* 'to not (be)', and *oroj* 'to not yet (be)' never take -PR when acting in a verb phrase with another verb (e.g. *mon-o-? sa ui-NEN ura?* (subject MAJ-NEN, 'they'), where—emphatic go-PR not, 'They don't go anywhere.' *ura?* and *oroj* can take -PR when the negative coupula is the (whole) verb form.

5K

a. See sentence 1b. iḍa? iṛ-o?-su uiḍe-loŋ

b. (Answer to 'What are they like after they drink (the liquor)?
bil-bil-ḍe-loŋ subject MAJ-NEN 'they
Redup-to be drunk-VAuxA-PrFu1
(They) must/would be drunk

c. din-ke ketek-laka ḍẽ-ḍem-ḍu-gu (subject 'they' MAJ-NEN)
daily how much Redup-make-VAuxA-Pst1
How much (solop liquor) were they making every day?

There are no examples in my data of VAuxA *ḍu-* without a preceding -PR where the pronoun is not 3 singular.

5KH

a. MAJ-NEN ketek lok tiarei-o?-NEN-ḍu-tu
they how many people to be ready-Pst2-PR
How many people are (being) ready (there)?

b. kõḍek-munaŋ biṛ-o?-NEI-ḍu-tu
a little-like sow-Pst2-PR-VAuxA-PrFu2
We have sown a little (millet).

The Aux *ḍem* is not very common. I find no examples in the sample (c 100 pages of text) of V1-tense-PR-ḍem-

5G

(earlier simra-gu-NEN-ḍuto they have (customarily) enjoyed (it), later (Muroli/Duaru, Conv 1)

a. simra-gu-ḍu-loŋ-NEN
enjoy-Pst1-VAuxA(ḍu)-PrFu1-PR
They will have enjoyed (it).

The auxiliaries don't treat -PR the same way: with *ḍu* 5KH is very common, 5G occurs, but rarely. With *ḍem-* (which is much rarer) there were no examples of V-tense-PR-*ḍem-*, perhaps because Redup-V-PR-VAux is uncommon, even with Vaux *ḍu,* but there are examples of that. It is possible that these VAuxA with *ḍem-* are better analysed as impersonal constructions, which would be in line with some *ḍem-* constructions where *ḍem-* is not an auxiliary. In that case 1b. would be, more literally, 'after you eat the gruel (or after the (your?) eating of the gruel, there will be a going. This too looks like a borrowing from Indo-Aryan.

2.6

The most common usage by far with VAuxB is 6G, with -PR on the auxiliary. There are a few cases of 6KH. The three common B auxiliaries (all of them calques, taken directly from Oriya) are *beḍ-*, literally 'to give', meaning motion away from and/or benefitting someone other than the speaker, *ui-*, literally 'to go', completive, and *suŋ-*, literally 'to throw', intensive. -VAuxB acts on a past-marked V1.

This is an answer to a 'what do they do then' question

6K

a. ḍuri?-gu beṛ-be? (subject MAJ-NEN, 'they')
to sleep (ḍuṛig-)-Pst 1 Redup-VAuxB
infinitival present
They sleep (note the action of sleeping is, with beḍ-, action away from the speaker')

It looks as if third person (plural) subjects are more commonly deleted than are the others. On one possible historical reason for this, see the Remo section.

b. (with PR, but no -RP) NOM b-ob-ri-o?- beṛ-o?
You fill-caus infix-Pst2 VAux-Pst2
You filled (it) (up)

6KH

a. A *-su,* non-finite, construction, but it can be made finite (keeping the -PR-placement) by ending the sentence here and deleting the *-su. loṭei-o?-NIŋ-beṛ-o?-su* loṭ ei-

'to have sex with a woman

-Pst2-PR-VAuxB-Pst2-su

After having sex (with her)....

b. dire joŋ len-o?-su ob-gai-o?-NEI-be?-to

slowly thigh raise-Pst2-su caus-entrer-Pst2-PR-AuxB-customary

I slowly raise my thigh and enter (it—not the thigh—in her) (NEI 'we', here meaning 'I')

c. NIŋ niŋ-nu onoo?n beṛ-o?-NIŋ- suŋ- tu

I I-gen. daughter give-Pst2-PR-VAuxB-PrFu2

I will give/offer (intensive) my duaghter.

6G

a. naik+barik sobu su-sun-NEN-ḍu-tu pigs-o?-suŋ-tu-NIŋ headman

etc. all Redup-say-PR-AuxA-PrFu1 break-Pst2-AuxB-PrFu2-PR

The headman et al are all saying I broke (it) (intensive).

b. (MAJ-NEN) tur-gu ui-gi-NEN

(They) to go out-Pst1 VAuxB-Pst1-PR

They went out.

One example of 6GH—both verbs taking -PR:

a. NIŋ rĩ-o?-NIŋ-su biṛ-o?-NIŋ-beṛ-o?-NIŋ-ḍu-gu

I bring-Pst2-PR-su sow-Pst2-VAuxB-Pst2-PR-VAuxA- Pst1

I brought (the seed) and I sowed it.

2.7

The V1 V2 section treats what is the most common sequence of verbs, an action (V1) followed by a verb of motion or positioning. Series of more than two verbs are uncommon,—previous actions are set off in clausal clitic, *-su-*, phrases, although, as in parallel IA 'conjunctive participle' phrases, the *-su* can be deleted. The more common construction is V1-Past-V2-tense-PR. See Section 7a for examples of V1-PR-V2 and V1-V2-PR and some speculations of what may be conditioning placement here.

7K

a. hã, kete lok NOM ai-o? ri-loŋ, be
Yes, how many people you call-Pst2 take-PrFu1 Voc ptcle
How many people will you call and take (there)?

b. nei-nu bag paṭna(-)NIŋ sob-o? ri-loŋ
We-gen tiger settlement-I take-Pst2 take-PrFul hold of/grab
I will take hold of her and take her to our tiger settlement.

7KH

a. loṭei-NIŋ- beṛ- o?-su (for ?? loṭei-(o)?NIŋ-)
to have sex-(Pst2 ??)-I-VAuxB-Pst2-su...with
After having sex (with her) ... (non-finite, with-su)

b. (see 7A—from Barogaṭia story, Sent 15)
jom-lai bu-o?-NIŋ pi-loŋ
Jom- acc beat-Pst2-I come-PrFul
I will beat up Jom, and come (back home).

c. NIŋ jom-lai ui-gi bu-o?-NIŋ pi-loŋ
(ui-gi reduced from ui-gi-su)
I Jom-acc go-Pst1 beat-Pst2-PR come-PrFul
I will go, and beat up Jom and come (home).

7G

a. goi-o? riŋ-to-PEN
clear-Pst2 bring-customary-PR land
(You (pl)) clear (the land) and bring (something) back.

b. an-o?-su mo?ṛ-gu piŋ-gi-NIŋ
pull out-Pst2-su get up-Pst1 come-Pst1-PR
(I) will pull (it) out, and get up and come (back home).
(the next two are from the 7A Barogaṭia story)

c. (Sentence 42 of the Barogaṭia story)
jom-lai NIŋ bu-o? pi-loŋ-NIŋ
Jom-acc I beat-Pst2 come-PrFu-1-PR
I will beat up Jom and come (back).

d. NIŋ ui-loŋ jom-lai bu-o?-su pi-loŋ-NIŋ
I go-PRFu1-PR Jom-acc beat-Pst2-su come-PrFul-Pr
I will go and after beating up Jom I'll come back.

7A

-PR attachment in 'the same sentence' in a story.

In a long story [425 sentences—told by Muroli (Murolidor Kilo)], the orphan boy, Barogaṭia (Twelve knots), is asked the same question, 'Where are you going, Barogaṭia?' (ũbo? ui, barogaṭia?) by various people and creatures he meets on his way to see Jom (Sanskrit Yama, Oriya Jɔmɔ), the Lord of the Underworld and the dead. The tale comes from Oriya. He gives essentially the same answer (see below), but varies it, and the variations, involving different placement of -PR, are revealing. He answers the question eight times, three of the answers being identical:

Sent. 9 jom-lai bu-o?-NIŋ pi=loŋ (same as S 29, and S 53)
Jom-acc beat-Pst2-PR come-PrFul
I will beat up Jom and come back.

Sent 15 NIŋ ui-loŋ jom-lai bu-o?-su pi-loŋ-NIŋ
I go-PrFu1-PR Jom-acc beat-Pst2-su come-PrFul-PR
I will go, and after beating up Jom will come back.

Sent 18 jom-lai ui-gi bu-o?-NIŋ pi-loŋ
Jom-acc go-Pst1 beat-Pst2-PR come-PrFul
After going, I will beat up Jom and come back.

There is a problem in translating these sentences into more or less colloquial English that comes from a problem in the analysis of Gutob (and the awkwardness of dealing with serial verbs in an English that can reflect the Gutob structure directly): does one take *ui-gi* in 18. as from *ui-gi-su,* and, further: does one take *bu(g)-o?*—both *ui-gi* and *bu-o?* are past forms—as *'from bu-o?-su'*? In Gta?, there would be a single three-verb sequence with only the final verb being inflected (e.g. Ga 1. (m æ) *e-liŋ-raŋ-ke,*

(He) go-buy-bring back-past, He went and bought (the meat) and brought it back.')

Basically, Gutob works more or less as Gta? does, but with the complications resulting from having borrowed more of Indo-Aryan conjunctive participle construction usage. The clausal clitic *-su* (its GRG cognates are Remo *-sa,* Plains Gta? *-ce(?),* Hill Gta? *-cī(?))* is old in GRG, but what its syntax was in GRG and what the overlap was with IA-like conjunctive participle constructions is unclear.

Sent 41 NIŋ jom-lai ui-gi bu-o?NIŋ pi-loŋ
I Jom-acc go-Pst1 beat-Pst2-PR come-PrFu1
I will go, and beat up Jom and come back.

Sent 42 jom-lai NIŋ bu-o? pi-loŋ-NIŋ
Jom-acc I beat-Pst2 come-PrFu1-PR
I will beat up Jom and come back.

A possible reading—an oral version would disambiguate this, but I can't now lay my hands on the taped version of the text—*jom-lai-NIŋ* has been rejected because we don't find -PR attached to accusatives elsewhere, and the transcription does not have -PR here. I take jom-lai to be emphasized, topicalized by being moved to sentence-initial position.

Sent 63 jom-lai bug-bug-NIŋ pi-loŋ (possibly bugbug NIŋ??)
Jom-acc Redup-beat-PR come-PrFu
I beat up Jom and (then) (I) will come back.

The proposal offered here does not fit—and, therefore, apply to—the sentences with *riŋ-* (7K a.,7K b., and in particular, 7G a., and 7G b.). How restricted it may be is not clear. That the Barogaṭia story is 'formulaic' stylistically, in a way some of the stories, and all the conversations are not, probably is relevant. Why *bu-o?-NIŋ pi-loŋ* in some of the sentences, *bu-o? pi-loŋ-NIŋ* in the others? Eight examples are hardly an 'adequate corpus'. That certain grammatical forms, clitics among them, presumably, are movable in ways that others are not in particular language systems, the shift in position more or less preserving meaning, is common knowledge. I will not try to apply any theoretical notions regarding such forms and systems here.

pi-loŋ-NIŋ is the less common form, occurring in only two of the eight examples. There is some evidence—or seemed to be, that the occurrence of free PR in the NP had something to do with conditioning *pi-loŋ-NIŋ,* but that hypothesis does not find much support. It looks as if the composition—or existence—of NP is largely irrelevant. What seems to be relevant, as relevent as anything I can identify, is a phonological—metrical—pattern (what meaning differences there may be between these two forms [(*bu-o? pi-loŋ-NIŋ* and *bu-o?-NIŋ pi-loŋ* in the various sentences) I can't judge, and the obvious guesses—

difference of emphasis, etc.—can be supplied by the reader)]. An alternative—non-phonological—accounting involving *-su* constructions is another option.

What is relevant is the verb phrase structure, which I will represent below for my purposes in the following way (it is useful to label the verb counting from the end -i.e. from right to left, i.e. in *ui-gi bu-o? -NIŋ pi-loŋ, piŋ-* is VN, *bug-* is VM, and *ui-* is VL):

9./23/53.VP: *jom-lai bu-o? pi-loŋ,* has three phonological phrases (or cola): *jom-lai, bu-o?,* and *pi-loŋ.* The final—second—finite verb phrase in 15., *jom-lai bu-o?-su pi-loŋ,* has three, *jom-lai, bu-o?-su* and *pi-loŋ;* 18. has four *jom-lai ui-gi bu-o?* and *pi-loŋ.* 41. has the same four. 42. has two (the object, *jom-lai,* here has been moved before the subject, *niŋ;* the verb phrase follows this and has two cola (and words): *bu-o?* and *pi-loŋ.* 63. has three: *jom-lai, bug-bug* and *pi-loŋ.* Note that the phonological phrases here are all single words, and one could reject this phonological analysis here as unnecessary. I talk of phrases because elsewhere, as I tentatively analyse some of the data, units of more than one word are involved. I take these as metrically definable; they are, of course syntactically constrained. The first word/phonological phrase of the verb phrase does not take -PR (unless it is the only word-necessarily a finite verb form—in the verb phrase). The second word/phonological phrase does take-PR if it is not VL, i.e. an antepenultimate verb (i.e. *ui-gi* in 18. and 41.) or the verb form takes *-su* (as in 15.). We take; *ui-gi* in 18. and 41. to be 'underlying *ui-gi-su*', but, if, as I think, phonological, i.e. metrical, features are primary, it is the phonology of the *-su* forms that is relevant—primary —and not the syntax that is relevant. I would rather not lean on the syntactic function of *-su* here. Thus, -PR attaches to the final verb here where it is the second word/phonological phrase in the verb phrase (42.), and where it follows a trisyllabic (*bu-o?-su*), or, alternatively, a *-su* verb form. (There are V-past-PR-*su* forms, but not here, and I have not examined the limits of their distribution elsewhere.) -PR attaches to the penultimate verb form where it follows an accusative or a VL. It would be neater phonologically if O VL (e.g. *jom-lai ui-gi* in 18. and 41.) occurred—were pronounced—in a single phonological phrase. They may be; I can't say. I have not tried to generalize these observations, and find larger scopes for these regularities—in the rest of the Barogatia text, or to others. See the general conclusions at the end of the Gutob section for some attempt to pull things together a little more.

2.8

-PR attaches to an adverb (preceding the verb complex) in the verb phrase. It was noted elsehwere in the paper that the phonetic 'clitic juncture' that identifies the -PR as a clitic and not as a separate word, PR, was not always consistently or accurately transcribed, and that this is particularly important in identifying -PR attaching to adverbs in the verb phrase. The clitic status of individual (-)PR instances can be questioned, but the general conclusions based on a corpus of accurately transcribed occurrences of -PR and PR are, I think, valid, although ADV-PR is not common in the tests. One would like to know whether—at, say, 'fast tempo'—ADV PR necessarily fuses to ADV-PR, or if either ADV-PR or ADV PR is possible. I assume there would be individual differences in usage.

See also Section 11. for examples of ADV-PR, and the 'extraordinary'—i.e. more than one -PR in the verb phrases—verb phrases where not just one ADV takes -PR, but where both V- and (one or more) ADV- are -PR-marked. The examples given here have one -PR in the verb phrase, and that on an adverb and not on a verb. c. and d. have ADV -PR and no V-PR a. has ADV1-PR ADV2-PR and no V-PR. b. has ADV-PR and V-PR.

(1) locative adverbs (the most common adverb class with (See *eke* 'here, in this region' in 11 d.)

a. a?-PEN mono?-PEN pi-loŋ ḍi-e? ḍi-e? ḍi?-to
now-PR where-PR come-PrFu1 quot 'it is said'
Note that there are two ADV-PR and no V-t-PR here
Where will you(pl) come to (i.e. go) now?

b. NIŋ miõ? maŋ-ḍem mospur-bo?-NIŋ ḍu-loŋNIŋ
I further/more why earth-loc-PR be/live-PrFu1-PR
Why will I go on living on this earth?

Here too there is more than one-PR in the verb phrase; the -PR attaches to the (preferred) locative which, here, follows 'further' and 'why', and must always precede the verb *ḍu-*, 'to be (located)/stay' with temporal adverbs [(ũḍoj 'when', dapre 'after (wards)']:

c. NIŋ ũḍoj-NIŋ sorpei-o? -be? -tu
I when-PR hand over-Pst2 VAuxB-PrFu2 give over
When will/do I hand over (the girl to the tiger)?

d. begi-NOM iḍa? ḍem
soon/you gruel make- (Imper2 zero) quickly
Make the gruel quickly.

The first adverb in the verb phrase is a preferred attachment place for -PR, but some adverb classes are more attractive to -PR than others, although we don't have the data to demonstrate this (i.e. which classes, where, how) clearly. Under higher rhetorical pressures—see the contexts described under 11. -PR attaches to adverbs, e.g. the sentence adverb *miõ?* 'further, again', not sufficiently attractive under lower pressures. There are very probably other contextual features constraining -PR attachment, e.g. the composition of the verb phrase, and the selection of particular verbs, about which I can't say anything. Thus, one finds *mono? ḍu-to-NEN* 'Where do they stay?' Is *mono?-NEN ḍu-to* possible? There are no examples of -PR on the accusative forms (Noun-*lai*, *a*-Pronoun-*lai*) which occur commonly verb phrase-initially, nor on any N-PR forms other than Noun-locative-. Again, the (stylistic) difference between c. *begi*-NOM..., and the possible sentence *NOM begi iḍa? ḍem,* i.e. with the PR in—as—an initial subject noun phrase is something I can't say much about. The usual assumption—plausible here—would be that putting *begi,* 'quickly' first, foregrounding it, gives it more emphasis. In *ũḍoj-NIŋ* and *begi-NOM* we have what can be called emphasis by prolongation (using 'prolongation' in the musicological sense of the term), the NIŋ prolongs the ũḍoj which takes the primary stress, and of course, prolongs—iterates—the 'I' (NIŋ). Multiple clitic-attachment is a kind of pedal point, or 'long component' (Firthian prosody?), the -PR applying through the phrase, attaching at every point where it is attachable (it is not easy to specify precisely what these points are). It can be no accident that three of these sentences are questions (there are other sentences in the corpus with *ũbo?* and *mono?,* 'where')—and the fourth is an imperative; clitical emphasis is, apparently, more common in such sentences. Prolongation in Gutob by vowel lengthening is found in some demonstrative forms, i.e. along with *hano? ((h)a-nV-bo?)* 'yonder' (further out than *uno?/tuno?,* 'there') we find *haaaaano?* (non-discrete lengthening) *'waaaaay* out there'. Gta? has a more elaborate demonstrative system, and lengthening for emphasis is common, this combined with a repetition of demonstrative stems which has something in common with the multiple -PR enclitic iterations, e.g. Gta? *nu,* 'yonder', *nu-ne,* but stretchable, e.g. to *nuuuu-ne* 'the one out yonder', but one can increase the 'yonderness' by using the emphatic *-o?-*, and, in addition, repeating *nu-* with or without the expressive prolongation—lengthening, i.e. *nuuuuuu nu-o?-nu-ne (nuuuuu no?nune),* 'the one (invisible) all the way out there'.

2.9

There are no examples in the sample (c 100 pages) corpus of -PR attaching to anything in the subject noun phrase. The final search for NP-PR confirmed earlier observations: that subject noun phrases—in the tales, narrative and conversations in this corpus—are minimal, particularly so for non-third person subjects, but also where the subject is some third person. Numeral adjectives, demonstrative adjectives, echo-words and repetitions of nouns occur, but in most sentences a subject noun phrase (whatever its clitic projection in the verb phrase) is not found.

2.10

NOM nei-nu kuruŋ pi-loŋ, ḍisel, NOM? (Duaru)

NOM nei-nu kuruŋ pi-loŋ-NOM, ḍisel? (Muroli)

you we- gen way/road/area -PR friend

Will you come (out) our way, friend?

This, and one other similar sentence from Duaru are the only examples of an extraposed, *de-(en)* cliticized -PR. Muroli uses a familiar construction. Duaru has moved (-)PR to the right, out of the verb phrase, making it a kind of apposed, second vocative. This is the only example of movement of this kind observed. Does one handle this in the same—syntax?—module in an autolexical grammar ? If there are complex vocatives elsewhere in Gutob, I have not seen them.

2.11

Multiple -PR attachment in the verb phrase is one of the more interesting features of Gutob clitic usage. The extreme cases of multiple -PR marking are in the speech of the irritated and frustrated tiger in The Story of the Old Couple, Their Son, Daughter and the Tiger Bridegroom, and the nagging old woman in the same story. If we had more example of angry tiger discourse, we could begin to set up a hierarchy of (valenced) attachment points of -PR where they can, under higher pressure, attach, but don't in 'ordinary speech', at any rate in the fairly large corpus I have of ordinary speech. There are a few examples in my corpus of multiple (double)— -PR-attachment (see 6 GH: *NIŋ rĩ-o?NIŋ-su biṛ-o?NIŋ-beṛo?-NIŋ-ḍu-gu*). See also 8. on Adverb -PR.

Another example—not from the tiger, from the old woman:

11 a. miõ? (i)ḍa?+sũol iṛ-o?-su kerekon(-)NOM mala
further gruel+ercho drink-Pst2-su how much you land
marei-o?(-NOM)-ḍu-tu-NOM ?
cultivate-Pst2-PR-AuxA-PrFu2-PR
cultivate-Pst2-PR AuxA-PrFu2-PR

The -PR after *marei-* was given in one version of the tale, not in the other. The nom after keṛekon is probably PR, not -PR.

How much land did you cultivate after drinking the gruel? (the implication, probably, is that he didn't do any work after eating)

b. (the old woman again, four sentences later)
NOM dapre-NOM mo?ṛ-guu-NOM piŋgi-NOM
you afterwards-PR get up-Pst1-PR come-PR
Then you got up and came back (doing no more work).

A few examples from the tiger:

c. (he first asks the old man *maŋ-ḍem miõ? NOM piŋ-gi?* 'Why have you come back again?)
sobu paiṭi NIŋ ḍem-o-NIŋ-beṛ-be?-NIŋ
all work I do-Pst2-PR-Redup-give-PR
I do all the work.

d. i-a, be; NOM maŋ-ḍem miõ?(-)NOM eke-NOM pi-loŋ-NOM
go-imper1 you why again(-) you here-PR come back
vocative particle -PrFul-PR
Go away! Why do you come back here again.

The old man keeps stalling on delivering the girl to the tiger, and the tiger gets more and more angry. 11 d. is repeated more than once in the story. Elsewhere in the story *dapre*-PR and *miõ?*-PR are explicitly recognized as adverb-enclitic structures. There is no simple, parallel way to convey the force of these repeated -PRs in Gta?,—or in English.

The old woman once more:

e. dapre-NOM biṛ-o?-NOM-beṛ-o?-su lo=o?+li-i?-NOM-ki ura?-ki
quickly-PR sow-Pst2-PR-AuxB-Pst2-su -PR-or not-or /soon
dig(hoe?)-Pst2+echo-Pst2
Have you sowed (the seeds) and dug (hoed?) so quickly or not?

There aren't enough examples of these multiple -PR sentences. Nor do I have available Gutob informants, much less the ones who could exemplify a variety of Gutob usages relevant to multiple attachment, answer questions about where -PR can be attached, preferred locations, differences in meaning, etc. It looks as if not only are there more -PRs in these sentences, but we have examples of -PR-attachment to words where they do not otherwise attach. See section 8. on Adverb -PR occurrences. The usual attachment, either to an adverb or a verb form in the verb phrase, deposits a single -PR in the verb phrase, and commonly no other subject marker in the noun phrase. Here, in d. we have PR (nom, 'you') in the noun phrase, and enclitic -PR three times in the verb phrase: after the adverbs 'again' (*miõ?*), 'here' (*eke*), and after the verb, 'will come/comes' (*pi-loŋ*), 'Why do YOU come back here again? 'There are examples in our corpus of -PR after *miõ?*, and after locative adverbs (*eke,* which is a rare—somewhat archaic?—form isn't one of them), and of course after *pi-loŋ,* but none of both ADVERB-and *pi-loŋ-*. In b. there is PR in the NP, and=PR on an adverb 'afterwards' (*dapre*), V1 'got up' (*mo?ṛ-gu*), and V2, *piŋ-gi* (came back). What restrictions there are on which words occurring in a VP can't take -PR (objects with-*lai,* e.g.

jom-lai in many of our examples?), and what hierarchy of preference there may be I can't say.

2.12

In summary, there is a common subject marking pattern in Gutob: for formal, committal discourse PR in (or often as) the noun phrase and -PR in the verb phrase. If the verb phrase has two verb forms and one is an auxiliary, -PR attaches to the V1 preceding the V2 (auxiliaryA) *ḍu-*, and to V2- where V2 is AuxB. Where the V2 is not an auxiliary but a verb of motion/positioning (but, apparently, not riŋ-) -PR attaches to V1, but under certain specifiable conditions—see Section 7—it attaches to V2. In informal discourse, almost all conversation, PR is dropped, and -PR marks the subject in the verb phrase. This 'common pattern' is subject to a great deal of variation: there are sentences with no (-) PR marked at all, sentences with PR but no -PR, sentences with several -PR, sentences where the -PR attaches to an adverb, and, for one informant, Duaru, the clitic is extraposed outside of (-) after (-) the verb phrase where it is a kind of (decliticized) vocative. With V1 and V2 the -PR sometimes occurs in the other position, i.e. not where the 'common pattern' puts it, and with ADVERB -PR—we don't have too many examples of this—there may be just the one -PR in the verb phrases or several. That discourse considerations affect -PR placement is likely, but what are these? What difference does it make (see 8 d.) if one says *begi-NOM iḍa? ḍem* or *NOM begi iḍa? ḍem!* 'Make the gruel quickly/soon!'? One talks of emphasis, the *begi* 'quickly'that comes at the beginning of the sentence getting more emphasis. And *ob-gir-o?-beṛ-o?-NIŋ* vs the much less likely but possible *obgir-o?-NIŋ-beṛ-o?* 'I taught' (see 3a.)? I don't know, but I don't think it has to do with more 'emphasis' on V1 'teach', and not on V2 (VAuxB *beḍ-*) 'action benefitting another or moving away from the speaker'. It may have to do with general phonological well-formedness, i.e. how the sentence sounds—in its (pragmatic?) discourse context. The examples in 11. of multiple-attachment are revealing, but we have too few of them. (I don't know what comparable data on multiple clitic-attachment exists in other languages. I assume that Gutob is not unique in its clitic-attachment grammar.) These sentences show that -PR can attach to some words (adverbs and verbs only) under extreme (rhetorical) conditions, words they do not attach to in 'ordinary sentences'. A hierarchy of these attraction valences could, perhaps, be established if we had enough data and informants providing and commenting on this data, but the complications of order permutations, cooccurrences of particular adverbs with particular verbs, lack of syntactic comparability, etc would make this a difficult job, if it were possible at all. The multiple -PR emphasis in the 11. sentences of the old woman and the tiger, however—which, ī would guess, is an innovation in Gutob, provide a useful rhetorical device which Gutob tales make good use of. Some of the sentences with more than a single -PR may be anticipatory forms, i.e. the -PR was attached before the full sentence—which would have placed it elsewhere—was formed. Some of them display a lesser degree of emphasis, perhaps (e.g. 6GH, 8 b.). Cltitic use also reflects—and is involved with changes in the serial verb construction (see the Gta? data for what I take to be the earlier situation), which is—probably under the influence of Oriya and Desia Oriya—broken down into smaller verb sequences (for Gta? four verbs is the largest common series), one (non-finite) verb form marked by the clausal clitic *-su* followed by no more than two verbs. (Remo breaks up verb series even more, but the data here are minimal.) But the *-su'* can be and often is deleted, which throws the form back to a Gta?-like three-verb series once more. And more complications.

As to how GR developed-PR: the three languages that keep the old SM subject prefixes are Juang, Gorum, and Gta?, all three small groups, and quite isolated (this is slightly less true for Gorum). Prefixes have been largely phased out (see North Munda), and no new ones innovated in Munda, new suffixation (again look at NM) becoming more and more important. Along with this the S of SOV, and a noun phrase with a more or less expanded S- this seems true of large parts of the Indian linguistic area—is losing ground. That the subject needs to be marked, if not in every sentence, is true, and it is in the verb phrase that this is done more and more. Munda has no person-marking verb suffixes, or number-gender markers on the verb. If Gutob, minimizing its S phrases, needs to mark the subject in the verb phrase, an enclitic seems the likeliest way of it could have done this. Pronominal information of a similar kind in that position is found in the old imperatives, and perhaps some residues of the old—pre-GRG—object suffixes and the syntactic arrangements that went with these (what might these be?) facilitated this development. As you see in the Gta? section the primacy of affixal/clitic marking in the verb phrase is found there too, and perhaps is old in GRG, and the frequent deletion of PR, similar in the two languages, goes back to GRG. But Gutob has certainly elaborated -PR usage and given it a variety and flexibility that it probably did not have in its earliest stages. It's stylistic way with -PR does things that Gta? cannot do. What, more precisely, the uses of the various positional variants may be is a relevant question, and something else we still can't say much about.

The Munda languages have considerable diversity and time depth, more so than either Dravidian or Indo-Aryan. The modern languages have a variety of subject- and object-marking patterns and syntactic arrangements using these. It should be possible—and would be interesting for the development of clitic formations, among other things—to reconstruct much of the morphology and syntax of, say, Proto-South Munda.

Remo

Remo is closely related to Gutob.. The two differ in the enclitic marking of third person subjects. Gutob-Remo has lost the GRG dual. Gutob marks the third plural with *-nen,* the usual noun plural suffix; the singular is unmarked. In Remo neither singular nor plural is marked on the verb form. The Gutob form is probably an innovation, but there are similar third plural-marking arrangements elsewhere in South Munda. In the skimpy text material (included in Bhattacharya's Dictionary) this makes for even fewer examples of -PR man and (an old) woman' in Gutob is:

kunig+ũ̆ḍam ḍi?-to ḍu-gu-NEN
(or ḍokra=ḍukri)
old woman-old man 'it is said' be-Pṣt1-PR (3P1)

In Remo a. ḍokra+ḍikri ḍi-ga to
or b. ḍokra-mwi+ḍikri-mwi ḍi-ga to

a. old-man+old woman be-Pst1 narrative particle
b. old man-one+old woman-one...

In Gta? ḍokra+ḍukri-pa m-ba-ya læ?-ge
old man+old woman-dual nominalizing prefix-
two-animate be/stay-GPst classifier

In Gutob the bound—enclitic—forms of the subject pronouns are copies of the free forms. In Remo this is true of all the pronouns but the first singular, *niŋ* when free, and as -PR everywhere except after the Present-Future tense suffix -tV-, where it is *-iŋ*. The *-iŋ* is more tightly bound than Gutob *niŋ*. Regarding movement in the complex verb from one verb form to another, only one Present-Future tense-marked form can occur, so there is no possible alternation of *-iŋ* and *-niŋ*, or an alternative marking. Historically, one can take -t-iŋ, not phonologically conditioned, as a reduced form of *-tV-niŋ*, and/or from, or influenced by older affixed *-iŋ* forms of the first person singular (i.e. old object suffixes).

Examples of clitic usage:

a. (with a single verb)
niŋ mwi buddi dem-t-Iŋ
i one trick do-PrFu-PR
I will play a trick (on the monkey).

b. (with (?) VAuxA ḍen- progressive)
No ma lu-lu? -ḍen-NO, lu?
You(sg) what Redup-ask/beg- Aux-PR ask (zero Imper2)
Whatever you are asking for, ask!, i.e. Ask (me) for whatever you want!

According to Fernandez [(on Hill Remo (Boṇḍa)]—Bhattacharya is recording the very similar Plains Boṇḍa—the form should be *lu-lu?-ḍen-ta-NO*. There are more examples of AuxB with *beṛ-*, 'to give' used as it is in Gutob, but the large majority with third person subjects:

c. a- mag- o(?) be?-t - Iŋ
caus-know-Pst2 AuxB-Pr-Fu-PR
I will teach (you a trick).

d. ḍora sun-o? ma-palay bug-o(?)-beṛ-o(?)-NIŋ
old man sayPst2 what-for beat-Pst2-AuxB-Pst2-PR

The old man said: 'what did I beat (her) for?', i.e. 'for nothing, for no good reason

The -PR is on V2 in these (and all noted) cases. Fernandez gives other auxiliary verbs, *suŋ-* a completive (cognate with the Gutob intensive), *goŋ* -to be able- and *ḍuso?-* to want to, *-suŋ-* occurring in V1-Pst2-AuxB(*suŋ-*) tense constructions, the other two in Redup-V-Aux-tense-PR constructions, i.e.—more or less—as AuxA.

Remo, in Bhattacharya's texts has a clausal clitic, -sa, cognate with and functioning somewhat like Gutob *-su,* Plains Gta?*-ce(?),* Hill Gta? *-c-(?),* but breaks up verb phrases much more than Gta? does, and even more than Gutob does using a 'conjunctive particle/clitic', *-se?/ -se?-ta* where Gta? and Gutob would have a verb series. An example of *-se?*:

e. oy-baŋ-sa mwi-bo ḍaktor riṛ-o(?)-se? sum-NAŋ
today-from-emph one-loc
milk (to)milk-Pst2-se? eat-we
From today let us milk (the buffalo's) milk and eat in one (the same) place.

Here Gutob would use *-su* for Remo *-se?*, but in f. Gutob would have a -cliticless *ḍon-o? riŋ-gi*. The difference between Remo *-sa* and *-se?/-se?ta* is not clear. The former in these texts is not very common.

f. ḍokra mar ḍokri mwi mwi ḍon-o(?) se?ta ruŋ-ga
old man old woman one one to carry SE?TA bring- and/along with? on the shoulders Pst1
The old man and the old woman carrying them one by one on their shoulders brought them (home).

Neither the data nor Fernandez and Bhattacharya permit a more detailed analysis of verb sequences in Remo.

Gta?

Gta? has no pronominal clitics, but subject pronouns, the bound-prefixed to a verb stem-pronouns, and the free pronouns in the sentence-initial noun phrase work in most ways as subject pronouns do in Gutob: the free subject pronoun in the initial noun phrase is commonly deleted in 'casual discourse' if it is markable on the verb form; the bound-prefixed-subject marker is obligatory. Third person pronouns are not markable on the verb form: verb forms with third person subject-third person singular, third person dual, and third person plural, are unmarked, and therefore identical. The initial subject noun phrase is commonly reduced to nothing (in the surface sentence) where the verb form has first or second person subjects. The presence of an overt noun phrase in a sentence in casual conversational style usually implies a third person subject.

What is interesting in Gutob is the placement of the enclitic (and the semantics of possible alternative clitic placement). It usually attaches somewhere in the complex verb piece, occasionally outside it on an adverb preceding the verb piece in the verb phrase or on a post-verb phrase vocative or particle, and, very occasionally, in the initial noun phrase. The placement of PR- in Gta? is almost always predictable. There are only two exceptional forms in the seventy-five examples of PR- in the hundred-odd pages of Mahapatra and Zide's Gta? Texts. Since the Gta? complex verb piece-PR-attaches to nonfinite verb forms as well as finite, but the elaborate finite complex verb forms are what we need to describe and analyse—is more and sometimes differently complicated than the parallel structures in Gutob, the relevant aspects of this complexity need to be described, the placement of PR- specified, and the two exceptional forms noted and commented on.

The 'subjects' of imperative sentences—all second persons: *na* you sg, *pa* you dual, *pe* you pl—are marked differently: *na* is not marked on the verb form [(thus (*na*) coŋ '(You) eat!', compare (*na*) *na-coŋ+e* 'You (sg) will eat.'; *pa* and *pe* are suffixed to the verb form: *coŋ-pe*! 'You (pl) eat!' (There is a 'zero imperative' for transitive verbs)]. The same pattern obtains in Gutob-Remo. This-presumably old-construction probably provided one model for the development of subject enclitic pronouns in Gutob-Remo.

Verb Complexes

PR- attaches before the final verb of a sequence of verbs whether this be an auxiliary of whatever class, or a non-auxiliary verb in a verb series. In bimorphemic verb stems where both morphemes are considered to be verb stems the PR- precedes the second morpheme (when the verb occurs finally) whether or not one or the other of the verb morphemes is 'empty', i.e. occurs independently as a verb. Thus, *lag-ḍo,* 'to run away' where *lag-* is empty, and *ḍo* means 'to run', and *jog-talig,* 'to throw away', where *jog-*, 'to pick up' occurs as an independent verb, but *talig-* (which the informants tell you 'doesn't mean anything') does not, are marked M1-PR-M2-. In the example sentences only *jog-talig-* in Sentence 2 is a bimorphemic verb stem. All the other verb morphemes constitute separate verb stems in serial construction. Where a bimorphemic stem has a noun—a monosyllable combining form of an incorporated noun—as the second morpheme the PR- comes before the verb stem, not before the noun. The one example in these texts, *bi?=coŋ-* is interesting because *coŋ* could be taken as the verb meaning 'to eat' as well as the combining form of the (derived by infixation) noun *c-n-oŋ,* 'something to eat, food'. The interpretation as an incorporated (object) noun makes more sense semantically, and simplifies the description of PR- attachment.

The common AUX types are Aux A, notably the perfective læ?- (intransitive), literally 'to stay'/ *bo-*(transitive), 'to put', and the progressive or continuous *ḍiŋ-*, 'to do' with transitive suffixes, 'to become' with intransitive. Aux B are borrowed-calqued-directly from Indo-Aryan, Aux A are not old in Munda or Gutob-Remo-Gta?, but the innovating was more complicated—are the completive, literally 'to go', Gta? *we-/e-,*Gutob *ui-*, and 'motion or benefit away from the speaker', literally 'to give', Gta? *bi?-*, Gutob *beḍ-*. Gta? uses the bare verb stem which is followed by the inflected Aux B; Gutob has a (frozen-there is no other option) past form before the Aux, perhaps modelling this on one analysis of the probable Oriya source form *kɔr (-)i*. Parallel forms are (Hindi) *mar ga-(y)aa,* (Oriya) *mɔri gɔla,* Gutob *goj-gi ui-gi,* and Gta? *gwe? we-ge,* all of these 'die go-past', with the Gutob V1 taking the intransitive past-*gu/-gi,* and the Indo-Aryan forms marking person (Oriya) and gender/number (Hindi) in one or another way.

The verb 'to go' occurs as the initial member of a series of Gta? verbs (as *e-*) in constructions similar to those in Gutob (see the various Gutob sentences from the Barogaṭia/Jom story) where the verb takes a tense suffix. The various serial constructions using, prominently, verbs of motion and positioning (come, bring, go, return, stay) will not be discussed here. With double verb stems, where+Vdb is either an echo (phonologically derived), or a second verb stem more or less idiomatically conjoined with V1, both verbs take-or don't take -PR (See Example 3):

1. (mæ) e-liŋ-ranŋ-ke (No Pr-, subject is 3 Sg (mæ 'he/she')
   he go-pick up/buy-bring-K-'past'
   (He) went and bought and brought back (the meat).
2. næŋ ba-gwe?-jog-N-talig+e
   I caus?-die jog-I-talig+Future (jog-talig bimorphemic stem
   'to throw away', jog- to pick up'
   I will kill (you) and throw (you - i.e. your body) away.
3. ḍokra, na bole+nturia? NA-coŋ+NA-ug-k(e)-ṛe?
   old man you(sg) rice+ millet gruel
   YOU-eat+YOU-drink-K'past'-interrog
   Old man, didn't you eat/drink your rice and millet gruel?
4. a?-kuṛe?-N- ḍiŋ-ke
   cause-meet-I- AuxA (progressive)-K'past'
   I am causing-to-meet, i.e. fixing (you) up (with a girl).
5. bobo, a-na-ke m-mwiŋ sela bihæ-M-bi?+e
   child, acc-you(sg)-acc one girl marry-I-give (AuxB)-Future
   Child (son), I will marry you off to a girl. (i.e. I will find a girl for you to marry.)
6. e-tur-N-ke+e
   go-look for-I-see/find+Future
   I will go and look for and see/find (a girl for you).
7. næŋ ḍugḍi e-ko-N-læ?+e
   I garden/vegetable patch go-sit-I-stay-Future
   I will go and sit down and stay in the garden.
8. e-hwe?-NE-raŋ
   go harvest/cut/reap -WE-bring
   Let us go and cut (the millet) and bring it home
9. jog-NE-bi?=coŋ+e
   pick up-we- raise/bring up-Future bi?=coŋ - lit. to give food
   Let us pick up and raise (the infant).

10. jibon b-a?-rwa-NA(M)-bo-ke
    life to live/be alive-cause-you-AuxA (transitive perfective) -K'past'
    the verb is *brwa-*, *-a?-*is a causative infix
    You caused me to live my life, i.e. You saved my life.

The two exceptional forms are:

11. N-wig-mia?-ke
    I-return-AuxA-K'past' mia?, lit. 'to know how', habitual, to be used to (V-ing)
    I habitually went back..
12. N-we?-gag-ce.... -ce the clausal clitic 'after having V-ed'
    I-swing-tie-CE 'V-ed and...'
    After I swung (in the swing made up creepers) and tied (the swing)...

What is different about these two is that PR- comes at the beginning of the verb sequence, and not, as expected, before the second verb. i.e. we would expect *we?-N-gag*...and *wig-M-mia?*.

I don't know why the expected forms were not produced, whether they are possible, preferred or non-preferred, and for what reasons. No Gta? informants are avilable in Chicago, and although there is a great deal of text material outside GTA? Texts I don't know that going through all those texts would clarify matters. Conceivably the PR- attachment was made in anticipation of a single V1, and not V1-V2. Almost all these texts were from a single informant, Dobek Pujari, whereas the Gutob texts came from four or five chief informants, and it is likely that greater variation would be found in a more diverse text sample. But it seems very likely that the sorts of alternative placements of enclitic subjects in Gutob, and the conditions governing them are not found for Gta? PR-, in the complex verb piece, in the large verb phrase, or anywhere else.

NOTES

1. The Fernandez data is from A Grammatical Sketch of Remo: A Munda Language, by Frank Fernandez, an unpublished Ph.D dissertation at the University of North

Carolina, 1967. Much of the research on Gutob and Gta? was supported by a greant from the National Science Foundation.

2. The Gutob data come from fieldnotes of Bimal P. Das, Richard DeArmond and Norman Zide from the summers of 1962, 1963 and 1964, and Das's and Zide's work in 1966-7. The Gta? material comes from Khageshwar Mahapatra and Norman Zide's *gta? Texts,* and lots of field notes. See also *Didayi, Vyaakaraṇa, Racanaavalii, Shabdakosha* (in Oriya) by P.K. Panda, Kh. Mahapatra, and D. Pujari, Academy of Tribal Dialects and Cultures, Bhubaneshwar, 1989. There is a literature on pronominal clitics, almost none of data paper. See Jerrold Sadock, *Autolexical Syntax*, University of Chicago Press, 1991, and Hagit Borer, editor, *Syntax and Semantics,* Volume 19, Academic Press, 1986, and the references in these works.

CHAPTER 18

TYPOLOGY OF LANGUAGE CHANGE* AND MAINTENANCE AMONG THE SANTALS AND MUNDAS

M. Ishtiaq

Introduction

Language change among the tribes in India is noticed throughout the country although its mangnitude varies from region to region and from tribe to tribe. Its variation depends upon the degree of exposure to external influences and other locational factors. The tribes living in the core of the tribal region have shown least inclination to change their traditional language. On the other hand, the tribal groups living on the peripheries of their heartland have shown a tendency of adaptability to communicate in more than one language (Ishtiaq, 1991:2). At their home, they speak their own traditional language while with the non-tribal people they communicate in the non-traditional languages. This tendency of bilingualism, in the due course of time has

*Footnote by the editor: the author uses the term 'language change' to refer to the general concept of 'change in the use of mothertongue', i.e. language shift.

led to the change, specially among the people belonging to the new generations who found their traditional language less functional as compared to the language of non-tribal communities. The learning of the non-tribal languages became an asset to them to enter the new social order (Chumaceiro, 1983:35). Besides growth of literacy, urbanization, industrialization and change in their traditional beliefs (Dalton, 1872:124) are some of the important factors to bring about a language change among the tribal communities in India. These factors, according to Moag, may be classified into demographic, political, social, and sociolinguistic (1987:49-63). Since all these factors do not play their roles uniformly at every place and in every tribal group, there exists variations in the degree of language change from place to place and from tribe to tribe.

Objectives

The objectives of the study are to find out the variations in the degree of language change and maintenance among the two major tribal communities namely, the Santals and the Mundas of India, and secondly, to develop the typology of language change and maintenance to demarcate the areas of mixed grades of language change and maintenance for both the tribes separately.

Data Base and Methodology

The data for this study have been derived from a secondary source. Since, the data on language change are not available from the census reports of 1971 and 1981, the study is based on 1961 census data. Special tables for Scheduled Castes and Scheduled Tribes, Vol. V-A for all the concerned states have been used for the collection of the data.

The data available on language are found in the discrete series fragmented into males and females as well as into rural and urban segments. To get the aggregate figure at the distict level, male and female population of rural and urban areas have been clubbed together. The degree of language change has been calculated for both the tribal communities with the help of percentages. Secondly, the maps of language change and maintenance have been superimposed to find out the typology in order to demarcate the areas of mixed grades of change and maintenance for both the tribal groups. The details of these methods have been discussed at the relevant places in the paper. The maps have been prepared by using the choroplething technique.

Language Change and Maintenance

The words 'change' and 'maintenance' of language have been used here to specify the language shift and preservation respectively. Linguistically, the change in language may be studied in both Apparent time and Real time (Chambers and Trudgill, 1980:88). The change in real time can be studied in more than one point of time while the apparent change can be studied at only one point of time. The former is known as diachronic study of language whereas the latter is known as synchronic study. Since, the data are not available for more than one point of time, the study is based on the language change in apparent time. An earlier study revealed that half of the tribal population in India have declared a non-tribal language as their mothertongue (Roy Burman, 1972:42). It indicated that this section of the tribal population have changed their traditional dialect with which they were linguistically attached. On the other hand, the remaining half of the tribal population of the country continued to be affiliated with their traditional language and declared one or the other forms of it as their tongue. The former group of the tribal population declared change of language while the latter group has maintained their affiliation with their traditional language.

Language Maintenance among the Santals

The Santals, despite having a long period of contact with the neighbouring areas are the largest tribal group who have been tenaciously holding onto Santali i.e. their traditional dialect as their mothertongue (Kochar, 1970:25). Sen observed that though they have given up their nomadic character, they retained their traditional language (1984:23). The degree of language maintenance among the Santals varies from less than one per cent to hundred per cent. Such a large variation has been classified into five groups with the interval of 20 per cent. Out of the 37 districts including Tripura in which the Santals are above 100 persons in number, there are 35 districts in which the Santals have declared Santali as their mothertongue although its share varies from district to district. There are four districts—Purnia, Saharsa, Malda, and Cuttuck in which almost hundred per cent Santals have returned to their traditional language as mothertongue. The share of Santali goes to more than 80 per cent in the other 17 districts. Out of these 13 districts have more than 90 per cent Santals declared Santali as their mothertongue. There are nine districts in which the degree of language maintenance varies from 40 to 80 per cent while in another two districts it varies from 20 to 40 per cent. The degree of maintenance is less than 10 per cent in three districts only (Table 1).

TABLE 1

Language change and Maintenance among the Santgals

%	Traditional	Other trib.	Regional	non-Trib./non-Reg.
100	4	—	1	—
> 80	17	—	4	—
60-80	6	—	2	—
40-60	3	—	1	—
20-40	2	2	3	—
< 20	3	10	20	8

Language Maintenance among the Mundas

The Mundas are believed to be the only primitive tribes of the country who belong to Munda or Kolarian, a pre-Aryan tongue which has been wonderfully preserved by different tribes of Bihar and Bengal (Dalton, 1872:123 and Roy, 1970:284). The degree of language maintenance among the Mundas also vary widely. Out of the total 41 districts including Tripura in which Mundas are above 100 persons in number, there are 28 districts in which the Mundas have declared varying degrees of Mundari as their mothertongue. There are two districts—Patna and Singhbhum in which more than 80 per cent Mundas have declared Mundari as their mothertongue. On the other hand there are 11 districts in which the share of Mundari is less than 20 per cent. The share of Mundari varies between 20 and 40 per cent in eight districts while it ranges from 40 to 80 per cent in another seven districts (Table 2).

TABLE 2

Language Change and Maintenance among the Mundas

%	Traditional	Other trib.	Regional	non-Trib./non-Reg.
100	—	—	1	—
> 80	2	2	8	—
60-80	4	6	5	2
40-60	3	3	6	1
20-40	8	3	12	2
< 20	11	21	8	18

Language Change among the Santals

The degree of language change among the Santals varies from less than one per cent in the district of Santal Parganas to hundred per cent in Puri and Sundargarh districts of Orissa. As much as 20 districts of the region in which less than one-fourth of the Santal population declared non-traditional language as their mothertongue. The degree of language change is more than 60 per cent in five districts only. In the remaining six districts the degree of the change varies between 20 and 60 per cent.

A closer investigation reveals that the language change among the Santals is multidimensional. In other words, the Santals have adopted a regional language, a invariably the non-tribal language belonging to the people of higher socio-economic and political background. Secondly, a small section of the Santals specially from West Bengal have shown a tendency of declaring the languages of other tribal groups with whom they had developed a close association. Thirdly, there are a group of Santals who live along the border areas of various states who have shown a tendency towards declaring a language which is neither tribal nor regional. These are the three broad dimensions in which the language change of the tribes may occur. The majority of the change may be found under the first category i.e., the regional language. It is to be noted that out of the total, there are 31 districts in which the change is found towards the regional language. There are 12 districts in which the Santals have declared other tribal languages and in eight districts non-tribal non-regional languages as their mothertongues. In both these cases the degree of change remained less than 40 per cent and less than 20 per cent respectively. On the other hand, the share of regional languages reaches to hundred per cent in Puri district (Table 1).

Language Change among the Mundas

The degree of language change among the Mundas also varies greatly. Out of the total there are 13 districts in which cent per cent Mundas have changed their traditional language and declared non-traditional language as their mothertongue. The degree of language change is found more than 80 per cent in 11 districts. The share of the change varies from 60 to 80 per cent in eight districts while there are seven districts in which the degree of change varies between 20 and 60 per cent. There are only two districts in which less than 10 per cent of the Munda population have declared non-traditional language as their tongue.

The multidimensional language change among the Mundas also reveals that a majority of them have adopted the regional language (Grierson, 1967:79). The share of the regional language reaches to hundred per cent in Purnia district, while it is more than 60 per cent in the other 13 districts. Of these, there are nine districts in which more than 80 per cent Mundas have declared the regional language as their mothertongue. The share of the regional language varies from 20 to 60 per cent in 18 districts while the remaining eight districts have less than 20 per cent share of regional language. There are eight districts in which more than 60 per cent Mundas have declared other tribal languages as their tongue. Its share varies from 20 to 60 per cent in six districts only. In the remaining 21 districts the share of other tribal languages remained less than 20 per cent. The share of non-tribal non-regional languages is more than 60 per cent in two districts only whereas it varies from 20 to 60 per cent in three districts. The remaining 18 districts have less than 20 per cent of Munda population, who have declared non-tribal non-regional languages as their mothertongue (Table 2).

Typology of Language Change and Maintenance

The degree of language change and maintenance among the Santals and the Mundas varies from less than one per cent to hundred per cent. Such a large variation in the data has been classified into four categories with the interval of 25 per cent to demarcate the areas of various degrees of change and maintenance—very high, high, medium, and low (See Table 3 and 4). It must be remembered that the percentages have been transferred into round figures for the purpose of convenience and less than 0.5 per cent has been considered as zero whereas more than 99.5 per cent as 100.

TABLE 3

Typology of Language Maintenance and Change among the Santals (Maintenance)

Percentage	No. of Districts	Name of Districts
> 75	19	Mongher, Singhbhum, Darjeeling, West Dinajpur, Murshidabad, Nadia, Hooghly, Burdwan, Birbhum, Bankura, Midnapore, Balasore, Mayurbhanj, Tripura, Bhagalpur, Santal Parganas, Hazaribagh, Ranchi, Dhanbad,
50-75	7	Jalpaiguri, Calcutta, Howrah, Purulia, Ganjam, Keonjhar, Dhenkanal,
25-50	2	Cooch Behar, 24-Parganas
< 25	3	Gaya, Palamau, Koraput
100% Maintenance in		Saharsa, Purnia, Malda, Cuttuck.
100% Change in		Puri, Sundargarh.

TABLE 4

Typology of Language Maintenance and Change among the Mundas (Maintenance)

Percentage	No. of Districts	Name of Districts
> 75	3	Patna, Ranchi, Singhbhum
50-75	4	West Dinajpur, Malda, Midnapore, Sundargarh
25-50	7	Palamau, Hazaribagh, Dhanbad, Murshidabad, Howrah, Burdwan, Bankura

Percentage	No. of Districts	Name of Districts
< 25	14	Shahabad, Santal Parganas, Raigarh, Raipur, Nadia, 24-Parganas, Calcutta, Hooghly, Purulia, Cooch Behar, Boudhkhandmals, Mayurbhanj, Dhenkanal Tripura.
100% Change in		Bhagalpur, Purnia, Surguja, Darjeeling, Jalpaiguri, Ganjam, Balasore, Cuttack, Keonjhar, Bolangir, Sambalpur, Kalahandi, Koraput

In order to find out the typology, the above identified categories of language change and maintenance have been shown on the maps for both the tribes separately. The maps of maintenance and change have been superimposed to demarcate the mixed degrees of change and maintenance. The following types of areas of the change and maintenance emerged out of superimposition of the maps:

a) Areas of very high maintenance with low change (VI);
b) Areas of high maintenance with medium change (Hm);
c) Areas of medium maintenance with high change (Mh);
d) Areas of low maintenance with very high change (Lv).

A Case Study of Santals

Areas of VI type: There are three pockets of this type consisting of 19 districts. The largest pocket comprising of 16 districts lying on the Chotanagpur plateau and its adjacent areas. An another pocket is located in the north in West Bengal. Tripura which is lying in isolation has also been classified under this type. It is the third pocket of the VI type lying in the north east India.

Areas of Hm type: There are five small pockets classified under this type. Except Purulia district, which lies in the midst of VI type on the Chotanagpur plateau, the other two pockets lie on the south of the VI type in Orissa. The remaining two pockets are located in West Bengal comprising of Calcutta and Howrah districts in the south and Jalpaiguri district in the north of the state.

TYPOLOGY OF LANGUAGE CHANGE AND MAINTENANCE (1961)

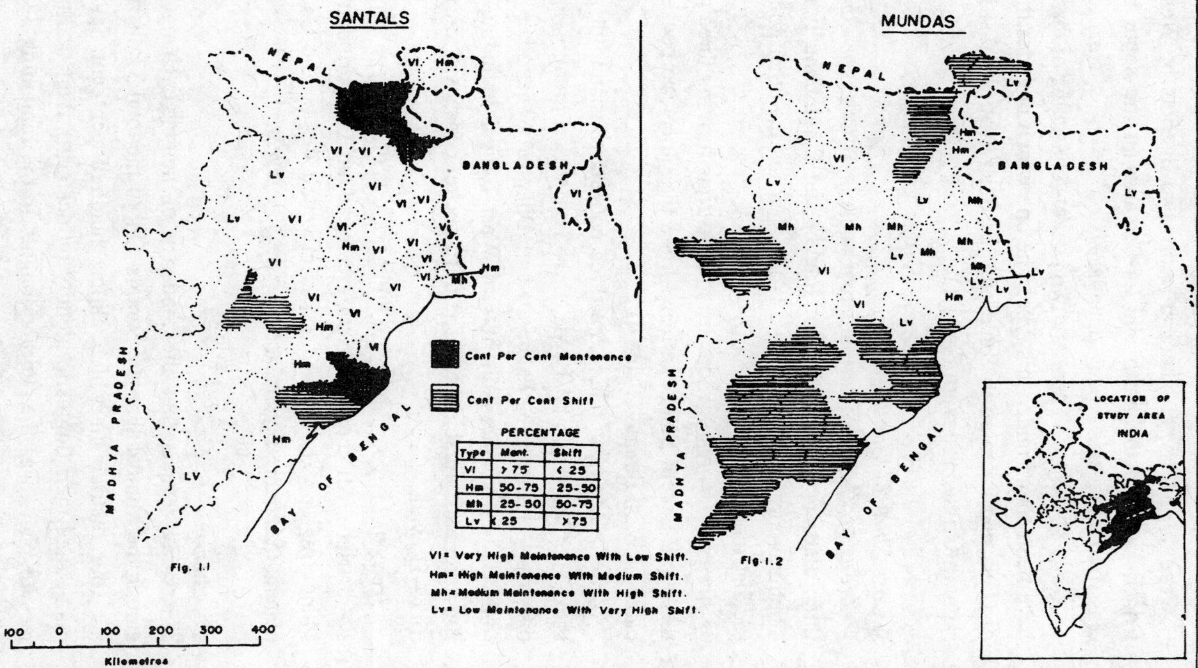

Fig. 1.1

Fig. 1.2

Areas of Mh type: There are only two districts of West Bengal-Cooch Bihar in the north and 24-Parganas in the south have been classified under this type (Appendix I).

Areas of Lv type: There are two pockets consisting of three districts have been found under this type. The one which includes the districts of Gaya and Palamau in Bihar and the other is in the district of Koraput in Orissa (See map; Fig. 1.1).

A Case Study of Mundas

Areas of Vl type: There are two pockets of this type consisting of three districts. The districts of Ranchi and Singhbhum lying on the Chotanagpur plateau forming a larger area and the other pocket lies in the district of Patna.

Areas of Hm type: There are four districts forming three pockets of this type. Except Sundargarh in Orissa the other two pockets are located in West Bengal (Table 4).

Area of Mh type: There are three pockets consisting of seven districts. To the north of Vl type, there is a pocket comprising of three districts—Hazaribagh, Palamau, and Dhanbad. The other pocket is found in the southern districts of West Bengal including Bankura, Burdwan and Murshidabad. The third pocket consists of only one district—Howrah.

Areas of Lv type: There are eight pockets of this type consisting of 14 districts. All these districts are found on the peripheries of the Munda region except Purulia district which lies on the Chotanagpur plateau (See map; Fig. 1.2).

Conclusion

The study reveals that the tendency of language change is more among the Mundas than the Santals. Out of the total 37 districts, there are four districts in which almost hundred per cent Santals have maintained their linguistic identity by declaring their traditional dialect i.e. Santali as their mothertongue. In the remaining 33 districts, 19 have been classified under very high degree of language maintenance with low degree of change. There are seven districts which have been classified under high degree of maintenance with medium degree of change while two districts under the medium degree of maintenance with high degree of change. There are three districts falling under the low maintenance with very high change. Besides, there are two districts in which cent per cent Santals have switched over to non-traditional language. On the other hand there are 13 districts in which cent per cent Mundas have declared non-traditional languages as their tongues. The degree of change is very high with low maintenance in 14 districts, high change with medium maintenance in seven districts, medium change with high maintenance in four districts and low change with very high degree of maintenance is found in three districts only.

The study of typology of change and maintenance reveals that the areas of Vl type are located in the heartland of the tribal region whereas the areas of Lv type lie on the peripheris. The areas of Hm and Mh types are commonly found in between these two above-mentioned types. Some irregular pattern in the distribution of these types can also be seen. It may be due to the development of mining centres, industries, and urban centres in the tribal region and the migration of tribal population to the non-tribal region.

The values of coefficient of variation for language maintenance are 39.6 among the Santals and 82.4 among the Mundas indicating lower regional variation among the Santals than the Mundas. On the other hand, the values for language change are 40.7 among the Mundas and 109 among the Santals indicating lower regional variation among the Mundas than the Santals.

REFERENCES

Chambers, J.K. and P. Trudgill (1980). *Dialectology*. Cambridge, Cambridge University Press.

Chumaceiro, R.M. (1983) "Language Maintenance and Shift Among Jerusalem Sephardim", *International Journal of Sociolinguistics*, Vol. 37, pp. 25-39.

Dalton, E.T. (1872). *Descriptive Ethnology of Bengal*, Calcutta, Office of the Superintendent of Govt. Printing.

Grierson, G.A. (1967). *Linguistic Survey of India*, Vol. IV, Delhi (reprint), Motilal Banarasidass.

Ishtiaq, M. (1991). "Dialectal/Linguistic Change among the Scheduled Tribes in India and Its Correlates—A Geographical Analysis:" Ph.D. dissertation, Jawaharlal Nehru University, New Delhi. Unpublished

Kochar, V. (1970). *Social Organisation among the Santals,* Calcutta, Editions India.

Moag, R.E. (1987). "Causal Factors in the Loss/Maintenance of Minority Language: The case of Tamil in Fiji," *International Journal of Dravidian Linguistics,* Vol. 16, No. 1, pp. 49-76.

Roy Burman, B.K. (1972). "Tribal Demography: A Preliminary Appraisal" in K.S. Singh (ed.) *Tribal Situation in India,* Simla, Indian Institute of Advanced Study, pp. 39-50.

Roy, S.C. (1970). *The Mundas and Their Country,* Bombay, Asia Publishing House.

Sen, S. (1984). *The Santals of Jungle Mahals,* Calcutta, Ratna Prakashan.

CHAPTER 19

WORD ORDER IN KHASI*

K.S. Nagaraja

Introduction

A language is said to have a single type of Word Order, say S-O-V for Indo Aryan and Dravidian languages. However, what if the various dialects of a language display different word orders? What order should be considered as basic or representative of the language in such situations? In this paper data from an Austroasiatic language—Khasi, is presented, wherein different dialects display different/divergent orders. However, theoretical issues connected with this are not touched upon here.

Khasi is a member of Mon-Khmer branch of Austroasiatic family. It is spoken mainly in the state of Meghalaya by around six lakh speakers. Khasi has many dialects. Some of these dialects display interesting divergences in the aspect of Word Order. The main dialects (among others) of Khasi are the following: Standard Khasi, Bhoi-Jirang, Langrin, Nongtung, Lyngngam and War. In the following paragraphs word order in the first five dialects will be discussed in some detail. In the process of discussing word order, various other features of these dialects will also be discussed, briefly wherever relevant.

Standard Khasi

The Standard Khasi has an S-V-O order. Within this order, in the subject NP, the attribute follows the noun. This variety displays an interesting aspect of agreement. It is between the subject and the verb (predicate) of the same clause. Here the agreement markers are none other than the third person pronouns. The third person pronouns are: *u* masculine singular, *ka* feminine singular, and *ki* common plural. There is one main limitation in the use of these agreement markers. That is, these function as agreement markers only when they occur with nouns. In this variety all nouns invariably have to take either *u* or *ka* in singular and *ki* in plural. These are placed before the nouns as such. But the combination of these and nouns give rise to 'phrases' instead of 'words'. Having SVO order means that the subject occurs first in a sentence. However the agreement markers occur preceding the nouns. When there is a pronoun as the subject, these agreement markers themselves function as personal pronouns. (So these have been called pronominal markers in K.S. Nagaraja, 1985.) In a possessive construction, the genitive maker follows the head noun. In the verbal complex, the correlative agreement marker occurs at the extreme left of it. The t/a/m elements occur preceding the main verb but after the agreement maker. If there is a negative element it occurs preceding the tense markers but after the agreement markers. Similarly, the auxiliaries also occur after the agreement markers. An adverb occurs after the verbal complex sometimes as part of the verbal complex itself; but could have some freedom of occurrence.

The 'Object' occurs after the verbal complex in a prepositional structure (This is true of all the dialects). So, the prepositions precede the nouns. In the standard variety the case markers are the following: nominative: ϕ, accusative (objective): *va,* instrumental: *da,* dative and locative: *ha,* ablative: *na,* goal (motion): *š̆a,* sociative: *bad,* and possessive: *joŋ.*

The tense distinction is (i) present: zero, (ii) past: *la,* and (iii) future: *īn; sa* is definite marker used in future tense. The negative marker is *īm.* It usually occurs immediately after the tense markers. In past negatives, a particle *šīm* occurs.

The interrogative markers belong to two types. The first group contains two bound forms *-no* and *-ey* which take pronominal, prepositional and a few other elements for their occurrence. The interrogative formed using *-no* conveys definiteness, whereas with *-ey* conveys indefiniteness. The free form is: *ayu* 'what'. *ayu* occurs sentence finally. The combinations of *-no* are more extensive than with those of *-ey*. To illustrate: u/ka/ki-no 'who', la/mīn-no 'when', ya-no 'whom'(obj.), joŋ-no 'whose'; u/ka/ki-ey 'who' etc. They occupy either sentence initial or final position. The data on interrogatives in other dialects is not sufficient enough to provide a comparative picture. Hence this aspect will not be discussed in this paper.

The following constructions of Standard Khasi (spoken around Cherrapunjii) illustrate the above features:

(1) (a) u leyt
he go-prs (ϕ)
'he goes'

(b) u la leyt
he pst go
'he went'

(2) *u* briew *u* la wan
man pst come
'the/a man came'

(3) ka n sa ba:m
she-fut def eat
'she will eat'

(4) *ka* briew *ka* la leyt ša (ka) iyeŋ
woman pst go to home
'the woman went home'

(5) *ka* khīnna? *ka* n leyt sukisuki
girl she-will go slow-slow
'the girl will go slowly'

(6) *u* kīnsay *u* n sa pīn-yap ya u bseñ
Kynsai will cause-die obj snake
'Kynsai will kill a snake'

(7) *ka* khīnna? *ka* a:y ya ka kot ha ka
girl give obj book to her
'the girl gives the book to her'

(8) *ka* briew *ka* la ba:m ya u so?
woman pst eat obj a fruit
'a woman ate a fruit'

(9) u khīnna? u *m* ba:m
boy neg eat
'the boy does not eat'

(10) ka khīnna? kan *īm* trey ya ka ka:m
girl fut neg do obj work
'the girl will not do the work'

(11) *ŋam šīm* la leyt
I-neg pst go
'I did not go'

Some of the other dialects show interesting divergences:-

Langrin

This variety (spoken in West Khasi hills, in Mawkyrwat block) on the whole follows the above order. But it shows certain other differences:

(12) (a) u dayt
he go-prs+ϕ
'he goes'

(b) ga dayt wa?
she go pst
'she went'

(13) u lu? i wa? ba ga kot ka ga-saw
he ? give pst obj book IO (?) she
'he gave the book to her'

(14) *u* skaw *u* kluŋ ba ga miyu
dog chase obj cat
'the dog chases the cat'

(15) u dayt chay-kot
he go-prs purchase-book
'he is not going'

(16) u dayt rie
he go-prs neg
'he is not going'

(17) *ga* khəndañ *ga* su? chri rie ba ga kam
girl fut do neg obj work
'the girl will not do the work'

(18) gi dayt wa? ciluk
they go pst neg
'they have not gone'

From the above sentences it will become clear that while the basic order is S-V-O, in the verbal complex some differences are observed. 1. While present tense is unmarked in both; past tense marker (which is different), is placed after the verb in this variety while it is opposite in the standard. The future marker is different as well. But it occurs preceding the verb in both. This variety seems to prefer compound verb formation rather than to have infinitive construction(?). The object case marker is *ba* here, while it is *ya* in the standard. Similarly, indirect object case marker in this variety is *ka* (as in 10 (?)), while *ha* in the standard variety.

The personal pronouns of this variety are quite distinct: First person: *ye* 'I', *hi* 'we', (in the standard- *ŋa* and *ŋi* respectively), second person: *phi* 'you' (sg.), *khyew* 'you'(plural), (in the standard- *phi* both in singular and plural), and third person: *u* 'he', *ga* 'she', and *gi* 'they' (in the standard: *u, ka* and *ki* respectively). As can be clearly noted, first person forms are different, in second person the plural form appears to be an innovative feature; and in third person masculine, the form is the same. The other forms appear to be the same too, though there is voice change in the consonant.

In the case of negative formation these two differ significantly, in that here the negative markers are *rie* (as in 13 and 14) and *ciluk* (as in 15) which are placed at the end of the verbal complex; while in the Standard it is *īm,* which is placed before the verbal complex; but after the agreement markers.

Bhoi-Jirang

Bhoi and Jirang dialects (spoken in the East Khasi hills—in Nongpoh block) behave similarly to a large extent (though there are some differences between them). The word order in this variety is intriguing and complex (as well as inconclusive, due to the limited data) as various possibilities are found. All these are exemplified from the sentences listed below:

Bhoi:

(19) VS (a) ley u
go-prs he
'he goes'

(b) la? ley u
pst go he
'he went'

(20) la? ba:m ḍa
pst eat I
'I ate'

(21) ci ba:m ka
fut eat she
'she will eat'

(22) VS+adv: wën ka teñteñ
come-prs she sometimes
'she comes sometimes'

(23) ci wən ka rabit lastep
fut come N tomorrow
'(the) hare will come tomorrow'

(24) VOS: ley thiet-kot u
go-prs buy-book he
'he goes to buy (a) book'

(25) VSO: la? a:y u ka kot ha ka
pst give he book to her
'he gave a book to her'

(26) SVO: *u* bru la? pən-yəp *u u* psñ
man pst cause-die snake
'the man killed a snake'

(27) *u* kīnsay la? chne *u* īŋ iñ
Kynsai pst build obj house
'Kynsai built a house'

(28) V neg S: ci ley re u
fut go neg he
'he will not go/he is not going'

(29) chem ley re ka
pst-part go neg she
'she did not go'

(30) *u* khīnna? ba:m re *u*
boy eat-prs neg
'the boy does not eat'

The above constructions demonstrate the differences between langrin and the standard variety. The interesting point to note here is that it has a complex word order: The word order is either VS(adv) (as in 19-23) or VOS/VSO (as in 24 and 25), or SVO (as in 26-27).

In VS(adv) order the subject could be either a noun or a pronoun, but the object is not present; when the object is present the order is either VOS or VSO. Here the subject can be only a pronoun and cannot be a noun. No agreement markers occur in these.

In SVO order the subject is a noun and not a pronoun. Only here agreement markers are used. Similar to that of the standard the agreement marker occurs preceeding the subject, but its correlative agreement marker occurs after the verbal complex instead of before it.

In 24-26 no case marker is used; whereas in 27 *īn* seems to have been used in this function(?). (Probably there is a preference for compounding here as well.)

A negative element in a sentence occurs after the verb unlike the standard variety where it does so before the verb, as in 28-30. Even here the correlative agreement marker occurs after the negative marker as in 30. In 29 *chem* is used only in past tense. It is similar to *šīm* of the standard variety.

Nongtung

Nongtung is spoken in East Khasi hills- in Umsning block. If an object is not present, but has a subject which could be either a pronoun or a noun, then the word order is VS (as in 31-35). If an object is present then the order could be either VOS/VSO (as in 36-39). Out of the four instances available here, 36 and 37 are representative of VOS. In 36 the subject is a pronoun while in 37 it is a noun. Out of the two representative samples of VSO as in 38 and 39, the first one has a pronoun as subject while 39 has a noun as the subject. None of these have any agreement feature. Further, item 40, provides an instance of SVO, which is similar to that of the standard form, with a difference that agreement marker appears after the object noun. So except for item 40, all others have different orders as compared to the standard. That way this variety is very significant. These aspects are illustrated below:

(31) VS: (a) li u
go-prs he
'he goes'
(b) da li u
pst go he
'he went'

(32) da ba:m ka
pst eat she
'she ate'

(33) porpor la? ka
adv come-prs she
'she comes sometimes'

(34) advVS: da li pənsmat ka bru
pst go adv woman
'the woman went quickly'

(35) adv VS: lamrit ci?la? ka skey
tomorrow fut-come hare
'the hare will come tomorrow'

(36) VOS: li thit kot u
go buy book he
'he goes (to) buy a book'

(37) VOS: da chna jiŋ u kīnsay
pst build house Kynsai
'Kynsai built a house'

(38) VSO: da ay u ka kot ha ka
pst give he book to-her
'he gave a book to her'

(39) VSO: da takara u ksəw ha ka miyu
pst chase dog obj cat
'the dog chased the cat'

(40) SVO: *u* bru pīnjap psəñ *u*
man cause-kill snake
'the man killed a snake'

(41) (a) le re u
go neg he
'he is not going'

(b) em-re ci? li ka
neg fut go she
'she will not go'

(42) bam re u khənna?
eat-prs neg boy
'the boy does not eat'

(43) *ka* khənna? tre re *ka* / tre re ka khənna?
girl do neg do neg girl
'the girl will not do the work',

This variety is highly complex and very interesting. The item 43 provides both the orders, one with subject noun beginning and another, verb beginning. It appears that the first order, i.e., subject noun occurring first seems to be secondary while the other order is primary. As far as the agreement aspect is concerned, it is marked very marginally. Only when the subject noun occurs as the first member in a sentence, then only the agreement is marked (as in 40 and 43). Otherwise no aspect of agreement is shown.

There seems to be a great flexibility as far as the negative constructions are concerned. In general the negative marker occurs after the verb and before the subject or before its agreement marker.

Lyngngam

Lyngngam is spoken in West Khasi hills- in Mawshynrut block. This dialect does not pose much of a problem from the word order point of view. Here the word order is as that of the standard variety, i.e., SVO. However within this, there are some differences as to the placement of the tense markers, negative markers, etc. The position of this variety can be explained from the following illustrations:

(44) (a) tu dənni
he go-prs(zero)
'he goes'

(b) tu di-la?
he go-pst
'he went'

(45) (a) nə baŋla
I eat-pst
'I ate'

(b) gju bənnən di?
she eat fut
'she will eat'

(46) gju līnnar əsonson
she come-prs sometimes
'she comes sometimes'

(47) ju di la? bən thot o kot
he go pst inf buy obj book
'he goes to buy a book'

(48) ju a:y la? o kot hə nam gju
he give pst obj book to her
'he gave a book to her'

(49) kīnsa:y ju əŋ la? o yeñ
kynsai build pst obj house
'Kynsai built a house'

(50) brä phnyap la? sa bəseñ
man cause-die pst obj snake
'the man killed a snake'

(51) ksu wënna-la? sə myəw
dog chase-pst obj cat
'dog chased the cat'

(52) (b) na di? ən-ji
I go-? -neg
'I did not go'

(53) khondañ *gju* di?trey ji
(girl) she work not
'the girl (will) not do the work'

(54) khondañ *tu* baŋ ji
(boy) he eat neg
'the boy does not eat'

Another interesting feature of this variety is that it does not have any sort of agreement. However one aspect has been observed in some constructions where a noun is used as a subject (but not in all). Here, immediately after the noun (as in 49, 53-54), an appropriate pronoun in the third person is used before any other element is used. In a way the pronouns make clear to what class the nouns belong. In other words, nouns by themselves are not distinguished for gender and number. Thus, by using third person markers these distinctions are marked (as clearly shown in 53-54). Similarly it is possible to have a distinction between number, as in: *brä ju* 'man', vs. *brä kyu* 'people'.

The personal pronouns show some variation as compared to other varieties—First person: *nə* 'I', *ya:w* 'we', second person: *mi* 'you' (masc. sg.), *phe* 'you' (fem. sg.), *ma:mi* 'you' (masc. plural), *ma:phe* 'you' (fem. plural), third person: *tu, ju* 'he', *gdu, gju* 'she', and *kyu, kudu* 'common plural'. This system, particularly the second person gender distinctions, remind us of the earlier stage of standard Khasi (where similar distinction existed), but which is no longer in use. Except for the second person forms, other are different. That way this system is very significant.

As stated above, the tense markers occur after the verb. The negative markers occur after the verbal complex. In this aspect also it differs from the standard form. Another important difference is in the verbs. Here the verbs (most of them:) have two forms, one full form and another—contracted form. The full form is used when the verb takes a non-past tense marker, while the contracted form is restricted to past tense, as could be observed above.

Among the case markers, objective case has two markers- *o,* when the object is inanimate (as in 47-48) and *sa,* when the object is animate (as in 50-51).

Conclusion

To conclude, the foregoing discussion on various dialects of Khasi, namely standard Khasi, Langarin, Bhoi, Nongtung and Lyngngam show the extent of diversity found amongst them mainly from the word order point of view. Among the five varieties discussed, standard Khasi, Langrin and Lyngngam are similar from this point of view, whereas Bhoi and Nongtung are very different. Lyngngam though is similar to the first, is quite different in various other aspects. (Infact some question have been raised about its dialecthood). In an attempt to understand the word order of these varieties, various related aspects of these languages have become known to us. No attempt has been made here to provide an exhaustive statement of differences between these varieties. The comparison has been restricted strictly to between standard variety and others. The questions, doubts need to wait for some time before a satisfactory answer can be provided (which demands extensive field work). It is really intriguing to explain how this diversity has came into existence. The significance of the above diversity rests in the change of word order—opposite order in some! Given this state of affairs, 'which order' should be considered as basic for the language? What is the significance of this diversity from the language universals point of view? These and other questions need to be answered in due course of time. This also perhaps shows that for a better understanding of the language structures, detailed studies of various dialects of languages is essential.

NOTES

* (i) This article is based on the data collected using a questionnaire, in 1987 and 1988. (ii) The fieldwork was funded by the University Grants Commission, New Delhi. (iii) In the collection of data I was assisted by my colleague Dr. S.R. Sharma. (iv) Preliminary version of this paper was presented at the 19th International Conference of Dravidian Linguists, held at Trivandrum in July, 1991. (v) ï=unrounded, high central

REFERENCES

Comrie, Bernard, 1981. *Language Universals and Linguistic Typology, Syntax and Morphology.* Oxford Basil Blackwell.

Nagaraja, K.S., 1985. *Khasi, a Descriptive Analysis.* Poona, Deccan College.

CHAPTER 20

COMPOUNDING IN KHASI

Mayjee Philip

Introduction

A compound is a linguistic unit, composed of elements that function independently in other circumstances. There are two sets of compounding:

i. Primary or root compounding.
ii. Synthetic or verbal compounding.

In primary or root compounding the two elements put together to constitute the compound either belong to the same or different categories. Synthetic or verbal compounds are closer to syntax than morphology and the verb is a primary element in such constructions.

Types of Compounds

Basically there are three types of compounds:

Endocentric compounds: One element in the compound functions as the head. The modifier element of the compound has the function of attributing a property to the head, much like the function of an attributive adjective.

Exocentric compounds: A compound which lacks a head is called exocentric. Such compounds are called *bahūvrīhi* compounds by Sanskrit grammarians.

Appositional compounds: A compound of this type is a simple conjunction of two elements, without any further dependency holding between them. The Sanskrit term *dvandva* is used to describe these compounds.

General Features

The head modifier, predicate argument and appositional relations together with the constituent structure all tend to align compounding with syntax. However, compounds also have a number of features which make them resemble words:

(i) Compounds are often lexicalised. They are often subject to semantic drift of a kind associated with stored words, which means that their meaning becomes non-compositional or even totally idiosyncratic.

(ii) A second property that links compounds with words is that of non-referentiality (i.e. they never refer to specific objects; this is also the reason for non-head elements being used attributively). Related to this is the fact that non-heads of compounds fail to be inflected.

(iii) A property that distinguishes words from phrases is morphological integrity: i.e. their elements cannot be split up by other words or phrases, e.g. by parentheticals. This is generally true of the constitutents of compounds.

(iv) There are often phonological features that apply to compounds but not to phrases. A well known example of this comes from English, where we have the Nuclear Stress Rule which places main stress on the right most constituent of a syntactic phrase, and the Compound Stress Rule which stresses the left member of a compound.

Compounds in Khasi

Khasi, a rigid SVO (subject verb object) language, has a copious stock of compounds that can be classified as endocentric and appositional.

Endocentric Compounds

The first striking difference as compared to other Indian languages in Khasi endocentric compounds is that they are left headed, e.g.,

'wrist'	rndaŋ	- kə̀tti
	neck	hand

'waiting room' jaka - aṗ
place wait
'magazine' ka -kət - də̀r
FSM -paper -picture
'weeping willow' u - diɛŋ - yàp - lɔk
MSM - tree - dead - spouse
'spectacles' yid - kəməd
glass - eye
'divorce' pillaid - sun - šiỳaŋ
release - five - shell
'cousins' šipara? - a:r - kỳie
sibling - two - mother
'high heeled shoes' juti - jrɔŋ - kɔ̀ŋ - dɔŋ
shoe - tall - corner
'gossip' sim - lai - diɛŋ
bird - three - tree
(the bird that does not stay on one tree)
'hair parting' linti - khilie?
path - head
'student' khanna - sk̀ul
child - school
'earring' sau? - šak̀or
fruit - ear
'useless person' nud - mάu
weed - stone
(a kind of moss)
'patriot' 'riyo/briyo - šiur
man - courage

Leiber (1980) Feature Percolation Convention IV helps exemplify this further. According to this the whole compound is labelled, guaranteeing its left-headedness.

'wrist' rndəŋ - kətti
neck - hand

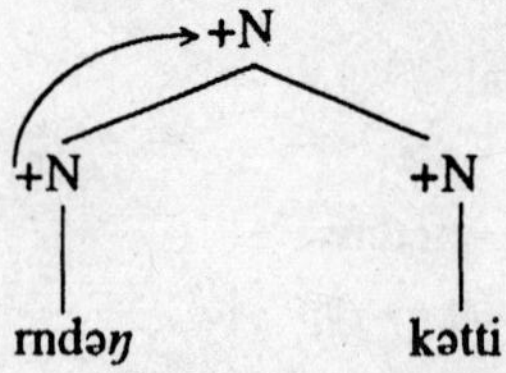

'useless person'	nud	-	máu
	weed	-	stone

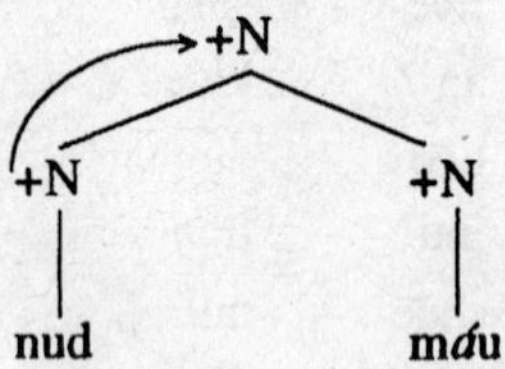

'patriot'	'riyo/briyo	-	šiur
	man	-	courage

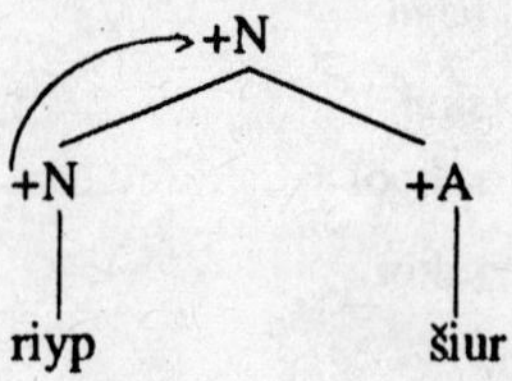

In all these examples the non-heads are used attributively. Being a strict SVO language, even at the word level, the two elements put together in a compound are of the modified-modifier order.

A unique feature of Khasi compounds is that the first element of a compound takes the gender number marker (GNM) and unlike in a sentence, GNM does not precede every constituent of the endocentric compound. When used in a sentence the left most elements or modified element takes the GNM—*'u'*, *ka* and *ki*.

Khasi compounds deviate from the standard assumption that in a true compound of two elements the first element is stressed. This can be seen in the examples given, where the compounds are left headed and the stress falls on the second element or the non-head element.

This feature of left headed compounding that is typical to Khasi indicates that it is a morphological process and the two elements that are collocationally fixed, have a dependency holding between them, as that between modified and modifier.

From the data collected it does not seem that Khasi has Exocentric Compounds.

Appositional Compounds

Khasi has a sizeable stock of compounds that is the result of a simple conjunction of two elements, without any further dependency holding between them.

e.g.,

'fodder'	ki -	plaŋ	+	ki -	kinbat
		grass			medicinal herbs
'furniture'	ki -	mài	+	ki -	šuḱi
		table			chair
'feast'	ka -	bà:m	+	ka -	dí?
		food			drink
'spine'	bu:d	+	lu:m		
	follow		mountain		
'january'	kalà	-	liŋḱəd		
	turn	-	short		
	(change)				
'limbs'	kət̀i	-	kjə́t		
	hand		leg		
'musical instruments'			pūt	-	tɛ̀m
			blow	-	play
'pine'	dìɛŋ	-	kśe?		
	tree	-	resin/lac		
'indigestion'	sɔ̀?	-	kpɔ?		
	prenetrating pain		stomach		

'december'	nɔ̀?	-	pərə́h		
	dip	-	winnoing tray		
'fidgety'	kh̀i?	-	ksə́in		
	move	-	maggot/worm		
'fascinated'	yàp	-	biỳed		
	died	-	awe struck		
'foul mouth'	krìn	-	sí?		
	say	-	foul		
'little finger'	'tì	-	kh̀ɔn		
	kətti				
	hand	-	offspring		
'last year'	m'n	-	šəm̀	-	snəm
	duration	-	meet	-	year
'palimony'	bài	-	bə́:m		
	cost	-	eat		
	(one's contribution to the expenses at home)				

It must be noted that all adverbial compounds in Khasi are reduplicated words and consequently fall into this category. In these elements the stress falls on both elements.

e.g.,

'anywhere'	šàno	-	šə́no
	where	-	where
'anyone'	inó	-	inó
	which one		which one
'anybody'	yàno	-	yə́no
	whom		whom
'whenever'	làno	-	lə́no
	when		when
'everywhere'	klə̀ŋ	-	klə̀ŋ
	around		around

'which (man)'	unó	-	unó
	which male		which male

Synthetic Compounds

Compounding, in a way represents the interface between morphology and syntax. This is particularly true of synthetic compounds. There are compounds whose head is derived by affixation from a verb, such as 'truck driver' in which truck appears to be an argument of the verb 'drive'.

Two distinctions that have to be made in relation to this argument are:

i. Predicate Argument Structure (PAS).

ii. Lexico Conceptual Structure (LCS).

The PAS is essentially the verb's theta grid and as such is part of the synthetic structure of the verb. The LCS is closer to a representation of the actual meaning of the verb. There are no morphological operations defined over the theta role. At most we find rules which refer to external or internal arguments. Many of the rules that are alleged to theta roles are actually rules affecting the LCS. In this case the agentive 'er' affixation accounts for 'er' nominalizations such as driver and is interpreted as agent. This is the consequence of the semantic operation induced by 'er' affixation. This has the effect of binding the subject position in LCS.

truck driver:

-er: the x such that [x drives y].

The same is true of synthetic compounds in Khasi.

nɔŋ	-	thuŋ	-	sintiyo	=	gardener
agent		plant		flower		
nɔŋ	-	ɔt	-	pləŋ	=	mower
agent		cut	-	grass		

When an argument in the LCS is bound in this way it does not show up in the PAS. Then the only remaining theta role for

nɔŋ	+	ɔt
agent	+	cut

is that of theme. The agent role of *'ɔt'* is not inherited because that role has been bound, a semantic effect of *nɔŋ* affixation. Therefore, the only other role which can be inherited is the theme role.

Lexical Categories in Khasi Compounds

In Khasi all major categories—nouns, verbs, adjectives, adverbs and prepositions are productively involved in word formation. Nouns are the most productive class of possible heads compounding with:

N + N + N

ka - sŋi - hət - maĵai - 'tuesday'

FSM - day - market - maĵai

N + N

u - sau? - səkɔ 'earring'

MSM - fruit - ear

N + ADJ

ka - kut - ĵrɔŋ 'overcoat'

FSM - coat - long

N + N + ADJ

u - diEŋ - sau? - ĵau 'lemon tree'

MSM tree - fruit - sour

N + ADJ + N

u - diEŋ - yəp - lɔk 'weeping willow'

MSM tree - dead - spouse

N + V

ki - khiyo - šət 'utensils'

NPM vessels - cook

N + V + V

u - nɔŋ - lEit - kurim 'bridgeroom'

MSM person - go - marry

N + V + N

u - brud - šud - binniyəd 'toothbrush'

MSM brush - clean - tooth

N + V + N + N

u - nɔŋ - tho? - kɔt - kubɔr 'journalist'
MSM person - write - person - news

N + ADV

ka - sŋi - baləŋ 'wednesday'
FSM day - together

N + ADV + N

u - thau - ləŋ - kayaubei 'ancestors'
MSM one who - together - first mother creates.

In all these compounds the left noun is the head element.

Compounds are formed with adjectives also. However adjectives do not head compounds, they combine with nouns; in such compounds the modified-modifier position is switched and is instead modifier-modified. The data indicates that compounds of the adjective-noun combination have a reversed order of modifier-modified in the case of physical attributes.

kənriaŋ - khəmət 'squint'
crooked - eye
kinde? - šadem 'palpitation'
heaving - breast
luŋ - minsεm 'compassionate'
tiny/tender - heart

In these cases Khasi compounds are exactly like compounds in English with the only difference that the second element still takes the stress.

Verbal compounds found in Khasi are found in combinations such as:

V + V

kaput - katεm 'musical instrument'
blow play

V + ADJ

krin - si? 'foul mouth'
say foul

V + N

sɔp - kətti 'glove'
cover hand

V + ADV

u - thau - ləŋ 'creator'
MSM make together

V + ADJ + N

sŋau - sî:d - med 'feverish'
feel hot body

V + N + P + N + N

ba:m - kuwai - ha - yəŋ - ublai 'departed'
eat betelnut in house God

In the verbal compounds the verbs take the head position if the compound is not appositional. Being an SVO language the verb is given almost equal importance as that of the subject.

In the case of prepositional compounds, prepositions combine with nouns, and the noun is the head. This is one universal feature that is true of Khasi compounds as well prepositions which usually do not head compounds.

P + N

šiliyaŋ - duriau 'overseas'/'abroad'
across sea/ocean

Adverbial compounds:

As pointed out earlier since most of the adverbial compounds are reduplicated words they fall under the appositional category.

ADV + ADV

šane - šantai 'around'
here there

kɛno - kɛno 'what'
what what

muno - muno 'who'
anyone anyone
(anyone from a group)

hɛŋno - hɛŋno - 'anywhere'
where where

kiɛi	-	kiɛi	'something'
something		something	

Bound Morphemes in Compounds

In Khasi most words are monosyllabic and therefore to identify a compound is fairly simple. But there are words that have derivational affixes that are taken only by certain words.

e.g. the derivation prefix *$m^y n$* is affixed to words that indicate a certain time span.

m^yn	-	step	'morning'	
duration		rising (sun)		
m^yn	-	sŋi	'afternoon'	
duration		shining (sun)		
m^yn	-	šəm	-	tayio 'last week'
duration		meet		week
m^yn	-	šəm	-	snəm 'last year'
duration		meet		year
m^yn	-	ta	-	kasŋi 'today'
now		day		
m^yn	-	ta	-	kamiɛd 'tonight'
now				night

These can also perhaps be considered compounds by a slight alteration of the earlier definition:

Compounds are linguistic elements that are collocationally fixed, and in such a fixture a bound morpheme with a restricted field of meaning attaches itself to an independent morpheme thereby constituting a compound.

This definition would restrict the possibility of all affixes being considered as parts of compounds. The restriction has a more semantic criterion rather than a syntactic or morphological criterion.

Conclusion

Compounding is a very productive word formation process in Khasi. It is obvious from the examples given that both root compounds and synthetic compounds illustrate ways in which morphology and syntax interact. The morphology-syntax interface, has been dealt with elaborately in the paper and it further reiterates that compounding cannot be wholly syntactic or morphological, instead it incorporates both morphology and syntax in its organization and structuration. Compounding best represents this interface and the dependency between lexical items and syntactic process.

NOTES

Abbreviations are used as follows:
MSM—MASCULINE SINGULAR MARKER
FSM—FEMININE SINGULAR MARKER.

REFERENCES

Di Sciullo, Ann-Maria & Williams, Edwin, 1987. *On The Definition of Word.* Massachusettes. M.I.T.

Grierson, G.A., 1904. Mon-Khmer and Siamese: Chinese Families. *Linguistic Survey of India.* ed. by Grierson G.A., New Delhi, Vol. 2.

Kageyama, Taro & Shibatani, Masyoshi, 1988. Word Formation in a Modular Theory of Grammar: Post Syntactic Compounds in Japanese. *Language.* Vol. 64. No. 2.

Kale, M.R., 1992. *A High Sanskrit Grammar.* New Delhi. Motilal Banarsidass.

Mathew, P.H. 1974. *Morphology: An Introduction to The Theory of Word Structures.* London. Cambridge University Press.

Spencer, A., 1991. *Morphological Theory: An Introduction to Word Structure in Generative Grammar.* Oxford. Basil Blackwell.

VI

TIBETO-BURMAN

Spring here, Spring there
And spring is everywhere.

On this forest and on that
On this tree and on that
On the leaves, in the leaves,
On the flower, within the flowers,

Spring here, spring there
And spring is everywhere.

Above, below, the red and the green
Sky, lands, filled with laughter and dance
The cuckoo and the nightingale, coos and sings
My heart pierced with all these things.

Spring here spring there
And spring is everywhere.

Upon this cornfield and on that
In this underwood and through that
The fragrant wind jostles through
Clouds in the sky and clouds on earth
And the wind blows my heart about.

Spring here, spring there
And spring is everywhere.

(A Children's song written by Tabu Taid.
Translated by Satish C. Abbi)

CHAPTER 21

PRONOMINALIZATION IN THE HIMALAYAN LANGUAGES OF HIMACHAL PRADESH AND UTTAR PRADESH

D.D. Sharma

Introduction

The language taken up for analysis in this paper belong to the Tibeto-Himalayan group, a subgroup of Tibeto-Burman family, spoken in Himachal Pradesh, currently being spoken in the districts of Lahul-Spiti, Kullu and Kinnaur, usually termed as Western pronominalized group, and in Uttar Pradesh, currently being spoken in the districts of Uttarkashi and Pithoragarh, normally termed as Eastern pronominalized group. In the latter group the languages spoken in the district of Pithoragarh have been designated as Rangkas group too.

Pronominalization

The linguistic phenomenon termed as 'Pronominalization' is a widely practised morphological feature of Munda, Dravidian and Tibeto-Himalayan languages of this sub-continent. It takes place in two ways: (i) Nominal pronominalization; and (ii) Verbal pronominalization. In the former type short forms of personal pronouns, as prefixes, are added before a governing noun in order to repeat the governed genitive, and in the latter type abbreviated forms of personal pronouns, acting as a subject or object of a verb, are prefixed, suffixed or infixed in the verb form itself to denote the particular person as the subject or the object of the verb concerned. In this paper, however, we shall confine ourselves to indicate the forms and functions of this feature in Tibeto-Himalayan languages spoken in Himachal Pradesh and Uttar Pradesh only which exhibit the latter type of pronominalization. Briefly, it may be presented as under:

In the languages under consideration the phenomenon of pronominalization is attested in their verbal forms only, there being no traces of nominal pronominalization. However, the feature of verbal pronominalization is attested both as simple as well as complex. In the case of complex pronominalization the finite verb forms of a transitive verb, other than including the morphological markers, incorporate pronominal signs representing the subject and the object of the verb concerned, while the simple pronominalization incorporates the subject only.

In this context it may be pointed out that though the phenomenon of pronominalization, in varying degree, is current in all the speeches of this group, yet the patterns of pronominalization are not uniform. The languages of the Western Pronominalized Group considerably differ from the languages of the Eastern Group, both in the matter of pattern and degree of pronominalization. There is a considerable variation even among the languages of the Western group. The feature of incorporating the pronominal object in the verb form takes place in Kinnauri, Chhitkali, Kanashi and Gari only. In others, as in the languages of the Eastern Group, only the phenomenon of subject incorporation is favoured and even this is not regular.

In the matter of subject incorporation, it may be said that, the representation of the pronominal subject is restricted to 1st or 2nd persons. Moreover, the representation may be in its full form as in Raji; or in reduced (truncated) forms or in symbolic forms, as we shall soon see.

Similarly, in the case of object incorporation, the practice of incorporation of the object is limited to the indirect pronominal objects only, there being no incorporation of the direct object.

Besides, in some speeches it is a regular feature and is attested in the verbal forms of all the tenses and moods, but in some it is quite irregular and is attested in particular tenses and persons, only.

In the matter of affixation too, there are no uniform patterns. In most of the cases they are suffixed, but there are speeches like Gari, Darmiya, Johari in which it is infixed in the past tense forms. The pattern of prefixation of the pronominal signs is, however, not attested in any speech of this group.

With regard to pronominalization another notable point is that, under the influence of other regional languages, it is becoming a diminishing feature and is even lost in many cases. A synchronic analysis of various forms and patterns of pronominalization, as attested in various speeches of the Himalayan group, may be represented as follows:

Subject Incorporation

Subject incorporation, in its abbreviated or symbolic form, is attested in almost all the speeches of this group. It is suffixed to the inflectional base of the verb concerned, and in case of object incorporation it follows the object particle. Moreover, the feature of subject incorporation is confined to the 1st and 2nd persons only. Its absence automatically denotes the verb form of the 3rd person. Normally, 1st person pronoun is represented by /g~k/ and 2nd person by /n/ and 1st, 2nd plural by /-c, -ñ/. These are, in synthetic constructions directly annexed to the inflectional base of the verb concerned, and in analytical constructions are appended to the auxiliary concerned. Consider:

Kinnauri:

Present	**Past**	**Future**
bio-du-k	bio-k	bi-to-k
'I go'	'I went'	'I will go'
bio-du-n	bio-n	bio-to-n
'you go'	'you went'	'you(sg.) will go'
bio-du	bio	bio-to-č

'he goes'	'he went'	'you(pl.) will go'
		bi-to-č
		'we will go'
		bi-to
		'he will go'

Pattani:

Past

lha-ri-g	'I did'
lha-ri-n	'you did'
'lha-ri	'he did'

Tinani:

Present		**Future**	
ibi-to-g	'I am going'	il-to-g	'I will go'
ibi-to-n	'you are going'	il-to-ñi	'we will go'
		il-to-n	'thou willst go'
		il-to	'he will go'

Gari:

Although in our data we could not obtain pronominalizing suffixes for the 2nd person, yet the data recorded for the LSI attests this feature for the second person as well, as in:

Present

la-to-k	'I do'
la-to-n	'thou doest'
la-to	'he does'
la-to-č	'we/you(pl) do'

Gari forms are identical with the Kanashi forms.

Chhitkali:

Past

la-te-k	'I did'
la-te-č	'we/you(pl) did'
la-te-n	'thou didst'
la-te	'he did'

Kanashi:

Past		**Present**	*lan* 'to do'
bo-ke-k	'I went'	la-to-k	'I do'
bo-ke-ñ	'we/you (pl) went'	la-ton-ñi	'you (pl) do'
bo-ke-n	'you(sg) went'	la-to-n	'you (sg) do'
		la-to-č	'we do'
la-te-k	'I did'	la-to-č	'you(hon) do'
la-te-č	'we did'		
la-te-n	'you(sg) did'		
la-te-č	'you(pl) did'		
la-te-ñi	'you(hon) did'		
Future			
la-no-k	'I will do'		
la-no-č	'we will do'		
la-no-n	'you(sg) will do'		
la-no-č	'you(pl) will do'		
la-no-ñi	'you(hon) will do'		

In the languages of the Eastern pronominalized group, though the pattern of suffixation of the subject particle is, more or less, similar to that attested in the languages of the Western group, yet its use is declining, particularly, with regard to the 1st person, in which it has also undergone some change. However, Marchha has maintained the general pattern to some extent, as in (Maṇa)—*rhəna* 'he comes'; *rhənani* 'you come'; *rhənagi* 'I come'; (Niti)-*rhəcya* 'he comes'; *rhəcən* 'you come'; *rhəce-ki* 'I come'. But here too, this feature of pronominalization is on its decline in both Maṇa and Niti dialects of Marcha. Consequently, in the dialect of Niti it is no more attested in the present indefinite and in the 1st person of the future tense, as in *rhan* 'I will come'; *zah* 'I will eat', etc. Similarly, in the dialect of Maṇa the subject particle *gi* has been reduced to *-i,* as in *za-na-i* * *za̱-na̱-gi* 'I eat', 'I shall eat'; *za-i* <* *za̱-gi* 'I ate', etc. Moreover, in it, as in Kanashi, the distinction of the present and future tenses is also lost, identical forms are being used for both, e.g. *rhətti* 'he will come', but *rhənani* 'you come', 'you will come'; *rhənagi.* 'I come, I will come', etc.

In Darmiya too the use of the pronominal personal terminations with the verb forms is on decline. By now it has lost must of its pronominalized character. It is only in the second person that the subject particle *n* has survived, as in *da-da* 'he gives': *da-dən* 'you give'; *da-di* <* *da-da-gi* 'I give'; *daŋ-da* 'he will give': *daŋ-dən* 'you will give'; *daŋ-di* <**daŋ-di-gi,* 'I will give'. It seems that in Marccha too the 1st person pronominal suffix *gi* ~ *ji* 'I' is reduced to *-i*.

In Chaudangsi too, the phenomenon of pronominalization is totally lost in the past tense. Though recorded by Grierson in the form of an infix, as in *de-n-a* 'goest', *se-n-s* 'struckest', *di-n-as* 'wentest' (L.S.I.III pt.I,506), yet in our data we could have only one indeclinable form which represents all persons and numbers. Its existence is, however, attested in the present and future tenses. But here, too, the pronominal subject particle of the 1st person, viz. *je* ~ *ji* seems to have developed into *ye~e*; but the pronominal personal termination of the 2nd person is very much there, as in *sɛtən* 'strike'. Byangsi: *za-gən* 'he eats'; *za-gə-no* 'you eat'; *zag ye za-ye* 'I eat'; *za-yəŋ* 'he will eat'; *za-yaŋ-no* 'you will eat'; *za-yəŋ-ye~za-ye* 'I will eat' etc. In Johari too the use of the subject particle is attested in the second person forms only, as in *diš* 'I do'; *diš-ŋ* 'you do'; *rhɛ-sə-n* 'thou livest', etc.

Raji which belongs to the languages of the Austro-Asiatic family, does exhibit the phenomenon of pronominalization, but unlike other Himalayan tongues of the pronominalized groups the pronominal subjects and objects are neither contracted nor represented by consonantal signs like *-g, -n, -c* etc. as we find them in other speeches. They rather retain their original pronominal bases, e.g. *həmu-re-a-nə* 'I strike him' (lit.strike-he-I); *həmu re-na-ni* 'he strikes me' (lit.strike-I-he). There the order of placement of the pronouns is invariably as verb + object + subject, as we find in other complex pronominalized languages. It has been noted that Raji too is losing its pronominalized character.

However, the untruncated use of pronominal forms differentiates Raji from the complex pronominalized languages of the Himalayan groups in which these are represented by consonantal signs representing respective persons and numbers.

Infixation

In our data the phenomenon of infixation of the pronominal subject was attested in Gari, Darmiya & Johari in their past tense formations only, e.g. (Gari) *lig-ki-za* I did (=do-1-past); *ni-n-za* 'thou werst', 'he was'. It is, however, dropped in many cases as in *ni-za* 'I was'. In Darmiya this infixation takes place in the 2nd person only, as in *da-n-su* 'you gave'; otherwise *da-su* 'I gave', 'he gave', *ra-n-su* 'you come', etc. It is attested in old Johari, as in *taŋ-na-su* 'you got' (sg.), *dia-nu-s* 'you gave', etc. A further investigation of this phenomenon may reveal its existence in other speeches as well.

Moreover, in the dialects of Chaudangs and Byangs the phenomenon of infixation is attested in respect to 1st person as well Chaudangsi: *se-gə-s* 'I struck', *da-gə-s* 'I gave/have given'; Byangsi: *sa-k-so* 'I struck'; *da-ka-s* 'I gave', etc.

In this context it may be interesting to note that above noted feature of infixation was current when the data for the LSI was recorded from the languages of the Rangkas group, though not pointed out by Grierson, but, has been attested in Darmiya by us. But we in our data have come across a few forms in which the pronominal element representing the 1st person seems to have been infixed in the future tense forms as well, as in *za-g-ne* 'we shall eat'; *de-g-ne* 'we shall go', etc.

Object Incorporation

The complex pronominalized languages, in their transitive verb forms, incorporate the pronominal subject as well as the pronominal object. Generally, the object particle precedes the subject particle. Structurally, it is verb stem + object particle + subject particle. Among the Himalayan tongues under consideration this feature is attesied in the speeches of the western pronominalized group only, and is normally represented with the particle /ca~sa/ for both first and second persons. In Kinnauri we also have /e~nme/ for first, dual and plural (inclusive), as in /kasaŋ bio tonme/ 'I and you go'. The third person is represented by /ta~da/ in some cases, e.g.

Kinnauri:

za-to-k	'I shall eat'
za-to-n	'you shall eat'

za-cə-k	'I shall eat you'
za-cə-n	'you shall eat me'
gəstoŋ-cə-bog	'I strike you'
khya-cə-k	'I saw you' (lit. see-you-I)
khya-cə-n	'you saw me' (lit. see-I-you)
khya-cə-n	'you(hon) saw me'
khya-ci-d	'he saw me/you'
khya-k	'I saw'
khya-n	'you saw'
khya-d	'he saw'

Gari:

khyed-ce-g	'I strike you'(lit. strike-you-I)
kan-ca-re	'you see him'
kan-ce-g	'I see you'
da-ca-re	'he/I/you give to you'

Besides *kyu~ku* the phonetic variation of *gye* 'I' is also attested in a few cases, as in *lig-ku-ni* 'you make for me' *khyed-kyu-za* 'I was beaten', etc.

Chhitkuli has, however, lost the regular feature of object incorporation. Synchronically, it is attested in a few sporadic cases only. For instance, in forms like *taŋ-c-i* 'I saw'; *tha-c-i* 'I strike', 'I struck', etc. The consonantal element *-c-* seems to be the remanant of object infixation, similar to that attested in Kinnauri forms like *ke-cə-k* 'I will give to you', *khya-cə-n* 'you saw me', etc. Thus the meaning of the Chhitkali forms like *taŋ-c-i* would be 'I saw you'. Moreover, the suffixal element *-i* may be representing the subject particle *-gi,* as is attested in the dialect of the Rangkas group.

Besides, the existence of *-c* in imperative forms like *ro-c* 'go' (=you go); *de-c* 'come' (=you come), etc. clearly indicate that in these forms too the pronominal element *-c* represents the pronominal object of the 2nd person. This is a regular feature in Kinnauri imperative as well, e.g. *za-č* 'eat', *khya-č* 'see'; *ləni-č* 'do', *toš-ič* 'sit'.

So far as Kanashi is concerned, it may be said that though the limited data is available to us yet it does not clearly exhibit the presence of this feature. Perhaps, the pronominal object is on its way to decline. Grierson too has not admitted its existence in this language. Yet in the data preserved in the LSI there are a couple of verbal forms which indicate that in the past, the verbal structure of this dialect too possessed the feature of object incorporation. For instance, in the utterance, *an-p-pici-gu-n* 'you make me (your servant)', the infixed particle *gu* as the Gari *ku*, seems to represent the object of the verb *pici* 'to make'. A detailed investigation is sure to bring to light a few more examples of this declining feature.

The aspect of pronominalization is totally missing in the speeches of the Eastern Pronominalized Group. The specimen recorded for the LSI in the beginning of this century also does not indicate the existence of this feature in these speeches at all.

REFERENCE

Grierson, George Abraham, 1903-28, *Linguistic Survey of India,* Vol. III, Pt. I. Reprinted Motilal Banarsidass, 1967.

CHAPTER 22

NEGATION IN KUKI-NAGA LANGUAGES

Chungkham Yashawanta Singh

Introduction

The concept of negation and the study of its expressions in languages have had philosophers, linguists and psychologists worried. Negation itself occupies a central position in the system of communication and in the system of logical representation. Through negation very ironical expression in natural languages can be expressed easily and naturally. Many scholars have already worked on different aspects of negation and the system of its realization in natural languages.

Jespersen's classic "Negation in English and other Languages" (1917), a revised and abridged form of which appears as Chapter XXIV of Jespersen (1924), remains unsurpassable for its insight and comprehensiveness. Other works published after 1960s took a new dimension on the study of negation. Klima's seminal paper (1964) highlights some of the central characteristics of English negation, particularly its syntactic aspects, within the framework of early transformational grammar. Klima distinguishes the so-called sentence and constituent negation. Zimmer's work (1964) is an exploration of the logical and linguistic diversity of types of affixal negation. Smith's dissertation (1969) is an "investigation of the consequences of adopting (generative semantics) for the analysis of certain aspects of negation including polarity, "until" and adverbials, negative transportation and the interaction of negation and quantifiers." An approach based on interpretive semantics is explored by Jackendoff (1969) and Lasnik (1972).

Hajicova's (1975) study was to contribute to the description of the semantico-syntactic structure of the sentence in the framework of the functional generative description, as proposed by P. Sgall in the early sixties and elaborated since then by the Prague group of algebraic linguistics.

Horn (1978) in his paper "Some aspects of Negation" deals with several manifestations of the functionally marked status of negative sentences, and semantics of negation including its interaction with other scope—including operators, lexically incorporated negation, the phenomena of negative polarity and negative transportation, multiple negation and the constraints on negation within embeded clauses. Near to Horn is John Payne's (1985) thesis. His article makes a typological study with the different syntactic forms of sentential negation dealing with the negation of quantifiers and adverbials as forms of sentential negation, negation in subordinates clauses and derivational negation. He takes care to establish language—independent criteria for the various ways in which negation has scope within the syntax of sentences and then surveys the variety of forms that these different kinds of negation can take.

The main thrust of this present study is to show how negation is formed in Kuki-Naga group[1] of Tibeto-Burman languages. The study excludes the analysis of Meitei.

It is known that there are two types of negative constructions that appears in many languages. One of these is formed by verbal modifiers such as *no, not, never, hardly,* etc., in English and *na* in Japanese (sentence negation). The other type is the negative formed by prefixes, such as *in-, dis-, un-,* etc., in English and *hi-, hu-, mu-,* etc. in Japanese (Affixal negation)[2]. In Kuki-Naga languages, namely, Thadou, Paite, Hmar, Kom, Vaiphei, Anal, Moyon, Tarao, Liangmei, Tangkhul, Sema, Ao, Lotha, Mao etc. it is found that negation is constructed by affixes, i.e. some are by prefixes and mostly by suffixes.

Prefixation

Out of 14 Kuki-Chin languages of Tibeto-Burman family spoken in North-East India only three languages namely Ao, Lotha and Tangkhul use prefixation for negative construction. Ao uses prefixes *mə-*, and *ti-* in prohibitive sentences.

1. pa tza mə-zam-ə
   he water neg. drink-asp.
   'He does not drink water'

Like Ao, Lotha also uses a negative marker *nə-* which is prefixed to the verb, as in sentence 2.

2. ə-nə nə-tso
   I-nom. neg-eat
   'I don't eat'

Like the two languages, Tangkhul also uses a negative prefix *mə-* but there is a particle *-mənə* which is suffixed to the verb root. Both *mə-* and *-mənə* occur simultaneously. Without the particle *-mənə* the sentence becomes ungrammatical.

3. i bazar-li mə-va-mənə
   I bazar-loc. neg-go-particle
   'I don't go to bazar'
4. i bazar-li mə-va-mələ
   'I shall not go to bazar'
5. *i bazar-li mə-va

In these prefixal negative languages prohibitive sentence is also formed by prefixation. Ao and Lotha have a similar marker *ti-* while Tangkhul uses the same negative marker *mə-*. Illustrations are given here.

6. ka muda*ŋ* ti-jəja*ŋ* (Ao)
   me before neg-command walk
   'Don't walk before me'
7. ə va*ŋ*we ti-nəvə (Lotha)
   me before neg. command walk
   'Don't go before me'

8. cithate mə-haŋ-lo (Tangkhul)
this neg. say-command
'Don't say this'

Suffixation

In Naga group of languages, there are some languages in which negation is formed by suffixation of negative marker to the verb. Liangmei is also one of them. In Liangmei, negation is formed by suffixation of a marker *-mək* (used in simple and in realized aspect) and *-lək* (used in unrealized aspect), as in sentences 9 and 10.

9. pa jəw sək-mək-e
he liquor drink-neg. asp.
'He does not drink liquor'

10. pa jəw sək-lək-e
'He will not drink liquor'

Sema also constructs negation by suffixation of a negative marker *-moy* to the verb, as in sentence 11. The marker *-moy* remains in all aspects and in all types of sentences.

11. niye skul-lo wu-moy
I school-loc. go-neg.
'I don't go to school'

In the Northern-Chin sub-group of Kuki-Chin languages, negation is constructed by suffixation. Paite has two negative markers, namely, *-kəy* and *-ləw*. They have a separate semantic status. The negative marker *-kəy* is used in confirmative negation, that is, the scope of negation is absolutely confirmed. The other marker *-ləw* is used to express a simple negation, as in sentences 12 and 13 respectively.

12. ken ən kə-ne-kəy
I-nom rice pro. eat-neg.
'I do/did never take my meal'

13. ken ən ne-ləw
'I do/did not take my meal'

Here it is noticed that the two negative markers have different grammatical property, i.e. whenever the negative marker *-kəy* occurs in a structure the main verb is to be prefixed by a pronominal marker *kə* as in sentence 12, but no pronominal marker is used in the case of *-ləw,* as in sentence 13.[3] This constraint is not found in the case of Thadou even though it (Thadou) has three separate negative markers, viz., *-ləw, -poy* and *-hi?*[4] occurring in different environments and in some cases two of the negative suffixes (*-poy* and *-ləw*) occur in free variation.[5]

Thadou and Paite of Northern-Chin subgroup have a typologically similar negative construction with that of Old-Kuki languages, viz., Kom, Anal, Hmar, Tarao etc. (i.e. negative is constructed by suffixation of the negative markers). Kom has only one negative marker *-mək* which is also used in prohibitive sentence along with command marker *-ro* as in sentence 15.

14. əma bu sak-mək
    he rice eat-neg.
    'He does not take his meal'
15. nəŋ zu in-mək-ro
    you liquor drink-neg.-command
    'Don't drink liquor'

In Moyon also the negative is constructed by suffixation of the marker *-mə* and even in prohibitive sentence this very marker is used, as in sentence 17.

16. ki tsə in-mə-iŋ
    I water drink-neg.
    'I don't drink water'
17. jo in-mə
    liquor drink-neg.
    'Don't drink liquor'

Anal is closer to Moyon in negative construction. Anal uses the negative marker *-mi*. Tarao and Hmar use the negative marker *-noh.* consider:

18. kəy zu in-noh-aŋ (Tarao)
    I liquor drink-neg.cont.
    'I don't drink liquor'

19. zu kədon-noh (Hmar)
liquor drink-neg.
'I don't want liquor'

Prohibitive Construction

Among the discussed languages only six languages have a separate negative marker for the prohibitive meaning. Lotha and Ao (of Naga subgroup) have the same prohibitive marker *ti-* which differs from other prohibitive markers of Thadou, Paite, Vaiphei and Liangmei.

20. ka madaŋ ti-nəjaŋ (Lotha)
me before neg.command-walk
'Don't walk in front'

21. ə vaŋwe ti-nəvə (Ao)
me before neg.command-walk'
'Don't walk in front'

In Thadou, it is formed by suffixation of a marker *-hi?* which is to be followed by a command marker *-in,* as in sentence 22 and 23.

22. zu don-hi? -in
liquor drink-neg.command
'Don't drink liquor'

23. nəŋ sinema-cu ve-hiə-in
you cinema-det. see
'Don't see that film'

Similarly, Paite uses the negative marker *-kəy* along with a command marker *-in,* here syncope comes in the assimilation (kəy + in > ken)

24. kəp-ken
cry-neg.
'Don't cry'

25. nəŋ zu don-ken
you liquor drink-neg.
'Don't drink liquor'

In the case of Liangmei, it is expressed by a marker *-du* along with the command marker *-lo,* as in the sentence 26 in request sentence also, the very markers *-du* and *-lo* also occur along with a request morpheme *-khay,* as in sentence 27.

26. nəŋ kəbuyduy sək-du-lo
you cow-milk drink-neg.command
'Don't drink milk'

27. nəŋ tek tiyu-khay-du-lo
you rice eat-neg. neg-command
'Please don't have your meal'

Unlike the examples cited above, languages such as Vaiphei has a specific marker, viz., *-kin* ~ *-kiwu* without using any command marker (*-kin* is used with singular while *-kiwu* with plural pronoun), as in 28 and 29 respectively.

28. nəŋ tuy don-kin
you(sg) water drink
'Don't drink water'

29. nəŋho tuy don-kiwu
you(pl) water drink
'Don't drink water'

'Let' Negative

In "let" negative construction, Paite has a separate negative marker -*da?* which is used along with suggestive marker *-ni* which occurs finally in a construction, as in sentence 30.

30. en gel?-da?-ni
us write-neg.proposal
'Let us not write'

But in Thadou, the negative marker *-poy* remains as it is and it occurs with "let" marker *-te* as in 31.

31. əyhon philəm-tu ve-poy-te
we film -det see
'Let us not see that film'

In Hmar, the negative marker *-noh* occurs with the "let" marker *-məy*, as in 32.

32. kha philm kha en-noh-məy-ni
det. film det. see-neg.let
'Let us not see that film'

In the case of Liangmei, the prohibitive marker *-du* occurs with the proposal marker *-khe*, as in 33.

33. aliyu paliyu-gu jəw pi-du-khe
 we they-dat liquor give-prohb-proposal
 'Let us not give liquor to them'

The Lexicalized Negator

Various languages of the world, namely Tongan, Fijian, Maori (of Loninesian), Diegueno, Majave (of Yunan languages), Evenki (of Siberian group of Tungus family), Nenets, Nganasan (of Somoyedic languages), Erzja (of Mordvin languages), Udmurt, Komi-Zyrian and Komi-Permjak (of Permic languages) and dialects of Lappish, Estonian, Veps, have negative verb or auxiliary verb or both.

Like the languages mentioned above, some of the Kuki-Chin languages have negative verb too. In Moyon, there is a negative verb functioning as a higher verb. The negative verb *mave* (in Moyon) functions as a linking verb in equative sentence of identification sentence as in 34 and 35.

34. əvay uti mave
 this dog neg.vb.
 'This is not a dog'

35. əma tomba mave
 he Tomba neg.vb.
 'He is not Tomba'

It is to be noted that this negative verb is also used in double negation. In other languages like Hmar, Thadou and Paite, the construction goes like this "He John is not". In Hmar, the negator is formed in such a way that the "be" verb + negative marker *-poy* becomes *əhi-poy* (əhipoy) as it occurs in 36 and 37.

36. əma john əhi-poy
 he John be-neg.
 'He is not John'

37. əma doctor əhi-poy
 'He is not a doctor'

Paite is very much similar to Hmar, that is, the negative marker *-ləw* is added to the verb "be" *hi* (əhi-ləw) and (əhi-kəy) as in 38.

38. əma john əhi {ləw kəy}
'He is not John'

Negative Strengthening

Jespersen mentioned that generally, negation is strengthened through some additional words (1917:4). In French the normal form for negation has been strengthened by accrual of postverbal elements like *mic* 'crump' *point* 'a point', specially *pas* 'a step'. The word selected for this strengthening effect may be an adverbial element, either intrinsically negative (English *not, nothing, never* or originally positive forms (like Danish *ikka* 'not') which acquired a negative signification through constant employment in negative sentence.

In Kuki-Naga, negation is strengthened or emphasised by either a word, or by a suffix. In Tarao, negation is strengthened by a word *ləw* (which is a negative marker in Thadou) which occurs before the verb as in 39.

39. kəy yu ləw in-noh a*ŋ*
I liquor drink-neg.
'I never drink liquor'

40. *kəy *ŋ*a ləw sa- a*ŋ*
I fish eat
'I never eat fish' (Supposed to be)

This strengthening element *ləw* occurs only in negative environment. That's why sentence 39 is grammatical while 40 is ungrammatical and *ləw* can be treated as a negative polarity item (NPI).[7] In Vaiphei, it is derived by the addition of a morpheme *-himhim* to the verb, as in 41.

41. kəy kani ne-*himhim* po*ŋ*ka
I opium eat-at all -neg.asp.
'I will not take opium at all'

42. kəy kani ne-po*ŋ*-ka
'I will not take opium'

Sentence 41 gives stronger negative meaning than 42. The NPI *himhim* can occur with any one of the negative marker, viz., *-poy*, or *-ləw* or *-poŋ*. It cannot occur in positive environment as in 44.

43. kəy əthum kə-ne-himhim poy/ləw/poŋ
I sweet pro.-eat
'I don't take sweet at all'

44. *kəy əthum kəne-himhim

Other negative polarity items in Vaiphei are *baŋməca* 'nothing', *koma* 'no one' or 'none', *khoyma* 'no where' *baŋtiklay* 'never'.

i. baŋməca 'nothing'
(a negative indefinite quantifier)

45. əma baŋməca əne-poy
he nothing pro.eat-neg.
'He does/did not eat anything (at all)'

ii. Koma 'no one' or 'none'

46. koma skul-la ce-poy
none school-loc. go-neg.
'No one goes to school'

iii. khoyma 'nowhere'

47. khoyma kəy ce-ponka
no where I go-neg.asp.
'I will not go anywhere'

iv. baŋtiklay 'never'

48. əma baŋtiklay phay əhuŋ-poy
he never Imphal come-neg.
'He never came to Imphal'

There is a prefix *mok-* which is grammatically different from the above NPI. With the addition of this prefix, the higher verb is reduplicated. Moreover, this prefix occurs both in negative and positive environments. In positive environment, the meaning of *mok-* is 'often' while it connotes the meaning of 'hardly' in negative environment.

i. *mok-* in positive environment 'often'

49. kəy lekha kə-mok-sim sim-ehi
I book pro.often-learn learn-be
'I often read the book'

50. *kəy lekha kə-mok-sim əhi

ii. *mok* in negative environment 'hardly'

51. kəy əthum kəmok-ne ne-poy
    I sweet pro-hardly-eat eat-neg.
    'I hardly eat sweets'

52. *kəy əthum kə-mok-ne-poy

The above sentences 50 and 52 are ungrammatical because the verb is not reduplicated. In the same way, in Kom also, the verb is reduplicated when the NPI prefix *sup*-is prefixed to the verb, as in 53, otherwise the construction is ungrammatical as in 54.

53. kəy yu sup-in in-mək
    I liquor NPI-drink drink-neg.
    'I don't take liquor at all'

54. *kəy yu sup-in-mək

Two negative morphemes NPI and negative marker are not treated as double negation here.

Double Negation

In Mathematics and Algebra, there is a principle or formula that two negatives become a positive. But "language is not mathematics" (Jespersen, 1924, p. 331). What can be applied to mathematics cannot be applied to language. Jespersen gives here his opinion . . . . "whenever two negatives really refers to the same idea or word (as special negative) the result is invariably positive . . . ." (Jespersen, 1924, p. 332). The two negatives, however, do not exactly cancel one another so that the result (*of no uncommon, no infrequent*) is identical with the simple *common, frequent,* the longer expression is always weaker. Such views of Jespersen can be observed in Kuki-Chin languages also. Some sentences are given below in support of the view.

Liangmei

55. pa niŋtiŋ-mək-bəw mək-e
    he wise-neg-inf. neg.-
    'He is not unwise'

Tarao

56. əmar əmel thra-noh wa-noh
    he face beauty-neg be-neg.
    'He is not ugly'
    (he is not not beautiful)

Unlike the two languages mentioned above, Vaiphei uses two separate negative markers *-ləw* and *-poy* in a construction. But there is a constraint that the marker *-ləw* is added to the verb while the other marker *-poy* is suffixed to the verb 'be' as in 57 otherwise the construction is ungrammatical, as in 58.

57. kəy lekha sim-ləw kəhi-poy
    I book read-neg pro.be-neg
    'It is not that I don't read'

58. *kəy lekha sim-poy kəhi-ləw

Vaiphei differs from Moyon in which a negative verb *məvə* is used and it (məvə) occurs sentence finally, as in 59.

59. en-mi its-mə məvə
    curry-det tasty-neg neg.vb
    'It is not that the curry is not tasty'

The construction of double negation in Kom is simple that the negative marker *-mək* occurs twice: first *-mək* is suffixed to the verbal noun, simultaneously it is again suffixed to the verb 'be' (cəŋ-mək), as in sentence 60.

60. juniŋə yen-hi əkətuy-mək cəŋ-mək
    today curry-det tasty-neg. 'be' neg.
    'It is not that today's curry is not tasty'

Conclusion

From the discussion above what can be concluded is that negation in Kuki-Chin is constructed by affixes, i.e. by prefixation or by suffixation. Typologically it can be concluded that Tangkhul, Ao and Lotha can be categorized in one group: Negation by Prefixation; and the remaining others are in another group: Negation by Suffixation.

NOTES

1. There are five very significant classifications of Tibeto-Burman family suggested by five scholars namely, Grierson-Konow, (1903-1928), Shafer (1955) and (1966-73), Benedict (1972), Egerrod (1974), Voegelin (1965). The hills of the subgroup "Kuki-Naga" is taken from Benedict.

2. Cited from McGloin's article "Negation" in Syntax and Semantics (ed.) by Masayoshi Shibatani. Vol. 5: 9.371.
3. Saratchandra reported in his book "A Descriptive Grammar of Paite" (1983) that in colloquial sentence pronominal concord prefix is not used while it is used in non-colloquial forms. But he did not mention the semantic difference of the two negative forms *-kəy* and *-ləw*.
4. This is according to Krishan' Thadou: A Grammatical Sketch, 1980.
5. *Ibid.*
6. Cited from John Payne's article 'Negation' in Language Typology and Syntactic Description. Vol. 1, (ed.) by Timothy Shopen, p. 207.
7. The 'Negative Polarity Items' is used by Buyssens (1959), Klima (1964) and Baker (1970).
8. juniŋə yen-hi kə-tʰɪy
   today curry-det. pro.tasty

REFERENCES

Baker, C.L., 1970. "Double Negatives," *Linguistics.* 169 ff.

Benedict, Paul K., 1972. *Sino-Tibetan: A Conspectus.* Cambridge. Cambridge University Press.

Buyssens, E., 1959. Negative Contexts *English Studies,* 40, 163 ff

Chomsky, N., 1981. *Lectures on Government and Binding.* Dordrecht: Foris.

Chhangte, L., 1986. *A Preliminary Grammar of the Mizo Language.* M.A. thesis, Arlington: University of Texas.

Egerod, Soren C., 1974. "Sino-Tibetan Languages," *Encyclopedia Britannica,* 16:796-806.

Grierson, George A. (ed.), 1930-28. Sten Konow: *Linguistic Survey of India,* Motilal Banarsidass, Delhi (Reprinted 1987).

Hajicove, Eva, 1975. *Negace a Presuposice Ve Vyznamove Stave be Vety Studic A Prace Lingvisticke,* Prague.

Hermon, G., 1985. *Syntactic Modularity.* Dordrecht: Foris.

Horn, Lawrence R., 1978. 'Some aspects of Negation' in *Universals of Human Language* (ed.) by J.H. Greenberg. Vol. 4, Standford, California. Standford University Press.

Jackendoff, R., 1931. 'An Interpretive theory of negation' in *Foundations of Language.* Vol. 5, pp. 218-241.

Jespersen, O., 1917. 'Negation in English and other languages,' *Selected Writings,* Longman.

Jespersen, O., 1924. *The Philosophy of Grammar.* London. Allene and Unwin. Reprinted by Norton, New York.

Klima, E., 1964. 'Negation in English,' in *The Structure of Language* (ed.) by Fodor and Katz. New Jersey. Englewood Cliffs.

Krishan, Shree, 1980. Thadou: *A Grammatical Sketch.* Calcutta, Anthropological Survey of India. Calcutta.

Lalitha, B. and K.V. Subbarao to appear. Agreement in Mizo. In Davison, A. and M.K. Verma (eds.) *Agreement in South Asian Languages.* John Benjamin's.

McCloin, N. Hanoka, 1978. 'Negation' in *Syntax and Semantics* (ed.) by Masayoshi Shibatani, Vol. 5, New York, Academic Press.

Payne, John, R., 1985. 'Negation' in *Language Typology and Syntactic Description,* (ed.) by Timothy Shopen, Vol. 1, Cambridge, Cambridge University Press.

Singh, Saratchandra, 1988. *A Descriptive Grammar of Paite.* Manipur, Tribal Development Centre.

Smith, S., 1969. *Meaning and Negation.* Doctoral Dissertation, UCLA. Printed by Mouton, The Hague, 1975.

Subbarao, K.V. and B. Lalitha. ms. *Aspects of Mizo Syntax.* University of Delhi.

Zimmer, K., 1964. Affixal negation in English and other languages. Word monograph. No. 5, New York.

CHAPTER 23

THE PASSIVE IN MIZO

K.V. Subbarao and
B. Lalitha

Introduction

In this paper we shall focus our attention on the formation of the various types of passive sentences in Mizo and the devices involved therein. We shall demonstrate how the formation of passive sentences of the native speakers of the older generation differs from that of the younger generation. We shall show that the passive of the older generation is basically a FOCUSING operation, that is, the passive is formed by focusing the direct or indirect object of the active sentence to the left or to the right of the original sentence. We shall also discuss the two types of passive forming strategies in the speech of the younger generation and shall show that an extra sentence node with verb *o:m* 'be' (existential)' or *ni* 'be (copula)' as the matrix verb has to be created. We shall label the first type of the passive of the younger generation as the Linker strategy as there is a linker which links the matrix and embedded sentence. We shall label the second type of the passive as the juxtaposition strategy as the embedded and the matrix sentence are juxtaposed. There are two distinct patterns exhibited in the Linker strategy, namely, (i) the retention of the ergative marker with the embedded subject and agreement marker with the embedded verb, (ii) the deletion of the ergative marker of the embedded subject and the consequent deletion of the agreement marker. We shall show these two strategies are identical to the ones found in the formation of relative clauses in Mizo. We shall provide data from Quechua, an American indian language, to show how the passive formation in the speech of the younger generation in Mizo is similar to the one found in Quechua in terms of having an embedded structure in passives. Finally, we shall hint at the problems that would arise in the analysis of passives in Mizo in the Government and Binding framework proposed in Chomsky (1981).

Passive in Older Generation

Let us first Consider the Passive in the Speech of the Older Generation.

(1)	tluanga	-cu[2]	indaun-a	zova-	le?
	tluanga	-foc	battle-in	zova	and
	la:la-n	an	-that		
	lala -erg	3pl	-kill		

'Tluanga was killed by Zova and Lala in the battle.'

(2)	le:khabu	cu	zovi-n	a	-chiar
	book	foc	zovi-erg	3sg	-read

'The book was read by Zovi.'

Notice that in (1) and (2) the logical object is fronted[3] and the rest of the constituents of the sentence remain in their original position of occurrence. What is crucial to note here is that the verb still agrees with the logical (original) subject in number and person. That is, passivization does not demote or effect the status of the active subject.

There is no difference between the active and passive sentences in the speech of the speakers of the older generation, when pronominal objects are incorporated in the verb.[4] A native speaker of Mizo therefore provides the same sentence either for the active or passive sentence.

(3)	min	-ha:u oam
	1p	scold

'Somebody scolded us' / 'We were scolded.'

(4) an -ha:u -ceu
3p scold -2pl
'They scolded you (pl.)' / 'You (pl.) were scolded by them.'

The explanation for the non existence of formal passive sentences in our opinion is the following. There is no overt object noun phrase available that is to be fronted in such cases becuase pronominal objects occur as agreement markers incorporated in the verb.

However, if the pronominal object is overtly present, it is fronted and the focus marker *cu* is attached to it. For example:

(5) keini -cu zova-n min-vua:
we foc zova-erg 1pl-beaten
'We were beaten by Zova.'

(6) nangma -cu la:li -n a -hau -ce
you -foc lali -erg 3sg -scold-2sg oam
'You were scolded by Lali.'

Sentences (5) and (6) clearly demonstrate that the passive is different from the active in Mizo only in terms of (i) fronting the direct object and (ii) the occurrence of the focus marker *cu* with the direct object of the active sentence.

Passive in Younger Generation

We shall now discuss the other two types of the passive in Mizo which are found only in the speech of the speakers of the younger generation.

We shall first discuss the Linker strategy. Let us consider the following sentences:

(7a) zovi-n thei -te a -ei
zovi-erg fruit-pl 3sg -eat
'Zovi ate (some) fruits.'

(7b) thei -te -cu zovi-n a -ei in an -o:m
fruit pl -foc zovi-erg 3sg-eat [-fin] linker 3pl -be
'The fruits were eaten by Zovi.'

(7c) thei -te -cu [zovi - ø ø -ei] in an -o:m
fruit-pl -foc zovi eat [-fin] linker 3pl be
'The fruits were eaten by Zovi.'

(8a) zova-n Tluanga indaun-aa -that
zova-erg tluanga battle-in 3sg -kill
'Zova killed Tluanga in the battle.'

(8b) tluanga cu [indaun-a zova-n a -tha?] in a -o:m 3sg -be
Tluanga foc battle-in zova-erg 3sg -kill [-fin] linker
'Tluanga was killed by Zova in the battle.'

(8c) tluanga cu [indaun-a Zova-ø ø-tha? in] a -om
Tluanga foc battle-in Zova kill [-fin] linker 3s -be
'Tluanga was killed by Zova in the battle.'

Notice that in sentences (7b) and (8b), (i) the logical subject carries the ergative marker and the verb agrees with the agent[6] which is FRONTED and the focus marker *cu* is attached, (ii) the original finite verb becomes nonfinite but still retains the agreement marker of the original subject, (iii) there is an extra verb *o:m* 'be' and this verb exhibits agreement with the fronted noun phrase (derived subject) and, (iv) there a linker *in* which links the original verb and the newly-added verb *om* 'be'.

Schematically, the passive in (7b) and (8b) can be represented as:

(9) logical object focus mkr [original subject+erg ↔
agr+v [-fin] linker] agr+o:m ('be')

The double direction arrow ↔ indicates that the presence or absence of the ergative marker and agreement marker is mutually dependent.

Let us consider the derivation of sentences (7c) and (8c). They are similar to the derivation of (7b) and (8b) respectively except for the fact that the ergative marker is not present with the original subject and consequently, the original verb does not carry any agreement marker. Schematically, this type of passive can be represented as:

(10) Logical Object Focus Mkr [Original Subject + ø ↔ ø + V
[-fin] o:m] Linker] Agr+o:m ('be')

The double direction arrow ↔ indicates that the presence or absence of the ergative marker and agreement marker is mutually dependent.

Let us now consider the second type of the passive (the JUXTAPOSITION strategy) in the speech of the younger generation.

(11) a:pil cu [zova-ø ø -ei] a -ni
apple foc zova eat 3sg -be
'The apple was eaten by Zova.'

(12) eleksan la:y mi tamtak -cu [ø ø -tha?] an -ni
election during person many -foc -kill [-fin] 3pl -be
'During the election many people were killed.'

To derive sentence (11), (i) the logical object is fronted and the focus marker *cu* is attached, (ii) the original verb becomes non-finite, (iii) the ergative marker with the original subject and the agreement marker with the original verb are together absent and, (iv) there is an extra verb *ni* 'be' added which now exhibits agreement with the fronted noun phrase as in the Linker strategy. It should be noted that there is no linker in this sentence and the existential verb *o:m* 'be' cannot occur in such cases.

Let us consider the case of sentence (12). The derivation of (12) is identical to that of (11). The new verb *ni* 'be' exhibits agreement with the derived subject noun phrase *mi tamtak* 'many people'. The original unspecified subject is marked as ø and, consequently there is no agreement marker with the original verb.

Thus, in sentences (11) and (12) the nonfinite clause is juxtaposed next to verb *be*. This type of passive can be schematically represented as:

(13) Logical Object Foc Mkr [Original Subject -ø ø+V [-Fin]]
Agr+ni

Thus, the juxtaposed variety differs from the linker variety (i) in having *ni* 'be' and not *o:m* 'be' (ii) in not having an option to have the ergative marker with the original subject and (iii) the absence of agreement marker with the original V. It should be emphasized that the embedded verb in both the strategies is non-finite.

The question that one may wish to raise is: why can't sentences such as (11) and (12) be treated as cases of nominalization, and not as passives? Under the nominalization hypothesis, the active sentence is nominalized and a new sentence node is created (by Chomsky adjunction) with *ni* : 'be' as the higher verb. The logical object 'raises' to the position of the subject of the newly created sentence and the verb *ni* 'be' exhibits agreement with the new subject. Since it is a case of fronting, the focus marker *cu* obligatorily occurs with the noun phrase. The absence of the ergative marker as well as the agreement marker on the original verb and the nonfinite nature of the original verb can be explained as a result of nominalization. The non-availability of a second pattern, namely, the pattern in which the original subject has an ergative marker and the original verb has an agreement marker with the verb in juxtaposed passives strengthens the nominalization hypothesis.

Both the passive analysis and the nominalization analysis seem to be equally plausible. However, native speakers of Mizo feel that sentences such as (11) and (12) are the passive equivalents of the English passive. We shall therefore prefer to analyze examples such as (11) and (12) as passives.

According to Hermon (1984), in Imbabura Quechua too, there are two types of passives. The following examples are illustrative:

Type A:

(14) nuka -ka juan maka- shke ka-rks-ni
i-nom-top juan hit passive be-pst- 1
'I was hit by Juan.'

Type B:

(15) nuka -ka maka -y tuku -rka -ni
i nom top hit inf become pst 1
'I was hit.'

In type A in sentence (14), the verb is nominalized within the passive marker *shka* following the nominalized verb and verb be is added. Verb be carries tense and exhibits agreement with the derived subject. In type B in sentence (15), the verb is nominalized too but the verb *tuku* 'become' is added and this too exhibits agreement with the derived subject.

The juxtaposition strategy of the Mizo passive discussed above shares the following characteristics with the Quechua passive:

(i) The original verb is nonfinite in both the cases.
(ii) An extra verb be/become is added and this exhibits agreement with the derived subject.
(iii) There is no linker linking the original verb and the newly added verb be.

In this section, we have presented an analysis of the passive of the speaker of the older generation and that of the younger generation. We have also shown how the passive in Mizo shares features with the passive in Imbabura Quechua.

Salient Features

We shall now consider some further characteristics of the Mizo passive.

Just as in English and unlike in Indo-Aryan languages, the indirect object of the active sentence can be the derived subject of the passive sentence. Let us first consider an active sentence (16).

(16) zova-n le:khabu zovi hne:na a -pe -tɔ
zova-erg book zovi dat 3sg -give perf
'Zova gave a book to Zovi.'

The indirect object in (16) is zovi and it carries the dative case marker *hne:na*. Sentences (16), (17) and (18) below are examples in which the indirect object is Fronted in the passive.

Indirect Object Passivized

The passive in the speech of the older generation:

(17) zovi cu zova-n le:khabu a -pe -tɔ
zovi foc zova-erg book 3sg give perf
'Zovi was given a book by Zova.'

The passive in the speech of the younger generation-Linker strategy:

(18) zovi cu [zova-n le:khabu a -pek] in] a -o:m
zovi foc zova-erg book 3sg -give [-Fin] linker 3sgbe/exist

The passive in the speech of the younger generation-Juxtaposition:

(19) zovi cu [zova-ø le:khabu ø-pe:k] -a -ni
zovi foc zova book give [-fin] 3sg -be

Direct Object Passivized when IO is Present

Sentences (20), (21) and (22) are examples in which the direct object is Fronted in the passive:

The passive in the speech of the older generation:

(20) le:khabu cu zova-n zovi hne:na a -pe- tɔ
book foc zova-erg zovi to 3sg-give -perf asp
'A book was given to Zovi by Zova.'

The passive in the speech of the younger generation-Linker strategy:

(21) le:khabu cu [zovi hne:na zova-n a -pe:k] in 3sg be
book foc zovi to zova-erg 3sg give [-fin] linker a -o:m

The passive in the speech of the younger generation-Juxtaposition strategy:

(22) le:khabu cu [zova-ø zovi hne:na ø- pe:k] a -ni
book foc zova zovi to give [-fin] 3sg be

The above data clearly illustrates that the passivization of a sentence with an indirect object is similar to the passivization of a sentence with a direct object in terms of the permissible options.

The perfect aspect marker *tɔ* and the secondary aspectual verb *ta* can occur either with the embedded (original) verb or with the newly-added verb be. The following sentences are illustrative:

(23) in cu [ø-nikumah ø-sak - tɔ] in] a -o:m
house foc last year build perf asp linker 3sg -be
'The house was built last year.'

(24) in cu [ø nikumah ø-sak] in] a -o:m tɔ
house foc last year build linker 3sg be perf asp
'The house was built last year.'

(25) zova cu [ø ø-vua:k ta] in a -o:m
zova foc beat sec verb linker 3sg -be
'Zova was beaten.'

(26) zova cu [ø ø-vua:k] in] a -o:m ta
zova foc beat linker 3sg -be sec verb
'Zova was beaten.'

Though the occurrence of the aspect and the secondary verb is permitted both with the matrix verb as well as with the embedded verb, the native speaker of Mizo prefers sentences in which aspect marker and the secondary verb occur with the matrix verb.

Consider the following active sentences (27) and (28) with an overt future tense marker *ang* with the newly-added verb *o:m* 'be':

(27) zovi cu [naktuk-a zova-n a -tha? in]a -o:m ang
zovi def tomorrow zova-erg 3sg -kill linker 3sg -be fut
'Zovi will be killed by Zova tomorrow.'

(28) in cu nikumah zova-n a -sak in -a -o:m ang
house foc next year zova-erg 3sg -build 3sg be fut
'The house will be built by Zova next year.'

Notice that both in sentence (27) and (28) the future tense marker *ang* occurs only with the verb *o:m* 'be' of the newly-created sentence node.

The future tense marker *ang*[7] cannot occur with original verb as the following ungrammatical sentences show:

(29) *zovi cu [naktuk-a zova-n a -tha? -ang] in a -o:m
zova foc tomorrow zova-erg 3sg -kill [-fin] -fut linker 3sg -be
'Zovi will be killed by Zova tomorrow.'

(30) *in cu[nakuma zova-n a -sak -ang [in] a -o:m
house foc next year zova erg 3sg build [-fin] -fut linker
3sg -be

Another interesting characteristic feature of the passive in Mizo is that the derived subject can occur to the right as sentences (31) and (32) illustrate:

(31) [zovi-n a -ei tɔ] in] *thei -te cu* an -o:m
zovi-erg 3sg -eat [-fin] perf linker fruits -pl foc 3pl -be asp
'The fruits were eaten by Zovi.'

(32) [induan -a zova-n a -tha?]in] ṭluanga- cu a -o:m
battle -in zova-erg 3sg -kill -fin linker tluanga foc 3sg -be
'Tluanga was killed by Zova.'

It is worth pointing out here that a similar phenomenon also occurs in relative clauses too. The modified noun phrase can occur to the right of the embadded clause as well.[8]

Let us now consider passive sentences in which the agent of the action is unspecified:

(33) (kei ma: cu) a -ha:u in ka -o:m
I 3sg scold linker 1sg be
an -ha:u
3pl -scold
ø -ha:u
-scold
'I was scolded.'

(34) hetiang in (keima:cu) a -hril in ka -o:m
like this adverbial I 3sg -scold linker 1sg -be
an -hril
3pl -tell
ø -hrill
-tell
'I was told like this.'

It can be noticed that (i) since the agent of the action is unspecified, the original verb can take an agreement marker either in singular or plural and (ii) if the derived subject is a pronominal, the occurrence of the derived subject in the surface structure is optional. For example, the occurrence of *keima:cu* 'I' in sentence (33) and (34) is optional. The derived subject is 'recoverable' because, the verb *om* 'be' or 'exist' of the higher sentence carries the agreement marker of the deleted pronominal which is the derived subject.

Relative Clauses

In this section, we shall discuss the relative clauses containing an embedded passive. Consider, for example, a simple passive as in (35) and a passive sentence containing a relative clause as in sentence (36):

(35) thei -te-cu [zova-n a -ei tɔ in] an -o:m
fruit -pl-foc zova-erg 3sg -eat perf linker 3pl -be asp
'The fruits were eaten by Zova.'

(36) thei -cu [zova-n a -ei tɔ in ø-o:m te cu/kha an -tui
fruits foc zova-erg 3sg -eat linker -be pl def 3pl -tasty
'The fruits which were eaten by Zova were tasty.'

In the simple passive sentence in (35) the plural marker *te* occurs with the derived subject *thei* 'fruit'. In sentence (36) the relative clause containing an embedded passive, the plural marker *te* occurs to the right of the higher verb *o:m* 'be' or 'exist' and it is followed by the demonstrative pronoun *kha/cu.*

It is worth noticing that the higher verb in the passive sentence *o:m* 'be' does not carry any number and person agreement marker because the agreement marker is carried by the predicate of the matrix sentence namely, *tui* 'tasty'.

We have mentioned earlier that in passives the focus marker *cu* is attached to the derived subject. However, if the noun phrase is specified by a definite demonstrative pronoun such as *kha—khan, so—so, cu—cu, he—he* in the active sentence, the derived subject in passive too would contain the same split demonstrative pronouns that occur with the noun phrase. In such cases there is no need to have an extra *cu* which otherwise normally occurs with the derived subject in passive sentences. The following sentences are illustrative:

(37) so hla so [zovi sak] in]a -o:m tɔ
def song def zovi sing linker3sg -be perf asp
'The song was sung by Zovi.'

(38) he le:khabu hi [zova chiar]in a -o:m tɔ
def book def zova read linker3sg -be perf asp
'This book was read by Zovi.'

(39) kha: n le:khabu kha [zova-n zovi hne:na amerika
def book def zova-erg zova to america
atšangin a -thon tɔ te kha an -tou
from 3sg -send perf perf def 3pl -expensive asp
'Those books which were sent by Zova to Zovi from America were expensive.'

It is interesting to note that Mizo passives and relatives share certain similarities which are as follows:

(i) In relative clauses the head noun phrase can occur either to the left or right of the modifying clause (cf. sentences (40a) and (40b). In passive sentences too, the derived subject which is the focused noun phrase can occur either to the left of the logical subject or to the right of the matrix sentence (cf. sentences (41a) and (41b)):

(40a) (kha) mipanaupang lo:man do:n tu] -kha] kha-in
def boy prize receive nom -def our -house
a? a -loukal
to 3sg -come
'The boy who won the prize came to our house'.

(40b) loman d:on tu (kha) minanaupang kha kan-in
prize receive nom def boy def our- house
a? a -loukal
to 3sg -come
'The boy who won the prize came to our house.'

(41a) theite cu [zova ei tɔ] in an -om
fruits foc zova eat perf linker 3pl -be
'The fruits were eaten by Zova.'

(ii) Both in relative clauses and passive there are two options available with regard to the retention (cf. sentences (42a) and (43a) or deletion (cf. sentences (42b) and (43b)) of the ergative marker and, consequently, the retention or deletion of the agreement marker. The following sentences are illustrative:

(42a) zova-n [zovi-n le:khabu a -lei-tur cu] a -chia:r -ang
zova-erg zovi- erg book 3sg buy-fut def 3sg read -fut
'Zovi will read the book which Zova will buy.'

(42b) zova-n [zovi -ø le:khabu ø- lei -tu:r] cu a -chiar -ang
zova-erg zovi book buy-fut def 3sg -read -fut
'Zova will read the book which Zovi will buy.'

(43a) le:khabu cu zova- n a -zia? in a -o:m
book foc zova- erg 3sg -write linker 3sg -be -fin
'The book was written by Zova.'

(43b) le:khabu cu [zova-ø ø-zia?] in a -o:m
book foc zova -write linker 3sg -be
'The book was written by Zova.'

Notice that both in relative clauses and in passives, the embedded verb invariably has to be non-finite. However, the retention of the agreement marker is directly dependent on the retention of the ergative marker in both the cases. Thus, if the ergative marker is deleted, the agreement marker is also deleted, both in relative clauses and in passive.

(iii) The other common factor both in relatives and in passives is that a noun phrase is focussed in both the processes and the noun phrase focussed must contain a focusing marker *cu* or a definite demonstrative pronoun such as *kha-kha, so-so* etc.

Conclusion

Finally, it is important to point out that the various types of passive sentences discussed in this paper cannot be accounted for by the rule of Move α proposed in the Government and Binding framework (Chomsky, 1981). Move α moves an NP from an uncase-marked θ position to a case-marked non-θ position. In Mizo, the NP that moves either to the right or to the left in passives is not moved to satisfy the Case Filter. Further research needs to be done to investigate the intricate nature of the passive in Mizo.

To sum up the discussion so far, in this paper we have shown that there are three types of passive constructions in Mizo and the choice of the construction depends on the age group that the speaker belongs to. The passive in Mizo basically is a focussing device where the noun phrase is moved either to the Left or Right of the original sentence. We have pointed our that the rule Move proposed in the Government and Binding framework cannot account for the various types of passive sentences in Mizo as the noun phrase is not moved to satisfy the Case Filter.

NOTES

1. This paper is a part of the findings of the University Grants Commission's Major Project on *Syntactic Typology, Language Universals and Convergence in South Asian Languages.* We are grateful to our informants Mr. O. Rosanga, Ms. Zovi Tulangi. Ms. Pui and Rev. Zaithanga. We thank Professor F.K. Lehman for helpful discussions. We are thankful to Ms. Shashi K. Nigam and Mr. A.K. Rohtagi for their help in word processing. Mizo (also called Lushai) is a Tibeto-Burman language spoken in the north-eastern part of India bordering Myanmar. A broad transcription is used in transcribing data.

   The abbreviations used in this paper are as follows: acc-accusative, agr-agreement, asp-aspect, dat-dative, def-definite, erg-ergative, foc-focus, [-fin]-

nonfinite, fut-future, nom-nominalizer, oam-object agreement marker, perf-perfect, pl-plural, sg-singular and sec vb-secondary verb.

2. *cu* is treated as an anophoric marker and it refers to something the addressee has seen or heard of but the speaker has only heard of (Chhangte 1989:142). Lehman (personal communication) labels *cu* as a discourse anaphoric marker. In this paper, the marker *cu* which occurs in passive sentences is treated as a FOCUS Marker and the *cu* which occurs in relative clauses is treated as a definite marker. It may be pointed out that *cu* functions as an accusative marker when it occurs with the direct object in unmarked word order.
3. We are aware of the fact that active and passive sentences are not derivationally related in recent theories like the Government and Binding framework. As the aim of this paper is mainly to provide a descriptive account of the passive in Mizo, the active and the passive are derivationally related for clarity in exposition.
4. For a detailed discussion of agreement in Mizo, see Lalitha and Subbarao (to appear).
5. It may be noted that *cu*, the accusative marker, is Optional in the active sentence whereas its occurrence is Obligatory in a passive sentence.
6. For a detailed discussion of ergativity in Mizo, see Subbarao and Lalitha (ms.)
7. Note that *ang* is not permitted to occur with the non-finite embedded verb. In our analysis, *ang* is treated as future tense marker. However, Chhangte (1989) and Lehman (personal communication) treat *ang* as an aspect marker. The question that arises now is: is *ang* an aspect marker or a tense marker? Note that the aspect marker *to* can occur with a non-finite embedded verb as in sentence (23) where as *ang* cannot occur with the embedded non-finite verb as the ungrammaticality of the sentences (29) and (30) show. It is worth mentioning that *ang* cannot occur with the non-finite verb in relative clause too (see Subbarao and Lalitha, ms).
8. See Subbarao and Lalitha (ms) for a detailed discussion.

REFERENCES

Chomsky, N., 1981. *Lectures on Government and Binding.* Dordrecht: Foris.

Chhangte, L., 1986. *A Preliminary Grammar of the Mizo Language.* M.A. thesis, Arlington: University of Texas.

Hermon, G., 1985. *Syntactic Modularity.* Dordrecht: Foris.

Subbarao, K.V. and Lalitha, B., *Aspects of Mizo Syntax.* University of Delhi.

Lalitha, B. and K.V. Subbarao to appear. Agreement in Mizo. In Davison, A. and M.K. Verma (eds.) *Agreement in South Asian Languages.* John Benjamin's.

CHAPTER 24

EXPRESSIVE MORPHOLOGY AS MANNER ADVERBS IN KHASI, TANGKHUL NAGA AND KUKI-CHIN LANGUAGES

Anvita Abbi and Ahum Victor

Introduction

If one ever undertakes to identify the antiquity of various linguistic structures of South Asian languages, one is sure to find expressive morphology or simply **Expressives** as the oldest, most widespread and most stable[1] lexicon of the modern and indigenous languages of India.

The term 'expressives' as used in this paper is inclusive of ideophones, onomatopoeics, mimics, imitatives, and sound symbolism (for details on each of these to avoid the confusion created by the overlapping definitions see Abbi, 1992). Although many writers today use, the term 'expressive' there has been something or a naming frenzy in the past. In earlier works, especially on African and South Asian languages, expressives have also been given labels such as 'interjections', 'descriptive adverbs', 'picture words', 'onomatopoeic adverbials', 'intensives', 'emphatics', 'impressifs', and so on. Again, different scholars give different definitions of expressives.

According to Childs (1989:1), the term 'expressives' seems to have been first coined by Durand (1961) in his analyses of Vietnamese. The term was later adopted and defined by Gerald Diffloth (1972)[2] and Murray B. Emeneau (1978). The term 'ideophone' is widely used, however, for the African phenomenon, as in Doke (1953) for Bantu. He seems to have first suggested the term, he defined or at least described an ideophone as a vivid representation of an idea of sound, a word, often ononmatopoeic, which describes a predicate, qualificative or adverb in respect to manner, colour, smell, action, state or intensity. This seems to suggest that ideophones are a grammatical class of words, a type of adverbial, but no formal criterion is given for distinguishing them from other adverbs. In the Bantu languages with which Doke was concerned, the invariable or indeclinable nature of ideophones had often been noted, in contrast with adverbials like those formed with the locative class prefixes.

It has also been noted that expressives, for some languages, are frequently phonologically anomalous. They may contain phonemes not found in other types of words, or unique sequences of phonemes, and they may be aberrant in respect to the rules of tone that apply to them. Diffloth holds a similar opinion (u.d.). Diffloth (1976), for Semai, considers expressives as a 'third basic word class' of the same order of magnitude as nouns and verbs. Describing the morphological, syntactic and semantic properties of Semai expressives, he proves that they are not even subject to the condition of 'lexical discreteness' and are indeed 'a totally different kind of linguistic animal'.

Diffloth very strongly advocates (in his undated paper) the iconicity point of view of expressives, "iconicity is the very *raison d'etre* of the whole word class called Expressives", as well as suggests that the linguistic theory has to be overhauled completely to incorporate this phenomenon, "it will be necessary to create an **asethetic component** (our emphasis) of grammar, distinct from, but incorporated into, the logicophonological component which has been the sole preoccupation of generativists" (u.d. p. 50).

Emeneau (1978) in his study of Kota onomatopoeics, opines that expressives can be identified by having syntax and morphology different from that of the major classes of the language. Abbi (1987) rejects such a position. For her, expressives do not necessarily have distinct morpho-syntactic properties than the other lexical items in the language. For example, verbal onomatopoeics and imitatives in Hindi and Tamil operate as normal verbs and take normal affixations allowed. Emeneau, however, rightly comments that:

> perhaps it would be more just to say that expressives denote varied types of sensation, the impingement of the material world, outside or within the person, upon the senses—not merely the five conventionally identified senses, but also the feelings both internal and external (1978).

Abbi (1987, 1990, 1992) discusses expressives from the point of view of reduplication, the linguistic structuration, which is more common and widespread in all the South Asian languages than the non-reduplicated ones. Whether the expressive form is reduplicated or non-reduplicated each form is a unit lexeme and a single stuctural category. Almost all (nearly 99%) reduplicated expressives are formed by iterating a meaningless syllable. The resultant structure thus acquires a menaing, constitutes a single morpheme as well as a single lexeme in that language. Abbi (1987) considers all expressives as instances of morphological reduplication as opposed to the lexical reduplication where the units before iteration are meaningful words of the language concerned. The question of expressive being iconic cannot be established without some doubt. Had these been totally iconic, languages of a *sprachbund* would share their expressives. Nonetheless, some sound symbolism is involved but no one can be sure about their total iconic nature.

Before we begin our investigation into the languages of North-East, we must remind our readers that the most significant aspect of Indian expressives is that they, without fail, indiacte five senses of perception, and as mentioned earlier, they behave and function like regular words and thus form a part of the lexicons of Indian languages. Another semantic area most widely covered by expressives is that of the 'manner' of an action/event stated. Every society and its members percieve the world distinctively. The perception of the manner in which any activity can be undertaken is culture-specific. That is, each culture has its own views and models for the manner in which any activity is undertaken. Society and culture-specific 'manner' in Indian languages are expressed by expressive morpology more than by prosaic words of manner adverbs. The phenomenon is in greater abundance in the indigenous languages of India than in the modern languages and, among the indigenous ones more prevalent in the languages of the North-East, both in Tibeto-Burman and Khasi (Austro-Asiatic). Interestingly, South Asian expressives are not restricted to the perceptual words and manner of actions alone. There are many in various languages which lay bare a large number of feelings, situations, attributes, disorder, disturbance, confusion, untidiness and, as Emeneau says, our internal and external feelings.

Tibeto-Burman and Mon-Khmer

We are going to investigate into two broad areas: (1) the area of five senses of perception; and (2) the area of expressive manner adverbs. We would like to take into consideration the languages of the North-East, primarily Naga languages of the Tibeto-Burman family, Meitei of Kuki-Chin group and Khasi of Mon-Khmer group of Austro-Asiatic family. We do not find much evidence of language convergence between these languages despite the geographical proximity. What strikes one is the use of the similar linguistic material for shared semantic constructs by these languages. The structural similarities are the significant linguistic truths of the area (for detail see Abbi, 1993).

Though Meitei is not listed under the scheduled tribal languages of the constitution yet it constitutes our object of investigation for the sake of cross comparison among the languages of the same geographical area, specifially with other tribal languages of the vicinity. This helps us to get a holistic picture of the North-East area.

Expressive Morphology and (Panchendriya) Five Senses of Perception

Expressives in these languages are used to emote all the five senses of perception, i.e. of smell, sight, touch, hearing and taste. Consider the range of perceptive powers of the speech communities of Naga, Kuki-

Chin, Khasi and Meitei. A word of caution. Khasi is an SVO language unlike other languages of the area and hence adverb follows the verb.

1. Acoustic Noises

(a) Animal noises

Khasi	ŋəŋ- ba to make echo sound 'mosquito noise'	ŋəŋ ŋəŋ expr.
Tangkhul	sip sip	'sound of cicada twittering'
Meitei	ŋiyau ŋiyau	'mewing sound of cat'
	məu məu	'dog's barking'
	ci ci	'crying sound of mouse'
Chakashang	krü krü	'sound of hen 'calling' the newly hatched chicken'
Yimchunger	cik cik	'hissing sound of snake'
	trıyak trıyak	'monkey's chattering when about to sleep'
Mizo	bao? bao?	'sound of dog's barking'
	crit crit	'twittering sound of a house cricket'

(b) Noises made by humans

Khasi	nok-ba khe khe laugh expr. 'to giggle'	
Tangkhul	thi thi	'giggle'
	rok rok	'sound of snoring'
Meitei	khi khi	'giggle'
	wa: wa:	'laughter (heartily)
Yimchunger	ha ha	'sound of laughing in a silly manner'
	khəm khəm	'threatening noise with a serious look'
Chakhashang	tü tü	'sound of mourning or crying due to pain or extreme fear'

(c) Noises made by natural phenomenon

Khasi	khom-ba grəŋ grəŋ 'blow expr.	'thundering noise'
Tangkhul	cək cək	'sound of a drizzle'
	kuŋ kuŋ	'sound of thunder'
Meitei	cro cro	'sound of heavy rains'
	krəŋ krəŋ	'sound of thunder'
	brek brek	'sound of discontinous rain accompanied by hail'
Nagamese	tak tak	'sound of rain pattering'
Konyak	pruk pruk	'sound of water flowing in small streams'

(d) Noises made by miscellaneous inanimate objects

Khasi	lau-ba tchrin tchrin to make sound expr. 'to jingle (of anklets, bangles etc.)'	
Tangkhul	khok khok	'sound of wood chopping'
	ten ten	'sound of tin or plates falling on the ground'
	šeo šeo	'sound of fermented rice bubbling'
Meitei	phrak phrak	'sound of bamboo breaking'
	pak pak	'sound of slapping, kicking'
Yimchunger	thrak thrak	'sound of fire cracker, bursting of bamboo when put into fire'
Chakhashang	kruŋ kruŋ	'sound of ringing bell'
Konyak	phruk phruk	'sound of boiling water'

2. Sense of Sight

Expressives of sight usually refer to flickering, glimmering and shimmering aspects of objects:

Khasi	thəwan star	micak	ŋan-ba shine	kuphet kuphet expr.
	'stars are twinkling'			

Tangkhul	phik phik	'twinkling'
	han han	'glare, unbearable to the eye'
Meitei	hiŋ hiŋ	'shining of metallic objects'
	raŋ raŋ	'brightness seen by a weeping person'
Yimchunger	rək rək	'twinkling, spearkling'
	nciŋ nciŋ	'shining of metallic objects'
Nagamese	camo camo	'twinkling or momentary shining'

3. Sense of Touch

Khasi	tsənap tsənap pa-pɔt expr. thing 'sticky thing'	
Tangkhul	hat hat	'feeling of sharpness such as knife, thorns etc.'
	lər lər	'feeling hard when pressed (solid muscles, cycle tyres etc.)'
Meitei	pet pet 'soft such as overcooked rice or overriped fruits' khək khək 'hard feeling of wood, bones, stones etc.'	
Chakhashang	to to 'to feel hard to chew, break or press' pa: pa: 'loose or sticky like overriped fruits or overcooked rice' tü tü 'very sticky (hard to be removed or peeled off)	
Yimchunger	əyik əyik 'very hard, such as underdone meat, tough' thrim thrim 'feeling of rubbing hands, legs etc. or touching only the hairs not the skin'	
Konyak	yiŋ	'feeling of electric shock'

Nagamese	syap syap	'sticky like overcooked rice'

4. Sense of Smell

Khasi jiŋ sma hek hek
smell expr.
'unpleasant smell'

Tangkhul hik hik
'strong smell (good or bad) causing irritation in the nose'

Meitei swe swe
'intense bad smell such as rotten things or stool'

5. Sense of Taste

Nagamese	sətə sətə	'tangy taste'
Tangkhul	mat mat	'extremely hot (chilli hot)'

6. Other Senses

Apart from these five senses, there are many expressives describing various bodily and psychological feelings:

Khasi	huri hura	'confusion'
Tangkhul	khak khak	'feeling of foreign particle in the eye'
	tuk tuk	'beating of heart due to longing or depression'
Meitei	ciŋ ciŋ	'feeling of pain rhyming with the beating of pulse'
	uru uru	'nauseating feeling'
	thuk thuk	'feeling of depression or longing'

There is a certain amount of overlapping among the various senses and feelings expressed by the expressives, specially seen between the auditory and visual senses and sometimes between visual sense and feelings. Some expressives express, for example, both the sound of crying and also the action of crying, or taste and sound of chewing simultaneously. From the above discussion it is clear that expressives are common features of the North-East linguistic area. However, we have to remember that the semantic fields are cultural-specific, language specific, and not language universal.

Usage

The primary function of expressives is that of a modifier. As mentioned earlier, in languages of South Asia expressive words with appropriate affixes can operate as either nouns or verbs. Consider:

Tangkhul:

yaŋ yaŋ-ə
expr. pres
'extremely cold'

thə thə-lu
expr. imp
'be smart and act/do/go fast producing the sound of trodding'

thək thək tə-cətlu
expr. adv. imp
'go smartly and fast'

ŋa ŋa ci məsa
expr. prn. neg.- hear
'don't you hear the baby crying na na?'

Collocations

There are expressives that have specific co-occurrence restrictions. The expressive *rop rop* (Tangkhul), when collocated with *wuk* 'stomach', expressess gas formation or gastric trouble; 'pregnant' is collocated with *sunau wuk* 'woman's belly'; 'anger' is collocated with *məluŋ* 'heart'; 'gossiping' is collocated with *nəcek* 'talk', 'growing very fast' (human/plant) is collocated with *ka* 'rise up' or 'grow up'. Similarly, *həm həm* 'reddening of face due to shyness or anger' or *rik rik* occurs with *kuyha* 'hair' for feeling of extreme fear/hair raising'; *cot* 'tire' with *cir cir* 'being tired of mental and/or physical work'. We would now like to consider one of such collocationally restricted expressive in Tangkhul Naga and Khasi which draws the attention of any linguist to its magnificient semantic range, minute subtelities and intensive perceptive power of its users.

Expressives as Manner Adverbs

As stated earlier, languages of this region excel in using expressive morphology for indicating 'manner' of an action/event. It has been observed that specially in Khasi, the speakers use a very wide range of expressives for modification of a single action. The range of manner expressives seem to surpass the range of available verb or noun class (perhaps a study in the expressive lexicon would be very revealing for future exploration in the word-formation processes of these languages).

Mind Your Walk! Khasis and Nagas are Watching!

Most of the intransitive action verbs can be modified in various subtle ways by adding an expressive word to them. This is particularly true of Khasi and Tangkhul Naga. One such verb is *'to walk'*. The following list gives an indication of the range of modification that the action verb 'go' can undergo.

Khasi:

The verb for 'go' or 'walk' in Khasi is *yaid* which precedes the manner adverbial expressive:

yaid (v) 'go, walk, proceed'.
— bak'-bak' 'go hurriedly'
— bia*ŋ*-bia*ŋ* 'walk continuously'.
— bran-bran 'go very fast'.
— brum-brum 'go with heavy steps'
— hai-hai 'walk shakingly as if very heavy'
— han'-han' 'walk like a duck'
— kep'-kep' 'go slowly not sure to keep the equilibrium'
— ker'-ker' 'walk trembling'
— khne?-khne? 'walk like a lame man'
— khni*ŋ*-khni*ŋ* 'walk lamely' (as if very tired or there is a stone in the sole)
— khrup' khrup' 'walk quickly and stamping the floor with the steps
— kjik'-kjik' 'walk as if on pins'
— knia?-knia? 'walk nicely and willing to speak'.
— knip'-knip? 'walk with pain'
— kor'-kor' 'walk trembling (from sickness)
— kthai-kthai 'walk well-dressed'
— kthek'-kthek' 'walk like dancing as on springs'

— kui-kui 'move a short but large body'
— kynrum'-kynrep' 'go on pouncing'
— kyrthek'-kyrthek' 'walk like dancing'
— kyntup'-kyntup' 'walk dressing very modestly'
— dar-dar 'walk briskly'
— der-der 'walk about with flying clothes'
— dat' dat' 'walk quickly without turning to left or right'
— doy'-doy' 'walk quickly (small boy)'
— don'-don' walk like a bird or child'
— dop'-dop' 'walk like a child, who has just learned to walk'
— dot-dot 'move as an old person'
— neŋ-neŋ 'walk like an intoxicated'
— ner-ner 'move shakingly'
— nuŋ'-nuŋ 'went on walking'
— hir-hir 'go longingly'
— yor-yor 'walk slowly from weakness'
— jaw-jaw 'go about in poorly wet clothes'
— lbeŋ-lbeŋ 'go completely naked'
— luŋ-luŋ/ leŋ-leŋ 'go in a hurry'
— suki-suki don-don 'went out very slowly as an old person'
— mlen-mlen 'go about very healthy and muscular'.
— rymphat'-rymphat' 'go about dirty and poorly dressed'
— sak-sak 'walk straight on'
— san-san 'daddle, walk as if not sure
— dain̲-ši-dain̲ 'going ahead successfully'
— šey-šey 'walk with long strides'
— šen-šen 'go as a drunkard'
— šop-šop 'walk with caution'
— sar-sar 'go steelthily'
— suki lwen'-lwen' (v) 'creep slowly'.
— tai-tai 'go about very dirty'
— ter-ter 'proceed in order'
— thaid'-ši-thaid' 'proceed on and on'
— then'-then' 'walk steady'
— thew-thew 'walk with strong legs'

— thiaw-ši-thiaw 'walk uphill with strong legs'
— thir-thir 'go quickly'
— thnet'-thnet' 'walk as if on the point of falling'
— thud'-thud' 'walk as stumbling'
— thut'-thut' 'walk tremblingly'
— twet'-twet' 'walk too fast'
— tub'-tub' 'walk as if not liking it'
— tub pa-tub' 'go slowly'
— tuin̲'-tuin̲' 'go slowly like an elephant'
— wai-wai 'walk weekly'
— wey-wey 'go in a zig-zag way'
— wet-wet 'go on hurriedly'
— wit'-wit' 'walk with many obstacles'
— wut'-wut' 'go on hurriedly'

Similarly, in Tangkhul Naga walking is perceived in various subtle ways. The verb for 'walk/go' is *kəzət* which follows the manner adverbial expressives of several types. Consider:

'*Walking Expressives*' (*kəzət* 'to go/walk')

yaŋyay kəzət	— 'to waddle like a child (by grown-up people)'
šiŋšiŋ	— 'to walk with heavy footstep in a direct manner without stopping or looking about'
thuŋthuŋ	— 'to walk heedlessly and laborously, usually with anger or worriness'
yuryur	— 'to walk in batches at a time'
thutthut	— 'to walk stealthily and slowly'
camcam	— 'to walk blindly and slowly; walk like very old people'
həyhəy	— 'to walk limpingly'
nutnut	— 'to walk unprogressingly with frequent backward motion, as while forcing to go by pushing or dragging'
wuywuy	— 'to walk waveringly, as when one is drunk'
yəyə	— 'to walk in a leisure way without any purpose'
wakwak	— 'to walk with long strides, especially by tall persons'

hiŋhiŋ — 'to walk fast with rather long strides'
rutrut — 'to walk silently and carefully, usually said of thief or persons with suspicious look'
təytəy — 'to waddle (by around one-year old children)'
phutphut — 'to walk very fast (as if getting late for some place to reach)'
namnam — 'to walk straight and quickly not caring for hindrances'
kuku — 'to walk tiringly with bowed posture'
həkhək — 'to walk quickly with light steps'
yokyok — 'to walk swinging the upper part of the body from back to forth, especially by thin and tall persons'
haphap — 'to walk carelessly without looking for what lies on the surface/ground'
yapyap — 'to walk uneasily with bowed legs, as when one has got boils in the thighs or buttocks'
rinrin — 'to walk carefully with hesitation, as on thorny surface'
pəkpək — 'to walk lightly looking back and forth'
thəkthək — 'to walk mincingly'
nennen — 'to walk slowly with hesitation, as with shyness in front or a crowd or someone'
pikpik — 'to walk fast and swingingly, as in a crowded street or place'

The North-East, perhaps could be declared as a 'Walking Area', the area characterized by a very high range of expressive morphology designating manner of 'walk' and 'go'. An intensive study in other languages of the Tibeto-Burman family of the region might validate the hypothesis.

A recent research conducted at Jawaharlal Nehru University (Victor, 1992) identifies a total of 342 expressives in Tangkhul Naga. Similarly, another study conducted at the same university (Pratiti Bhattacharya, 1993) has identified 20 Khasi expressives collocating with the verb *ba:m* 'to eat', 28 expressives with the verb *khin* 'to tremble', 38 with the verb *krin* 'to speak, say' and 18 expressives collocate with the verb *mareh* 'to run'. The largest number of expressives in Khasi begin with *k-* and *kh-*. A dictionary of expressive morphology in these languages is definitely warranted as the structure under consideration is an integral part of the linguistic competence of these speech communities. The richness in sheer number of expressives in these indigenous languages exposes the poverty of manner expressives in modern Indian languages. We would like to inform our readers that it had been an extremely difficult task to translate these expressives in simple English due to lack of available equivalent terms, unfamiliar situations of the use of the expressives, as well as due to our limited perception.

Non-translatability or the limitation of the availability of equivalent terms or similar structural configurations is not a new problem. Whorf (1937, 1941)[3] and Sapir (1924)[4] had encountered this problem while conducting field work in Hopi and Nootka respectively, the American-Indian languages. The resultant famous Linguistic Relativity Theory proposed by Sapir- Whorf can be summarized, As Stuart Chase (1955) puts it, in two cardinal hypotheses:

First, that all higher levels of thinking are dependent on language. Second, that the structures of the languages one habitually uses influences the manner in which one understands his environment. The picture of universe shifts from tongue to tongue.

Whorf spoke of "our linguistically determined thought world" and held that "we dissect nature along lines laid down by our native languages" (J.B. Carroll, p. 213). For him each language was not merely an instrument for expressing ideas but rather itself the 'shaper of ideas' (J.B. Carroll, p. 216). Thus according to Whorf the individual is 'considered to certain modes of interpretation even while he thinks himself most free (J.B. Carroll, *op. cit.*). Now, this has been the most debatable issue—"linguistic relativity". Whether language determines thinking and perception or that thinking and perception determine the language and its structure.

The richness of expressive morphology in Naga and Khasi contrasted with moderate (not the kind of collocationally extensive application as we just witnessed) existence of parallel systems in Hindi, Tamil, Bangla, Gujarati, Telugu and other languages is rather striking. According to Edward Sapir[5] "the outstanding fact about our language is its formal completeness . . . . By 'formal completeness' I mean a profoundly significant peculiarity which is easily overlooked". Thus the framework of linguistic forms of any given language provides a complete system of reference.

> 'The world of linguistic forms held within the framework of a given language, is a complete system of reference, very much as a number system is a complete system of quantitative reference or as a set of geometrical axes of coordinate is a complete system of reference to all points of a given space....To pass from one language to another is psychologically parallel to passing from one geometrical system of reference to another'. (Sapir in Mandelbaum, 1963, p. 153)

Is it really true that Whorf's Theory of Oligosynthesis[6] where the key notion is that of a 'broad idea or complex or related ideas which might be associated with linguistic elements is right? The question is relevant because it is related to the concept that languages with different collocations of semantic ideas might provide different "maps" of the realm of the possible ideas. Whorf believed that different languages might provide different 'segmentation of experience'.

This belief that our language effectively creates our perceptions of reality has been much debated in the linguistic literature. But then there is another side of the picture. There are essentialists who believe in the theory that language encodes or expresses the perceived reality. Language is simply a medium which reflects social condition, and changes in response to social changes. Language is perceived as something which is constructed by reality. This issue of language and reality—the linguistic determinism—is central to the dispute between theoretical reformists and radicals. Or, should we agree with Roy Harris, "the central indeterminacy of all communications is indeterminacy of what is meant" (Harris, 1981).

We feel that language structure reflects the societal pattern and the world view of the speech communities. Since these two change from place to place, languages and linguistic structures tend to follow suit. It is in this context we would say that an enquiry into a distinct and distanced community can begin by analysing its language. Looking at the structure of a language is the surest way of perceiving reality of its speech community.

NOTES

1. It has been observed by the authors that expressives remain unchanged over an extended period of time. The dialectal differences can be identified on the basis of avaialable cognate like expressives.
2. Diffloth (undated) in 'Expressive Phonology and Prosaic Phonology in Mon Khmer' (49-59) mentions that he coined the term expressive by reference to Jakobson (1966) who was following Pierce in equating expressive meaning with iconicity.
3. See Discussion of Hopi Linguistics (1937) and Language and Logic (1941). Both of these articles are reprinted in J.B. Carroll's *Language Thought and Rality,* 1971 (sixth printing).
4. Originally the article was published in American Mercury, 1924. 1, pp. 149-155. Reprinted in Mandelbaum 1963. *Selected Writings of Edward Sapir*.
5. Mandelbaum (ed.), 1963, p. 153.
6. Whorf developed his theories of Oligosynthesis with characteristic originality and acumen, and it is perhaps unfortunate that he never was able to bring himself to publish any full and mature description of the theory. (J.B. Carroll, *op. cit.*, p. 32 in his 'Introduction').

REFERENCES

Abbi, Anvita, 1987. *Reduplicative Structures in South Asian Languages. A Phenomenon of Linguistic Area.* UGC Report. Advanced Research Project. New Delhi. Jawaharlal Nehru University.

—, 1992. *Reduplication in South Asian languages. An Areal, Typological and Historical Study.* New Delhi. Allied.

—, 1993. *Semantic Universals in Indian Languages.* Simla. Indian Institute of Advanced Study.

Ahum, Victor, 1992. *A Grammatical Study of Expressives and Echo Formations in Tangkhul Naga.* M. Phil. dissertation. Jawaharlal Nehru University. New Delhi. Unpublished.

Bhattacharya, Pratiti, 1993. *Reduplication in Khasi.* M.A. Field Report. Jawaharlal Nehru University, New Delhi.

Carroll, J.B. (ed.), 1971. (sixth printing). *Language, Thought and Reality.* Writings of Benjamin Lee Whorf. Cambridge. Massachusettes. The M.I.T. Press.

Chase, Stuart, 1955. 'Foreword' to J.B. Carroll edited 1956 (first printing).

Childs, G. Tucker, 1989. *African Ideophones.* Mimeo.

Diffloth, Gerald, 1972. Notes on Expressive Meaning. *Papers from the 8th Regional meeting.* Chicago, Chicago Linguistic Society.

—, 1976. Expressives in Semai. *Austro Asiatic Studies.* Oceanic Linguistics. Special Publication, No. 13, Hawaii, University of Hawaii Press.

—, u.d. *Expressive Phonology and Prosaic Phonology in Mon Khmer.*

Doke, Clement, 1953. *Bantu Linguistic Terminology.* London. Longmans.

—, 1954. *The Southern Bantu Languages*. London. Oxford University Press.

Durand, M.,1961. Les impressifs en Vietamien, ètude prèliminaire. *Bulletin de la Socièè des Etudes Indochinoises*. New Series 36.1. Saigon.

Emeneau, M.B., 1978. Some notes on Dravidian intensives. In *Collected Works of Emeneau*. Berkeley. University of California at Berkeley.

Harris, Roy, 1981. *The Language Myth*. Great Britain. Duckworth.

Mandelbaum, D.G. (ed.), 1949. 1963 (fourth printing). *Selected Writings of Edward Sapir in Language, Culture and Thought*. Berkeley and Los Angeles. University of California Press and London, Cambridge University Press.

CHAPTER 25

SCRIPT AND ETHNOLINGUISTIC IDENTITY:

THE MEITEILON QUAGMIRE

Kailash S. Aggarwal

> "Frontiers are estabilished by power, and maintained by the constant and known readiness to defend them by arms. It is absurd to think that professors of linguistics and collectors of folklore can do the work of statesmen and soliders. What does happen is that academic enquiries are used by conflicting interests to bolster up their claims, and their results prevail only to the extent that somebody has the power to make them prevail. He who exercises the power exercises it while he can and as he can, and if he ceases to exercise power, then he ceases to rule. Academic research does not add a jot or a title to the capacity for ruling, and to pretend otherwise is to hide with equivocation what is a very clear matter.
>
> (E. Kedourie, 1961, *Nationalism,* London, Hutchinson, p. 125)

Introduction

Most modern societies today are confronted with many different, often conflicting, languages and language varieties and thus have to grapple with the complexities of intra- and inter-ethnolinguistic group relations. A number of alternative solutions have been offered, most of which may be categorized into the frameworks of the two American metaphors: the melting pot and the salad bowl (see, e.g., Aggarwal, 1990). The melting pot or the theory of assimilation advocated a course whereby a state can impose one official, national language, usually the dominant, legitimized language of the ruling elite, upon the entire population by devalorizing, pretermiting, winking at or eliminating all other languages. This solution(?) has been invariably adopted in the history of the western world till about the 60s of the present century, when the Civil Rights Movement and struggle of the Blacks forced the U.S. Administration to allow for the 'salad bowl' or the pluralistic model. The 'assimilation approach', in fact, had led to the virtual extinction of a number of minority and regional languages. France is the classic case in point. In its fixation for national unity and integrity, the French State, using all means, successfully imposed the Parisian dialect of the ruling elite upon the entire population of France and most of its overseas colonies (for details, see, e.g., Bourhis, 1982).

Today, however, apart from the turn around to the 'salad bowl', be it token or whatever, the states have oriented themselves towards the use of the subtler instrument of language planning, which is after all a particular form of social, cultural, political and economic planning. However, "Too many works on the subject fail to examine the assumptions upon which language planners base their practices, namely the legitimizing philosphy of the dominant group(s) in society." (Hamers and Blanc, 1989:169). One thing, however, is crystal clear. Language planning can be and mostly has been a tool for domination and control in the hands of the state. But it can potentially be a revolutionary force also for the minorities, the dominated and the underprivileged-, the- ruled. Thus though one notices the widespread conviction among linguists that there are no primitive languages and that there is no way to rank the overall structural complexities of languages along an evolutionary continuum, we all know that the facts of life and society are different. "Only before God and the linguists are all languages equal. Everyone knows that you can go further with some languages than you can do with others." (Mackey, 1978:7)

What is an Ideal Script?

In spite of this dichotomy between theory, or rather the assumptions among linguists, and the reality, Ferguson (1968:28) suggests three dimensions along which the development of languages can be compared: "*graphization*—reduction to writing, *standardization*—the development of a norm which overrides regional and social dialects, and for want of better terms, *modernization*—development of intertranslatability with other languages in a range of topics and forms of discourse characteristic of industrialized, secularized, structurally differentiated, 'modern' societies".

Our primary concern in this paper is 'graphization', but of a unique kind, with rather unique dimensions. Here we are not concerned with the provision of a writing system for an unwritten language, either by using an existing system or inventing a new one. We are rather faced with the problem of reviving and 'standardizing' an archaic script to replace an existing one in the context of reassertion of ethnolinguistic identity. There is no doubt a growing literature which postulates criteria and principles for evaluating and judging the adequacy of writing systems. Cooper (1989:126) divides these principles and criteria into two categories: (1) Psycholinguistic or technical; and (2) Sociolinguistic.

Psycholinguistic Considerations

The psycholinguistic, technical principles and criteria are concerned with the extent to which the writing system is easy to learn, easy to read, easy to write and easy to reproduce by modern technology. Berry (1958) points out that these criteria may conflict with one another. What is easy to read is not necessarily easy to write and print. What is easy to learn is not necessarily easy to use. Venezky (1977) makes a distinction between persons becoming literate and those who can be called advanced readers. For a literacy programme, an orthography should indicate the sounds of the words but for advanced readers it should indicate meanings rather than sounds.

While the goals may conflict, there may also be conflicts with regard to the means of attaining a goal. For example, if ease of reading is a goal, how could this goal be optimized? If we presume that reading involves the matching of written symbols with sound units, then we need to design a writing system where each grapheme represents a phoneme (if one is using alphabets) or each syllable (if one is using a syllabary) with a unique symbol. That is how the writing system can represent the phonological realization of a word. But if we presume, on the other hand, that a fluent reader does not recognize the correspondence between graphemes and phonemes but rather the correspondence between the written symbols and meanings, we need to design a system which reflects underlying grammatical and lexical forms. Thus the last symbol in the plural forms of, for example, 'cats' and 'dogs' would be the same because it represents the plural morpheme rather than its phonetic realization.

Berry (1977) points out that if this second view is taken to its limits one would have to conclude that the alphabetic principle is irrelevant for fluent reading, that fluent readers treat a text as if it were ideographic. Though many may not buy Berry's extreme argument, most of those who believe that an ideal writing system should adopt a phonetic transcription might be persuaded to modify their approach when it proves impractical. The basic question as to whether and to what extent should a writing system represent the phonological realization of a text and to what extent should it represent abstract underlying grammatical and lexical structures remains a controversy. Still more basic a question is does it all really matter? Whether it does or not, we need to realize that in the field of graphization, in the Indian context particularly, there are more questions than answers and rather than attempting to freeze the issues, which in any way cannot be done, we might as well attempt to formulate the questions in the context of social totality, not simply in the linguistic or 'sociolinguistic' context.

Sociolinguistic Considerations

The sociolinguistic perspective might be invoked at this stage to see what it has to offer. An obvious reason for a relaxed attitude towards technical niceties and details is that historically they have proved to be of much lesser significance for the acceptance or rejection of a writing system than sociopolitical considerations. That European Jews wrote Judezmo, a Romance language, and Yiddish, a Germanic language, in Hebrew script had little to do with the technical adequacy of Hebrew to represent those languages. Similarly, that non-Arab Muslim peoples until recently wrote their languages in Arabic script and that Roman Catholic Slavs wrote their languages in Latin script while Orthodox Slavs wrote theirs in Cyrillic script is a function of social not technical constraints (Cooper, 1989:128). The primacy of socio-geopolitical considerations is clearest when we see the same language written in different scripts. For example, in India, Konkani is written in Nagari, Roman, and Kannada scripts, while Sindhi is written in both Nagari and Perso-Arabic scripts.

Many of these examples in fact reveal the influence of religious factors upon the acceptability or otherwise of writing systems. Indeed the scripts associated with the religious texts gained acceptability along with the texts themselves. Muslims decorate their mosques with passages from the Quran, written in exquisite Arabic calligraphy, while Roman Catholic Bishops trace the letters of the Latin alphabets on church floors during consecration rites. That the writing systems are divine gifts has been a common claim since the dawn of history across the globe. The claim of divine origin of writing systems in fact helps the rulers, the representatives of 'God on earth', legitimize their authority. Take, for example, a quote from the six page introduction to Elio Antonio de Nebrija's grammar, *Grammatica Castellana,* which came off the press on 18 August, 1492, just fifteen days after Christopher Columbus had sailed.

"My Illustrious Queen. Whenever I ponder over the tokens of the past that have been preserved in writing, I am forced to the very same conclusion. Language has always been the consort of empire, and forever shall remain its mate. Together they came into being, together they grow and flower, and together they decline (Illich 1981:6)." Having translated the quote which is an address to Queen Isabella, Illichi comments on Nebrija's attempt as a fundamental attempt of engineering of a new social reality.

Script: The Double Edged Weapon

Writing systems, like other instruments of power, can be wielded by those who can grasp it. Rulers use writing to perpetuate their rule and power, and the ruled attempt to use it to subvert the balance of power. The subjugated minorities have often wanted their languages to be written in the system of their rulers, whether or not this system adequately represents their own languages. This will and does facilitate their acquisition of literacy in the ruler's language. At other times, minorities want a system different from their rulers. They want a system unique to themselves—to claim a sociocultural, historical status superior to neighbouring peoples as well as to claim an enhanced prestige and status owing at least partly to their posession of a unique script. Other motives may also contribute to the creation or revival and acceptance of indigenous scripts. While the minority in a macro context might envy the power and material advantages associated with the knowledge of the dominant script and see these scripts as a means of its own subjugation, the same minority might function as a dominant power with its unique script, created or revived, in a macro context. Thus, the indigenous script may become a double-edged weapon, resisting the authority of alien powers on the one hand and establishing its own superior authority on the other. It must, of course, be admitted that a unique, indigenous script, designed and modified properly, may permit its users to benefit from modern technology, without sacrificing traditional beliefs and practices. It can provide an elegant solution to the problem of how to be modern and traditional at one and the same time.

On this premise, we might propose that social, political, economic and cultural considerations and power relations far outweigh technical factors in determining a particular script's creation or resurgence and acceptance.

Script Planning in India: Assimilationist Bias

It is high time that experts and specialists in India, as perhaps anywhere else, seriously committed to understanding and contributing to the solution of language-related problems recognize their position and role and also admit explicity whose interest do they represent and serve. Fishman elegantly and aptly admits that his own views on language and ethnicity are not unbiased, stating that he would not take seriously any one else's claim to an unbiased viewpoint on this subject. He then says:

> "The best I can hope for is (a) to state my biases; (b) to seek as much contact with emprical evidence as is possible, since such contact may lead me to revise my views; and (c) where

> no such contact is really possible, as is the case with many of our most central convictions, to accept the fact that social scientists (including myself) are only human, i.e. that they have values and these values do show, must show, whether they are on my side of the fence or on the other."
>
> (Fishman, 1989:2)

Again this is especially necessary given the recent trend for linguists (as in Australia) to be interventionists rather than participant/ observers. That would hopefully be a step forward toward not only progressive resolution of conflicts but also towards truer reconciliation of theory and practice.

In India, however, we have trapped and frozen overselves in quagmires, vacillating between Euro-centric disciplines of thought, theories, categories and local perceptions. What is necessary is to reconcile the snap-shots and the moving pictures, the particular and the universal, the being and the becoming, the product and the processes, and all this in the socio-historical context of the peoples, groups and communities in our country. Indian linguistics, let us confess, has been star-crossed and has moved exactly in the opposite direction. A couple of representative examples will help clarify our point of view.

Outrightly ruling out the ethnic identity, political, religious, and emotional positions and approaches, Pattanayak (1981:106-8) suggests five principles as guidelines for rational language planning in regard to the use of scripts in India. They are:

(a) *Discouraging the creation of new scripts.* Since they add to the existing multiplicity of scripts in India which come in the way of national integration and dispersal of knowledge across segments.

(b) *Use of dominant script systems by non-literate languages.* From the point of view of the development of the typing-printing and telecommunication technology. In other words, their economic interests are tied up with the dominant script.

(c) *Rationalising and consolidating the allied scripts.* This kind of consolidation will be a great step towards the rationalization of printing technology, the creation of a wider book market and national integration.

(d) *Script reform.* In the interest of efficient research and the introduction of new technology, there is a great need of coordination in this area.

(e) *Quick learning of the scripts.* For the accelerated learning of reading and writing.

A more recent work (Ranjitha, 1989) asserts: National integration in its truest sense can never be achieved but through the footstool and prelude of language integration. Language integration can not be realized but through a common script. A common script will not be accepted unless it is easy and scientific, suitable for any form of writing and does not create confusion for any language when applied. (283)

On this premise, Ranjitha (1989) pleads for the Bharati script for all the languages in India: Bharati script promises to solve many related problems concerning the languages in India. The problems involved in its implementation are dwarfed before the colossal problems that India faces in the field of languages and communication. The advantages of Bharati can be listed as follows:

(1) Technical provision to introduce primary education in mothertongue for all non-literary language groups of India.
(2) Creation of a common language from the existing resources.
(3) Fabrication of national integration.
(4) Making an aesthetic experience of the subjective experience of writing and the objective experience of reading.
(5) Formation of cultural bridge between the North and the South, East and the West through the tribal communities. (*op. cit.*, 291).

Lastly, let us see what Miranda (1988) recommends for Konkani. Even after presenting the figures of non-periodical publications in Konkani in different scripts (Nagari=Around 80, Roman=Over 1000, and Kannada=Around 400), Miranda (1988:2) prefers the adoption of Devanagari script on the following two grounds:

(i) It is the script of three major Indian languages (Marathi, Hindi and Sanskrit) which have a rich literature and an established status in the educational institutions of the Konkani areas.

(ii) It will be learned in course of time by all school-going Konkani speakers because of the introduction of Hindi in schools in all the areas.

The above three and many more are reflections of policies of linguistic assimilation, shrouded in technicalities which are supposedly meant to lead to national unity and integrity. But have they? The Indian scenario, both linguistic and non-linguistic, remains enveloped in crisis and is faced with fundamental questions of identity.

The Meiteis: The Relegion and Script

Manipur as a border state of India is unique but at the same time it is a typical mosaic like many other societies in India in the sense that it is multi-ethnic, multi-religious, multi-lingual, multi-cultural and multi-racial (for details, see Aggarwal, 1992). Within the rubric of this paper, what is of direct relevance is the religious, linguistic, and historical background of the Manipuris or Meiteis as they call themselves.

There are various accounts on the origin of the Meiteis. Grierson (1904) traces their origin from the upper courses of the Yangtze and the Hoyang-Ho in China. Johnstone (1971:97) concludes: "The Manipuris themselves are a fine stalwart race descended from an Indo-Chinese stock with some admixture of Aryan blood, derived from the successive waves of Aryan invaders that have passed through the valley in prehistoric days. Since then the race has been constantly fed by additions, from the various hill tribes surrounding the valley." Pemberton thinks that "the Manipuris of the present-days are the desceandants of the Tartar colony, which probably emigrated from the north-west borders of China . . . . " (1835). According to Chatterji (1958:87):

> The Mongoloids appear to have been already established in the southern Himalayan slopes and in easten India by about 1000 B.C. for there is mention of the Kirata people in the Yajur Veda and the Atharva Veda. They represent two or three different peoples racially, all speaking forms of Sino-Tibetan and belonging to the same culture type which originally developed somewhere in eastern China either in the east of the Hoynag-Ho valley or about the head waters of the Yang-Tze Kiang.

According to the local legends and manuscripts, the Meities believe themselves to be the creation of Lord Atiya Guru Sidaba, when the valley was divided into seven small kingdoms under the rules of the seven clan dynasties, namely Khaba, Chenglei, Luwang, Ningthouja, Khuman, Moirang and Angom. In course of time, the clean dynasties merged to form a composite Meitei people who now form the majority (about 60%) of the total population of Manipur. And their history, as recorded in the royal chronicle, Cheitharol Kumbhaba started from the first half of the first century A.D.

As regards the indigenous Meitei script, the most commonly accepted version is that it evolved during the reign of Meitei King Kiyamba (1469-1503 A.D.). This has been corroborated by the stone inscriptions found at Khoibu in Tengnoupal District in Manipur. The composition of Cheitharol Kumbhaba started during this period itself. Another version is that Choupha Khe Khomba, the King of the neighbouring Pong (now Shan State in Myanmar) country sent a person Louta Seng by name, for doing the job of reading and writing in the court of the Meitei King. However, not a single manuscript written in the Shan script has been traced yet. European scholars like Damant (1875) and Hudson (1975) point out that the Meitei script has been developed as late as the 16th/17th century. On the contrary, W. Yumjao Singh, a local scholar, has pushed back the date to as early as 3rd century A.D. (1935:19). Unfortunately there is no valid historical evidence to corroborate any of the views.

As stated earlier, each script available in the world has a mythological background and divine intervention/assistance. Meitei script is no exception. Myths about its divine origin are in wide circulation. One myth says that the Meitei script was invented by Lai-Pakhanga, the legendary Meitei deity. In fact, the letters constituting the Meitei script have corresponding divine attributes. One description is as follows: 'Ka' is male and represents the deity of the Ningthouja clan; 'Kha' is male and represents the deity Atiya Sidaba, the household deity; 'Ga' is female and represents Laisana, the consort of Pakhangba; 'Gha' is feamle and represents Leimaren, the consort of Sanamahi; 'Nga' is eunuch and represents Ashiba, an important deity and so on and so forth. According to the version of a contemporary scholar, the first letters of the seven rows are taken to be representatives of seven days in a week (Manihar, 1988).

Apart from historical accounts and myths, there have been epigraphic and numismatic studies as well as analysis of old manuscripts to determine the letters in the indigenous script. A number of stone inscriptions, found in the length and breath of the Manipur valley have been studied. Of particular importance are the ones at Khoibu in Tengnoupal District (1467-1508), at Ngapram Chingjen in the West District (1702 A.D.), at Ningel in Thoubal District (1709-1748), at Leishang Khong (1813-1819) and lastly within the compound of 1st Battalion, Manipur Rifles (1844-1850). In all these stone inscriptions 35 letters have been found used. (see Appendix I). The same number of letters have been found in the genealogies of Meitie families inscribed on copper, brass and bronze plates which have been kept in the custody of paterfamilias handed down from generation to generation.

For numismatic studies, the coins issued by successive Meitei Kings have been used. However these coins have proved to be of little help as they bear no full names of the Kings except some initial letters and dates of issue.

Learning and production of Meitei manuscripts were taken up seriously during the reign of king Khagemba (1597-1652 A.D.) and up to the close of the 17th century, i.e. until the imposition of Hinduism. These manuscripts dealt with different topics like myths, astrology, study of natural phenomena, administration and pure heroic and romantic literature. An important point that emerges from the study of the manuscripts is the fact that uptil about the begining of the 18th century they were completely free from any loan words. In fact loan words from Sanskrit and Bengali languages particularly have been found in manuscripts produced from 1709 onwards.

The findings from the study of loan words in the old Manuscript lead us to see the linkages between religion and script. The Meiteis were proselytised into Hindusim in the 17th century. First, the King of Manipur himself was converted by a Vaishnavite missionary from Sylhet (now in Bangladesh), namely Shanti Das Gosai. The King whose Meitei name was Pamheiba was rechristened as King Gharib Nawaz (interestingly an Urdu name). King Gharib Newaz then, by royal decree, converted the entire Meitei population into Hinduism. Thereafter, in a massive cataclysm, all facets of indigenous Meitei culture and history were sought to be destroyed, involving the pulling down of each and every Sanamahi (the ancestral deity of Meiteis) temple. Most of the old manuscripts in the original Meitei, script, were burnt down in an event popularly known as *Puya Meithaba* (for details see Das, 1985). The original script was replaced by the Bengali script and Sanskrit and Bengali vocabularies were infused into the language in a big way. Commenting on this intimate link between religion and script, Chatterji (1971:18) comments:

> From the time of King Gharib Newaz Singh of Manipur (1709-1748), the Manipuri people, through the influence of the Bengali Vaishnava of Chaitanya school from Nawadwip and Sylhet, accepted the Bengali script for their language (c.1740) and now this has become fully established.

Local Meitei scholars, however, contest this theory of acceptance of Hindu religion and Bengali script. They assert that it was rather a "period of anguish and resentment among the Meiteis at the burning of old Meitei manuscripts by Santidas (Gosai), the Ramanandi missionary. The issue at stake was the imposition of a new royal faith upon the Meiteis, that also at the instigation of Santidas" (Resistance, 1976). The other contention of Chatterji *(ibid.)* that "now this has become fully established" again does not hold water in view of the fact that the movement to restore the indigenous Meitei script had already started by then and the demands for its revival was taken on to the floor of the Manipur Legislative Assembly by 1978. We shall return to it a little later.

Spelling Reform

From the early 20s to the mid 70s, the basic language concern in Manipur can be said to have been spelling reform of the Bengali script. A Spelling Reform Committee was constituted in 1925 under the Chairmanship of Raja Dumbra Singh, then a Judicial Member of the Durbar. After three years, the Committee submitted its report but reactions came about the pitfalls of the system from various quarters. Then the Education Standing Committee (E.S.C.) took over charge from the Spelling Committee. The E.S.C. modified and imporoved the spelling system of 1925. The Government of Manipur accepted the modified system on February 6, 1935. The Maharaja of Manipur also gave his assent on March 26, 1935.

This spelling system then became the only standard. All textbooks were produced according to this system. Uniformity in spelling could be maintained because in those days all books were produced by the Government and printed at the Government Press. For about two decades this systems continued.

Later, when the Government of Manipur was no longer the only publisher of the textbooks and as private publishers started publications of their own, the standard spelling system of the Government gradually lost its status and power over the writings by people. Different publishers of books as well newspapers etc. and different writers started using their own spelling systems with a vengeance. As a result, after 1960, comments and suggestions from individual pandits and scholars on the degenerated spelling systems started pouring in. A more vigorous wave of controversy came when the Manipur Sahitya Parishad (MSP) published three articles on the issue in its Journal *Sahitya* in January 1965. The main observations and suggestions made by the three scholars in those articles may be summed up as follows:

(a) In Meitei script the tonal differences can be expressed in writing but not in the Bengali script;

(b) For the sake of Bengali script, even speech sounds from Bengali language were thrust onto Manipuri language; and

(c) The loan words from Sanskrit and Bangali etc. could retain their original spelling but for the native words alien sounds like the retroflex, sibilants, voiced palatals, uvular nasals etc. should be done away with.

Though these suggestions apparently are based on technical considerations, their genesis lied in socio-religious-ethnic factors, as we shall see later. In fact, there were sharp reactions when in 1967 the MSP published the book *Manipuri Lon-gi Banan-gi Pathap* [Rules of spelling of Manipuri Language]. The reactions were sharper since the authors had quoted Panini's 'ślokas' in Sanskrit.

As the reactions and controversies grew unabaited, the Government of Manipur again constituted an Expert Sub-Committee to reconsider and modify the spelling system. The draft of this Committee was approved by the Government and was published in the Manipur Gazette (Extraordinary No. 117-E-101) on July 28, 1969. This 1969 spelling system proved to be no better than that of 1925 since the confusion and controversies persisted as they were. Though the 1969 system attempted to take care of tonal distinctions, it allegedly allowed inordinate room for Bengali and Sanskrit words in preference to the native ones.

After 1969, interest in the spelling system of Manipuri with the Bengali script declined. Some sections of the Manipuri speakers rather started emphasizing the Meitei script. Of course there were some people who thought of Romanization while others silently discussed the adoption of the International Phonetic Alphabet. Public statements such as the following were made in the mid-70s:

"No doubt there was a conspricay to murder the Meitei script . . . . . However, the death blow to the Manipuri script was given by the British after 1891" (Resistance March 23, 1976). The common people accused that the British colonial Government had brought into Manipur a large number of Bengali babus, clerks, revenue officers, interpreters etc. In fact, Bengali script was introduced in Manipur quite effectively through the schools established by the British from the last quarter of the 19th century. Thus the people felt that the British colonial regime and the Bengali babus under them accomplished the unfinished task of Santidas i.e. destroying the indigenous script. People now started asserting that "Meiteiron belongs to Sino-Tibetan Phylum; it has its own phonetic system and everything should be subservient to this system "(Resistance April 13, 1976). Thus, the *Manipuri Phonetic Reader* (Singh, 1976) was outright rejected since it was "purely from the technical point of view."

Resurgence of Ethnolinguistic Identity: The Quagmires

By 1977-78, ethnolinguistic consciousness among the Meiteis took a different direction and reached its pinnacle. On the 31st March, 1978, the Manipuri Official Language Bill, designating Manipuri written in Bengali script as the Official Language of the State was unanimously passed by the Legislative Assembly of Manipur (for details, see, Aggarwal, 1992). After receiving the assent of the Governor on 24 October, 1979, the Manipur Official Language Act, 1979 came into force. The Act's definitions included "'Manipuri language' means Meiteilon written in *Bengali script* and spoken by the *majority* of Manipur population (emphasis mine)." Although this was an occassion of rejoicing, the two main ethnolinguistic concerns, revival of indigenous script and inclusion of Meiteilon in the Eighth Schedule of the Constitution of India remained the bones of contention. The statements made by different Members on the floor of the Assembly considering the merits of the adoption of the indigenous Meitei script on 30 June, 1978, reflect the seriousness of the issue:

Mr. Ibotombi (Janata): "We owe it to our self-respect to restore our indigenous script to its rightful place."

Mr. L. Jugeswar (CPI): "An ancient and developed script, it was displaced from its unchallenged status as the repository of our culture as well as the instrument of its advancement by the machinations of one man Santidas Gosai, a Bengali Hindu missionary."

Mr. Nguklkholao (Janata): ". . . a self-respecting nation or community needs a script of its own as an emblem of its pride."

Mr. Parijat (CPI): ". . . the continued use of Bengali script in preference to our own (as is being done now) amounts to self-debasement."

Mr. Th. Chaoba (Janta): "Our religion, language and script were displaced by alien ones. Our books and manuscripts were burnt. Death was the penalty for anyone found reading any book that escaped the burning." (Aggarwal, 1992:30-31)

Lastly, it is interesting to refer to Mr. R.K. Dorendra, then a Janata MLA who emphasized the revival of the indigenous script from two angles:

(1) Script is a vital instrument for defining our separate identity.

(2) In the whole of the north-eastern region barring the Assamese and Bengali areas ours is the only exising script which has nurtured and consolidated a mature civilization. It is an index of our Mongoloid roots as well as our Oriental affinities. (Resistance, 4 July, 1978)

In response to the mounting pressure, the Government of Manipur constituted the Meitei Mayek Expert Sub-Committee on 16 November, 1978 and approved the report submitted by this Committee on 22

April, 1980 (Manipur Gazette Extraordinary No. 1/2/78-SS/E). The Government of Manipur accepted the Meitei script consisting 27 alphabets and issued orders for its acceptance. In a second order on 19 January, 1983 the Government asked all educational institutions in Manipur to introduce the indigenous script as recommended by the Expert Sub-Committee from the Class VI level during the academic session, 1983-84.

It may be noted that controversy regarding the fixation of the number of alphabets of Meitei Meyek dogged the Expert Sub-Committee and out of the total 7 members 3 gave notes of dissent. The majority of 4 members favoured to fix the number at 36 i.e. the old 35 alphabets plus the Anji. They argued that these alphabets were found published during the reign of Maharaja Chandra Kirti Singh of Manipur, as also by the then political Agent of Manipur, Mr. G.H. Damant, in his article in the *Journal of the Asiatic Society of Bengal* (1877) and further in the *Linguistic Survey of India,* Vol. III, Part III (Grierson, 1904).

Of the three members who had given notes of dissent, two recommended only 30 letters (24 consonants and 6 vowels) whereas one suggested 32 (24 consonants and 8 vowels). However, the majority of 4 recommending 35 letters plus the Anji prevailed on the argument that these were "used in Manipur from time immemorial by the Maharajas and Pundits . . . in the old manuscripts, family genealogies, epigraphy and royal chronicles . . .". The Expert Sub-Committee was however, unanimous in recommending the continuance of the use of Bengali-Assamese numerals and also in their suggestion that the alphabets should be read as Ka, Kha, Ga, Gha. . . and so on and not as Kok, Sam, Lai, Mit. . . etc.

In his paper of dissent Dr. Mangi Migomba argues that "Reading those old manuscripts are for the researchers and epigraphers; not for school going students." On this premise, he recommends 24 consonants, 8 vowels and any numerals. He also pleads for reading the alphabets as Ka, Kha, Ga, etc.:

> In this system of reading there is possibility of pronouncing the letters by minimum addition of extraneous sounds . . . If we follow the tradition of reading the alphabets by a speakable name such as 'Kok' (for k), Sam (for s), Lai (for l), Mit

> (for m), Na(for n), Pa(for p) etc., the consonants may not be spoken of easily by a minimum of addition of extraneous sound.

The Government of Manipur, however, arrived at what can be called an uncomfortable compromise. While it approved the recommendation of 'modernist' experts of fixing the number of alphabets at 27, it succumbed to the 'traditionalist's pressure to read the letters as Kok, Sam, Lai etc. (See Appendix I. These speakable names of the alphabets refers to the different parts of the human body, human actions and natural phenomena e.g. *kok* means 'head'; *sam* means 'hair'; *lai* 'forehead'; *pa* 'eyebrow'; *ee* 'blood'; *atiya* 'sky' and so on.

We shall not go into further details of the technical matters as they would not in any way help us understand the script crisis in Meiteilon. An editorial published in Resistance (January 31, 1978) titled "Muddle in Meitei Script" makes interesting reading and hence parts of it are reproduced below:

> "The Meiteis have something to learn about script from the Bodos of Assam. The latter wanted, still want, to use the Roman script for their Bodo language instead of the Assamese script they use at present. In the early seventies, their movement gained momentum, but it was crushed by the police who hunted down the activists like assasins. the Union Home Minister bluntly told the Bodos either to continue with Assamese script or to start introducing the Devanagri script. The Bodos chose the status quo . . . . . There is of course a fundamental difference between the case of the Bodos and that of the Meiteis. The Meiteis are not asking for changing into a new script like the Bodos, but only re-introduction of their own script in place of the Bengali script they are using. But such niceties are unlikely to make any difference in the attitude of the Centre towards the meiteis script."
>
> "Advocates of Meitei script, who run into thousands, only look at the problem from their own angles. They consider that the greatest obstacle to reintroduction of the Meitei script is the lack of unanimity about the number of alphabets among the scholars. They blame the State Government for not being a judge in the academic controversy, as though the

> government is competent to do so . . . . What they require is not Government's intervention, but a little common sense and an understanding about the dynamic link between a language and its script. To the credit of India's brain-washing efforts, they do not seem to consider that the greatest hurdle is New Delhi's attitude to the issue."

In the meantime, in a mystifying feat, the Lok Sabha [Lower House of the Indian Parliament] on August 20, 1992 passed the 71st Constitutional Amendment Bill to include the Nepali, Manipuri, and Konkani languages in the Eighth Schedule of the Constitution of India. While this lead to great jubiliation among the Meiteilon speaking people in Manipur, it also led to the re-emergence of the Meitei Mayek controversy with greater intensity. On 19th March, 1993, Dr. H. Borobabu Singh, the Speaker of the Manipur Legislative Assembly, announced in the House that the Committee to "re-examine for addition of Meitei Mayek (script) and its introduction in Manipur had been reconstituted" consisting of nine members. (Manipur Legislative Assembly Secretariat Bulletin Part I, No. 6). What is interesting to note here is that all the members of the reconstituted committee are elected Members of the House and not language experts and, more significantly, they represent the seven clans which had converged into the Meitei ethnic group in the past.

The other important development has been a protracted protest movement by a locally strong organization, namely, Apunba Meitei Kanba Kanglup (AMKK), against what they call the 'GENOCIDE' of Meitei language, culture, script and people at the hands of both the State Government and the Central Government. On January 9, 1993, AMKK sent a telegram to the President of India making a 'Constitutional Protest' against naming their language 'Manipuri' in place of 'Meiteilon'. The overall socio-historical context in which they see this as a 'GENOCIDE' may be glimpsed through from a paragraph in the telegram *(ibid.)* reproduced below:

> Such a heinous act of the complete extermination of the said ASIATIC MEETEI ethnic people, by burning those Meetei Puyas (Scriptures) and Kangleirons (Scriptures of Spritual Foundation of Science and Art of conducting State Affairs)—by burning such Puyas and Kangluirons under a high motiva-

tion of castrationizing the highly civilized and cultured MEETEI and Seven Yeks (Natural Genetic Codes) into an unnatural Gotras of the Aryan Hindus, with an aim at rewriting the story and history of the Meetei Puyas and Kangleirons for Sankritizing them (the said Puyas and Kangleirons) to impose the caste system of the Hindus upon the Non-Aryan Meetei as well as to cut off the traditional link between the hill and plain people—is tantamount to a commitment of an international crime globally called "GENOCIDE".

Thus we are back into the trap of quagmires. As we said earlier, there are more questions than answers at this stage of development of our understanding of the dynamics of ethnolinguistic identity and of language in social totality. We only hope that we have moved towards grasping the issue and formulating the problem.

NOTE

I am thankful to Dr. R.S. Gupta and Dr. S. Jha for their patient hearing of and suggestions on an earlier draft of this paper. The usual disclaimers of course apply.

(For Appendixes to this Chapter please see pages 475 & 477).

REFERENCES

Aggarwal, K.S., 1990. 'American bilingual education revised'. *Scandanavian Journal of Development Alternatives.* Vol. IX, No. 4, pp. 97-105.

—, 1992. 'To include or not to include: An Attempt to study the language conflict in Manipur.' *Language Problems and Language Planning.* Vol. 16, No. 1. pp. 21-37.

Berry, Jack, 1958. 'The making of alphabets.' *Proceedings of the Eighth International Congress of Linguists.* Oslo: University Press, pp. 752-764.

—, 1977. "'The making of alphabets' revisited." In Joshua A. Fishman (ed.), Advances in the Creation and Revision of Writing Systems. The Hauge: Mouton, pp. 3-16.

Bourhis, R., 1982. 'Language policies and language attitudes: Le monde de la francophonie.' In E. Ryan & H. Giles (eds.), Attitudes towards language variation, London: Edward Arnold.

Chatterji, S.K., 1958. *Cultural Heritage of India.* Vol. 1, No. 1, p. 87.

—, 1971, 'Manipuri as a language of literature and culture.' *In Indian Literature: Adivasi Literatures of India.* New Delhi:Sahitya Akademi, pp. 18-197.

Cooper, Robert L., 1989. *Language Planning and Social Change.* Cambridge: Cambridge University Press.

Damant, G.H., 1875. 'Specimen of Manipuri Alphabet'. In *Proceedings of the Asiatic Society of Bengal.* ASB, Calcutta.

Das, R.K., 1985. *Manipur Tribal Scene.* New Delhi, Inter-India Publications.

Ferguson, Charles A., 1968. 'Language development'. In Joshua A. Fishman et al (eds.), *Language Problems of Developing Nations.* New York: John Wiley and Sons, pp. 27-35.

Fishman, Joshua A., 1989. *Language and Ethnicity in Minority Sociolinguistic Perspective.* Clevedon & Philadelphia: Multilingual Matters.

Grierson, G.A., 1904. *Linguistic Survey of India.* Vol. III, Part III. Reprinted by Motilal Benarsidass, Delhi.

Hamers, J.F. and Blanc, M.H., 1989. *Bilinguality and Bilingualism.* Cambridge: Cambridge University Press.

Hudson, T.C., 1975. *The Meitheis.* New Delhi, Neeraj Publishing House (Reprint).

Illich, Ivan, 1981. 'Taught mother language and vernacular tongue.' In D.P. Pattnayak. *Multilingualism and Mothertongue Education.* Delhi. Oxford University Press.

Singh, Inder, 1976. *A Manipuri Phonetic Reader.* Mysore: Central Institute of Indian Languages.

Johnstone, Sir James, (1971). *My Experience in Manipur and Naga Hills.* Delhi (reprint). Originally published in 1896. London. Sampson and Law, Marstone & Co. Ltd.

Kedousi, E., 1961. Nationalism. London. Hutchinson.

Mackey, W., 1978. 'The Importation of bilingual education.' In J. Alatis (ed.), *Georgetown University Roundtable on Language and Linguistics.* Washington D.C.: Georgetown University Press.

Manihar, Ch., 1984. 'Meiteis: origin and affinity.' *Journal of Manipur University.* Vol. 1, No. 1, pp. 22-29. Canchipur: Manipur University.

Miranda, Rocky V., 1988. 'Language Development in the Konkani Region.' Paper presented at ICLAND. Hyderabad: Osmania University.

Pattanayak, D.P., 1981. *Multilingualism and Mothertongue Education.* Delhi. Oxford University Press.

Pemberton, R.B., 1835. *The Eastern Frontier of British India.* Gauhati. Department of Historical and Antiquarian Studies in Assam.

Ranjitha, J.A., 1989. *Writing Non-Literary Languages in the Indian Context.* Unpublished Ph.D. Dissertation. New Delhi: Jawaharlal Nehru University.

Resistance Weekly, 1976-1986. Imphal: Pan Manipuri Youth League.

Venezky, Richard L., 1977. 'Principles for the design of practical writing systems.' In Joshua A. Fishman (ed.), 1989.

Yumjao Singh, W., 1935. *Reports on the Archaelogical Studies in Manipur.* Imphal, W. Gourachandra Singh.

VII

ANDAMANESE

The day is just about to break
Don't go on living as if you are over sleeping
Lift up your head and look
The people of the earth are waiting
For your reaction and action
Let all the people of this earth
Live together.
Bring your glory, your intellect, and
Your strength together
Let us rebuild this world.

(A Rongmei song)

Translated by Khaleb

CHAPTER 26

PRONOMINAL PREFIXES AND FORMATIVE AFFIXES IN ANDAMANESE LANGUAGE

S. Manoharan

Introduction

The Andamanese belong to the Negrito stock and are different from the Negro or Negroid population of Africa. They are considered to be the surviving representatives of the Negrito race that once flourished and held sway in the entire South-East Asia region. The other representatives of this great Negrito race found in the Andaman group of Islands are the Onge of Little Andaman Island, the Jarawa of South Andaman Island and the Sentinelese of the North Sentinel Island. The Semang of Malaysia and the Aeta of the Philippines are the other representatives of the Negrito stock found outside India. Though, the Semang and the Aeta have physical and cultural resemblances with the Andamanese, they recently have adopted the language of their alien neighbours to a great extent (Radcliffe-Brown, 1948:6). But the linguistic identity of the Negrito of the Andaman group of Islands are still preserved. The people who are now called Andamanese or Great Andamanese are differentiated from the other Negrito of the Andaman group of Islands, who were formerly ten different tribes and who had a separate linguistic identity of their own. Now they are known under a common nomenclature as many of them are extinct.

The present day Andamanese are so called as they are the inhabitants of the Andaman Islands or they are referred to as Great Andamanese to avoid confusion from the other tribes: Onge, Jarawa and Sentinelese as they are also inhabitants of the Andaman Islands. The various ten different tribes are: Bale, Bea, Bo, Cari, Jeru, Juwoi, Kede, Kol, Kora and Puchikwar.[1] Apparently some of the tribal names like Kol and Kora are well comparable with that of the Austro-Asiatic languages speaking tribes of the Indian subcontinent bearing similar names. The Onge tribe who are the inhabitants of the Little Andaman Island call themselves *ëŋe* meaning 'man', having a parallal etymology to that of the Ho tribe who also derive their name from the word *hor* meaning 'man'. The etymology of the name of the tribe of Jarawa is from a word meaning 'stranger' belonging to the earlier Bea tribe. The Sentinelese are called so, as they inhabit the North Sentinel Island. So the Jarawa and the Sentinelese tribes still are known by means of other references and not by their own.[2] But in the absence of proper etymology of the names of the various tribal groups of Andaman Islands, such comparison, though possible, could not be attempted and established concertely. The etymology of Andaman is considered to be from Hanuman, related with the Hindu mythology (Bonington, 1931: 172). The Chinese and the Japanese had referred to these Islands as Yeng-t'o-mang and Angaman respectively. The Malays had referred to them as Handuman, a corrupt form of Hanuman.

Andamanese Family of Languages

The languages of the Andaman Islanders form a separate linguistic family which has been designated as "Andamanese Family of Languages" (Manoharan, 1980) and their affinity with the other known languages of the world has yet to be studied. The ten different languages of the ten different Great Andamanese form a separate subgroup and the other three languages, the languages of the Onges, Jarawas, and the Sentinelese, form a separate subgroup, namely, the Little Andaman Group. The interrelation between the Great Andaman group and the Little Andaman group is such that:

> "it would not be possible from a consideration of the vocabulary alone, to prove that they belong to the same language stock. It is only when the grammatical structure of the language is examined that it is possible to show that they are really all dervied from one original language."
>
> (Radcliffe-Brown, 1914)

Thus the Little Andaman group of languages when compared with the Great Andaman group shows only a distant affinity. Man (1885) subgroups the Great Andamanese into three different subgroups as South, Middle, and North, while Radcliffe-Brown (1948) subgroups them into two different groups-South and North. A comparative study based on the available linguistic materials on the different languages of the Great Andaman and Little Andaman subgroups shows the following picture. (Manoharan, 1983)

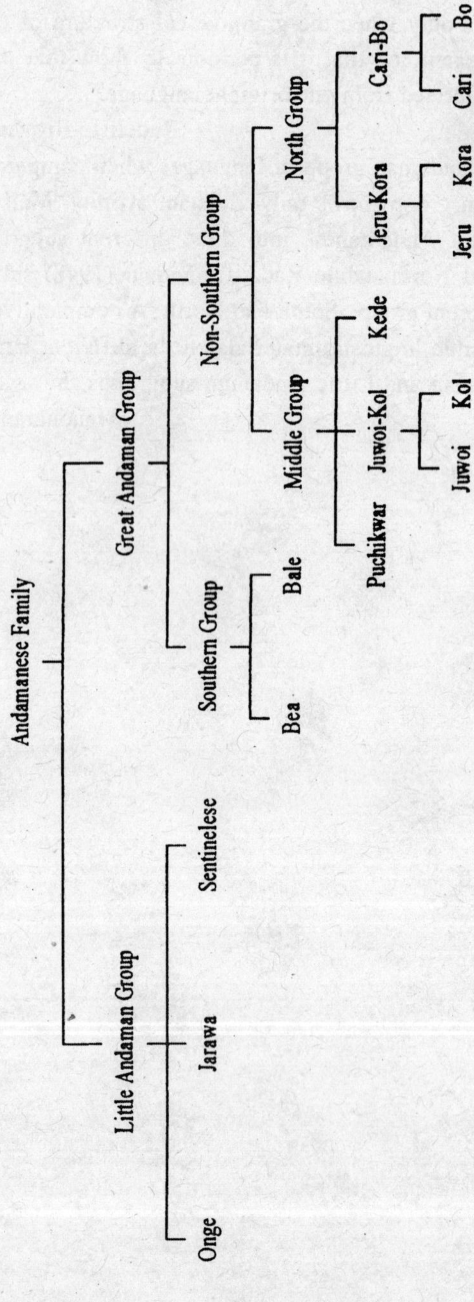
Andamanese Family
Little Andaman Group
Great Andaman Group
Onge
Jarawa
Sentinelese
Southern Group
Non-Southern Group
Bea
Bale
Middle Group
North Group
Puchikwar
Juwoi-Kol
Kede
Jeru-Kora
Cari-Bo
Juwoi
Kol
Jeru
Kora
Cari
Bo

Fig. 1.

Affixes

The pronominal prefixes and the formative affixes are the important characteristic features of the noun morphology of not only the Andamanese language but also of the other languages belonging to the Andamanese language family.[3] The pronominal prefixes have two kinds of functions. When it occurs before a noun, it gives the meaning of possession and when it occurs before a verb, it is a subject noun. In Andamanese languages, the words denoting body parts always occur having possessive meanings. The formative affixes are those prefixes and infixis which modify the concept of a stem or a root into words having specific meaning. Since they form the words from a concept, they are called **formative affixes.** In this paper the account of these two characteristic features are dealt with only for the Andamanese/Great Andamanese language. Based on the type of pronominal prefix that occurs with the words denoting body parts, the entire set of words of the same category can be classified into three distinct classes.

Noun Classes

Class I—Nouns:[4] These are the nouns that take *ṭɔ-* 'my' as the first person singular pronominal prefix:

ṭɔ-otbe:c	ṭɔtbe:c	'my hair'
ṭɔ- otcow	ṭɔtcow	'my head'
ṭɔ- tra:p		'my head (bald)'
ṭɔcĩiso:ŋɔ		'my body'
ṭɔmøoŋ		'my armpit'
ṭɔntow		'my wrist'
ṭɔŋkɔ:rɔ		'my palm of hand'
ṭɔŋka:ra		'my nail'
ṭɔŋkena:p		'my finger'
ṭɔtca:r		'my chest'
ṭɔtbothurḍe:lɔ		'my heart'
ṭɔtkarno		'my spleen'
ṭɔnḍrɔ:nɔ		'my ankle'
ṭɔma:ṭɔ		'my feet'

Class II—Nouns: These are the nouns that take *ṭa-* as the first person singular pronominal prefix:

ṭa-tha:t	ṭatha:t	'my tongue'
ṭa-kɛ:r-totlo:coŋ	ṭakkɛ:r - totlo:conŋ	'my throat'
ṭaøŋ		'my mouth'
ṭalɛmo		'my uvula'
ṭakkɛ:r		'my neck'
ṭara:bucow		'my leg'
ṭara:kka:ra:p		'my waist'

Class III—Nouns: These are the nouns that take *ṭe-* as the first person singular pronominal prefix:

ṭe-erbe:ñ	ṭerbe:ñ	'my forehead'
ṭerulu		'my eye'
ṭermixu		'my forehead'
ṭercow		'my head'
ṭerji:li		'my joint of eye brows'
ṭerulutobɔ:k		'my eye brows'
ṭerkɔtho		'my nose'
ṭerbuwa:		'my lips'
ṭerøi:lɛ		'my teeth'
ṭertara:lɛ		'my gum of teeth'
ṭernɔxo		'my cheek'
ṭerta:p		'my chin'
ṭerxolme		'my cheek bone'
ṭerbuwo:		'my ear'
ṭerta:ŋɔ		'my temple of ear'
ṭercɔ:k		'my face'
ṭermine		'my brain'
ṭeṭṭɔ:y		'my bone'
ṭerxiṭ		'my arm'
ṭeburɔ:ŋɔ		'my rib'
ṭermettay		'my breast'
ṭemeyca		'my lungs'
ṭetteyco		'my kidney'

ṭeŋŋe:ṭ 'my navel'

ṭekkɔtra 'my stomach'

ṭeba:la: 'my hand'

ṭecca:wɔtho:mɔ 'my thigh'

ṭecco:rak 'my knee'

ṭertɔ:ŋ 'my hand'

ŋeli—Pronominal prefix

The following nouns denoting bodyparts take */ŋeli-/* as the second person honorific pronominal prefix:

ŋeli-erbe:ñ ŋelirbe:ñ 'your (hon.) forehead'

ŋelirulu 'your (hon.) eye'

ŋelirmine 'your (hon.) brain'

ŋelirburɔ:ŋɔ 'your (hon.) ribs'

ŋelirji:li 'your (hon.) joint of eye brows'

akka—Pronominal prefix

The following nouns denoting bodyparts take */akka:-/* as the third person singular pronominal prefix:

akka:tha:t 'his/her/its tongue'

akka:kkɛ:rtotlo:coŋ 'his/her/its throat'

akka:øoŋ 'his/her/its mouth'

akka:lɛmo 'his/her/its uvula'

akka:ccɛxu:yi 'his/her/its gullet'

akka:kkɛ:r 'his/her/its neck'

akka:cca:r 'his/her/its chest'

akka:jji:ra: 'his/her/its intestine'

ara—Pronominal prefix

The following nouns denoting bodyparts take */ara:-/* as the third person singular pronominal prefix:

ara:buccow 'his/her/its leg'

ara:kka:ra:p 'his/her/its waist'

Free variation is found between */o- /* and */akka:- /* and */o- /* and */e- /* in the following words:

otca:r~akka:ccar 'his/her/its chest'

ercow~otcow 'his/her/its head'

akka- and *ara-* pronominal prefixes, correspond to the *ṭa-* class of words:

Free variation is found between *ṭe-* and *ṭɔ-* in the word ṭercow~ṭɔtcow 'my head' where the formative affixes -er- and -ot- also are in free variation.

Third person honorific pronominal prefix

The pronominal prefixes that are used as third person singular honorific are: */amma:ye/* and */ammimi/* which are used according to the gender of the possessor noun. They are derived from the words *ma:ye* 'father' and *mimi* 'mother'.

amma:yetcow 'his (hon.) head'

amma:yerbe:c 'his (hon.) hair'

ammimitcow 'her (hon.) head'

ammimitbe:c 'her (hon.) hair'

The pronominal prefixes[5] used for the various personal pronouns are given in table 1:

TABLE 1

Pronominal Prefixes in Andamanese

Classes	I	II	III
First person singular	ṭɔ-	ṭe-	ṭa-
First person plural exclusive	mɔ-	me-	ma-
First person singular exclusive	ṭeŋŋɔ-	ṭeŋŋe-	ṭeŋŋa-
First person plural inclusive	meŋŋɔ-	meŋŋe-	meŋŋa-
Second person singular	ŋɔ-	ŋe-	ŋa-
Second person plural and honorific	ŋɔle-	ŋele-	ŋale-
Third person singular	o-	e-	—
Third person plural	nɔ-	ne-	na-
Third person honorific	nɔle-	nele-	nale-

TABLE 2

The Pronominal System of the Andamanese Language

First person singular	ṭiyo	'I'
First person singular inclusive	ṭeŋŋiyo	'we (inc.sg.)' (I and you)
First person plural exclusive	miyo	'we (excl.)'
First person plural inclusive	meŋŋiyo	'we' (we and you)
Second person singular	ŋiyo	'you'
Plural	ŋiliyo	'you (pl.)'
honorific	ŋamale	'you (hon.)'
Third person singular	o	'he/she/it'
plural	niyo	'they'
Third person singular honorific		
masculine	amma:ye	'he (hon.)'
feminine	ammimi	'she (hon.)'
Third person plural honorific	niliyo	'they (hon.)'

In the pronominal system, Andamanese distinguishes three persons viz., first person, second person and third person. Number is distinguished in all the three persons. In first person plural pronoun, apart from the inclusive-exclusive distinction, the inclusive plural is further differenciated into two which I treat as first person singular inclusive and first person plural inclusive. This system of having inclusive singular and inclusive plural in the first person plural is a special feature of this language. The first person inclusive singular and the first person inclusive plural are formed by adding the second person singular pronoun */ŋiyo/* 'you' to the first person singular pronoun /ṭe-/ 'I' and the first person exclusive plural pronoun */me-/* 'we (excl.)'respectively.

The Possessive Pronouns are:

ṭicco	'my'
misso	'ours'
ṭeŋŋisso	'ours (inc. sg.)'
meŋŋisso	'ours (inc. pl.)'
ŋisso	'yours (sg.)'

ŋilisso	'yours (pl.)'
isso	'his/her/ist'
amma:yesso	'his (hon.)'
ammimisso	'her (hon.)'
nisso	'theirs'
nilisso	'theirs (hon.)'

The *ṭi-* pronominal prefix which does not come as a possessive pronominal prefix for the body parts occurs with other nouns as *ṭicco:*

ticco kɔ:wbe	'my bow'
ticco lɛcbe	'my arrow'
ticco kɛ:wbe	'my crap'

Verb Classes

It is the pronominal prefixes and not the pronouns that occur before a verb in sentences. According to the pronominal prefixes that they take, the Andamanese verbs are classified into four classes. Otherwise the verbs of this language are classified into seventeen classes depending on the imperative suffixes they take.

Class I—Verbs

These are the verbs which come after *ṭɔ-* pronominal prefix:

-otterta:-	'to tell (story)'
-esere:p-~-essere:w-	'to cut'
-otco:-~-otco:ne:-	'to go'
-ijo:-	'to eat'
-ca:-	'to do'
-berulu:-	'to catch'
-iñci-	'to wander (intr.)'
-ɛno:-	'to wander (tr.)'
-era:su:ya-	'to cook'
-cer-	'to seneeze'
-era:yetto:-	'to stand up'
-ɛlo:w-	'to read'
-ɛbo:-	'to beat'
-ṭɔ:p-	'to bathe'

-ɛlɛ:y-	'to descend'
-ikku-	'to set fire'
-ɛtco-	'to row'
-bekasi:-	'to clean (utensil)'
-be:-	'to sweep'
-erbora:-	'to blow'
-ekka:tto:-	'to close (tr.)'
-etta:lo:ṭṭa-	'to change (tr.)'
-era:su:ya-	'to cook'
-ekka:ccɔ-	'to bind'
-ṭɔ:wɔ-	'to make (canoe)'
-atta:bi-	'to think (tr.)'
-yatte:-	'to put'
-ɛra:yi-	'to take'
-ɛbokco:-	'to join'
-akka:yi-	'to open (tr.)'
-ɛra:øu:ya-	'to smoke (tr.)'
-ɔtco:-	'to cut (hair)'
-ke:r-	'to snore'
-etta:se:-	'to change (dress)'
-akka:xi:-	'to fill up (tr.)'
-erendara:ji-	'to show (tr.)'

Class II—Verbs

These are the verbs which come after */ṭe-/* pronominal prefix:

-ño-	'to come'
-ce:-	'to go'
-etco:-	'to get'
-ebisi:-	'to clean (teeth)'
-erjim-	'to sleep'
-ŋɔ:c-	'to itch (intr.)'
-erɛñce:w-	'to fight'
-eruñu:m-~-erñyu:m-	'to sleep'
-jire:-	'to scold'

Class III—Verbs

These are the verbs which come after the /*ṭu-*/ pronominal prefix:

-unde:-	'to call'
-ṭi:bitcellɛ-	'to cry'
-ce:-	'to go'
-ijo:-	'to eat'
-ijiy-	'to eat'
-ixu-	'to drink'
-iyɛ:-	'to catch'
-eserɛ:p-	'to cut'
-be:no:-	'to sleep'
-ili-	'to urinate'
-ecco:w-	'to build (tr.)'
-ɛrɛ:p-	'to ascend'
-juro:y-	'to dance'
-mo:-	'to give'
erte:-~-ertede̩:-	'to see'
-iḍḍuwo:-	'to hear'
-ikkusu:ya-	'to fire'
-irøo:-	'to dig'
-jo:-	'to take'
-ikkulo:-	'to untie'
-jire:-	'to scold'
-iya:retta:-	'to teach'
-ikku-	'to bring'
-itle:øitu:-	'to smoke (intr.)'

Class IV—Verbs

These are the verbs which come after /*ṭa-*/ pronominal prefix:

-ña:-	'to eat'
-ijiyo:-	'to eat'
-eramla:ṭ-	'to be afraid'
-ew- ~ -ewno-	'to sit'
-yeṭi-	'to bluff'
-le-	'to swim'

Formative Affixes

Andamanese language uses a stem or root for designating one concept and then classify that concept differently using different affixes commonly called as 'formative affixes'. The abstract concepts are formed according to a particular quality or quantity in terms of shape, size, position etc. in compound words, the noun is compounded with the stem which convey the particular concept. Examples:

/-be:c/

i-be:c	'honey comb'
ara:-be:c	'tail (of birds)'
tot-be:c	'feather'
ṭɔ-ot-be:c	'hair-my'
ṭɔw-ter-be:c	'cloud'(tɔ:w 'sky')
ṭe-erjuxu-be:c	'mustach-my'
ṭe-erulu-to-be:c	'eyelash-my'
ṭe-erta:p-be:c	'beard-my'
ṭa:jiyo tot-be:c	'bird'

/-cow/

et-cow	'fruit (of tree)'
ekko-cow	'knot (n)'
ettay-cow	'kidney'
ŋɔ-ot-cow	'head-your'

/ce/

ce	'thorn'
et-ce	'gill of the fish'
ara:-ce	'sting'

/xuḍo:y/

ir-xuḍo:y	'circle'
it-xuḍo:y	'ring'

/kɔw/

kɔw	'bow'
kɔw-bu	'umbrella'
kɔw-øo	'banana fruit'
ɔt-kɔw-bo	'bark (of tree)'
ŋerulu to- kɔwbo	'eye lid-your'

/øoŋ/

øoŋ	'hole'
myo:-øoŋ	'cave' (myo: 'rock')
inɔ-tɛr-oŋ	'well' (n) (in 'water')
eø-o:ŋ- øŋe	'dig' (v)
bilixu tara:øoŋ	'east' (bilixu 'god')
ṭi:-ta:-øoŋ	'well' (n) (ti: 'place')
ṭerkɔ:tho tara:- øoŋ	'nostril-my'
ṭa-øoŋ	'mouth-my'
ṭɔ-om-øoŋ	'armpit'

It seems, the various formative affixes used in derving words from a particular concept have its own specific function in difining the quality, quantity according to the shape, the size and the postition of the particular object for which the word is formed. For example *ir-* and *er-* occur as formative prefixes with such words which convey the front or tip of the object:

ir-øiḍe	'edge of rudder'
ir-juxu	'edge of arrow'
ir-øi:le	'edge of weapon'
ir-xume	'front portion of the bow'
er-juxu	'beak of a bird'

In the following examples *era:-* or *ɛra:-* or *ara:-* mean the back or middle part of an object:

era:- xume	'back portion of the bow'
ɛra:- wrɔ	'tail of animal'
ara:- be:c	'tail of bird'
ara:-ce	'sting of a scorpion'
era:-ṭɔwøo	'middle holding portion of a bow'
era:- bu:cco	'roots of a tree'
era:-ṭɔwlɔ	'middle string of a bow'

It is assumed that the formative affixes had a specific elaborate system of their own in the derivation of words. But, now since the language has been highly creolized resulting in the use of more than one formative prefix for a particular derivation,[6] their are three different formative prefixes *era:-*, *ɛra:-* and *ara:-*. Multiple affixes for a similar derivation is also viewed as the resultant of creolisation. In the process of creolization the affixes of the different languages spoken earlier are retained resulting in multiplication of the number of affixes. Some of the affixes might have been lost also. Hence, the clear semantic structure of the concept and the further derivation of words from a concept using various formative affixes becomes difficult to analyse.

NOTES

1. The 1901 Census was the last census which could record the distinct population figures of the different tribes of the Great Andamanese. The same has been reproduced here:

Population: Great Andamanese, 1901

Name of the Tribe	Adults		Children		Total
	male	female	male	female	
Bale	5	10	3	1	19
Bea	14	16	3	4	37
Bo	15	16	7	10	48
Cari	16	15	6	2	39
Jeru	98	80	26	14	218
Juwoi	21	19	7	1	48
Kede	24	30	3	2	59
Kol	6	2	3	–	11
Kora	31	32	14	19	96
Puchikwar	31	14	2	3	50
Total	261	234	74	56	625

The Bea, Bale and Puchikwar tribal groups occupied the South Andaman Islands. The Juwoi, Kede and Kol tribes ocupied the Middle Andaman Islands. The Cari, Bo, Jeru and Kora ocupied the North Andaman Islands. The vast differences between the adults and children population may be observed.

2. It may be worth to note that contacts with the Jarawa and the Sentinelse have been difficult to establish in the recent past, as the two communities have been rather hostile to outsiders. Hence language data of their speech communities are still awaited. For the Jarawa language, very little data is available (c.f. McCarthy, 1940).
3. The ten different languages that were spoken by the earlier ten different tribes of the Great Andaman group and the languages of the Onge, the Jarawa and the Sentinelese form Andamanese language family. Though no language data is available on the language of the Sentinelese. It is treated under this language family because of the

physical and cultural resemblances of Sentinelese with those of other Negrito tribes of the Andaman Islands and their geographical proximity to the latter (Manoharan, 1983).

4. ñ : voiced palatal nasal
   ë : high mid rounded vowel
   ø : voiceless bilabial fricative
5. For Onge, Ganguli (1966) speaks of two kinds of pronominal prefixes; one with a single consonant of C-type and the other with a consonant and vowel of CV-type. For Great Andamanese language also Man (1885, 1923), Portman (1898), and Radcliffe-Brown (1914,1948) have taken only the C-type of pronominal prefixes. But a detailed analysis of the present Great Andamanese language shows that the pronominal prefixes are of CV-type and the morphophonemic rules that govern the changes have not been noticed by the earlier authors and hence they have taken the pronominal prefixes as of C-type. And for the Onge language also, I hope if studied in detail, it will reveal that the pronominal prefixes exists as of CV-type with some morphophonemic rules. The following are the examples showing the use of pronominal prefixes with the noun denoting bodyparts, in Onge language (Ganguli, 1966):

mejale	'my face'
etajalle	'our faces'
ŋejale	'your face'
ŋejalle	'your faces'
gajale	'his, her, its face'
ekwejalle	'their faces'
ëŋejale	'human face'
ëŋejalle	'human faces'

6. For example the word for 'well' is derived from the concept /-oŋ/ 'hole'. But it is derived from two sources of compounding the concept using two formative prefixes:

inɔ-ter-øoŋ	'compounding *inɔ* meaning water
ṭi:- ta:- øoŋ	'compounding *ṭi:* meaning place.

These two words may be from two different languages but both are in use now as the present language is a creole evolved by mixing the various languages of the past.

REFERENCES

Basu, D.N., 1952. 'A Linguistic Introduction to the Andamanese,' *Bulletin of the Department of Anthropology*. Vols. 1-2, pp. 55-70.

Bonington, M.C.C., 1931. Extract from the Census Report on the Andaman and Nicobar Islands, *Census of India*. 1931, Vol. 2, Part III, pp. 172-176.

Ganguli, Pranab, 1966. 'Vocabulary of the Negritoes of Little Andamanese with Grammatical Notes and Materials'. *Bulletin of Department of Anthropology*. Vol. 15, pp. 1-30.

Man, E.H., 1885. *On the Aboriginal Inhabitants of the Andaman Islands*, Reprinted 1932, Bibling and Sons Ltd. Great Britain, 1885.

—, 1923. *Dictionary of the South Andaman Language*. Bombay: British India Press.

Manoharan, S., 1980. 'Language of the Present Great Andamanese, *Journal of Indian Anthropological Society*. Vol. 15, pp. 43-55.

—, 1982. 'Linguistic Effect of Culture Contact: Present Andamanese Linguistic Situation.' *Journal of Indian Anthropological Society*. Vol. 17, pp. 223-227.

—, 1983. 'Subgrouping Andamanese Group of Languages,' *International Journal of Dravidian Linguistics*. Vol. 12:1, pp. 82-95.

—, 1986. 'Linguistic Peculiarities of Andamanese Family of Languages,' *Indian Linguistics*, Vol. 47. (1-4), pp. 25-32.

—, 1989. *A Descriptive and Comparative Study of Andamanese Language*, Anthropological Survey of India, Calcutta.

McCarthy, A.D.M., 1940. *Notes on the Jarawa Language*. Chief Commissioner's Press, Port Blair.

Portman, M.V., 1898. *Notes on the Languages of the South Andaman Group of Tribes*, Calcutta.

Radcliffe-Brown, A.R., 1914. 'Notes on the Languages of the Andaman Islands,' *Anthropos*, Vol. 9, pp. 36-52.

—, 1940. 'The Andaman Islanders, Illinois: Free Press.

APPENDIX I

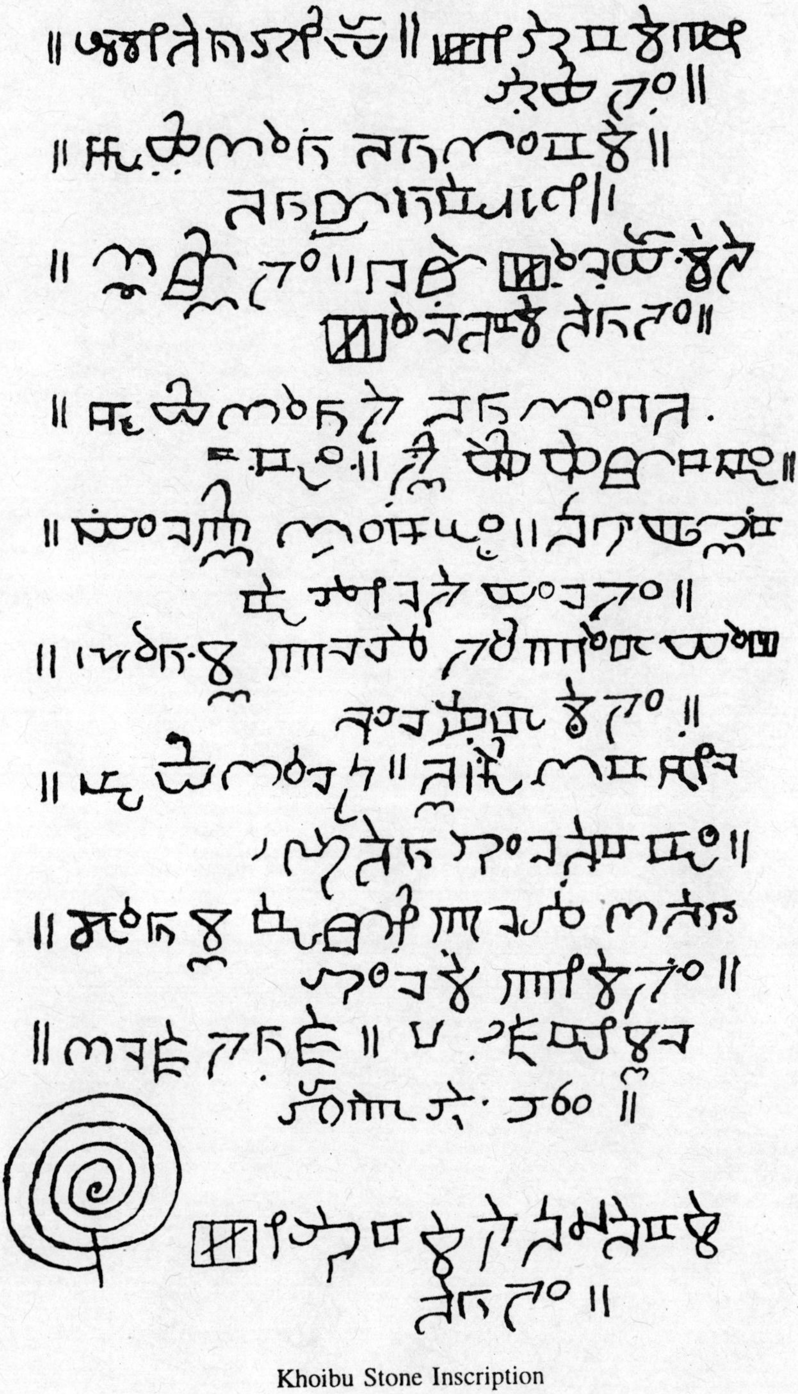

Khoibu Stone Inscription

APPENDIX II

Meitei Numbering System

INDEX

Languages of Tribal and Indigenous Peoples of India

CONTRIBUTORS

1. Anvita Abbi
   Centre of Linguistics & English
   School of Languages
   Jawarharlal Nehru University
   New Delhi 110 067 (India)
2. Kailash Aggarwal
   Department of English
   University of Manipur
   Imphal (India)
3. M.S. Andronov
   Institute of Oriental Studies
   12/1, Rozhdestrenka St.
   Moscow 103777
   Russia
4. E. Annamalai
   Institute for the Study of Languages and Cultures of Asia and Africa, Tokyo University of Foregin Studies
   4-51-21, Nishigahara, Kita-ku
   Tokoyo, 114, Japan
5. D.N.S. Bhat
   1174, Nandadeep
   T.K. Layout
   4th Stage
   Mysore 570 023
6. M.B. Emeneau
   Dept. of Linguistics
   University of California at Berkeley
   California, U.S.A.
7. Syed Imtiaz Hasnain
   Department of Linguistics
   Aligarh Muslim University
   Aligarh (India)
8. M. Ishtiaq
   Department of Geography
   Jamia Millia Islamia
   New Delhi (India)
9. M. Israel
   Department of Linguistics
   Madurai Kamraj University
   Madurai (India)
10. Lachman Mulchand Khubchandani
    Centre for Communication Studies
    Pune (India)
11. B. Lalitha
    Department of Linguistics
    University of Delhi
    Delhi-110 007 (India)
12. S. Manoharan
    Anthropological Survey of India
    Southern Regional Centre
    Mysore (India)

13. B.P. Mahapatra
The Registrar General of India
Language Division
Calcutta (India)
14. Panchanan Mohanty
Centre of Applied Linguistics and Translation of Studies
University of Hyderabad
Hyderabad (India)
15. K.S. Nagaraja
Dept. of Linguistics
Deccan College
Post-Graduate and Research Institute
Pune (India)
16. Mayjee Philip
Centre of Linguistics & English
Jawaharlal Nehru University
New Delhi 110 067 (India)
17. Christian Pilot-Raichoor
LACITO (Laboratoire de Langues et Civilizations a Tradition Orale)
44 Rue de l'Admiral Monchez
75014 Paris
18. D.D. Sharma
Jal Nigam Street
Nawabi Road
Haldwani-II
Pin: 263 139
19. Kumar Suresh Singh
Former Director General of Anthropological Survey of India
New Delhi (India)
20. Chungkham Yashwanta Singh
Department of Linguistics
Manipur University
Imphal (India)
21. Stanley Starosta
Department of Linguistics
University of Hawaii at Manoa
Honolulu, Hawaii 96822
U.S.A.
22. K.V. Subbarao
Department of Linguistics
University of Delhi
Delhi-110 007
23. Ahum Victor
Centre of Linguistics & English
Jawaharlal Nehru University
New Delhi 110 067 (India)
24. Arlene Zide
Washington College
Department of Foreign Languages/ESL and Humanities,
University of Chicago
Chicago IL 60615
U.S.A.